SELF-DETERMINATION AND SECESSION IN INTERNATIONAL LAW

Self-Determination and Secession in International Law

Edited by
CHRISTIAN WALTER,
ANTJE VON UNGERN-STERNBERG,
and
KAVUS ABUSHOV

OXFORD
UNIVERSITY PRESS

OXFORD
UNIVERSITY PRESS

Great Clarendon Street, Oxford, OX2 6DP,
United Kingdom

Oxford University Press is a department of the University of Oxford.
It furthers the University's objective of excellence in research, scholarship,
and education by publishing worldwide. Oxford is a registered trade mark of
Oxford University Press in the UK and in certain other countries

First Edition published in 2014

Impression: 1

Published in the United States of America by Oxford University Press
198 Madison Avenue, New York, NY 10016, United States of America

British Library Cataloguing in Publication Data
Data available

Library of Congress Control Number: 2014932547

ISBN 978–0–19–870237–5

Printed and bound by
CPI Group (UK) Ltd, Croydon, CR0 4YY

Preface

The present volume is the result of co-operation on the issue of self-determination and secession with a specific focus on conflicts in the CIS region. It started with a workshop which was organized by the Institute of International Law on 16 and 17 February 2012 at the Ludwig-Maximilians-University in Munich. At the workshop, discussions were held on the general issues of self-determination and secession on the basis of four case studies related to the CIS region (Nagorno-Karabakh, Abkhazia, South Ossetia, and Transnistria). Three remaining case studies were added for comparative purposes (Kosovo, Eritrea, and Western Sahara).

The publication of these case studies (parts II and III of the book) and the general international legal considerations in part I of the book were made possible by the Azerbaijan Diplomatic Academy which generously funded the workshop in Munich. We are grateful for invaluable linguistic and technical support by Stefanie Hempel, Melanie Kühn, Markus Vordermayer, and Carl Robert Whittaker.

Munich and Baku, November 2013
Christian Walter
Antje von Ungern-Sternberg
Kavus Abushov

Contents

Table of Cases

PCIJ

ICJ

ICTY

ECHR

AFRCOM

BADINTER COMMISSION

NATIONAL COURTS

List of Abbreviations

AFISMA	African-led International Support Mission to Mali
AOU	Organization of African Unity
AQIM	Al-Qaida in the Islamic Maghreb
ASSR	Abkhazian Autonomous Soviet Socialist Republic
CERD	Committee for the Elimination of Racial Discrimination
CIS	Commonwealth of Independent States
EC	European Community
ECHR	European Court of Human Rights
ECOWAS	Economic Community of West African States
ELF	Eritrean Liberation Front ELF
EPLF	Eritrean People's Liberation Front
FPA	Fisheries Partnership Agreement
FRY	Federal Republic of Yugoslavia
FTA	Free Trade Agreement
FYROM	Former Yugoslav Republic of Macedonia
HRC	Human Rights Committee
ICC	International Criminal Court
ICCPR	International Covenant on Civil and Political Rights
ICESCR	International Covenant on Economic, Social and Cultural Rights
ICJ	International Court of Justice
ICR	International Civilian Representative
IDP	Internally Displaced Person
JCC	Joint Control Commission
KFOR	Kosovo Force
KLA	Kosovo Liberation Army
MINURSO	United Nations Mission for the Referendum in Western Sahara
MINUSMA	United Nations Multidimensional Integrated Stabilization Mission in Mali
MNLA	National Movement for the Liberation of Azawad
MUJWA	Movement of Unity and Jihad in Western Africa
OSCE	Organisation for Security and Co-operation in Europe
SADR	Sahrawi Arab Democratic Republic
SRSG	Special Representative of the Secretary-General
TPLF	Tigrean People's Liberation Front
UNMIK	United States Interim Administration Mission in Kosovo
UNOVER	United Nations Observer Mission to Verify the Referendum in Eritrea

List of Contributors

Kavus Abushov is an Assistant Professor of Political Science at the School of Public and International Affairs at ADA University. His major research interests include international relations theories, international security and territorial issues in international law.

Bill Bowring is Professor of Law at the School of Law, Birkbeck College, University of London, and Director of the LLM/MA in Human Rights. His teaching and research interests include human rights, minority rights, international law, and the law of the USSR and of the Russian Federation and the other states of the former USSR.

Thomas Burri is Assistant Professor in International and European Law at the University of Saint Gallen (HSG). His research interests include issues of self-determination, secession, and autonomy, the law of European integration and battle robots.

Joshua Castellino is Professor of Law & Dean of the School of Law at Middlesex University, London, UK. He works on comparative constitutional law, public international law and international human rights law.

Gregory Fox is a Professor of Law and Director of the Program for International Legal Studies at Wayne State University Law School. He has published on international law and democratization, the law of occupation and the international administration of territory, among other topics.

Heiko Krüger is an attorney at law specializing in international and European legal affairs. Beside his research activity, he is mainly engaged in the realization of development projects in Africa and Asia financed by international public funds.

Farhad Mirzayev is a practicing lawyer based in London and Baku. He is Senior Partner of BM Morrison Partners international law firm. His main fields of academic interests are public international law, disputes settlement, territorial and boundary problems.

Stefan Oeter is Professor of Public International Law and Public Law at the Institute of International Affairs at Hamburg University Law School. His major research interests concern human rights, humanitarian law, international institutions and international peace and security as well as theory of internattional law and international relations.

Anne Peters is Director at the Max Planck Institute for Comparative Public Law and International Law, Heidelberg (Germany) and a professor of international law at the University of Basel (Switzerland). She is a member (substitute) of the European Commission for Democracy through Law (Venice Commission) in respect of Germany (since 2011) and served as the President of the European Society of International Law (2010-2012). Born in Berlin in 1964, Anne studied at the universities of Würzburg, Lausanne, Freiburg, and Harvard.

Sven Simon is Assistant Professor of Public Law, International and European Law at the Franz von Liszt Institute for International and Comparative Law at the Justus Liebig University Giessen. His major research interests include constitutional adjudication in the era of globalization, international economic law, and international peace and security.

James Summers is a Lecturer in International Law and Director of the Centre for International Law and Human Rights at Lancaster University. His research interests lie in public international law and particularly the rights of peoples.

Antonello Tancredi is Professor of Public and Private International Law at the University of Palermo. His research interests cover public international law in general, WTO and EU law.

Antje von Ungern-Sternberg, a lawyer and historian, is a Lecturer in Law at the Institute of International Law, Ludwig-Maximilians University in Munich. She works on comparative constitutional law, public international law, and law and religion.

Christian Walter is Professor of Public International Law and Public Law at the Institute of International Law at the Ludwig-Maximilians University, Munich. His major research interests concern human rights, international institutions and international peace and security.

Christopher Waters is Professor at the Faculty of Law, University of Windsor, Canada. His research interests are in the areas of international human rights law, the law of armed conflict, and law and politics in Eastern Europe.

1

Introduction

Self-Determination and Secession in International Law—Perspectives and Trends with Particular Focus on the Commonwealth of Independent States

Christian Walter and Antje von Ungern-Sternberg

I. The Problem

Self-determination and secession constitute central issues of international law. Peoples and minorities in many parts of the world assert a right to self-determination, autonomy, and even secession which conflicts with the respective mother states' sovereignty and territorial integrity. Apart from its practical relevance, this conflict also demonstrates how modern visions of international law, promoting rights of individuals and groups against the state, might clash with older visions that emphasize the role of the sovereign state for the protection of stability and peace. After the Advisory Opinion of the International Court of Justice concerning the Declaration of Independence of Kosovo, rendered in 2010,[1] many questions of self-determination and secession remain open. In particular, debate surrounds the question of how the right of self-determination—predominantly shaped in the period of decolonization following World War II—has developed in the post-colonial era. The Commonwealth of Independent States (CIS), emanating from the former Soviet Union, provides a good starting point for examining the current state of the law of self-determination and secession because it hosts four corresponding conflicts, concerning Transnistria (Moldova), South Ossetia, Abkhazia (both Georgia),[2] and Nagorno-Karabakh (Azerbaijan). These four entities claim

[1] *Accordance with International Law of the Unilateral Declaration of Independence in Respect of Kosovo, Advisory Opinion of 22 July 2010* [2010] ICJ Rep 403.

[2] Georgia formally declared her withdrawal from the CIS on 18 August 2008. It became effective one year later.

to be entitled not only to self-determination but to secession, and they base that claim on historic affiliations and on charges of discrimination and massive human rights violations committed by the mother state.

Where does international law currently stand on self-determination and secession? Self-determination started off as a political concept which was promoted by the protagonists of the American Declaration of Independence and the French Revolution, by socialist leaders and by Woodrow Wilson, and which played a certain role in the post-World War I settlement of territorial arrangements within Central and Eastern Europe,[3] but materialized into a legal right only after World War II. Even though the principle of self-determination incorporated into Art. 2 (1) and Art. 55 UN Charter[4] is generally considered to be too vague to provide a right to self-determination,[5] subsequent developments led to the acknowledgement of such a right in customary[6] and treaty law, as evidenced by the following documents: the 1960 *Declaration on the Granting of Independence to Colonial Countries and Peoples* of the UN General Assembly states that all peoples have a right to self-determination (N° 5) and laid the legal foundation for the decolonization policy of the UN;[7] Art. 1 of the two Covenants on Civil and Political and on Economic, Social and Cultural Rights (1966) established the right to self-determination as a treaty right; and, last but not least, the *Friendly Relations Declaration* of the UN General Assembly (1970)[8] confirms the right to self-determination, which entails the right of all peoples 'freely to determine, without external interference, their political status and to pursue their economic, social and cultural development' (Principle 5).

However, the exact contents of the right remain a matter of dispute: who is entitled, ie what constitutes a people—and may other groups, such as indigenous groups or ethnic, linguistic, religious, or other minorities also rely on it? Is the right, due to its historical origins, solely applicable in situations of decolonization and of military occupation, as the ICJ acknowledged in 2004,[9] or also to the many other conflicts of self-determination? And what exactly does self-determination comprise: minority rights, autonomy or, as a matter of last resort, a right to secession if the incumbent state does not honour its obligations? This volume, which

[3] Cf. A Cassese, *Self-determination of People–A Legal Reappraisal* (CUP 1995) 11–27.

[4] According to Art. 1 (2) UN Charter one of the purposes of the UN is to 'develop friendly relations among nations based on respect for the principle of equal rights and self-determination of peoples, and to take other appropriate measures to strengthen universal peace'. This is reaffirmed in Art. 55 UN Charter in which the UN commits itself to several goals concerning international economic and social co-operation '[w]ith a view to the creation of conditions of stability and well-being which are necessary for peaceful and friendly relations among nations based on respect for the principle of equal rights and self-determination of peoples'.

[5] Cf. Cassese (n 3) 42; D Thürer and T Burri, 'Self-Determination' in R Wolfrum (ed), *The Max Planck Encyclopedia of Public International Law* (OUP online 2013) MN 8.

[6] Acknowledged in *Western Sahara Case* (Advisory Opinion) [1975] ICJ Rep 12, para 54 et seqq.

[7] UNGA Res 1514 (XV) (14 December 1960) UN Doc A/RES/1514 (XV).

[8] *Declaration on Principles of International Law concerning Friendly Relations and cooperation among States in Accordance with the Charter of the United Nations*, UNGA Res 2625 (XXV) (24 October 1970) UN Doc A/RES/2625 (XXV).

[9] Acknowledged by the ICJ in *Legal Consequences of the Construction of a Wall in the Occupied Palestinian Territory* (Advisory Opinion) [2004] ICJ Rep 136, para 118.

is dedicated to the problem of self-determination and secession, attempts to find answers particularly to the latter question—which, however, requires examining the former ones as well.

Secession, ie the unilateral withdrawal from a state of one of its constituent parts with its territory and population,[10] is not duly received in international law. As a legal order based on sovereign states, international law favours stability and the integrity of its principal legal subjects. Formally, it neither prohibits nor authorizes secession, as has been confirmed by the ICJ in its recent Advisory Opinion on Kosovo.[11] But this indifference normally benefits the incumbent state since it allows the state to fight secessionist groups. According to the traditional view, the right to self-determination—which does not entail a right to secession—does not effectively counterbalance the strong position of the mother state. This view can rely on a strong commitment to the 'territorial integrity' of states that goes along with most commitments to self-determination.[12] However, tendencies in international law which strengthen human rights in general and the right to self-determination in particular might eventually give rise to a right to secession. It is argued, notably, that 'remedial' secession following severe and widespread human rights violations should be acknowledged.[13]

II. Perspectives and Trends

The chapters of this book depict different perspectives and trends concerning the problem of self-determination and secession. Some of the more general aspects will be specified in the following.

1. Self-determination and secession between national and international law: when and how does international law step in?

Self-determination and secession lie at the intersection of national and international law. Events which are originally governed exclusively by national law become matters of concern to international law at a particular point in time. At the same time, national law might continue to influence international law. The

[10] Cf. D Thürer and T Burri, 'Secession' in Wolfrum (n 5) MN 1.

[11] The Court stated that 'general international law contains no applicable prohibition of declarations of independence'; *Accordance with International Law of the Unilateral Declaration of Independence in Respect of Kosovo,* Advisory Opinion of 22 July 2010 [2010] ICJ Rep 403, para 84.

[12] Cf. Art. 2 (4) UN Charter; N° 7 *Declaration on the Granting of Independence to Colonial Countries and Peoples; Friendly Relations Declaration.* Common Art. 1 of the International Covenants, while not referring to territorial integrity, obliges all states to promote and respect the right to self-determination 'in conformity with the provisions of the Charter of the United Nations', thereby implying respect for territorial integrity.

[13] C Tomuschat, 'Secession and Self-determination' in MG Kohen (ed), *Secession—International Law Perspectives* (CUP 2006) 23, 42.

following chapters show, however, that this interplay between the national and the international legal orders may vary considerably depending on the specific legal question at stake.

First of all, it is interesting to note that a right to secession, though not (yet) established under international law, might exist under national law. The four case studies from the CIS refer in particular to the 1977 Constitution of the Soviet Union which provided for a right to secession. This right, however, was confined to Soviet Union Republics and did not extend to autonomous regions within those republics. Therefore Transnistria, South Ossetia, Abkhazia, and Nagorno-Karabakh, which did not enjoy the rank of a Soviet Union Republic but merely constituted autonomous regions within the Republics of Moldova, Georgia, and Azerbaijan, could not rely on such a right.

But when and how does international law step in? The relevant beneficiaries of the right to self-determination are comprehensively defined by international law, as **Joshua Castellino** describes in his contribution on 'Peoples, Indigenous Peoples, and Minorities'. He suggests a reading of the two Covenants on Civil and Political and Economic, Social and Cultural Rights that would strengthen the position of indigenous peoples by discerning five models of self-determination, ie (1) full political self-determination for 'peoples', (2) political self-determination including proprietary rights for territorially based indigenous peoples, (3) non-political self-determination for non-territorially based indigenous peoples in order to guarantee human rights and to address concerns of personal autonomy, (4) non-political self-determination for minorities which, again, comprises respect for human rights, notably non-discrimination, and allows for access to special measures promoting equal opportunities, but excludes self-determination in a political sense, and (5) a remedial right of secession in the event where widespread and consistent rights denial occurs against a recognizable vulnerable group (indigenous people or minority). However, he stresses that subsequent settlers have claims, too, which—as the example of the conflicts in the CIS shows—legally and politically complicates their solution.

The **use of force** in conflicts regarding self-determination is a further element shaped by international law. **Antonello Tancredi**, in his contribution on 'Secession and Use of Force', challenges the traditional view that the international regime on the use of force, conceived to apply in international relations, is totally unrelated to the problem of secession. He demonstrates that different factors can intervene to 'internationalize' separatist struggles. First, he exhibits tendencies in favour of the customary extension of the non-use of force to internal conflicts, but concludes that they have not yet matured into law. Examining the relationship between the incumbent state and third states, he then elaborates that foreign military interventions carried out upon the invitation of the former with a view to repelling a secessionist attempt are, in practice, well tolerated, whereas external intervention upon invitation by the secessionists or by a civil war party are prohibited—which can clearly be demonstrated by reference to the external support of the breakaway regions in Georgia (provided by Russia) and in Azerbaijan (provided by Armenia). Tancredi therefore concludes that the international regime on the use of force still favours the incumbent state.

Finally, **Anne Peters**, in her contribution 'The Principle of *Uti Possidetis Juris*: How Relevant is it for Secession?', claims that *uti possidetis* can potentially transform any type of internal territorial demarcation that has been established in domestic law prior to secession into an international one once secession has succeeded. She demonstrates, however, that the CIS member states which are affected by secessionist attempts are not constituted as federation-type states with internal domestic administrative boundaries but rather as unitary states, and that older administrative lines stemming from the pre-independence era cannot be opposed against the currently existing 'mother' states since they are not acknowledged in their domestic law. As a consequence, the breakaway territories cannot rely on *uti possidetis*. From a more general perspective, it seems that the internal, ie federal, structure of a state—a potential right to secession under national law notwithstanding—might be influential once a secession is successful.

2. The role of law and judicial law-making in the field of self-determination: caution or assertion?

As has become evident by now, the position of international law on the issue of secession is far from clear. There are counter-directional fundamental principles of international law (self-determination on the one hand, territorial integrity as part of a state's sovereignty on the other), which are not easily reconcilable. What is the proper role of the judiciary in such an unsettled area of law? Should it push developments into a certain direction or should it act rather cautiously and leave the active part to other actors? These issues of law-making are treated in the contributions by **Christian Walter** and **Stefan Oeter**. In his chapter 'The Kosovo Advisory Opinion: What It Says and What It Does Not Say', Christian Walter analyses the ICJ's Advisory Opinion as a tightrope exercise between different functions of an international judiciary. As a dispute settlement body, the Court has the task of facilitating the settlement of disputes which otherwise might (continue to) endanger international peace and security. At the same time, the ICJ, just as any national judicial organ, contributes to the development of the law. Walter argues that the judicial minimalism of the Court helped the settlement of the Kosovo conflict because it politically facilitated the acceptance of independence in the concrete case of Kosovo; yet while doing so, the Court resisted temptation to press the further development of international law into a secession-friendly direction.

But who, then, is to develop the law on secession? Here, the contribution by Stefan Oeter on 'The Role of Recognition and Non-Recognition with Regard to Secession' comes into play. Does recognition as a legal instrument help in assessing competing claims of sovereignty which are voiced both by a seceding entity and by the respective mother state? Oeter, who is also more critical of the Court's judicial minimalism, is sceptical. He analyses the role of recognition in international law as it currently stands as basically an instrument whose use is determined by interests of bilateral diplomacy. Hence, he argues, recognition is unable to process competing claims of sovereignty as issues which are of importance to the overall structure of the international community, in which interests of individual groups need to be balanced against general interests, such as stability of borders or foreseeability of decisions. In consequence, Oeter calls for the strengthening of the role of recognition, which under existing legal practice and doctrine is understood as being purely declaratory. In Oeter's analysis, the Kosovo declaration of independence and the developments which have ensued in the CIS area strongly argue for the development of mechanisms of collective recognition, a claim which would automatically imply the increased legal and political relevance of such collective acts of recognition.

3. Challenges to the traditional role of the state: from sovereignty and stability to legitimacy—a right to remedial secession?

The general question underlying a legal assessment of self-determination and secession is whether a modern conception of the state in international law will focus less on state sovereignty and the state's role in providing stability and more on the legitimacy of states. The ever-growing importance of human rights, the ideal of a state's responsibility to protect[14] and a nascent principle of democratic governance[15] stress the importance of a state's legitimacy and therefore point in this direction. If international law recognized a right to remedial secession as a response to gross human rights violations, this would be in line with this general trend: state sovereignty is no longer an end in itself, it is part and parcel of a state's responsibility to protect its population. If state sovereignty is no longer used to fulfil this purpose but, quite to the contrary, severely endangers human rights, it may be forfeited and a right to secession might result.

The authors of this volume's contributions present different views regarding this question. Whereas some authors, like **Joshua Castellino, Anne Peters**, and **Tom Burri**, claim that a very exceptional right to remedial secession exists, others remain sceptical. The authors of the case studies on the conflicts in the CIS come to the conclusion that the corresponding practice does not contribute to the establishment of such a right, whereas Tom Burri argues that the four examples do not contradict such a right. The legal assessment of the conflict in Kosovo seems to be equally mixed. Some, like **Antonello Tancredi** and Anne Peters, consider it to provide a possible argument in favour of remedial secession, while others, like Stefan Oeter and **James Summers**, the author of the case study on Kosovo,

[14] Cf. AB Bellamy et al. (eds), *The Responsibility to Protect and International Law* (Martinus Nijhoff Publishers 2010); A Peters, 'The Responsibility to Protect—Spelling Out the Hard Legal Consequences for the UN Security Council and its Members' in U Fastenrath et al. (eds), *From Bilateralism to Community Interest: Essays in Honour of Bruno Simma* (OUP 2011) 297; I Winkelmann, 'Responsibility to Protect' in Wolfrum (n 5).

[15] TM Franck, 'The Emerging Right to Democratic Governance' (1992) 86 AJIL 46; GH Fox, 'The Right to Political Participation in International Law' (1992) 17 YJIL 539; N Petersen, *Demokratie als teleologisches Prinzip–Zur Legitimität von Staatsgewalt im Völkerrecht* (Springer 2009); F Ehm, *Das völkerrechtliche Demokratiegebot–Eine Untersuchung zur schwindenden Wertneutralität des Völkerrechts gegenüber den staatlichen Binnenstrukturen* (Mohr Siebeck 2013).

deny that the corresponding practice is conclusive in this regard. However, the question of legitimacy regards not only the potential right of remedial secession, but also some of the related topics. Thus, Antonello Tancredi finds that even though the international regime on the use of force normally favours the incumbent state, a state can be sanctioned internationally, or in extreme cases even be considered devoid of the full prerogatives relating to the use of internal force, if it is deemed responsible for gross violations of human rights or humanitarian law or if it threatens or violates other collective interests of the international community. This follows from the idea that the preservation of the unity of the state, rather than being a right, is a state's responsibility towards its citizens and the international community. As regards the issue of recognition, Stefan Oeter stresses the importance of the new pattern of collective recognition as a tool in political conflict management, practised for the first time by the EU member states in the case of the dissolution of the former Yugoslavia, where recognition was made dependent upon a catalogue of criteria of legitimate statehood. He argues that the collective approach to recognition necessarily relies on a set of normative criteria as a guideline for such common action, which implies that it is less the effectiveness of a secession than some (normative) criteria of legitimacy that matter.

The traditional role of the state is further and very generally challenged in the chapter by Tom Burri, 'Secession in the Caucasus: Causes, Consequences and Emerging Principles', which brings the four case studies and the case of Kosovo together. Even though he admits that no international right to secession emerges from these cases (while stressing that the development does not rule out the notion of remedial secession), he puts some of the 'softer' arguments against secession and autonomy into perspective. He calls into question the notion that secession is contagious, that autonomy snowballs into secession, and that the layered nature of minority problems prevents conflict solution by territorial secession. In his conclusion, he claims that not secession but the status of statehood itself, due to its binary (all or nothing) quality, might be the underlying problem of the conflicts of self-determination, suggesting that statehood should either be freely available to all who desire it or rethought or abolished altogether.

4. Types of conflicts

A final layer of analysis concerns different types of conflicts. International law's traditional approach to secession makes a fundamental distinction between claims of secession deriving from a postcolonial situation and all other claims presented by entities which are distinguished from the mother country on the basis of ethnic, historical or cultural criteria without belonging to a postcolonial scenario. To illustrate the similarities and differences between these different types of conflicts, the book relies on case studies which primarily serve as a basis for the (comparative) analysis of developments in the CIS region. These case studies cover four conflicts in the CIS (**Bill Bowring** on Transnistria, **Farhad Mirzayev** on Abkhazia, **Christopher Waters** on South Ossetia, and **Heiko Krüger** on Nagorno-Karabach) and three further conflicts which, due to the use of military force, have entered the sphere of international law (James Summers on Kosovo, **Sven Simon** on Western Sahara, and **Gregory Fox** on Eritrea). The three additional conflicts were selected for comparative purposes. The situations in Western Sahara and in Eritrea both have a clear colonial background which, however, is superseded by additional claims for self-determination which do not belong exclusively to the decolonization process but rather can be viewed as typical minority/majority conflicts. The conflict in Kosovo, by contrast, is—at least geographically—situated outside the classical arena of decolonization, which focuses on Africa, Asia, and South America. Kosovo exhibits the specific problems of conflicts surrounding claims for self-determination in multi-ethnic or multicultural societies.

The comparative analysis of these conflicts, both in an intra-CIS and in a general perspective, reveals that the traditional assumption of international law that secession is, in principle, lawful when occurring in a postcolonial context and, in principle, unlawful in any other context rests on assumptions which seem at least questionable. The conflicts in Western Sahara and Eritrea have a clear colonial background, even though they do not concern secession from the colonial power; the CIS conflicts are a legacy of the Soviet empire and which entities were granted a constitutional right to secession under Soviet domestic law as republics and which entities were denied such a right because of their lower status in the internal federal hierarchy of the Soviet Union seems, at least to some extent, arbitrary. If, as is clearly shown in the chapter by Anne Peters, international law tends to transfer the *uti possidetis* principle from its formerly purely colonial application to the determination of borders in case of the dissolution of a complex multi-layered federal structure such as existed in the former Soviet Union (and the former Yugoslavia), the question may be raised as to whether the current legal distinction between postcolonial and other types of secession is still convincing.

On a more fundamental level, the historical background of both the former Soviet empire and the former Yugoslavia shows certain parallels to colonial structures which allow us to add a further question mark to the fundamental distinction between postcolonial and other types of secession. Even the very definition of colonialism becomes unclear in that context, given the fact that most multi-ethnic or multicultural societies have witnessed different periods with different groups settling or being resettled.

III. Outline of the Book

Methodologically, the general chapters of the book are all based on the factual and legal background provided for in the case studies, while at the same time, of course, also reflecting the general development of the law outside the specific context analysed in the case studies. The book starts from the more general questions and, from there, moves on to the specific issues dealt with in the case studies. The overall starting point for the chapters in the general part of the book is the current significance of the Kosovo Opinion, including its relevance for conflicts in the CIS region (Walter). The book subsequently treats the relevant beneficiaries of the right to self-determination and, thus, possibly also of secession (Castellino), and the possible influences of third parties, both by use of force (Tancredi) and by recognition (**Oeter**). It then covers the crucial questions of borders (Peters) and ends with a detailed comparative assessment of the CIS conflicts (Burri).

The second part consists of the four case studies concerning conflicts in the CIS, which provide the factual material and a legal analysis of the respective conflict. Finally, three further case studies are added to allow for a comparison outside the CIS and, notably, between conflicts with a clear colonial background (Western Sahara and Eritrea) and the CIS conflicts which stand at the centre of the book.

PART I

GENERAL ISSUES OF SELF-DETERMINATION AND SECESSION

2

The Kosovo Advisory Opinion

What It Says and What It Does Not Say

Christian Walter

I. Introduction: International Adjudication Between Dispute Resolution and Law-Making

Judgments may be looked at from different angles. The most obvious perspective for lawyers is an analysis of their legal reasoning: Is it convincing? Are the legal issues dealt with comprehensively? How does the judgment relate to existing case law? From a perspective of legal policy one may ask whether a judgment is progressive, implying a development of the law, or rather conservative, in the sense that an existing interpretation of the law is maintained although the views in society on the issue in question may have changed over time. Inevitably, courts fulfil a function of 'judicial law–making'. It has rightly been stressed that this function is particularly prominent in advisory proceedings,[1] so that the 'contribution made by the Court to the development of international law by giving advisory opinions can hardly be overestimated...'[2]

The primary function of judgments is, by contrast, to solve disputes. Therefore, they may be assessed with respect to their effect in the given dispute: Did the judgment contribute to the finding of a way out of an apparently difficult situation? Was the dispute solved by the judgment? At first sight, one might be tempted to limit the dispute resolution function to contentious proceedings.[3] However, although advisory opinions formally relate to abstract legal issues,[4] it is by no

[1] K Oellers-Frahm, 'Lawmaking Through Advisory Opinions?' (2011) 12 GLJ 1033, 1040.

[2] JA Frowein and K Oellers-Frahm, 'Art. 65' in A Zimmermann, C Tomuschat, K Oellers-Frahm and C Tams (eds), *The Statute of the International Court of Justice—A Commentary* (2nd edn, OUP 2012) MN 67.

[3] See K Oellers-Frahm (n 1) 1033 f; H Thirlway, 'Advisory Opinions', MPEPIL (online edn) para 2.

[4] See the ICJ statement in the Nuclear Weapons Advisory Opinion: 'The purpose of the advisory function is not to settle–at least directly–disputes between States, but to offer legal advice to the organs and institutions requesting the opinion', *Legality of the Threat or Use of Nuclear Weapons* [1996] ICJ Rep 226, para 15.

means excluded that a concrete legal dispute stands behind the abstract question.[5] To the contrary, many advisory opinions by the International Court of Justice (ICJ) have been triggered by concrete disputes.[6] Most of the concrete issues were either constitutional disputes within the UN system[7] or related to disputes involving international organizations which could not have been parties to a contentious case before the ICJ.[8] In fact, a genuinely abstract legal question seems to be the exception rather than the norm. The Nuclear Weapons Advisory Opinion probably comes closest to an abstract question, even though one might argue that, given the possession of nuclear weapons by some states, the issue was not purely abstract.[9] The Kosovo Advisory Opinion and the Advisory Opinion on the Palestinian Wall are the most important examples where a concrete legal dispute between a state and another entity under international law was dealt with under the disguise of an abstract legal question.[10] Such advisory opinions may also be analysed as to their effects concerning the peaceful settlement of a concrete dispute.

Looked at from the perspective of its effects on the concrete dispute concerned, it must be acknowledged that the Kosovo Advisory Opinion, even though it is otherwise often criticized for having left open decisive issues such as a right to (remedial) secession,[11] has had positive effects. Immediately after the opinion had been pronounced, Serbia presented a draft resolution in the GA in which the latter would have declared 'that unilateral secession cannot be an acceptable way for resolving territorial issues'.[12] In an accompanying position paper, Serbia stressed that the 'Court did not affirm the Province of Kosovo's right to secession from the Republic of Serbia'.[13] Kosovo was not an independent, sovereign state. The position paper concludes that 'the main issues arising from the unilateral declaration of independence of 17 February 2008 remain unanswered after the rendering of the advisory opinion of 22 July 2010'.[14]

[5] H Thirlway (n 3) para 2; P-M Dupuy, 'Comment' in R Wolfrum and I Gätzschmann (eds), *International Dispute Settlement: Room for Innovations?* (Springer 2013) 69, 74 f.; R Falk, 'The Kosovo Advisory Opinion: Conflict Resolution and Precedent' (2011) 105 AJIL 50, 53.

[6] See C Dominicé, 'Request of Advisory Opinions in Contentious Cases?' in L Boisson de Chazournes, C Romano and R Mackenzie (eds), *International Organizations and International Dispute Settlement: Trends and Prospects* (Transnational Publ. 2002) 91–103; P-M Dupuy (n 5) 74 f.

[7] *Certain Expenses of the United Nations* (Advisory Opinion) [1962] ICJ Rep 151; *Admission of a State to the United Nations* (Advisory Opinion) [1948] ICJ Rep 57.

[8] Generally C Dominicé (n 6) 91 f.

[9] See generally, for the possibility of both abstract and concrete legal issues as being subject requests for advisory opinions, JA Frowein and K Oellers-Frahm (n 2) MN 21.

[10] For a slightly different evaluation see H Thirlway (n 3) para 44 ('intensely politicized controversies').

[11] T Burri, 'The Kosovo Opinion and Secession: The Sounds of Silence and Missing Links' (2010) 11 GLJ 881 et seq.

[12] Draft Resolution on Agenda Item 77 of the 64th Session of the General Assembly <http://www.un.int/serbia/Statements/77.pdf> accessed 2 August 2013.

[13] Position of the Republic of Serbia concerning the Advisory Opinion <http://www.un.int/serbia/Statements/76.pdf> accessed 2 August 2013.

[14] Position of the Republic of Serbia concerning the Advisory Opinion (n 13).

This attempt at officially limiting the effects of the Advisory Opinion failed. Serbia did not find the necessary support and had to withdraw its draft resolution. Instead, it joined the sponsors of an alternative text which was finally adopted by consensus as Resolution A/64/298.[15] This resolution, apart from acknowledging the Advisory Opinion, merely states that the GA 'welcomes the readiness of the European Union to facilitate a process of dialogue between the parties; the process of dialogue in itself would be a factor for peace, security and stability in the region, and that dialogue would be to promote cooperation, achieve progress on the path to the European Union and improve the lives of the people'. The fact that no mention of the territorial issue and of a possible right to secession was made has convincingly been interpreted as a 'first step towards the regularization of Kosovo's international relations'.[16]

Thus, even if the Advisory Opinion did deliberately leave open the hot issue of a right to secession, it may have contributed *de facto* to the acceptance of the practical result in the case at hand. Also, the immediate effects on further declarations of recognition seem to be limited. Of the 96 states that have to date officially recognized Kosovo as an independent state, only 27 did so after 22 July 2010.[17]

So: is all well that seems on a solid track? As academics, we intend to look beyond the mere practical results. Building on the already impressive literature on the Kosovo Advisory Opinion,[18] the following chapter analyses the Court's solution from the different perspectives of its dispute resolution and its law-making functions. For that purpose it elaborates on three (partially) interrelated points: (1) Sovereignty and Legitimacy; (2) International Law as Interstate Law?; (3) The Lotus Debate. The analysis leads to the conclusion that the judicial minimalism chosen by the Court in its Kosovo Advisory Opinion was the right approach for this thorny issue. It channels the future development of the law concerning (remedial) secession without attempting to actively shape it. Precisely for that reason, it is important to closely observe further developments in state practice regarding secession.

[15] UNGA Res 64/298 (13 October 2010) UN Doc A/RES/64/298.

[16] M Weller, 'Modesty Can Be a Virtue: Judicial Economy in the ICJ *Kosovo* Opinion?' (2011) 24 LJIL 127, 146.

[17] Website of the Ministry of Foreign Affairs of the Republic of Kosovo <http://www.mfa-ks.net/?page=2,33> accessed 2 August 2013.

[18] J Summers (ed), *Kosovo: A Precedent?* (Nijhoff 2011); M Arcari (ed), *Questions de droit international autour de l'avis consultative de la Cour Internationale de Justice sur le Kosovo* (Giuffrè 2011); P Hilpold (ed), *Kosovo and International Law* (Nijhoff 2012); H Zygojannis, *Geburt aus Ruinen—Kosovo als neuer Staat in Europa?* (Duncker & Humblot 2013); M Bothe et al., 'Kosovo in the ICJ' (2010) 11 GLJ 837–918; J Cerone, 'The International Court of Justice and the Question of Kosovo's Independence' (2011) 17 ILSA JICL 335–54; T Christakis et al., 'Symposium: The ICJ Advisory Opinion on the Unilateral Declaration of Independence of Kosovo' (2011) 24 LJIL 71–161; R Tricot and B Sander, 'Recent Developments: The Broader Consequences of the International Court of Justice Advisory Opinion on the Unilateral Declaration of Independence in Respect of Kosovo' (2011) 49 CJMJTL 321–63; R Wilde, 'Accordance with International Law of the Unilateral Declaration of Independence in Respect of Kosovo' (2011) 105 AJIL 301–7.

II. Sovereignty and Legitimacy

1. Dispute settlement, law-making and state sovereignty

The tension between the Court's dispute settlement function and its law-making function relates to the legitimacy of international law in general and to the role of the concept of sovereignty of states more specifically. Whereas the dispute settlement function in contentious proceedings only affects the parties to the dispute, the consequences of law-making on the occasion of a concrete dispute potentially concern the international community as a whole. Furthermore, the parties to a dispute have consented to the dispute being settled by the ICJ and have had the opportunity, during the written and oral phases of the ICJ proceedings, to present their views concerning their dispute. Hence, the dispute settlement function, in principle, largely remains within the limits of traditional concepts of sovereignty. The law-making function, however, requires additional justification.[19]

Regarding advisory opinions, the perspectives are slightly different. Since, under its advisory jurisdiction, the Court is entrusted with answers to 'any legal question' (Article 96 UN Charter), its law-making function seems much more obvious here than in contentious proceedings.[20] There are, of course, important remaining issues, such as the question of the non-binding character of advisory opinions.[21] But, generally speaking, the law-making function of advisory opinions seems to be broadly accepted.[22] By contrast, the dispute settlement function seems less obvious in advisory than in contentious proceedings. If the parties to the dispute have agreed to the question to be answered by the Court, or even accepted the answer as binding for the resolution of their dispute, this can be quite easily squared with the exigencies of sovereignty. This is different, however, if such consent is unclear or even nonexistent.

Irrespective of Serbia's involvement in formulating the question to be answered by the Court, the reactions from the Serbian government referred to above make it abundantly clear that the country was not willing to accept the Advisory Opinion as binding. It is thus necessary to look for additional justifications for the factual support which the Advisory Opinion provided towards the independence of Kosovo.

[19] N Petersen, 'Lawmaking by the International Court of Justice—Factors of Success' (2011) 12 GLJ 1295, 1316; A von Bogdandy and I Venzke, 'Beyond Dispute: International Judicial Institutions as Lawmakers' (2011) 12 GLJ 979, 996 et seq.

[20] See for example R Falk, 'Towards Authoritativeness: The ICJ Ruling on Israel's Security Wall' (2005) 99 AJIL 42–52.

[21] *Interpretation of Peace Treaties* (Advisory Opinion) [1950] ICJ Rep 65, 71; *Applicability of Article VI, Section 22, of the Convention on the Privileges and Immunities of the United Nations* (Advisory Opinion) [1989] ICJ Rep 177 para 31; *Nuclear Weapons* (n 4) para 12; under exceptional circumstances advisory opinions may be given binding force by way of a respective treaty provision. See in that regard R Ago, '"Binding" Advisory Opinions of the International Court of Justice' (1991) 85 AJIL 439–51.

[22] See again JA Frowein and K Oellers-Frahm (n 2).

2. The concept of responsibility to protect

For such additional justifications, a closer look at the concept of responsibility to protect may prove helpful. Responsibility to protect is usually treated in the context of the use of force,[23] but the redefinition of sovereignty, which serves as a conceptual basis for the notion of responsibility to protect, may also be of relevance in the present context.

The notion of responsibility to protect was developed in order to address humanitarian concerns, which were traditionally dealt with under the concept of humanitarian intervention.[24] The concept was initially proposed by a Commission sponsored by the Canadian government.[25] It places emphasis on the victims' need to be protected rather than on an alleged right to intervention.[26] The concept was first adopted within the UN by the High-level Panel on Threats, Challenges and Change set up by Secretary General Kofi Annan in preparation for the World Summit 2005.[27] It made its way not only into the Outcome Document of the 2005 World Summit,[28] but also into resolutions of the SC dealing with challenges for international peace and security in general[29] or relating, more specifically, to particular conflicts,[30] the most prominent examples being Resolutions 1970 (2011) and 1973 (2011) concerning the situation in Libya before the fall of the Gaddafi regime.[31]

Conceptually, the responsibility to protect rests on the assumption that sovereignty implies the responsibility of a state to protect its own population. However, a residual responsibility also lies with the international community. When a state is unwilling or unable to meet its responsibility, this residual responsibility of the international community is activated.[32] In the Report presented by the High-Level Panel on Threats, Challenges and Change, the general idea is phrased in the following terms: 'Whatever perceptions may have prevailed when the Westphalian system first gave rise to the notion of State sovereignty, today it

[23] See A Randelzhofer and O Dörr, 'Art. 2 (4)' in B Simma et al. (eds), *The Charter of the United Nations—A Commentary* (3rd edn OUP 2012) MN 56.

[24] For details see M Vashakmadze, 'Responsibility to Protect' in Simma et al. (n 23) MN 1–25.

[25] Report of the International Commission on Intervention and State Sovereignty (ICISS), *The Responsibility to Protect*, December 2001 <http://responsibilitytoprotect.org/ICISS%20Report.pdf> accessed 8 August 2013.

[26] ICISS Report (n 25) para 2.28.

[27] UNGA, 'Report of the High-level Panel on Threats, Challenges and Change' (2 December 2004) UN Doc A/59/565.

[28] UNGA Res 60/1 (16 September 2005) UN Doc A/RES/60/1 paras 138–140.

[29] UNSC Res 1674 (28 April 2006) UN Doc S/RES/1674; UNSC Res 1894 (11 November 2009) UN Doc S/RES/1894; see also UNSC Res 1975 (30 March 2011) UN Doc S/RES/1975.

[30] UNSC Res 1706 (31 August 2006) UN Doc S/RES/1706; UNSC Res 1769 (31 July 2007) UN Doc S/RES/1769; UNSC Res 1778 (25 September 2007) UN Doc S/RES/1778; UNSC Res 1856 (22 December 2008) UN Doc S/RES/1856; UNSC Res 1861 (14 January 2009) UN Doc S/RES/1861; UNSC Res 1863 (16 January 2009) UN Doc S/RES/1863; UNSC Res 1923 (25 May 2010) UN Doc S/RES/1923; UNSC Res 1970 (26 February 2011) UN Doc S/RES/1970; UNSC Res 1973 (17 March 2011) UN Doc S/RES/1973; UNSC Res 2016 (27 October 2011) UN Doc S/RES/2016; UNSC Res 2031 (21 December 2011) UN Doc S/RES/2031.

[31] For details see M Vashakmadze (n 24) MN 37–41.

[32] ICISS Report (n 25) para 2.31.

clearly carries with it the obligation of a State to protect the welfare of its own peoples and meet its obligations to the wider international community'.[33]

3. Responsibility to protect and the Advisory Opinion on the Unilateral Declaration of Independence by Kosovo

In a mid-term or long-term perspective, the Kosovo Advisory Opinion may be also read in this context. Apparently there was a strong feeling by many states that Serbia had lost the legitimacy to govern Kosovo due to its massive human rights violations.[34] Seen from that perspective, it is probably correct to state that—in terms of her own interests—Serbia received a 'disastrous' Advisory Opinion from the Court.[35]

It is true that all considerations just mentioned are primarily of a political nature. But that does not mean that they are legally irrelevant. Even if self-determination does not grant a legal right (in terms of an entitlement) to secession,[36] it may be argued that in the case of Kosovo the international community was apparently ready to acquiesce in the results even though the Serbs' violations of human rights and discrimination against Kosovars, at the time of the Declaration of Independence, already dated back quite a while.[37] In sum: even though the Kosovo Advisory Opinion did not expressly say anything on a right to secession, it certainly contributed to the international community's acquiescence to the developments in the specific case of Kosovo.[38] And in that regard, it cannot be excluded that a precedent for other cases was set.

4. Consequences for Further Analysis

The foregoing considerations lead to an interim conclusion: in terms of dispute settlement, the Advisory Opinion facilitated the international community's acquiescence to a new independent state of Kosovo. In this regard, the Court's finding that the Declaration of Independence 'does not violate international law' mainly operates on a political or psychological level,[39] because the Court does not address the substantive issue of the legality of Kosovo's independence at all. This 'judicial

[33] UNGA, 'Note by the Secretary-General 59/565' (2004) UN Doc A/59/565 para 29.

[34] Falk (n 5) 56.

[35] T Christakis, 'The ICJ Advisory Opinion on Kosovo: Has International Law Something to Say about Secession?' (2011) 24 LJIL 73, 77.

[36] This is the overwhelming legal position, for details see S Oeter, 'Self-Determination' in Simma et al. (n 23) and S Oeter, this volume.

[37] P Hilpold, 'The International Court of Justice's Advisory Opinion on Kosovo: Perspectives of a Delicate Question' (2009) 14 ARIEL 259, 272 f.

[38] R Wilde, 'Self-Determination, Secession, and Dispute Settlement after the Kosovo Advisory Opinion' (2011) 24 LJIL 149, 153 et seq.; R Wilde, 'Accordance with International Law' (n 18) 306 et seq.

[39] Similarly A Peters, 'Does Kosovo Lie in the *Lotus*-Land of Freedom?' (2011) 24 LJIL 95, 108; *Accordance with International Law of the Unilateral Declaration of Independence in Respect of Kosovo* (Dissenting Opinion Bennouna) 2010 <http://www.icj-cij.org/docket/files/141/15999.pdf> accessed 8 August 2013 paras 39 et seq. and 65 et seq.

minimalism'[40] is even more obvious regarding the Court's law-making function, since the thorny relationship between self-determination and territorial integrity is entirely left to future developments. It thus seems that the Court, although deciding in advisory proceedings, placed its dispute settlement function above its law-making function. For the law on secession, this underlines the practical relevance of the approach taken by states and other actors of the international community in the CIS conflicts analysed in this book. But the question remains whether the Court succeeded in avoiding statements with possible repercussions on the development of international law. Two areas have been discussed in that regard: the concept of international law as interstate law (III) and the Lotus principle (IV). These two areas will be discussed in the following sections of this paper.

III. International Law as Interstate Law?

1. The Court's holding in the Kosovo Advisory Opinion

The Court holds in the Advisory Opinion that

> ... the scope of the principle of territorial integrity is confined to the sphere of relations between states.[41]

The Court reaches this conclusion as a result of some rather brief reasoning in which the principle of territorial integrity is linked to Article 2 (4), to the Friendly Relations Declaration and to the Final Act of the Helsinki Conference of 1975.[42] While it is true that territorial integrity is expressly mentioned in these provisions and documents and that, originally, they stem from interstate situations, it does not follow logically and necessarily that the principles contained in them *only* apply in interstate relations.

There can be no doubt that the Court was aware of the (many) parts of international law which are either applicable in the internal legal order of states[43] or have no cross-border aspects,[44] or even both if one considers the whole body of human

[40] See *Kosovo* (Separate Opinion Cançado-Trindade) 2010 <http://www.icj-cij.org/docket/files/141/16003.pdf> accessed 8 August 2013 para 35; Peters (n 39) 107; Wilde (n 18) 303; EM Brewer, 'To Break Free from Tyranny and Oppression: Proposing a Model for a Remedial Right to Secession in the Wake of the *Kosovo* Advisory Opinion' (2012) 45 VJTL 245, 261; DH Meester, 'The International Court of Justice's *Kosovo* Case: Assessing the Current State of International Legal Opinion on Remedial Secession' (2011) 48 CYBIL 215, 223; J Vidmar, 'The Kosovo Advisory Opinion Scrutinized' (2011) 24 LJIL 355, 358 FN 19.

[41] *Accordance with International Law of the Unilateral Declaration of Independence in Respect of Kosovo* (Advisory Opinion) 2010 <http://www.icj-cij.org/docket/files/141/15987.pdf> accessed 9 August 2013 para 80.

[42] *Kosovo* (n 41) para 80.

[43] eg *Avena and Other Mexican Nationals (Mexico* v *United States of America)* [2004] ICJ Rep 12 para 40.

[44] eg *Görgülü* case [2 BvR 1481/04], Federal Constitutional Court of Germany (19 October 2004) MN 15 ff. <http://www.bundesverfassungsgericht.de/en/decisions/rs20041014_2bvr148104en.html> accessed 16 August 2013.

rights law.[45] It follows that the background of the Court's statement cannot be a general concept of international law as interstate law.

2. Possible explanations

A narrower perspective could focus on the specific principles in question, namely the prohibition of the use of force and territorial integrity, and ask whether at least these principles are exclusively applicable in interstate relations. Olivier Corten reads the position of the Court as 'a reminder of its previous case law' in the *Wall Opinion* and in *Armed Activities (Congo* v *Uganda)*, in which he says the Court refused to apply '*jus contra bellum* to non-state actors'.[46] However, this is only in part convincing. In fact, in the two decisions mentioned, the Court did not refuse to apply *jus contra bellum* in total to non-state actors. Both decisions only relate to the right of self-defence and, even more specifically, to the notion of an 'armed attack'.[47] Furthermore, the Security Council used its Chapter VII powers against private actors,[48] which underlines that there are parts of international law in the area of international peace and security which operate even in the absence of an interstate scenario.[49]

Astonishingly, the Court itself, in the Kosovo Advisory Opinion, seems to apply the prohibition of the use of force to non-state actors.[50] In a passage in which the Court deals with certain SC resolutions condemning declarations of independence, it distinguishes these resolutions from the underlying situations from the Kosovo case:

> The Court notes, however, that in all of those instances the Security Council was making a determination as regards the concrete situation existing at the time that those declarations of independence were made; the illegality attached to the declarations of independence thus stemmed not from the unilateral character of these declarations as such, but from the fact that they were, or would have been, connected with the unlawful use of force or other egregious violations of norms of general international law, in particular those of a peremptory character (jus cogens). In the context of Kosovo, the Security Council has never taken this position.[51]

The use of force addressed here may be brought into the interstate paradigm if it is considered as addressing the use of force by other states (in the case of Northern

[45] See A Peters, 'Das subjektive internationale Recht' 59 (2011) Jahrbuch des öffentlichen Rechts der Gegenwart 411, 447 et seqq.

[46] O Corten, 'Territorial Integrity Narrowly Interpreted: Reasserting the Classical Inter-State Paradigm of International Law' (2011) 24 LJIL 87, 91.

[47] *Legal Consequences of the Construction of a Wall in the Occupied Palestinian Territory* (Advisory Opinion) [2004] ICJ Rep 136, para 139; *Case Concerning Armed Activities on the Territory of the Congo (DRC* v *Uganda)* [2005] ICJ Rep 168 paras 146 f.

[48] See UNSC Res 1127 (28 August 1997) UN Doc S/RES/1127; UNSC Res 1173 (12 June 1998) UN Doc S/RES/1173; UNSC Res 1373 (28 September 2001) UN Doc S/RES/1373; UNSC Res 1540 (28 April 2004) UN Doc S/RES/1540.

[49] For further details see N Krisch, 'Introduction to Chapter VII: The General Framework' in Simma et al. (n 23) MN 10.

[50] *Kosovo* (n 41) para 81.

[51] *Kosovo* (n 41) para 81.

Cyprus: Turkey; in the case of the Republika Srpska: the Federal Republic of Yugoslavia (Serbia and Montenegro)).[52]

Article 2 (4) UN Charter remains restricted to the interstate situation for other reasons, namely that it contains an obligation for the members of the United Nations. However, that does not exclude the possibility of a customary law principle of prohibition of the use of force to also apply to non-state actors.[53]

3. Distinguishing the principles of territorial integrity and of prohibition of the use of force

Furthermore, the principles of non-use of force and of territorial integrity may be distinguished. In fact, this seems to be the understanding underlying the Kosovo Advisory Opinion. The Court is explicit regarding the interstate character of the principle of territorial integrity:

> In General Assembly Resolution 2625 (XXV), entitled 'Declaration on Principles of International Law concerning Friendly Relations and Co-operation among States in Accordance with the Charter of the United Nations', which reflects customary international law (Military and Paramilitary Activities in and against Nicaragua (Nicaragua v. United States of America), Merits, Judgment, ICJ Reports 1986, pp. 101–103, paras 191–93), the General Assembly reiterated '[t]he principle that States shall refrain in their international relations from the threat or use of force against the territorial integrity or political independence of any State'. This resolution then enumerated various obligations incumbent upon States to refrain from violating the territorial integrity of other sovereign States. In the same vein, the Final Act of the Helsinki Conference on Security and Co-operation in Europe of 1 August 1975 (the Helsinki Conference) stipulated that '[t]he participating States will respect the territorial integrity of each of the participating States' (Art. IV). Thus, the scope of the principle of territorial integrity is confined to the sphere of relations between States.[54]

However, the Court did not limit the prohibition of the use of force in a similar manner to the interstate scenario.[55] At first sight this difference in treatment seems strange. First, and most importantly, the principle of territorial integrity is derived from the prohibition of the use of force.[56] Second, from a strictly legal point it seems difficult to discern decisive differences between the two principles. Both are general principles, both certainly have their main area of application in the interstate context, but both are equally transferable to non-state actors without there being any compelling obstacles. So are there other reasons?

a) *Hypothetical alternative*

A look at the consequences of the alternative solution (application of the principle of territorial integrity to non-state actors) might help to find at least a tentative answer: in the situation at hand, the Kosovars and, notably, the authors of the Declaration of

[52] It seems unclear to what extent another state was militarily involved in the South Rhodesian case.

[53] See generally on the issue of use of force in the context of secession Tancredi (ch 5, in this volume).

[54] *Kosovo* (n 41) para 80.

[55] See *Kosovo* (n 41) para 81.

[56] See the passage quoted at n 53; this point is especially emphasized by O Corten (n 46) 91.

Independence did not have a problem with the prohibition of the use of force. It was not suggested that they had tried to become independent by using means which are illegal under international law, notably by using military force. To the contrary, irrespective of their Declaration of Independence, they continued to respect the authority of the United States Interim Administration Mission in Kosovo (UNMIK). This is, after all, one of the reasons why the Court could operate with the idea of different perspectives in time, Resolution 1244 (1999) aiming at an interim solution and the Declaration of Independence being an attempt to finally determine the status of Kosovo. If the Court pursued the aim not to address the substantive issue of a right to (remedial) secession, it could, therefore, leave open the applicability of the principle of non-use of force.

By contrast, had the Court applied the principle of territorial integrity to non-state actors, it would have been, invariably, drawn into the debate on possible justifications for an infringement of that principle by the authors of the Declaration of Independence. Thus, for the path chosen by the Court, it was indispensable to restrict the application of the principle of territorial integrity to state actors.

b) Repercussions for global constitutionalism

This decision may be deplored from the perspective of global constitutionalism,[57] if global constitutionalism is understood as requiring strong institutions, or even a strong judiciary. If, however, global constitutionalism is conceived in a broader sense as including the gradual development of common values and substantive principles,[58] the reactions in the General Assembly after the Kosovo Advisory Opinion may be seen as a step towards a modern understanding of sovereignty. However, this development is not pushed by a single Court decision but—in the best sense—by the international community as a whole, including state and non-state actors, the judiciary and, last but not least, academics who, by now, have been debating these issues for several decades.

Nevertheless, one side effect must not be overlooked: since in the opinion of the Court the (international legal) principle of territorial integrity does not apply to groups within a state, international law does not protect states from disaggregation from within. Action which would be prohibited if committed by other states is left unregulated by international law when committed by non-state actors.[59]

[57] A Peters, 'Das Kosovo-Gutachten und Globaler Konstitutionalismus' in P Hilpold (ed), *Das Kosovo-Gutachten des IGH vom 22. Juli 2010* (Brill 2012) 229–58.

[58] Peters (n 57) 243 et seq.; JA Frowein, 'Konstitutionalisierung des Völkerrechts' (2000) 39 Berichte der DGVR 427, 428 f, 442 et seqq.; see also M Koskenniemi, 'Constitutionalism as Mindset: Reflections on Kantian Themes About International Law and Globalization' (2007) 8 TIL 9, 19 et seqq.; V Röben, 'The ICJ Advisory Opinion on the Unilateral Declaration of Independence in Respect of Kosovo: Rules or Principles?' (2010) 2 GoJIL 1063, 1076 et seqq.

[59] But see Wilde (n 38) 152, who concludes that the action by non-state actors is being 'sanction[ed] as lawful' by the Court. However, this conclusion seems to go too far. Again it should be stressed that unregulated does not automatically imply lawful.

4. Interim conclusion regarding the interstate character of international law

In conclusion, it may be said that the Kosovo Opinion is probably less assertive in pushing the interstate paradigm than it may seem. From the dispute settlement perspective suggested above, it was inevitable for the Court to highlight the interstate character of the principle of territorial integrity. This consideration, however, does not apply to the prohibition of the use of force. While this principle is, in fact, referred to quite prominently (and probably too prominently...) as a legal basis for the principle of territorial integrity, the Court does not explicitly limit the prohibition of the use of force to the interstate context.

IV. The Lotus Debate

1. Application of the Lotus Principle to non-state actors?

The Kosovo Advisory Opinion has triggered a debate concerning the applicability of the Lotus principle.[60] Although the Lotus principle was referred to by several states during the proceedings,[61] the origin of the academic debate seems to lie in the declaration by Judge Simma, who writes:

> The Court's reading of the General Assembly's question and its reasoning, leaping as it does straight from the lack of a prohibition to permissibility, is a straight forward application of the so-called *Lotus* principle. By reverting to it, the Court answers the question in a manner redolent of nineteenth-century positivism, with its excessively deferential approach to State consent. Under this approach, everything which is not expressly prohibited carries with it the same colour of legality; it ignores the possible degrees of non-prohibition, ranging from 'tolerated' to 'permissible' to 'desirable'.

This criticism, and the additional distinctions suggested, have been taken up by several commentators.[62] But can the Court's approach really be understood as 'a straight forward application' of the Lotus principle? The immediate objection that comes to mind is that the Lotus principle is a circumscription of the traditional concept of state sovereignty.[63] Hence, applying the Lotus principle presupposes

[60] One of the comments even takes this up in the title: A Peters, 'Does Kosovo lie in the *Lotus*-Land of Freedom?'(n 39).

[61] See *Kosovo* (n 41) Oral Statements by Croatia, Denmark, Germany, and Serbia <http://www.icj-cij.org/docket/index.php?p1=3&p2=4&k=21&case=141&code=kos&p3=2> accessed 14 August 2013.

[62] Peters (n 39); Weller (n 16) 130, 134 et seq.; Falk (n 5) 50; Cerone (n 18) 352 et seq.; Christakis (n 35) 78 et seqq.; R Muharremi, 'A Note on the ICJ Advisory Opinion on Kosovo' (2010) 11 GLJ 872 et seqq.; K Oellers-Frahm, 'Problematic Question or Problematic Answer? Observations on the International Court of Justice's Advisory Opinion Concerning Kosovo's Unilateral Declaration of Independence' (2010) 53 GYBIL 793, 812 et seqq.; A Orakhelashvili, 'The International Court's Advisory Opinion on the UDI in Respect of Kosovo: Washing Away the "Foam on the Tide of Time"' (2011) 15 Max Planck UNYB 65, 75, 77; Röben (n 57) 1075 et seqq.; S Yee, 'Notes on the International Court of Justice (Part 4): The *Kosovo* Advisory Opinion' (2010) 9 Chinese JIL 763, 771 et seqq.

[63] Peters (n 39) 100; Röben (n 61) 1076 et seqq.; see also Christakis (n 35) 79.

the existence of a state, which is precisely the question in the process of acquiring independence. In fact, one could make exactly the reverse claim: by applying the noble Lotus principle, which was until now strictly confined to states, to non-state entities in the process of achieving independence, state sovereignty may have been weakened, not strengthened.[64]

2. Secession: not prohibited, allowed, or unregulated by International Law?

But irrespective of whether or not the underlying concept is named 'Lotus', the question remains how the law in the absence of a positive and explicit regulation should look like. Here, the reformulation of the question asked by the GA, from 'is the Declaration of independence in accordance with international law?' to 'does the Declaration violate international law?', comes into play.[65] It has been strongly criticized as 'on the border of overstepping judicial competence' and as a 'decisive reshaping of the issue'.[66] I have doubts about whether the Court deserves this strong criticism. The reasons for these doubts lie precisely in the question concerning the applicable law in the absence of an explicit regulation. If a matter is not expressly regulated, the question of a residual rule arises. There are several options for such a residual rule. Under the Lotus principle, two alternatives are usually discussed. The residual rule could be either 'anything that is not prohibited is allowed' or the exact opposite, namely 'anything that is not expressly allowed is prohibited'. There is, however, a third option: the issue in question is not regulated by law at all. This is the position which has been advanced by many authors regarding secession.[67] This third option may be viewed as the key to the Court's reformulation of the question asked by the General Assembly.[68] The question is formulated on the basis of a presumption that the issue is in fact regulated by international law. The formula 'in conformity with' presupposes that the issue is regulated by law. It is either allowed or prohibited. The ICJ's formula 'not in violation of', by contrast, does not presuppose a regulation. 'Not in violation of' is not limited to 'allowed'. It can also mean 'not regulated'. If this understanding of the two formulae is correct, the reformulation merely reflects the approach taken by the Court: since the international legal principle of territorial integrity

[64] Peters (n 39) 100; Christakis (n 35) 79.

[65] Generally on the legal problems involving a reformulation of questions asked in advisory proceedings, see J Kammerhofer, 'Begging the Question? The *Kosovo* Opinion and the Reformulation of Advisory Requests' (2011) 58 NILR 409–24.

[66] A Peters, 'Remarks' on 'What the Kosovo Advisory Opinion Means for the Rest of the World' 105 (2012) ASIL Proceedings 264.

[67] O Corten, 'Are There Gaps in the International Law of Secession?' in M Kohen (ed), *Secession* (CUP 2006) 231, 232 et seqq.; J Crawford, *The Creation of States in International Law* (OUP 2006) 374 et seqq.; T Christakis, *Le droit à l'autodétermination en dehors des situations de décolonization* (Documentation française 1999) 74 and 118; see also the description of this position by M Kohen, 'Introduction' in M Kohen (ed), *Secession* (CUP 2006) 5; *Kosovo* (n 41) Written Statement by Germany (April 2009) <http://www.icj-cij.org/docket/files/141/15624.pdf> accessed 14 August 2013.

[68] See also Peters (n 39) 99.

is not applicable to non-state actors, and since no other international legal norms are applicable to the case, international law is silent. A positive ruling holding the declaration in question to be 'in conformity with' international law is therefore excluded.

V. Conclusion

What conclusions can be drawn from all this? The main point is that the judicial minimalism chosen by the Court must be viewed as an adequate response to the concrete factual and legal problem it was confronted with. The fact that it was tailored to the specific situation of the case at hand may be illustrated by the following hypothetical situation: imagine that after the Declaration of Independence of South Rhodesia, the UK had managed to convince the General Assembly to ask the Court for an Advisory Opinion on the question of whether the Declaration of Independence was in conformity with international law. Could one seriously imagine the Court stating, in a similar manner, that all it could say is that the Declaration as such did not violate international law? Certainly not. One reason for this may be found in para. 81 of the Advisory Opinion, where the Court explicitly states that there are circumstances which may render unilateral declarations of independence unlawful, namely 'unlawful use of force or other egregious violations of norms of general international law, in particular those of a peremptory character (ius cogens)'. Under such circumstances an Advisory Opinion would probably have highlighted the importance of these provisions and concluded that the Declaration, for this reason, was 'not in conformity with international law'.

The Advisory Opinion in the Kosovo case seems to have reached most goals of the peaceful settlement of international disputes. It contributes to the development of a solution, although not settling the issue itself. The position of the Kosovars and their claim for independence are *factually* and *politically* strengthened.[69] At the same time, fears that sanctioning the unilateral Declaration of Independence as lawful might open Pandora's box may be countered *in terms of law* by referring to the Court's judicial minimalism which, in strict legal terms, precisely avoided any pronouncement on the legality of secession under international law as it currently stands.

The Court thus leaves the further development of international law regarding secession to the future. Possibly, it nudges this development in a direction which has already received some support (remedial secession), but it refrains from pressing for remedial secession by exercising judicial authority.[70] It is for this reason

[69] Falk (n 5) 57; Oellers-Frahm (n 62) 829 et seq.; M Kohen and K del Mar, 'The Kosovo Advisory Opinion and UNSCR 1244 (1999): A Declaration of "Independence from International Law"?' (2011) 24 LJIL 109, 125.

[70] For a similar assessment see R Howse and R Teitel, 'Delphic Dictum: How Has the ICJ Contributed to the Global Rule of Law by its Ruling on Kosovo?' (2010) 11 GLJ 841, 843; Meester (n 40) 252.

that the analysis of international practice in the CIS case studies undertaken in this volume is so important.[71]

It has been said that the Court missed a date with history when it opted for its minimalist approach.[72] I don't believe that it missed the rendezvous. History is a continuous process and so is the development of law. There will be further rendezvous. And whenever the chances of meeting someone more than once are high, modesty is a virtue.[73]

[71] See chapters 8 to 11. [72] Burri (n 11) 888.
[73] See the title of the contribution by Weller (n 16).

3

International Law and Self-Determination

Peoples, Indigenous Peoples, and Minorities

Joshua Castellino

I. Introduction

The assumption of defined and fixed territoriality is one of the most fundamental facets of the recognition of statehood.[1] States remain the primary actors in international law and are entrusted with the privilege of direct participation in the creation of international law.[2] Thus the emphasis on territoriality and the attraction of statehood for various groups is not difficult to comprehend. Since the end of World War II, numerous states have been born or recognized, with the vast majority having emerged from processes of decolonization, others through the dissolution of larger states, and still others through a violent process of secession from postcolonial entities. In the course of these events there has been an array of confusing trends. First, 'self-determination', the process in international law usually attributed with the mythical status of creating states, has moved from a political concept to something akin to a legal tenet of uncertain contours.[3] Second, the unit or territory available for such 'self-determination' has often been deemed as existing within current boundary lines, irrespective of the manner in which these were drawn or their historical legitimacy.[4] Third, as will be seen in each of the four case studies presented from the CIS region, the mechanisms for achieving self-determination

[1] See Art. 1, Montevideo Convention 1934.

[2] For a general reading on issues of statehood in international law see eg J Crawford, *The Creation of States in International Law* (CUP 1979); RY Jennings, *The Acquisition of Territory in International Law* (Manchester University Press 1963); MN Shaw, *Title to Territory in Africa* (OUP 1986); OC Okafor, *Re-defining Legitimate Statehood: International Law & State Fragmentation in Africa* (Nijhoff 2000). Also see R Lapidoth, 'Statehood & Sovereignty' (1992) 46 JIA 1; A Anghie, 'Finding the Peripheries: Sovereignty and Colonialism in Nineteenth Century International Law' (1999) 40 HJIL 1.

[3] SR Ratner, 'Drawing a Better Line: *Uti Possidetis* and the Borders of New States' (1996) 90 AJIL 590. This issue is explored in the current volume by A Peters, 'The Principle of *Uti Possidetis Juris*: How Relevant is it for Issues of Secession?', Chapter 6, 95 et seqq.

[4] J Castellino and S Allen, *Title to Territory in International Law: An Inter-Temporal Analysis* (Ashgate 2003).

remains unclear, with law offering little by way of a remedy. In fact, as Bowring (Pridnestrovskaya Moldavskaya Respublika), Krüger (Nagorno-Karabakh), Waters (South Ossetia), and Mirzayev (Abkhazia) show, in each of the case studies in the region, it is not even clear whether it should be international or national law that applies in determining this question. At the heart of the doubt concerning self-determination lie two fundamental challenges: (a) the notion of territoriality remains contested in international law, in view of the arbitrary and colonialist nature of boundary-drawing, raising questions about its legitimacy—with significant implications for the human rights agenda, most visible in the treatment of indigenous peoples and their right to self-determination;[5] (b) while 'all peoples' have the right to self-determination',[6] the question of 'who' the people are, continues to defy clarity.[7]

This chapter is offered primarily to focus on question (b) above, detailing evaluation and discussion of the various entitlements of three recognizable groups within international society, viz. peoples, indigenous peoples, and minorities. To achieve this objective, the chapter is divided into three parts. The first part offers a working hypothesis of the 'right' of self-determination in international law, emphasizing its purposes, principles, and the applicable legal regime. The second part examines the definitions and claims of 'peoples', 'indigenous peoples', and 'minorities' against the applicable legal regime. The third part then seeks to reflect the experiences and issues raised in the context of self-determination for each of these groups. This chapter is also offered mindful of the analysis presented by the authors of the various case studies later in the volume.

In seeking to identify the applicable regime for self-determination, the opening section of this chapter will also briefly unpack its underlying tensions and scrutinize the mechanisms for the realization of the 'right'. Towards this end it will offer a summary of what constitutes self-determination, highlighting the fact that the single biggest difficulty with its realization remains the question of 'who' is entitled to exercise the right. The second section then examines the 'credentials' of the three distinct groups recognized in public international law, as identified above; namely, 'peoples', 'indigenous peoples', and 'minorities'. The objective of this section is to set down the broad elements that constitute these groups and to offer a position on their appropriateness in accessing the 'right' of self-determination. The final section seeks to offer some reflections on the question of entitlements.

[5] For a general reading on the issue of self-determination see A Cassese, *Self-determination of Peoples: A Legal Reappraisal* (CUP 1995); H Hannum, *Autonomy, Sovereignty & Self-determination: The Accommodation of Conflicting Rights* (University of Pennsylvania Press 1980); M Koskenniemi, 'National Self-determination Today: Problems of Legal Theory and Practice' (1994) 43 ICLQ.

[6] Joint Article 1, International Covenant on Civil & Political Rights, 1966 and International Covenant for Economic, Social and Cultural Rights, 1966.

[7] For an early articulation of this question see the comment attributed to H Lansing, see Jennings (n 2), 58.

II. Self-determination: Applicable Law, Underlying Tensions and Means

To be able to address any question concerning entitlements to self-determination it is first important to lay down a basic understanding of what constitutes self-determination, and how it has evolved in response to different challenges. For the purpose of this paper, the following is taken as a basic grounding of self-determination:

(a) The 'right', initially expressed in the American and French revolutions at the end of the eighteenth century, was considered as one of guaranteeing democratic consent within an entity.[8]

(b) Drawing inspiration from the notion of democratic entitlement, self-determination was used as the driving ideology in the context of Latin American decolonization (1810–1825), where the offspring of Spanish and Portuguese colonizers sought to establish independent states, separate from Europe.[9] In this guise self-determination was a process through which 'independence' was gained for territorially defined units. Such a determination accepted the boundary regimes drawn in Spanish ecclesiastical law and determined that all those within such boundaries would become subjects of the emerging 'independent' states.[10]

(c) The disruption attendant to the break-up of the Austro-Hungarian and Ottoman Empires in the era prior to the outbreak of World War I was significant enough for the League of Nations, born in the aftermath of that war, to seek to detail a process by which 'minorities' would be allowed to express an opinion about their future political aspirations. In this process US President Wilson directly applied the concept of self-determination to minorities, offering them a choice of political lineage, determined through plebiscites. He famously warned statesmen of the peril of ignoring the right to self-determination.[11]

(d) Immediately prior to the establishment of the United Nations, self-determination was also used by the Nazi regime to justify the reunification of 'German' nations.[12]

[8] TM Franck, 'The Emerging Right to Democratic Governance' (1998) 92 AJIL 46–91.

[9] A Alvarez, 'Latin America and International Law' (1909) 3 AJIL 269, 271.

[10] See J Castellino and S Allen, 'The Doctrine of Uti Possidetis: Crystallization of Modern Post-Colonial Identity' (2000) 43 GYBIL 205.

[11] For more on this issue see RS Baker and WE Dobbs (eds), *The Public Papers of Woodrow Wilson* (1925–1927). Also see A Whelan, 'Wilsonian Self-determination and the Versailles Settlement' (1994) 43 ICLQ 99.

[12] S Cvijic, 'Self-determination as a Challenge to the Legitimacy of Humanitarian Interventions: The Case of Kosovo' (2007) 8 GLJ 57–80.

(e) Self-determination reappeared in the UN era,[13] becoming the vehicle of choice for decolonization.[14] Three options were identified in clarification of its parameters in decolonization, namely: (i) secession to form a new state; (ii) association with an existing state; (iii) integration into an existing state.[15]

(f) The transformation from political tenet to legal norm was completed with its expression as the first human right in the Covenants of Human Rights in 1966,[16] though the land rights or proprietary element of the right was not made explicit.[17]

(g) The 1970 Declaration sought to enshrine this legal norm into a guiding principle of the United Nations, though it is clear that the context for that document remained traditional colonization.[18]

(h) Vital questions remain in contemporary society as to: (i) whether the principle has validity in a post-decolonization phase;[19] (ii) who is entitled to self-determination as currently expressed; and (iii) the extent to which the availability of appropriate solutions temper the appropriateness of the legal norm.[20]

There are a number of further underlying conceptual issues that have generated debate and been interpreted in different ways depending on the context to which they are being applied. Thus, in answering the fundamental question 'who are the people who may be entitled to self-determination?', various sources indicate

[13] For general commentary on the UN and decolonization see R Sureda, *The Evolution of the Right to Self-determination: A Study of United Nations Practice* (Sijhoff 1973); also FL Kirgis, 'The Degrees of Self-determination in the UN Era' (1994) 88 AJIL 304.

[14] As evidenced by three general Assembly Resolutions on the subject, namely *Declaration on the Granting of Independence to Colonial Countries and Peoples 1960* UN GAOR 1514 (XV); UN GAOR 1541 (XV); and *Declaration on the Principles of International law Governing Friendly Relations and Co-operation Among States in Accordance with the Charter of the United Nations 1970* UN GAOR 2625 (XXV).

[15] See UN GAOR 1541 (XV); for a commentary on self-determination within the United Nations see H Gros-Espiell, 'The Right to Self-determination: Implementation of United Nations Resolutions' (1980) UN Doc E/CN.4/Sub.2/405/Rev.1; A Cristescu, 'The Right of Self-determination: Historical and Current Developments on the Basis of United Nations Instruments (1981) UN Doc E/CN.4/Sub.2/Rev.1; R Emerson, *Self-determination Revisited in the Era of Decolonisation* (Harvard University Press 1964).

[16] See D McGoldrick, *The Human Rights Committee* (OUP 1991); also see S Joseph, J Schultz and M Castan, *The International Covenant on Civil & Political Rights: Cases, Materials and Commentary* (OUP 2000).

[17] J Castellino, 'Conceptual Difficulties and the 'Right' to Indigenous Self-Determination' in N Ghanea and A Xanthanki (eds), *Minorities, Peoples and Self-Determination* (Martinus Nijhoff 2004) 55–74.

[18] For a general reading of the significance of the 1970 Declaration see V Lowe and C Warbrick (eds), *The United Nations & the Principles of International law: Essays in Memory of Professor Michael Akehurst* (Routledge 1991).

[19] With 'decolonization' interpreted as being European domination over non-European peoples. However even this remains problematic in the context of indigenous peoples. For a discussion of the 'Belgian Thesis' and its relation to indigenous peoples see V Langenhove, 'The Question of Aborigines Before the United Nations: The Belgian Thesis' (1954) 89 Rec. des Cours 321. Also see UN Doc A/AC.67/2 pp. 3–31.

[20] See J Castellino, *International Law & Self-determination: The Interplay of the Politics of Territorial Possession with Formulations of 'National' Identity* (Martinus Nijhoff 2000) 43–44.

that these are 'colonial peoples'.[21] However what constitutes 'colonial' in this case remains undefined, especially in a post-Soviet context. Elsewhere, Judge Dillard famously stated that it is for 'the people to determine the fate of the territory and not the territory the fate of the people'.[22] Yet, as is often the case, this notion is not always borne out in practice.[23] The literature is also replete with writings about the conflict between a state's territorial integrity, protection for which is enshrined as a principle of public international law and captured in Article 2 (7) of the UN Charter, and the principle of self-determination.[24] Thus if questions concerning the potential disruption of the state are forestalled due to that state's territorial integrity, then self-determination necessarily becomes a dead letter, a stalemate visible in conflicts concerning Chechnya, Kurdistan, Kashmir, and Tibet as much as within the immediate subregion under study. Another significant issue that has merited consideration is the 'grounds' for self-determination. Classical writings argue that self-determination is an extension of the Grotian principle of *jus resistendi ac secessionis*.[25] In articulating this concept Grotius called for 'a people' to throw off their colonial yoke and aspire to freedom.[26] Yet once again, the notions of 'people' and 'colonial oppression' remain subjective. It would also seem clear that in terms of cases where self-determination was 'achieved' and those where it was 'denied' a number of political factors have played a significant role, not least the superior use of force[27] and political connections to 'friends in high places'.[28] In this connection one of the most significant questions that has emerged for self-determination, post-Kosovo, is whether there exists a scenario for 'remedial self-determination', whereby the perpetration of gross human rights violations against a 'people' or community may itself serve as a justification for self-determination. This is an argument that the Kurds have sought to make with some compulsion in the aftermath of the Halabja Massacre, with the opportunity to shape a new Iraqi constitution.[29]

Each of these conceptual difficulties has further obscured questions around 'entitlement' to self-determination, and with the strong emergence of human rights within customary international law both in *opinio juris* and in state practice, the

[21] See the Belgian Thesis argument (n 19).

[22] *ICJ Reports* (1975) 122 (Judge Harry Dillard, Dissenting Opinion).

[23] R Higgins, 'Judge Dillard and the Right to Self-Determination' (1983) 23 VJIL 387–94.

[24] See eg L Brilmayer, 'Secession and Self-Determination: A Territorial Interpretation' (1991), Faculty Scholarship Series. Paper 2434 <http://digitalcommons.law.yale.edu/fss_papers/2434> accessed 31 October 2012.

[25] For a discussion about this issue see RB Neuberger, *National Self-Determination in Postcolonial Africa* (Lynn Reiner Publishers 1986) 4.

[26] R Higgins, 'Grotius and the Development of International Law in the United Nations Period', in H Bull, B Kingsbury and A Roberts (eds), *Hugo Grotius and International Relations* (Clarendon Press 1992) 267.

[27] This can be seen in the contrast between how the claims of Bangladesh and Biafra were addressed and treated. See Castellino (n 20).

[28] This is visible in the contrast between the Western Sahara and the situation facing Kurdistan. See Castellino (n 20).

[29] See J McGarry and B O'Leary, *Iraq's Constitution of 2005: Liberal Consociation as Political Prescription* (2007) 5 ICON 670. Also see J Castellino and K Cavanaugh, *Minority Rights in the Middle East: A Comparative Legal Analysis* (OUP 2013).

clamour to widen the conception of self-determination itself has grown. While states have strongly resisted its charm, the idea of self-determination for various populations has found echoes in voices as diverse as the EC Commission on the Former Yugoslavia[30] and the calls of protestors involved in the events commonly referred to as the Arab Uprising.[31]

III. Assessing the Claimants' Right to Self-determination: Peoples, Indigenous Peoples, and Minorities

Many arguments pertaining to indigenous peoples' rights start from the premise that their self-determination ought to be located within the context of decolonization.[32] Many minorities, too, argue that the treatment meted out to them necessitates an automatic trigger for the right to self-determination. While many communities may allege that their treatment by an unrepresentative state may be unfair and quasi-colonial, the threshold for gaining the right to self-determination in international law is configured on the problematic grounds of 'peoplehood'.

This raises important questions concerning the status of the three distinct groups within international law who claim the right to self-determination and statehood. The three are:

(a) Peoples, also referred to as 'nations' or 'submerged nations';
(b) Indigenous peoples, also referred to as First Nations or 'Indians', and usually considered to subsume 'Tribal Peoples';
(c) Minorities, also referred to as 'ethnic, linguistic, or religious minorities' or, more problematically in Europe, as 'national minorities'.

The first task that confronts any assessment of these groups' claims to self-determination is an articulation of the definitions and constituents of each category. The following sub-section will thus seek to reflect on the characteristics and definitions attendant to each.

1. Peoples

Defining a 'people' would be extremely difficult and while several efforts have been made to identify the constituent elements of 'peoplehood', these usually involve

[30] See *Declaration on the Guidelines on the Recognition of New States in Eastern Europe and in the Soviet Union (16 December 1991)* reproduced as Annex One and discussed in D Turk, 'Recognition of States: A Comment' (1993) 4 EJIL 66–71.

[31] See MP Angrist, 'Morning in Tunisia: The Frustrations of the Arab World Boil Over' from www.foreignaffairs.com, reprinted in *The New Arab Revolt: What Happened, What it Means and What Comes Next* (Council on Foreign Relations: Foreign Affairs eBook 2011).

[32] See B Kingsbury, '"Indigenous Peoples" in International Law: A Constructivist Approach to the Asian Controversy' (1998) 92(2) AJIL 414–57.

the conflation of the notion with the concept of 'nationhood'.[33] This interpretation is necessarily subjective and has little normative value in law. Thus it is hard to see why 'Indians' as a category may be considered a 'people' while 'Kashmiris' might not; or similarly why the Chinese may be a people and Tibetans or Uighurs may not. Discussions on the categorization of peoples inevitably involve either aggrandizing or belittling historically significant communities or nations by emphasizing or denying them the right to call themselves 'peoples' in the sense that may generate claims for self-determination.

The literature around international law appears to accept the difficulties around the conceptualization of peoples, offering instead the idea that this refers to 'whole peoples', in other words an entirety of a nation, a discussion framed in the aftermath of what is referred to as the 'Belgian Thesis' and the 1970 Declaration discussed above.[34] Yet such a classification of 'whole peoples' pays much greater credence to the drawing of colonial boundaries delimiting entities rather than any congruence of cohesion in the communities that inhabit such a territory.[35]

As a result, while there is some evidence for support of the claims to peoplehood of the Palestinians, Tibetans, and Kurds, the claims of others, such as the Basque, Kashmiris, Tamils, and Chechens do not gain as much consensus for recognition. Despite the existence of various historical justifications that may indicate evidence to the contrary, it would be difficult to envisage communities in the Transnistria, Nagorno-Karabakh, South Ossetia, or Abkhazia being classed as a 'people' entitled to self-determination. In many instances there are also discrepancies between how two communities or nations within the same state are processed or perceived—for example, the treatment of Uighurs and Tibetans. This inevitably highlights the subjective and highly politicized nature of the determination of 'peoples', and the extent to which claims made under this banner gain credence from the international community.

2. Indigenous peoples

In contemporary society, at a theoretical level, indigenous peoples appear to have the best case for engaging the decolonization rhetoric and gaining the right to self-determination. Indigenous peoples have had their territory occupied by settlers from outside their territory and, in many circumstances, have lived as quasi-colonial subjects on their own land. The most widely cited, albeit flawed, definition of 'indigenous peoples' reflects this history:

> Indigenous communities, peoples and nations are those which, having a historical continuity with pre-invasion and pre-colonial societies that developed on their territories, consider themselves distinct from other sectors of the societies now prevailing on those territories, or parts of them. They form at present non-dominant sectors of society and are determined

[33] For a general reading and definition of these concepts see AD Smith, *Nationalism* (Polity Press 2001, reprinted in 2010).

[34] See P Thornberry, 'Self-Determination, Minorities, Human Rights: A Review of International Instruments' (1989) 38 ICLQ 867.

[35] Castellino and Allen (n 4).

to preserve, develop and transmit to future generations their ancestral territories, and their ethnic identity, as the basis of their continued existence as peoples, in accordance with their own cultural patterns, social institutions and legal system.

This historical continuity may consist of the continuation, for an extended period reaching into the present, of one or more of the following factors:

(a) Occupation of ancestral lands, or at least of part of them;
(b) Common ancestry with the original occupants of these lands;
(c) Culture in general, or in specific manifestations (such as religion, living under a tribal system, membership of an indigenous community, dress, means of livelihood, lifestyle, etc.);
(d) Language (whether used as the only language, as mother tongue, as the habitual means of communication at home or in the family, or as the main, preferred, habitual, general, or normal language);
(e) Residence in certain parts of the country, or in certain regions of the world;
(f) Other relevant factors.[36]

In articulating this definition as part of one of the first major studies of indigenous peoples issues, Cobo spent a considerable amount of time clarifying the importance of 'self-identification' or indigenous group consciousness. Thus acceptance by other indigenous peoples as indigenous inevitably becomes an equally crucial subjective factor in the definition. This facet is not merely a question of an individual's right to determine their own status, but rather recognition of the sovereignty of the peoples, in much the way that states' recognition of each other plays a crucial role in fostering relations between them.[37] While it remains challenging to apply the rubric of indigenous peoples to many areas of the world,[38] mainly where waves of settlement are less clear, there has been no concerted attempt to articulate claims in Transnistria, Nagorno-Karabakh, South Ossetia, or Abhkhazia through this lens. This is probably a consequence of what Krüger calls the phenomenon of 'transit and settlement... for many ethnic groups for thousands of years... [with] innumerable campaigns of conquest and ethnic dislocation'.[39]

3. Minorities[40]

With the minority rights discourse tracing back to the *Promise of St. Louis of France* in 1250,[41] it is perhaps unsurprising that much has been written about

[36] JM Cobo (Special Rapporteur of the UN Sub-Commission on Prevention of Discrimination & Protection of Minorities), *Study on the Problem of Discrimination against Indigenous Populations*, UN Doc E/CN.4/Sub.2/1986/Add.4.

[37] Cobo (n 36).

[38] See eg B Kingsbury, '"Indigenous Peoples" in International Law: A Constructivist Approach to the Asian Controversy' (1998) 92(3) AJIL 414–58.

[39] H Krüger, 'Nagorno-Karabakh: A Case Study on the Rights to Secession and the Legal Status of the Region', in this volume, Chapter 11, 214.

[40] For general readings on minority rights see J Castellino (ed), *Global Minority Rights: International Library of Essays* (Ashgate 2011).

[41] *Promise of St. Louis of France 1250*. General background information on St. Louis and the Treaty can be found on the *Encyclopaedia Britannica* website at: <original.britannica.com/eb/topic-348849/Louis-IX> accessed 31 October 2012.

what and who constitutes a minority.[42] Concern for minorities stemmed from their perceived vulnerability in the face of majoritarian rule.[43] Early minority treaties focused on seeking to guarantee certain basic rights for groups that were inferior in number to the rest of the population of the state and were usually distinct from that population.[44] For the purpose of this paper it is essential to have a working definition of who a minority is, and rather than seeking to discuss the merits of such definition it is proposed that Capotorti's definition be accepted, with all its conceptual weaknesses.[45] Thus for the purpose of this paper a minority can be considered as:

> [a] group numerically inferior to the rest of the population of a State, in a non-dominant position, whose members – being nationals of the State –possess ethnic, religious or linguistic characteristics differing from those of the rest of the population and show, if only implicitly, a sense of solidarity, directed towards preserving their culture, religion or language.[46]

Three caveats need to be briefly addressed with regards to the suitability of this definition. First, vis-à-vis the issue of nationality, the restrictive approach of law would require that 'minorities' be nationals of a state. Thus the prime focus of international minority rights law has often been concern regarding a state's treatment of minority groups within it, based on the accepted principle that distinguishing between nationals and non-nationals is a prerogative of state sovereignty. The allowable differentiation of a state's treatment of citizen and non-citizen is reflected in human rights law[47] but has subsequently been constricted.[48] Further, the traditional definition of 'national' minorities has not been useful beyond the borders of Europe, since this only accords status to groups living in one state with the nationality of another.[49] While national minorities are often

[42] J Pejic, 'Minority Rights in International Law' (1997) 19 HRQ 666; PV Ramaga, 'The Group Concept in Minority Protection' (1993) 15 HRQ 575; NS Rodley, 'Conceptual Problems in the Protection of Minorities: International Legal Developments' (1995) 17 HRQ 48; J Packer, 'On the Definition of Minorities', in J Packer and K Myntti (eds), *The Protection of Ethnic And Linguistic Minorities in Europe* (Turku/Åbo: Åbo Akademi Institute of Human Rights 1993) 23; O Andrysek, *Report on the Definition of Minorities* (Netherlands Institute of Human Rights, SIM Special No.8, 1989).

[43] P Thornberry, *International Law & the Rights of Minorities* (Clarendon Press 1991).

[44] J Castellino, 'The Protection of Minorities and Indigenous Peoples in International Law: A Comparative Temporal Analysis' (2010) 17(3) IJM&GR 393–422.

[45] MJ Aukerman, 'Definitions and Justifications: Minority and Indigenous Rights in a Central/ Eastern European Context' (2000) 22 HRQ 1011.

[46] F Capotorti, Special Rapporteur, 'Study on the Rights of Persons Belonging to Ethnic, Religious and Linguistic Minorities' UN Doc E/CN.4/Sub.2/384/Rev.1 (1977).

[47] See *The International Convention on the Elimination of All Forms of Racial Discrimination* (hereinafter the Race Convention), opened for signature 7 March 1966, 660 UNTS 195 at Art. 1(2).

[48] The Committee for the Elimination of Racial Discrimination (hereinafter CERD) is the monitoring body for the Race Convention. See CERD *General Recommendation XI* (42nd session, 1993) and *General Recommendation 30 Discrimination against Non-citizens* (64th session, 2004).

[49] For a comparative study of minorities beyond Europe, see J Castellino and E Dominguez Redondo, *Minority Rights in Asia: A Comparative Legal Analysis* (OUP 2006); J Castellino and DP Keane, *Minority Rights in the Pacific: A Comparative Legal Analysis* (OUP 2009) and J Castellino and KA Cavanaugh, *Minority Rights in the Middle East: A Comparative Legal Analysis* (OUP 2013).

as vulnerable as non-national minorities, the approach advocated is for a broader reading, to include non-national groups.[50] Second, the definition is only accepted as a working definition, so as to enable a basic understanding of the groups that would ostensibly come under the umbrella of protection afforded by international human rights law. A third issue that arises is over the relationship between a 'minority' and 'indigenous peoples'.[51] While Cobo's definition of indigenous peoples cited above is equally problematic,[52] it too can nonetheless be accepted on the same principle as the Capotorti definition. It could be argued in more general terms that indigenous peoples have all the rights that minorities have, but may in addition have the right to self-determination, with all its attendant problems of interpretation and application.[53] In addition, it is clear that prior to Cobo's important study, little attention was paid to indigenous rights issues within the emerging human rights regime, and thus in previous periods 'indigenous peoples' would have been subsumed under the general conceptual banner of 'minorities', problematic as this may be. With each of the case studies selected from the region the attendant historical processes would suggest that each group(s) be considered a minority within the context of these definitions, as a default of not fitting neatly within the few objective elements that exist for 'peoplehood', nor meeting the subjective criteria of having achieved global consensus with respect to their claim.

IV. Peoples, Indigenous Peoples, Minorities, and Self-determination

The first 'wave' of modern decolonization occurred between 1810 and 1825 in Latin America, and was driven by Enlightenment ideas concerning freedom and independence.[54] Yet this wave of self-determination specifically treated the 'peoples' entitled to self-determination as the offspring of the Spanish and Portuguese colonizers or the Creole, rather than the indigenous populations of Latin America who had been oppressed by colonial rule. As in many other contexts, indigenous peoples were deprived of their land through subterfuge.[55] Yet the articulation of

[50] This is also the approach taken in the OUP series cited in n 49.

[51] See T Makkonen, *Identity, Difference and Otherness: The Concepts of 'People', 'Indigenous People' and 'Minority' in International Law* (Erik Castren Institute: University of Helsinki 2000); also see JR Valentine, 'Toward a Definition of National Minority' (2004) 32 DJIL&P 445–74.

[52] Cobo (n 36).

[53] Xanthanki addresses this at some lengths in her monograph; see A Xanthanki, *Indigenous Rights & the United Nations Standards* (Cambridge: CUP 2007) 131–95. Also see J Castellino, 'Conceptual Difficulties and the Right to Indigenous Self-determination' in N Ghanea and A Xanthaki (eds), *Minorities, Peoples and Self-determination* (Martinus Nijhoff 2004) 55–74 and J Castellino and J Gilbert, 'Self-determination, Indigenous Peoples and Minorities' (2003) 3 MqLJ Special Issue: Self-determination 155–78.

[54] Alvarez (n 9).

[55] C Doyle, *Indigenous Peoples, Title to Territory, Rights & Resources: The Transformative Role of Free Prior Informed Consent* (thesis submitted for PhD, Middlesex University, October 2012).

the concept of freedom and independence specifically excluded them, treating them instead as objects rather than subjects of law.[56]

It would thus seem that any attempt to redress the balance would need to be similar to a quasi-decolonization process. In the UN decolonization era the options were straightforward, as articulated in GA Resolution 1541 (XV), namely: (i) the creation of an independent state; (ii) free association with an existing state; or (iii) integration with a pre-existing state.[57] When applied to indigenous peoples, however, these 'options' become tenuous, impractical, and politically undesirable for the sovereign states in which indigenous peoples live. The question of strategy vis-à-vis implementation of these rights is arguably the stumbling block that prevents expression of the political nuance of the right of self-determination for indigenous peoples.[58] As was shown in Nunavut, however, there might be other means by which the claim to self-determination can be expressed.[59]

As far as contemporary human rights law is concerned, the issue of self-determination is enshrined as the 'first human right' at the commencement of the two International Covenants on Human Rights, 1966. Article 1 of the Covenants states that:

1. All peoples have the right of self-determination. By virtue of that right they freely determine their political status and freely pursue their economic, social and cultural development.
2. All peoples may, for their own ends, freely dispose of their natural wealth and resources without prejudice to any obligations arising out of international economic co-operation, based upon the principle of mutual benefit, and international law. In no case may a people be deprived of its own means of subsistence.
3. The States Parties to the present Covenant, including those having responsibility for the administration of Non-Self-Governing and Trust Territories, shall promote the realization of the right of self-determination, and shall respect that right, in conformity with the provisions of the Charter of the United Nations.[60]

The colonial flavour of this article has been much discussed[61] and is made explicit in the text in sub-paragraph (3) above. From the spirit of the text, however, it is clear that self-determination, including the potential option of political status determination, should be made available to indigenous peoples just as it was to *colonial* peoples. One vital factor to this equation would need to be an acceptance of the

[56] RL Barsh, 'Indigenous Peoples in the 1990s: From Object to Subject in International Law?' (1994) 7 HHRJ 33–62.

[57] GAOR 1541 (XV).

[58] This is also true for the ILO Convention 169, *Convention Concerning Indigenous and Tribal Peoples in Independent Countries,* 5 September 1991 169 ILO 1989.

[59] For the official website of the government of Nunavut see <http://www.gov.nu.ca/>.

[60] Joint Article 1, International Covenant on Civil and Political Rights (1966) and the International Covenant on Economic, Social and Cultural Rights (1966).

[61] J Castellino (n 20).

territorial basis of a community, since it would be nearly impossible to realign states where indigenous populations do not live in a contiguous zone. To consolidate the situation and prevent a sliding scale of claimants to this right, it would also be necessary to reiterate the attitude of the UN Human Rights Committee (henceforth HRC, the monitoring body to the International Covenant on Civil and Political Rights) in relation to minorities' access to this right—i.e. that they do not have the right to self-determination.[62] Thus in the terms of the Civil and Political Rights Covenant, a hierarchy would develop whereby territorially based indigenous peoples would have rights akin to those of colonial peoples and would thus enjoy the full benefits of Article 1, including sub-paragraph 1 (1) as cited above. Meanwhile, indigenous peoples who do not inhabit distinct territories would have the right of self-determination as given by Article 1 (2), which can be identified as a 'resource-based right to self-determination'. By contrast, minorities would only have the rights guaranteed by Article 27 of the same Covenant—which is a combination of non-discrimination, equality, and the right to special measures that seek to give equal opportunities to minorities in the civil, political, economic, social, and cultural realms. Where minorities are based on contiguous territories, the notion of 'internal' self-determination may also be entertained.[63]

This approach would make some telling differentiations. First, it would distinguish between indigenous peoples and minorities: a differentiation that is readily accepted in the literature and in law.[64] Second, it would bring indigenous peoples within the parameters of 'peoples' due to the similarities between their situation and that of colonial peoples, and also in recognition of the dispossession of their lands, which first led to the incursion and creation of non-representative sovereign states upon their territories. This is particularly appropriate since dispossession usually occurred through a process of formal law either without consent or through consent gained by the subterfuge of unequal treaties[65] that would fail to satisfy the basic tenets of a contract between two parties, never mind customary legal norms or expressions of the Vienna Convention on the Law of Treaties, 1969.[66]

Another way of conceptualizing self-determination for indigenous peoples is to focus on the increasing jurisprudence of the HRC on the issue of the applicability of Article 1 (2). The Committee has found in favour of indigenous peoples in relation to their right to self-determination in the context of 'subsistence'. This approach is a significant improvement on the previous decisions on indigenous peoples' issues, in which the Committee was extremely reluctant to engage Article 1 at all.[67]

[62] CCPR General Comment No. 12: Article 1 (Right to Self-determination), The Right to Self-determination of Peoples (adopted at the 21st session, 13 March 1984).

[63] CERD General Recommendation XXI (Right to self-determination) (adopted at the 48th session, 23 August 1996).

[64] See especially T Makkonen, *Identity, Difference and Otherness: The Concepts of 'People', 'Indigenous People' and 'Minority' in International Law* (Helsinki: Eric Castren Institute 2000).

[65] See eg the discussions concerning the Treaty of Waitangi in J Castellino and DP Keane, *Minority Rights in the Pacific: A Comparative Legal Analysis* (OUP 2009) 122–9.

[66] For a general commentary on the law of treaties see A Aust, *Modern Treaty Law and Practice* (CUP 2000).

[67] See MikMaq Tribal Case Comm. No. 78/1980 UN Doc Supp. No.40 (A/39/40) at 200 (1984).

However, by ruling that indigenous peoples might have access to rights under Article 1 (2), the HRC could be argued to be taking a restrictive view. While the *travaux préparatoires* to the Covenant makes it clear that the notion of self-determination was framed in relation to colonial peoples, it would seem incongruent that the notion of peoples contained in Article 1 (1) would differ so radically from that in Article 1 (2). Rather it can be argued that since indigenous peoples are recognized as a 'people' for the purposes of Article 1 (2) then that ought to also hold for Article 1 (1), notwithstanding the political exception doctrine.[68] Thus the applicability of Article 1 (1) ought to be considered a derivative of acceptance of Article 1 (2) for the situation, since the article as a whole was in place to deal with the nuances of subjugated peoples.

The only permissible distinction then would be the one suggested above with regard to the potential of resolution to different situations, whereby indigenous peoples living on contiguous territory could access additional rights to those indigenous peoples who lived interspersed among other groups whose rights would need to be heeded. Of course, this approach would be in direct opposition to the HRC's approach in General Comment 12, though arguably that comment pertained to the previous, more conservative era of interpretation on Article 1.

Finally, irrespective of the nature of the group concerned, it can be argued that a new expression of self-determination is emerging in the face of groups who face a threat of physical extinction from within the state in which they exist. With the strength of conviction in the norms against genocide and crimes against humanity, it could be argued that should a state pursue such an agenda as a matter of policy then a natural right to self-defence would exist for the incumbent population; the expression of this right might well take the form of secession from the state, something that arguably occurred long before the recognition of Kosovo.[69] Framed in these terms, the right is arguably closest to *jus secessionis ac resistendi* as expressed by Grotius in *De Jure Pacis*.[70] This idea would also be in keeping with what Koskenniemi once described as the 'romantic notion of self-determination'.[71] In terms of international politics the secessions of East Timor, Eritrea, and Bangladesh would arguably come within this rubric, though the former were achieved through UN-organized plebiscites.[72]

Thus, despite the conceptual and practical weaknesses of self-determination as a discourse and 'right', it remains the vehicle of choice through which indigenous and other submerged nations' rights to territory are often expressed. The right

[68] See D Kretzmer, *The Occupation of Justice: The Supreme Court of Israel and the Occupied Territories* (State University of New York Press 2002) 22–4.

[69] This was the chief argument in J Castellino, 'The Secession of Bangladesh: Setting New Standards in International Law?' (2000) 7 AYBIL 83.

[70] For a general discussion of the framing of this right see Neuberger (n 25). Also see, generally, H Bull, B Kingsbury and A Roberts, *Hugo Grotius and International Relations* (OUP 1990).

[71] Koskenniemi (n 5).

[72] The Western Sahara Case is also scheduled for decision through a plebiscite though the decision of who is entitled to vote continues to cause much consternation. See eg *Report of the Secretary General* UN Doc S/2002/467 19th April 2002.

itself has seen numerous changes since its early expressions and on each occasion it has responded to political contexts and transformed its political nuances. Giving such a principle, of uncertain substantive content, the authority of a legal tenet was arguably fraught with danger: yet political forces seeking transformation have played a key role in sweeping up this principle and selecting it for expression of freedom in the face of oppression. In looking towards it as a tool for modern freedom from oppression, Kingsbury's warning vis-à-vis the future of self-determination is worth heeding:

> [The] argument from decolonisation has been reinforced by practice suggesting that self-determination in the strong form as a right to establish as separate state may be an extraordinary remedy in distinct territories suffering massive human rights violations orchestrated by governing authorities based elsewhere in the state...But the far reaching argument that self-determination in this strong form of statehood or almost complete autonomy is essential as a general precondition for human rights does not establish which groups or territories are the units of self-determination for the purposes of human rights enhancement; not does it overcome legitimate concerns about the threats to human rights and to human security posed by repeated fragmentation and irredentism. The remedial human rights justification for self-determination, while persuasive in some cases, is most unlikely to become normal rather than exceptional unless the sovereignty and legitimacy of states declines precipitously.[73]

V. Conclusion

While self-determination is likely to continue to have its detractors—mainly sovereign states, who view it as a threat to territorial sovereignty—the concept, with its attendant promises of freedom from oppression, keeps raising its head in various different contexts. In contemporary terms, five models of political self-determination could be discerned:

(a) Political self-determination for a 'peoples' or 'submerged nation', loosely understood as encompassing 'nationhood' in the sense of a long-shared historical cohesion and a territorially based identity;

(b) Political self-determination offered to territorially based indigenous peoples or 'submerged nations' living in a contiguous zone, including determination of and proprietary over the title to the territory they inhabit;

(c) Non-political self-determination to non-territorially based indigenous peoples that confers rights falling short of title to territory but guarantees access to human rights law and seeks to address issues of personal autonomy;

[73] B Kingsbury, 'Restructuring Self-determination: A Relational Approach' in P Aikio and M Scheinin (eds), *Operationalizing the Right of Indigenous Peoples to Self-Determination* (Institute for Human Rights 2000) 23.

(d) Non-political self-determination to minorities that guarantees human rights and access to special measures but does not confer the right of self-determination in a political sense;

(e) A remedial right of self-determination in the event where widespread and consistent rights denial occurs against a recognizable vulnerable group (indigenous people or minority).

Past injustices such as colonization are protected from legal scrutiny in modern international law via the *inter-temporal rule of law*.[74] The rule needs to be commended since it would clearly be unjust to seek to project a more progressive notion of law and its underpinning morality onto the actions of the past in a bid to determine culpability. This would violate basic legal entitlements against retrospection against revisionist notions. While the validity of revisionist notions is being questioned in other forums,[75] it is not the purpose here to seek to question the rule itself, but rather to demonstrate the extent to which the rule is incoherent and often applied inappropriately to situations governing the treatment of territory in modern international law. If the actions of European powers in annexing territories in Africa in the late nineteenth century are beyond culpability because they ought to be subject to the *inter-temporal rule*, then the temporal context of that time bears examination. The decolonization of Latin America provides as appropriate a temporal context as necessary. By analysing and discussing notions that concerned not only territoriality but also the manner of conquests of colonies, the tone was set in customary international law for the development and further solidification of norms of international law against wanton conquest and annexation of territory. Viewed from this perspective, a conclusion can be drawn that the norms that had developed and that were considered appropriate in Latin America were disregarded on purpose in the colonization of Africa. The situation was compounded by blatant violations of the norms governing the signing of 'treaties' as European powers sought to challenge each other in the bid to accumulate colonies in the continent.[76] Further, in decolonizing these territories, the need for 'international' order was considered so sacrosanct that it overruled the history and geography of postcolonial entities. Rather than seeking to accommodate and negotiate with diverse peoples that happened to fall within rigidly defined frontiers, the simplistic decision to maintain colonial boundaries was taken, with severe long-term implications. While nearly universally accepted by western-trained state leaders in Africa, this course of action failed to accommodate non-state actors who sought to gain legitimacy by seeking statehood themselves.[77] The result has been numerous

[74] For more on the intertemporal rule see TO Elias, 'The Doctrine of Intertemporal Law' (1980) 74 AJIL 285.

[75] See *Irving* v *Penguin Books Ltd. & D. Lipstadt* (2001) EWCA Civ 1197 (20th July 2001).

[76] See P Gifford and WR Louis, *France and Britain in Africa: Imperial Rivalry and Colonial Rule* (Yale University Press 1971); LH Gann and P Duignan, *The Rulers of British Africa 1870–1914* (Croom Helm 1978); JD Hargreaves, *West Africa Partitioned* vol. 1 (Macmillan 1974).

[77] This is often justified in an African context by recourse to the Cairo Declaration of 1963, which was adopted by the Heads of States of African countries. But this in itself is arguably not an effective

conflicts of 'post-modern tribalism',[78] as artificial colonial boundaries only of significance for roughly 50 years (and much less in some instances) are sought to be renegotiated along more historical lines.[79]

While the application of the doctrine of *uti possidetis*, which solidified the sanctity of colonial boundaries, does allow change in the face of consent, it is important to stress that this consent is required between existing sovereign states and thus generally rules out non-state actors. These actors have no explicit right to demand territorial adjustment, even though this is a facet of the first and foremost human right as recognized in the two International Covenants of 1966. Existing states have sought to minimize the impact of the right of self-determination by declaring it to be a right that only exists in 'internal' guises.[80] While notions of international order are to be cherished, self-determination is often downgraded by states, to the right to a form of limited autonomy. In this form it is inadequate in meeting the aspirations of indigenous peoples and submerged nations, who aspire to the rhetoric of promised emancipation. The artificiality of the boundaries and the failure to address the problematic nature of the acquisition of territory exacerbate this dilution and further reduce the impact of self-determination. This often results in aggrieved and unrepresented 'peoples' within a state seeking secession, and in a bid to access the international right to self-determination these groups may even seek to pierce the veil of domestic sovereignty and internationalize their conflicts with their respective state governments.[81]

Thus all entitlements of self-determination vis-à-vis the three groups essentially flounder on the need for order and the determination of that order through international politics. International law is keen to guarantee order and to stymie any norm that could potentially violate such order. In keeping with the process of self-determination it stresses that this should involve the accommodation of differing national identities within the confines of the state, rather than the creation and/or dismembering of older states. Human rights instruments take up this cause but, although recognizing the importance of self-determination, are less keen to make the connection between it and the proprietary rights, in deference to state parties. The attempt to enshrine property rights within the International Covenants was effectively sacrificed in the discussion between East and West.

test since it was the territorial rights of these very sovereigns that was guaranteed by the adoption of such a principle. See, generally, Neuberger (n 25); also A Mazrui, *Towards a Pax Africana: A Study of Ideology and Ambition* (Weidenfield & Nicholson 1967).

[78] See TM Franck, 'Post-modern Tribalism and the Right to Secession' in C Brölmann, R Lefeber, and M Zieck (eds), *Peoples & Minorities in International Law* (Martinus Nijhoff 1993) 3.

[79] See D Wippman (ed), *International Law & Ethnic Conflict* (Cornell University Press 1998).

[80] See P Thornberry, 'The Democratic or Internal Aspect of Self-determination with Remarks on Federalism' in C Tomuschat (ed), *Modern Law of Self-determination* (Martinus Nijhoff 1994) 101.

[81] As is occurring in several ethnic conflicts: see F De Varennes, 'Minority Rights and the Prevention of Ethnic Conflicts' (Working Group on Minorities, 6th session 22–26 May 2000). E/CN.4/Sub.2/AC.5/2000/CRP.3. Also see CO Quaye, *Liberation Struggles in International Law* (Temple University Press 1991).

Thus human rights instruments stress the availability of rights to all, are willing to make special concessions for indigenous peoples and minorities—but are reluctant for these concessions to take on the mantle of the title to territory. From the perspective of indigenous peoples and submerged nations, self-determination often has to include some manifestation of the relationship of the community to the territory, and more importantly the relationship of settlers vis-à-vis that territory. While the general growth of enfranchisement of indigenous peoples within the UN and most states' systems is commendable, it remains akin, in many cases, to the granting of full franchise to members living within a colonial setting. For a fully acceptable solution, the underlying basis of the self-determination claim needs to be addressed.

But the constraints to such an address remain clear, especially in the Transnistria, South Ossetia, Abkhazia, and Nagorno-Karabakh: populations that have subsequently settled upon the territory have claims too. The state often acts in the interest of these settler claims, and it is the state that consents to human rights law in the name of its inhabitants. The frustration of this particular debate has resulted in the slowing of several important legal documents within the UN system,[82] within regional settings[83] and also in the context of other organizations.[84] The stalling point remains the issue of land rights and while important case law is being developed on the subject,[85] this tends to occur within domestic rather than international settings.[86] Thus we remain a considerable way from being able to address the issue of the entitlement to self-determination in a manner that can guarantee any legal certainty. Instead, political factors such as the use of force and the cultivation of geostrategic relationships within the international community remain a more compelling force. Each of the authors of the case studies from the CIS region demonstrates these issues in detail in their chapter. In doing so they also highlight the fact that the discussions on self-determination seem to focus more on the

[82] Draft Declaration on the Rights of Indigenous Peoples, UN Doc. E/CN.4/1995/2; E/CN.4/Sub.2/1994/56, 28 October 1994 at 105–15; reprinted in (1995) 34 ILM 541. See S Wiessner, 'The 2000 Revision of the United Nations Draft Principles and Guidelines on the Protection of the Heritage of Indigenous People' (2000) 13 St. Thomas LR 383. For a general discussion see P Thornberry, *Indigenous Peoples & Human Rights* (Juris Publishing 2002) 370–396.

[83] See the *Proposed American Declaration on the Rights of Indigenous Peoples* approved by the Inter-American Commission on Human Rights at its 133rd session, Feb 26, 1997, OEA/Ser.L/V/II.9, doc.7, rev. 1997; also see Thornberry (n 82) 397–404.

[84] For a commentary on developing standards at the World Bank vis-à-vis Indigenous Peoples see F MacKay, 'Universal Rights or Universe Onto Itself? Indigenous Peoples' Human Rights and the World Bank's Draft Operational Policy 4.10' (2002) 17 AUILR 527; also see *Convention Concerning Indigenous and Tribal Peoples in Independent Countries,* Sept 5, 1991 169 ILO 1989, especially Articles 13–17.

[85] For a relatively wide comparison of developments see I Sansani, 'American Indian Land Rights in the Inter-American System: Dann v. United States' (2003) 10 HRB 2; O Kreimer, '"Indigenous Peoples" Right to Land, Territories and Natural Resources: A Technical Meeting of the OAS Working Group' (2003) 10 HRB 13.

[86] There have been numerous significant achievements at regional level, particularly within the Inter-American system. For more on this see SJ Anaya, 'Protection of Indigenous Peoples' Rights over Lands and Natural Resources under the Inter-American Human Rights System' (2001) 14 HHRJ 33.

territory than the people, with boundaries drawn on maps becoming significantly more relevant than issues such as 'identity', whether 'national', linguistic, ethnic, or religious. Against this, the fact remains that claims for self-determination *do not* disappear, but continue to grow in vehemence and, as viewed over a longer span of history, may eventually lead to a reconfiguration of the states, irrespective of the 'legitimacy' of such claims.

4

The Role of Recognition and Non-Recognition with Regard to Secession

Stefan Oeter

I. Introduction: After Kosovo—Has Kosovo Changed Anything?

The project from which the contributions to this book resulted was placed under the heading 'After Kosovo'. But when one looks, with a certain dose of scepticism, at the recent discussions on the Kosovo precedent—in particular the Kosovo authorities' unilateral Declaration of Independence (UDI) of 2010—as well as at the ICJ Advisory Opinion delivered upon the issue of this declaration,[1] a fundamental question immediately arises: has the Kosovo precedent really changed anything? Admittedly, quite an important group of states has recognized Kosovo as an independent state in the wake of the UDI—despite the Serbian claim of still possessing territorial sovereignty over Kosovo, and despite SC Resolution 1244, which still applies to the situation and which confirmed Serbia's title of territorial sovereignty.[2] The recognizing states thus clearly departed from traditional practice that tended to avoid recognition as long as territorial sovereignty over a seceding territory remained in dispute. The move towards recognition of Kosovo, however, has met strong resistance—and, by and large, the community of states remains divided over whether such recognition makes sense (or is even legally feasible).[3]

[1] *Accordance with International Law of Unilateral Declaration of Independence in Respect of Kosovo* (Advisory Opinion), ICJ Reports 2010, 141 (July 22, 2010)—in the following abbreviated as 'ICJ Advisory Opinion'.

[2] Concerning the intricate relationship between the 2010 ICJ Advisory Opinion and Res. 1244 see S Oeter, 'Secession, Territorial Integrity and the Role of the Security Council' in P Hilpold (ed), *Kosovo and International Law. The ICJ Advisory Opinion of 22 July 2010* (Brill 2012) 109, 122–8, and MG Kohen and K Del Mar, 'The Kosovo Advisory Opinion and UNSCR 1244 (1999)' (2011) 24 LJIL 109–26, but also C Schaller, 'Die Sezession des Kosovo und der völkerrechtliche Status der internationalen Präsenz' (2008) 46 Archiv des Völkerrechts 131, 145–62.

[3] See eg S Richter, 'The Political Future of Kosovo after the ICJ Opinion: Status Question (Un) Resolved?' in P Hilpold (ed), *Kosovo and International Law. The ICJ Advisory Opinion of 22 July 2010* (Brill 2012) 263–80; S Tierney, 'The Long Intervention in Kosovo—A Self-Determination Imperative?' in J Summers (ed), *Kosovo: A Precedent?* (Nijhoff 2011) 249–78; as to the internal

Thus, the Kosovo precedent has aggravated the tension over issues of recognition with regard to secession cases—and has given additional fuel to principled disputes over recognition vs. non-recognition in such cases.[4] As a result, the Kosovo precedent has definitely not brought new light into the disputed landscape of recognition policies and the underlying theoretical queries in international legal doctrine—quite to the contrary, it has added to the already visible confusion in the field.[5]

What about the Kosovo Advisory Opinion of the International Court of Justice of 2010? The ICJ remained silent in this Opinion on the decisive issues of recognition and non-recognition, although the questions of recognition and secession constituted a kind of 'elephant in the room' when the Kosovo case was debated before the ICJ.[6] The formula used by the court, namely that international law does not contain any prohibition on declarations of independence, is not really helpful in this regard, since it confuses the legal issues at stake more than that it delivers a fruitful contribution to their resolution. Such a statement, if it is to be taken seriously, rests on the assumption that the authors of the declaration of independence are mere civil society actors not bound by international law. Whether this was really true in the case of the elected members of the Kosovo Assembly that together issued the declaration, relying on their democratic credentials of being elected (to the Kosovo Assembly), is an issue open to dispute.[7]

disputes inside the EU see W Koeth, 'State Building Without a State: The EU's Dilemma in Defining its Relations with Kosovo' (2010) 15 EFAR 227–247, in particular 233–7.

[4] The Kosovo Assembly's UDI has given rise to an extended dispute in public international law writings—see A Orakhelashvili, 'Statehood, Recognition and the United Nations System: A Unilateral Declaration of Independence in Kosovo' (2008) 12 Max Planck UNYB 1 et seq., D Fierstein, 'Kosovo's Declaration of Independence: An Incident Analysis of Legality, Policy and Future Implications' (2008) 26 BUILJ 418 et seq.; R Muharremi, 'Kosovo's Declaration of Independence: Self-Determination and Sovereignty Revisited' (2008) 33 RCEEL 401 et seq.; B Jia, 'The Independence of Kosovo: A Unique Case of Secession?' (2009) 8 Chinese JIL 27 et seq.; P Šturma, 'The Case of Kosovo and International Law' (2009) 29 PYBIL 51 et seq.; J Vidmar, 'International Legal Responses to Kosovo's Declaration of Independence' (2009) 42 VJTL 778 et seq.; I Cismas, 'Secession in Theory and Practice: The Case of Kosovo and Beyond' (2010) 2 GJIL 531 et seq.; T Fleiner, 'The Unilateral Secession of Kosovo as a Precedent in International Law' in U Fastenrath (ed), *From Bilateralism to Community Interest* (OUP 2011) 877 et seq.; T Jaber, 'A Case for Kosovo? Self-determination and Secession in the 21st Century' (2011) 15 IJHR 926 et seq.; D Shelton, 'Self-Determination in Regional Human Rights Law: From Kosovo to Cameroon' (2011) 105 AJIL 60 et seq.

[5] See C Tomuschat, 'Recognition of New States—The Case of Premature Recognition' in P Hilpold (ed), *Kosovo and International Law. The ICJ Advisory Opinion of 22 July 2010* (Brill 2012) 31–46.

[6] See also T Burri, 'The Kosovo Opinion and Secession: The Sounds of Silence and Missing Links' (2010) 11 GLJ 881, 885 et seq.; RA Falk, 'The Kosovo Advisory Opinion' (2011) 105 AJIL 50 et seq.; T Christakis, 'The ICJ Advisory Opinion on Kosovo: Has International Law Something to Say About Secession?' (2011) 24 LJIL 73, 74–80.

[7] See in this regard Oeter (n 2) 125–8; A Gattini, '"You Say You'll Change the Constitution"—The ICJ and Non-State Entities in the Kosovo Advisory Opinion' in P Hilpold (ed), *Kosovo and International Law. The ICJ Advisory Opinion of 22 July 2010* (Brill 2012), 233–54; R Howse and R Teitel, 'Delphic Dictum: How Has the ICJ Contributed to the Global Rule of Law by Its Ruling on Kosovo?' (2010) 11 GLJ 841 et seq., 843; and Burri (n 6) 882 et seq.; M Bothe, 'Kosovo—So What? The Holding of the International Court of Justice is not the Last Word on Kosovo's Independence' (2010) 11 GLJ 837 et seq., 838, Kohen and Del Mar (n 2) 109 et seq., as well as E Cirkovic, 'An Analysis of the ICJ Advisory Opinion on Kosovo's Unilateral Declaration of Independence' (2010)

Be that as it may, the Advisory Question leaves completely unanswered the question of whether the declared new state of the 'Republika Kosova' really fulfils the criteria under international law to qualify (and be recognized) as an independent and sovereign state.[8] The ICJ thus leaves us international lawyers (and the international community in general) still alone with the confusing puzzle raised by conflicting claims of sovereignty.[9] There may have existed good reasons of judicial politics to narrow down the question answered in the Opinion, and accordingly to avoid any hint of an answer to the delicate (and very disputed) questions of secession, of statehood of secessionist entities, and of subsequent recognition of such 'de facto' units of statehood.[10] The court as a result managed to speak with one voice, not ending up in a kind of *non liquet* as was the case in the Nuclear Weapons Advisory Opinion—but the price paid is quite high. The decisive issue of the legality of recognition of secessionist entities like Kosovo has remained open, and still divides the international community (and also the European Union).

If we want to assess the questions of statehood and recognition (or non-recognition) of secessionist entities, we still have to look to traditional theories and have to analyse corresponding state practice. State practice on recognition, however, has ended up in a state of confusion anyway as a result of the events accompanying the dissolution of Yugoslavia.[11] Accordingly, the paper must take a very careful look at such

11 GLJ 895 at 903 et seq. and MD Öberg, 'The Legal Effects of United Nations Resolutions in the Kosovo Advisory Opinion' (2011) 105 AJIL 81 at 84 et seq.

[8] See eg Tomuschat (n 5) 36–40.

[9] As critical comments to the Kosovo Advisory Opinion see Bothe (n 7); Howse and Teitel (n 7); Cirkovic (n 7); C Ryngaert, 'The ICJ's Advisory Opinion on Kosovo's Declaration of Independence: A Missed Opportunity?' (2009) 57 NILR 481 et seq.; A Rusniah and DI Efevwerhan, 'The ICJ Opinion on Kosovo: Symphony or Cacophony?' (2010) 50 IJIL 545 et seq.; DH Meester, 'The International Court of Justice's Kosovo Case: Assessing the Current State of International Legal Opinion on Remedial Secession' (2010) 48 CYIL 215–54; V Röben, 'The ICJ Advisory Opinion on the Unilateral Declaration of Independence in Respect of Kosovo' (2010) 2 GJIL 1063 et seq.; Christakis (n 6) 73–86; JA Frowein, 'Kosovo and Lotus' in U Fastenrath (ed), *From Bilateralism to Community Interest* (OUP 2011) 923 et seq.; Falk (n 6) 50 et seq.; Kohen and Del Mar (n 2) 109 et seq.; M Weller, 'Modesty Can be a Virtue—Judicial Economy in the ICJ Kosovo Opinion?' (2011) 24 LJIL 127 et seq.; R Wilde, 'Self-Determination, Secession, and Dispute Settlement after the Kosovo Advisory Opinion' (2011) 24 LJIL 149 et seq.; D Jacobs and Y Radi, 'Waiting for Godot: An Analysis of the Advisory Opinion on Kosovo' (2011) 24 LJIL 331 et seq.; J Vidmar, 'The Kosovo Advisory Opinion Scrutinized' (2011) 24 LJIL 355 et seq.; J Summers (ed), *Kosovo—A Precedent?* (Nijhoff 2011); K Oellers-Frahm, 'Problematic Question or Problematic Answer? Observations on the International Court of Justice's Advisory Opinion Concerning Kosovo's Unilateral Declaration of Independence' (2011) 53 GYIL 793 et seq.; A Orakhelashvilli, 'The International Court's Advisory Opinion on the UDI in Respect of Kosovo' (2011) 15 Max Planck UNYB 65 et seq.; R Tricot and B Sander, 'The Broader Consequences of the International Court of Justice's Advisory Opinion on the Unilateral Declaration of Independence in Respect of Kosovo' (2011) 49 Columbia JTL 321 et seq.; Oeter (n 2) 109–138; P Hilpold, 'Secession in International Law: Does the Kosovo Opinion Require a Re-assessment of this Concept?' in P Hilpold (ed), *Kosovo and International Law. The ICJ Advisory Opinion of 22 July 2010* (Brill 2012) 47–78.

[10] See Oeter (n 2) 127–8; in addition CD Espósito, 'El discreto ejercicio de la función consultiva de la Corte Internacional de la Justicia en el asunto Kosovo' (2011) 63 Revista española de derecho internacional 125–47; H Hannum, 'The Advisory Opinion on Kosovo' (2011) 24 LJIL 155–61.

[11] See in detail R Caplan, *Europe and the Recognition of New States in Yugoslavia* (CUP 2005), as well as P Radan, *The Break-Up of Yugoslavia and International Law* (Routledge 2002) 160–243.

practice in the past two decades in order to develop a plausible reconstruction of the current state of the role of recognition and non-recognition with regard to secession. There is a big question mark here: can we really take the Kosovo case as a precedent and, following from such precedent, argue a new policy line on recognition to be required by international law with regard to cases such as Transnistria, Abkhazia, South Ossetia, and Nagorno-Karabakh,[12] and potentially other cases in future? Has Kosovo produced a change of tide in international recognition practice, or is this a minor incident of misguided policy in an unfortunate case, leaving unchanged the 'longue durée' of recognition patterns? Such questions are not easy to answer, but international legal practice needs answers to these questions in order to avoid the traps of 'subjective' misconstruction of what constitutes the state of the law.

II. Traditional Doctrines of Recognition

Recognition of new political entities may happen in various forms—usually by explicit declarations, but also in implicit ways.[13] The real problem about recognition, however, is less its practical mode of exercise than its legal nature and consequences.[14] The landscape of recognition doctrine has been ravaged by long and protracted turf wars between the so-called 'declaratory' and 'constitutive' theories.[15] Most treatises of international law still describe the 'declaratory theory' as the dominant doctrine governing state practice.[16] As main characteristics of the 'declaratory theory' on recognition, the writings of public international law usually describe that:

> sovereign statehood, ie the quality of being an independent and sovereign state, constitutes a mere fact which may be assessed in an empirical fashion;[17]

[12] See CJ Borgen, 'From Kosovo to Catalonia—Separatism and Integration in Europe' (2010) 2 GJIL 997–1033.

[13] On the various modes of recognition see J Ker-Lindsay, *The Foreign Policy of Counter Secession* (OUP 2013) 7–9; I Brownlie, 'Recognition in Theory and Practice' in R St. J MacDonald and DM Johnston (eds), *The Structure and Process of International Law. Essays in Legal Philosophy Doctrine and Theory* (Nijhoff 1983) 628–9.

[14] With regard to the theoretical debates on recognition, and how these fit to state practice, see J Dugard, 'The Secession of States and their Recognition in the Wake of Kosovo' (2011) 357 Recueil des Cours de l'Académie de Droit International 13, 45–57; M Fabry, *Recognizing States: International Society and the Establishment of New States Since 1776* (OUP 2009); WT Worster, 'Law, Politics, and the Conception of the State in State Recognition Theory' (2009) 27 BUILJ 115, 119–45; J Crawford, *The Creation of States in International Law* (2nd edn, Clarendon 2006), 17–28; J Dugard and D Raič, 'The Role of Recognition in the Law and Practice of Secession' in MG Kohen, *Secession: International Law Perspectives* (CUP 2006) 94, 96–101; S Talmon, 'The Constitutive versus the Declaratory Theory of Recognition' (2004) 75 BYIL 101–181; TD Grant, *The Recognition of States: Law and Practice in Debate and Evolution* (Praeger 1999) 1–38.

[15] See in detail U Saxer, *Die internationale Steuerung der Selbstbestimmung und der Staatsentstehung* (Springer 2010), 703–18; see in addition BR Roth, 'Secessions, Coups and the International Rule of Law: Assessing the Decline of the Effective Control Doctrine' (2010) 11 MJIL 393, 393, 396–8.

[16] See eg Ker-Lindsay (n 13) 16–17.

[17] See eg J Vidmar, 'Territorial Integrity and the Law of Statehood' (2012) George Washington ILR 697, 700–70; Roth (n 15) 396; S Talmon, *Kollektive Nichtanerkennung illegaler Staaten*

the underlying judgment of whether a political entity is a sovereign state constitutes a mere act of cognition oriented at criteria of effectiveness of state authority, and not a genuinely normative judgment;[18]

statehood in essence requires exclusive sovereignty over a distinct territory and people exercised by an effective structure of authority;[19]

a state worthy of recognition must be independent of foreign states and may not be subjected to a hierarchical relationship of authority exercised by another state.[20]

Such an empirical approach at first glance seems appealing because it avoids becoming entangled in a myriad of normative judgments on the political (democratic, constitutional) quality of a certain regime and the state-building process leading to its creation. The problems of such a strongly normative approach may still be seen in the problems raised by the recognition of governments[21]—does it make sense at all to recognize governments, and if we do so, what are the normative criteria guiding such recognition? Does it make sense to look merely for effectiveness of authority, ie sheer exercise of brute power, or should we look for criteria of constitutional legitimacy—and in the latter case, what are these criteria and where do they derive from?

There may be some wisdom in trying to avoid such normative questions, and it is no coincidence that most states stopped recognizing governments during the 1970s and 1980s.[22] But issues of recognition of governments are back on the stage of international relations: an 'emerging right to democratic governance' and the corresponding condemnation of coups d'état requires the community of democratic states to withhold recognition in cases of putsch governments based on mere force in order to create pressure towards the reconstruction of constitutional (and democratic) legitimacy.[23] Also, the recent case of recognition of the Libyan National Transitional Council as the government of Libya has indicated a change with regard to recognition patterns vis-à-vis governments.[24] A comparable stumbling block seems to exist with regard to recognition of secessionist entities.

(Mohr Siebeck 2006) 218–33; D Raić, *Statehood and the Law of Self-Determination* (Kluwer 2002) 50–82; J Castellino, *International Law and Self-Determination: The Interplay of the Politics of Territorial Possession with Formulations of Post-Colonial 'National' Identity* (Nijhoff 2000), 77–89.

[18] See Saxer (n 15) 705.

[19] See eg Roth (n 15) 398–404; Ker-Lindsay (n 13) 27–28; Crawford (n 14) 45–61.

[20] See eg Ker-Lindsay (n 13) 29; Crawford (n 14) 62–89.

[21] See eg MJ Peterson, *Recognition of Governments: Legal Doctrine and State Practice, 1815–1995* (Macmillan 1997); S Talmon, *Recognition of Governments in International Law* (Clarendon 1998); BR Roth, *Governmental Illegitimacy in International Law* (Clarendon 1999) 121–99.

[22] See Talmon (n 21) 3–14; Peterson (n 21) 88.

[23] See Roth (n 15) 422–39; J d'Aspremont, 'Responsibility for Coups d'État in International Law' (2010) 18 TJICL 451–475; Roth, *Governmental Illegitimacy* 365–412; SD Murphy, 'Democratic Legitimacy and the Recognition of States and Governments' (1999) 48 ICLQ 545–81.

[24] See A Schuit, 'Recognition of Governments in International Law and the Recent Conflict in Libya' (2012) 14 ICLR 381–402; G Nesi, 'Recognition of the Libyan National Transitional Council' (2011) 21 IYIL 45–59.

If analysed carefully, it remains open to doubt whether a simple, unreserved 'declaratory' approach really provides an accurate description of current state practice.[25] Secession is perceived by most states in the world to be a severe threat to international order and a menace to the orderly development of statehood in the nation states constituting the international society. Accordingly, there exists a strong bias against secession in state practice.[26] This bias can be easily seen if one looks to the persistent practice of non-recognition of secessionist entities as long as the previous territorial sovereign has not given up its title of territorial sovereignty over a disputed territory.[27] For a very long time this approach of non-recognition constituted the 'iron rule' of traditional recognition practice with regard to secession.[28]

The underlying value judgement is not difficult to discern. The traditional practice of non-recognition of secessionist entities is based upon a widespread perception in the international community that territorial integrity constitutes a primordial value for a system based upon the idea of peaceful coexistence of states.[29] To be exact: the addressees of such rule are not internal societal movements, such as rebels, insurgents, or revolutionary groups, but the other states. The civil society factions that struggle over the organization of statehood within a state are not bound by international law. In this regard, the ICJ was quite right in its Kosovo Advisory Opinion, at least in principle. Societal movements within a state quarreling over the way in which the state should be organized may act illegally from the perspective of a given legal (and constitutional) order. But the internal quarrel is not a matter of legitimate international concern, at least as long as the quarreling factions do not violate—in terms of a 'gross and consistent pattern'—fundamental human rights. Quite to the contrary, the substantial questions of political organization being at stake in such quarrels, as well as the ways and means by which such quarrel is carried out, are issues of internal self-determination to be decided solely by the people in question, if necessary even by civil war.[30] This does not change if the quarrel goes beyond questions of adequate political and constitutional organization inside a state and extends to questions of territorial organization of statehood as such, ie the question of whether diverse parts of a population want to live together in a state or would prefer separate statehood. The internal quarrel over separate statehood (and secession) remains in principle an issue of self-determination—at

[25] See Saxer (n 15) 706–9, but also J Vidmar, 'Explaining the Legal Effects of Recognition' (2012) 61 ICLQ 361–87 and C Hillgruber, 'The Admission of New States to the International Community' (1998) 9 EJIL 491, 492–5.

[26] See, in particular, Ker-Lindsay (n 13) 24 (and very much in detail, as regards the reasons of such bias, 109–29); see in addition MG Kohen, 'Introduction' in MG Kohen (ed), *Secession: International Law Perspectives* (CUP 2006) 1, 3–4, as well as Dugard and Raič (n 14) 94–5.

[27] See Vidmar (n 17) 709–19.

[28] See eg Vidmar (n 25) 363–4.

[29] See eg J Mayall, 'Secession and International Order' in A Pavković and P Radan (eds), *The Ashgate Research Companion to Secession* (Ashgate 2011), 11, 16; Vidmar (n 17) 706–9; Dugard (n 14) 31–2, 98–107; Fabry (n 14) 204–7.

[30] See S Oeter, 'Self-Determination' in B Simma et al. (eds), *The Charter of the United Nations. A Commentary* (OUP 2012, 3rd edn) 313, para 41.

its outset not of the 'people' claiming separate statehood, but of the entire population of the pre-existing state which must determine the question of continued joint statehood or separation.

The result of such a quarrel ultimately will not depend on matters of (internal) legality, which by definition will be disputed in such cases, but on essentially political factors: which faction has more support in the population, has more resources, and can consolidate its claim for legitimacy.[31] There will always exist some cause for secession, otherwise a secessionist movement could not mobilize enough public support to become politically relevant. Whether such cause justifies separation, however, is not a matter to be judged by the outside world. Accordingly, traditional doctrine has dealt with phenomena of secession as a mere factual issue not governed as such by international law.[32] It constitutes a legally neutral act whose consequences are regulated internationally.[33] Particularly regulated under international law is the permissibility of third-state reaction to quarrels over secession. Third states may not support armed opposition groups militarily, and also may not provide secessionist movements with military items, training, or other kinds of significant material support capable of changing the political balance of power—if provided nevertheless, such support would qualify as a prohibited intervention.[34] Such prohibition of intervention also applies to 'premature' forms of recognition of secessionist movements in terms of a separate statehood.[35] The resulting rule of non-recognition of (unfinished) secessions secures—at least in the perspective of a more traditional brand of international lawyers—peace and stability of the international order.

Does this established pattern of non-recognition tell us anything about the adequacy of traditional doctrines of recognition? Probably not, since a pattern of non-recognition of secessionist entities is also explicable to a certain degree in terms of the declaratory theory. The continuing claim of the previous territorial sovereign puts into doubt the claim of exclusive authority raised by the new political entity—the former territorial sovereign will continue to exercise some authority over parts of the territory, or at least has reserved such exercise of authority, and could potentially regain its authority without violating any rule of international law.

[31] See A Pavković and P Radan, *Creating New States: Theory and Practice of Secession* (Ashgate 2007) 33–163.

[32] See D Thürer and T Burri, 'Secession' in *The Max Planck Encyclopedia of Public International Law* (OUP online 2012) para 14, as well as AP Rubin, 'Secession and Self-Determination: A Legal, Moral, and Political Analysis' (2000) 36 Stanford JIL 253, 257 and Kohen (n 26) 4; but see also, as a critical analysis of such traditional doctrine, T Christakis, 'The State as a "Primary Fact": Some Thoughts on the Principle of Effectiveness' in MG Kohen (ed), *Secession: International Law Perspectives* (CUP 2006) 138–70.

[33] See Crawford (n 14) 390.

[34] See P Kunig, 'Intervention, Prohibition of' in *Max Planck Encyclopedia of Public International Law* (OUP online 2012) para 34, and—as far as direct military support is concerned—G Nolte, 'Secession and External Intervention' in MG Kohen (ed), *Secession: International Law Perspectives* (CUP 2006) 65, 76–93.

[35] See D Geldenhuys, 'Secession and Contested States' in A Pavković and P Radan (eds), *The Ashgate Research Companion to Secession* (Ashgate 2011) 285, 291, but also Raić (n 17) 92–104 and Dugard (n 14) 27–30.

But if there are competing contenders for public authority over territory and people, there does not exist 'exclusive' authority that constitutes the hallmark of sovereignty. There exists a limit, at least in terms of the 'declaratory theory'. Can the previous territorial sovereign indefinitely uphold claims of territorial sovereignty, even if it has factually lost all his control over territory and people? The phenomenon of 'stabilized de facto regimes'[36] creates severe problems for a purely declaratory approach, since it is difficult to explain why long-standing factual authority of one sovereign effectively excluding the other does not constitute effective authority, and thus sovereign statehood. If 'effectiveness' is the only decisive criterion, effective authority over a certain period of time must lead to independent statehood, and thus to the admissibility of recognition by third states.

State practice, as such an intellectual experiment with radical insistence upon effectiveness demonstrates, definitively relies on normative criteria when dealing with issues of secession.[37] This is relatively easy in cases where the intervention of third states, constituting illegal use of force under international law, has brought about the effective separation. In such situations, the Stimson doctrine, ie the rule of non-recognition of the results of illegal use of force, overrides all considerations of effectiveness.[38] The same might in principle be true for arguments resulting from the right of self-determination, which undoubtedly constitutes a rule of *jus cogens*. The broad support for anti-colonial struggles of liberation demonstrates the point.[39] States did not care about the claimed 'territorial integrity' of colonial powers, since the quest for self-determination of 'non-self-governing' peoples of colonial entities was perceived as legitimate. The same judgement does not hold true for claims of self-determination raised by parts of the population of 'self-governing', established states: this constitutes the backbone of postcolonial international practice. The community of states shows a strong reluctance to support processes of secession—many states feel threatened by separatist movements and perceive secession to erode the stability of the international order.[40]

[36] See JA Frowein, 'De Facto Regime' in *Max Planck Encyclopedia of Public International Law* (OUP online 2012); S Pegg, *International Society and the De Facto State* (Ashgate 1999) 26–52, 173–202; see in addition N Caspersen and GR Stansfield (eds), *Unrecognized States in the International System* (Routledge 2011); E Berg and R Toomla, 'Forms of Normalisation in the Quest for De Facto Statehood' (2009) 44 International Spectator 27–45; D Geldenhuys, *Contested States in World Politics* (Palgrave Macmillan 2009) 29–44.

[37] See also, with an argument in the same direction, Grant (n 14) 83–119.

[38] See eg Vidmar (n 25) 381–386; Christakis (n 6) 82–83; Kohen (n 26) 8; Talmon (n 17) 239–258; D Turns, 'The Stimson Doctrine of Non-Recognition: Its Historical Genesis and Influence on Contemporary International Law' (2003) 2 CJIL 105–43; Raić (n 17) 122–8.

[39] The argument is also made in Roth (n 15) 393–440; see in addition TD Grant, 'Regulating the Creation of States: From Decolonization to Secession' (2009) 5 JLIR 11, 23–36.

[40] See Geldenhuys (n 35), 293, but also R Higgins, 'Self-Determination and Secession' in J Dahlitz (ed), *Secession and International Law* (T.M.C. Asser Press 2003) 21–38.

III. International Legal Perspectives on Secession

Counterclaims have been made in legal doctrine, but these claims are difficult to sustain in terms of customary law, ie as a result of practice and *opinio juris*. Arguing that every group of persons having something in common in terms of language, culture, religion, or ethnicity forms a 'people' in the sense of the doctrine of self-determination, having a title to statehood,[41] does not really make sense, at least not as long as self-determination is directed towards separate statehood.

A brief look into the historical evolution of the right of self-determination tells us that there is only one clear core area where the bearer of the right is beyond dispute: the case of decolonization, where state practice has confirmed that non-self-governing territories (as well as trusteeship territories) enjoy an unconditional right to self-determination, understood as a right to freely determine their political status.[42] The 'people' in the sense of self-determination in these cases is the autochthonous population of the non-self-governing territories that has been grouped together into a polity in colonial times by its constitution as a distinct entity.[43] These territories became independent states on the basis of the principle of *uti possidetis*, which means that the territorial shape of the territories had been definitely established in colonial times—and they simply inherited the boundaries from their colonial rulers.[44] Self-determination clearly did not mean that a local people was completely free in its decision of whether they wanted to belong to the newly independent state, or instead to a neighbouring state. State practice clearly banned such a far-reaching claim, making the inherited territorial boundaries inviolable.[45]

Whether this excludes other 'peoples' from the right of self-determination is still an open issue. An important strand in international legal scholarship argues that every group of persons bound together by common objective characteristics, like language, culture, religion, or race might be qualified as a 'people', as long as such a group also has a common (subjective) understanding of belonging together and being distinct from all the other surrounding groups.[46] Such an understanding

[41] See the contributions in M Moore (ed), *National Self-Determination and Secession* (OUP 1998), but also VP Nanda, 'Self-Determination under International Law: Validity of Claims to Secede' (1981) 13 CWRJIL 257–80; D Turp, 'Le droit de secession en droit international public' (1982) 20 CYIL 24–78; D Murswiek, 'The Issue of a Right of Secession—Reconsidered' in C Tomuschat (ed), *Modern Law of Self-Determination* (Kluwer 1993) 21–40; A Cassese, *Self-Determination of Peoples: A Legal Appraisal* (CUP 1995) 119–20; D Raič, *Statehood and the Law of Self-Determination* (Kluwer 2002) 316–72; P Radan, 'International Law and the Right of Unilateral Secession' in A Pavković and P Radan (eds), *The Ashgate Research Companion to Secession* (Ashgate 2011) 321, 326–7.

[42] See in detail Grant (n 39) 23–42 and S Oeter, 'Self-Determination' in B Simma et al. (eds), *The Charter of the United Nations. A Commentary* (OUP 2012, 3rd edn) 313, paras 8–14.

[43] See Saxer (n 15) 278–81 and Grant (n 39) 37–42.

[44] See on the details of *uti possidetis* Saxer (n 15) 763–79; Dugard (n 14) 100–7; Fabry (n 14) 160–8; Castellino (n 17) 109–43; A Beaudouin, *'Uti possidetis' et sécession* (Dalloz 2011).

[45] See J Fisch, *Das Selbstbestimmungsrecht der Völker* (CH Beck 2010) 56–61.

[46] See D Ronen, *The Quest for Self-Determination* (Yale University Press 1979) 39–45; C Gusy, 'Selbstbestimmungsrecht im Wandel. Von der Selbstbestimmung durch den Staat zur Selbstbestimmung im Staat' (1992) 30 Archiv des Völkerrechts 385–410.

might be termed a 'naturalist' concept of peoples. Another line of thinking insists on the territorial element of self-determination. Self-determination, the argument goes, has always been linked to historically pre-constituted political entities with a specific territory. 'People' in this understanding is not simply a group of persons—one could also say an ethnic group—but the constituent people of a certain territorial entity formed by history.[47]

A careful analysis of state practice clearly supports the second understanding. There has never been any serious international support for a claim of self-determination raised by a simple 'ethnic group' having no firm territorial basis in a pre-existing political entity.[48] Colliding claims of self-determination of (non-territorial) ethnic groups cannot be solved without taking recourse to a defined territory—a plebiscite or referendum where the majority might determine the political status of the territory only makes sense where a territory is given. Although a traditional, 'naturalist' understanding of a 'people' can point to the intuition that the term 'people' does not in itself have a territorial connotation, a functional perspective of self-determination, construing the concept in light of the political and legal system in which it is embedded, leads to the insight that a certain degree of 'territoriality' is unavoidable if the concept of self-determination is to operate productively.

In essence, the whole debate concerns the question of whether 'ethnic groups' which qualify as 'minorities' in the sense of modern concepts of minority protection may qualify also as 'peoples' enjoying a right of self-determination.[49] In principle, one should definitely keep both concepts apart.[50] The term 'minorities' covers all groups linked together by some commonalities, such as language, culture, religion, race—as long as these groups do not form the majority in a given state. Some of these minorities might have a clear territorial basis, a historical settlement area where the group used to live together in high concentration in former times. In modern times even such groups will tend to lose their territorial roots to a certain degree, because personal mobility and consequent waves of migration will spread these groups across a much larger area. Many minority groups never had clear territorial strongholds but were always scattered among other population groups. To accept a 'right of self-determination' for each of these historically formed groups would definitely be to open a Pandora's box of never-ending disputes on territory and political dominance, at least as long as self-determination is understood in terms of separate statehood.[51] The only way to avoid such endless quarrel is

[47] See TM. Franck, 'Clan and Superclan: Loyalty, Identity and Community in Law and Practice' (1996) 90 AJIL 359–83; Saxer (n 15) 310–26.

[48] Saxer (n 15) 324–6, but also C Tomuschat, 'Secession and Self-determination' in MG Kohen (ed), *Secession: International Law Perspectives* (CUP 2006) 23, 25–38.

[49] See J Castellino, 'Order and Justice: National Minorities and the Right to Secession' (1999) 6 IJMGR 389–415; J Wright, 'Minority Groups, Autonomy, and Self-Determination' (1999) 19 OJLS 605, 612–29; Castellino (n 17), 45–74; Saxer (n 15) 286–300, 310–25.

[50] See eg S Wheatley, *Democracy, Minorities and International Law* (CUP 2005) 124–6, and Kohen (n 26) 9–10.

[51] See TM Franck, 'Postmodern Tribalism and the Right to Secession' in C Brölmann et al. (eds), *Peoples and Minorities in International Law* (Nijhoff 1993) 3–27 as well as TM Franck, 'Clan and Superclan: Loyalty, Identity and Community in Law and Practice' (1996) 90 AJIL 359–83.

the path taken by the community of states in twentieth-century state practice, by insisting upon a close linkage between (predetermined) political entities and self-determination. Self-determination is a right that can only be granted sustainably to polities linked to a historically defined territory—here self-determination may easily work, with a majority deciding in a plebiscite upon its political status and clearly defined boundaries that must be accepted by the neighbours according to the principle of *uti possidetis*.[52]

Such predetermined entities may be established states, where it is beyond dispute that the peoples of such states enjoy a continuing right of self-determination protecting them against foreign intervention, alien domination, or illegal occupation.[53] They may also be historical entities traditionally enjoying a certain degree of autonomy within states, or member states of federations or federal states.[54] The fact that a certain territory has formed a distinct political entity, with a population living together in such an entity for a long time, usually results also in a strong sense of collective identity irrespective of language, culture, or religion. This does not exclude divergences of opinion—the members of the previously dominant group will not like being separated from their kin-state and thus being made a minority in a new state, as was the case with Russians in the former republics of the Soviet Union.[55] But the international community accepted the claims of such republics, as well as the claims of the former republics constituting the Socialist Federal Republic of Yugoslavia, to form their own states.[56] Although in both cases the recognition was mostly based on arguments regarding dismemberment of the former federations, the international community had no problem accepting their claims of self-determination.

Beyond these specific constellations of predetermined political entities, a claim that a certain group of persons with distinct characteristics enjoys a right to self-determination can only be made in terms of 'internal self-determination', exercised in the various forms of autonomy, in federal constructs, or by mere political participation complemented by arrangements of minority protection.[57] This is of particular importance for federal states.

[52] See MC Johanson, 'Secession and Territorial Borders: The Role of Law' in A Pavković and P Radan (eds), *The Ashgate Research Companion to Secession* (Ashgate 2011) 303, 314–17.

[53] See K Doehring, 'Self-Determination', in B Simma et al. (eds), *The Charter of the United Nations: A Commentary*, Vol 1 (2nd edn, OUP 2002) 56 para 33.

[54] See eg O Kimminich, 'A "Federal" Right of Self-Determination?' in Tomuschat (n 41) 83–99, as well as P Thornberry, 'The Democratic or Internal Aspect of Self-Determination with some Remarks on Federalism' in Tomuschat (n 41) 101–38; see also E McWhinney, 'Self-Determination of Peoples and Plural-Ethnic States: Secession and State Succession and the Alternative Federal Option' (2002) 294 Recueil des Cours de l'Académie de Droit International 171, 236–55.

[55] See WC Allison, 'Self-Determination and Recent Developments in the Baltic States' (1991) 19 DJILP 625–84.

[56] See M Weller, 'The International Response to the Dissolution of the Socialist Federal Republic of Yugoslavia' (1992) 86 AJIL 569–607.

[57] See eg Crawford (n 14) 127–8; as concurrent voices from political theory see W Kymlicka, 'Federalism and Secession: At Home and Abroad' (2000) 13 CJLJ 207–24; R Bauböck, 'Why Stay Together? A Pluralist Approach to Secession and Federation' in W Kymlicka (ed), *Citizenship in Diverse Societies* (OUP 2000) 366–93; J Wright, 'Minority Groups, Autonomy, and Self-Determination' (1999) 19 Oxford JLS 605, 612–29.

The historical feature of federated states, autonomous regions, and member states of federations is the fact that they are integrated into a roof state, although provided with a certain degree of political and institutional autonomy. The principle of territorial integrity works not only in favour of centralized, unitary states, but also protects federations, federal states, and quasi-federal constructs. The result of such precedence of territorial integrity is the legal assumption that in these cases self-determination is bound in the constructs of federation or autonomy. The 'people' of such entities historically had reasons for entering into a close relationship with another political entity, and as long as there are no exceptional grounds rebutting such a presumption in favour of territorial integrity, the internal dimensions of self-determination will prevail.[58]

Doctrinal debate over the last two decades has placed significant emphasis upon this dimension of 'internal self-determination'.[59] In terms of legal politics, it provides a productive alternative to endless claims for independent statehood in ever smaller political entities, leading to a vicious circle of ever new claims of secession.[60] In constructs of federation and/or autonomy it is much easier to balance competing claims of political participation and dominance, with the central state taking over the role of guarantor for the complex arrangements balancing the competing interests of regional majorities and minorities.[61] 'Internal self-determination' grants the possibility for majority populations of certain historical entities with ethnic, linguistic, cultural, and/or linguistic characteristics different from those of the 'state nation' to enjoy a high degree of self-government without involvement in counterproductive quarrels over statehood, territory, boundaries, and citizenship. Accordingly, the broad range of solutions of 'internal self-determination' is also the preferred toolbox of diplomatic mediators when trying to contain (often secessionist) conflicts over title to territory and self-government.[62]

[58] See W Kymlicka, 'Is Federalism a Viable Alternative to Secession?' in PB Lehning (ed), *Theories of Secession* (Routledge 1998) 111–50, but also M Moore, *The Ethics of Nationalism* (OUP 2001) 165–201.

[59] As to 'internal self-determination' see H Hannum, *Autonomy, Sovereignty, and Self-Determination* (University of Pennsylvania Press 1990); P Thornberry, 'The Democratic or Internal Aspect of Self-Determination with some Remarks on Federalism' in Tomuschat (n 41) 101–38; A Rosas, 'Internal Self-Determination' in Tomuschat (n 41) 225–52; G Welhengama, *Minorities' Claims: From Autonomy to Secession* (Ashgate 2000), 125–205; Doehring (n 53) 56–7 paras 32–4; W Danspeckgruber, 'A Final Assessment' in W Danspeckgruber (ed), *The Self-Determination of Peoples: Community, Nation and State in an Interdependent World* (Lynne Rienner 2002) 335–57; Raić (n 17) 272–88; M Moore, 'An Historical Argument for Indigenous Self-Determination' in S Macedo and A Buchanan (eds), *Secession and Self-Determination* (NYU Press 2003) 89–118; M Seymour, 'Secession as a Remedial Right' (2007) 50 Inquiry 395–423; Saxer (n 15) 335–51; Fisch (n 45) 61–3; Dugard (n 14) 85–8; M Seymour, 'Internal Self-Determination and Secession' in A Pavković and P Radan (eds), *The Ashgate Research Companion to Secession* (Ashgate 2011), 385–97; M Sterio, *The Right to Self-Determination under International Law: 'Selfistans', Secession, and the Rule of the Great Powers* (Routledge 2013), 18–22.

[60] See A Eide, 'In Search of Constructive Alternatives to Secession' in C Tomuschat (ed), *Modern Law of Self-Determination* (Kluwer 1993) 139–76.

[61] See, as a forceful argument in this direction, M Weller, *Escaping the Self-Determination Trap* (Nijhoff 2008), in particular 78–90.

[62] See MW Doyle, 'UN Intervention and National Sovereignty' in W Danspeckgruber (ed), *The Self-Determination of Peoples: Community, Nation and State in an Interdependent World* (Lynne Rienner

For such solutions to work, they must include a certain guarantee of (limited) self-government. The concrete modalities of federation and/or autonomy cannot be cast in iron, but must to a certain degree remain flexible. If the federation or autonomy is drastically changed or abolished without the consent of the entity concerned, the question of self-determination is revived. Usually, the claim will go towards restoration of the previous state of autonomy, but in cases of brute and violent oppression, it might also convert into a claim for independent statehood, ie 'secession'.[63] The arbiter of these claims finally should be—and will be—the international community.

Only if the fundamental right to survival of such distinct groups are put in danger, by forms of genocide, massive 'ethnic cleansing', gross and consistent patterns of violations of fundamental human rights that threaten to destroy the group, may a legal claim directed towards separate statehood make sense. Separate statehood is 'remedial' in these cases since it cures a proven impossibility to live together in one state.[64]

If a state completely blocks any 'internal self-determination', erodes existing arrangements of autonomy, and takes recourse to brutal forms of violent oppression, ending in gross and consistent patterns of crimes against humanity, forms of 'ethnic cleansing', and perhaps even genocide, a 'right to secession' as an emergency tool seems to be arguable.[65] Usually such a claim is founded on assumptions of natural law or general principles of law, such as self-defence in situations of extreme emergency.

2002) 67–99; see in addition C Borgen, 'Imagining Sovereignty, Managing Secession' (2007) ORIL 477, 483–5.

[63] See S Oeter, 'Selbstbestimmungsrecht im Wandel. Überlegungen zur Debatte um Selbstbestimmung, Sezessionsrecht und "vorzeitiger" Anerkennung' (1992) 52 ZaöRV 741, 753–55.

[64] See Radan (n 41), 324–7.

[65] See EM Brewer, 'To Break Free from Tyranny and Aggression: Proposing a Model for a Remedial Right to Secession in the Wake of the Kosovo Advisory Opinion' (2012) 45 VJTL 245–92; JR Ablan, 'Signals and Affirm: How the United Nations Should Articulate the Right to Remedial Secession' (2012) 45 VJTL 211–43; TW Simon, 'Remedial Secession' (2011) 40 GJICL 105–73; Dugard (n 14) 112–22, 211–13; Meester (n 9), 215–54; Cismas (n 4) 543–54; M Sterio, 'On the Right to External Self-Determination: "Selfistans", Secession and the Great Powers' Rule' (2010) 19 MJIL 137, 145–6; M Ott, *Das Recht auf Sezession als Ausfluss des Selbstbestimmungsrechts der Völker* (BWV Berliner Wissenschafts-Verlag 2008); Weller (n 56) 59–69; J Summers, *Peoples and International Law. How Nationalism and Self-Determination Shape a Contemporary Law of Nations* (Nijhoff 2007) 343–4; A Pavković and P Radan, *Creating New States: Theory and Practice of Secession* (Ashgate 2007) 213–37; Dugard and Raič (n 14) 106–9; Tomuschat (n 48) 38–42; AE Buchanan, *Justice, Legitimacy, and Self-Determination: Moral Foundations for International Law* (OUP 2004), 331; P Groarke, *Dividing the State: Legitimacy, Secession and the Doctrine of Oppression* (Ashgate 2004) 149–68; DL Horowitz, 'A Right to Secede?' in S Macedo and A Buchanan, *Secession and Self-Determination* (NYU Press 2003) 50–75; A Buchanan and M Moore, *States, Nations and Borders: The Ethics of Making Boundaries* (CUP 2003) 247; J Dugard, 'A Legal Basis for Secession: Relevant Principles and Rules' in Dahlitz (n 40), *Secession and International Law* (T.M.C. Asser Press 2003) 89–96; Raič (n 17) 366–72; C Tomuschat, 'Self-Determination in a Post-Colonial World' in C Tomuschat (ed), *Modern Law of Self-Determination* (Nijhoff 1993) 9; H Hannum, 'Rethinking Self-Determination' (1993) 34 VJIL 1, 46–7; LC Buchheit, *Secession: The Legitimacy of Self-Determination* (Yale University Press 1978).

There are a number of cases where such a right has been argued in practice. State practice, however, is extremely reluctant to accept such a line of argument as justification for a legal entitlement to secession.[66] For good reasons, states are afraid of secessionist movements. Secession does not usually solve the political problems lying beneath the surface, but often tends to escalate the situation. Claims of secession regularly produce counterclaims of secession of smaller sub-entities and lead to endless conflicts over territory and boundaries.[67] It must be borne in mind that, in the end, it is not an ethnic group that is legally and factually seceding, but a certain territory that must be separated from the territory of the former sovereign in order to become a new state.[68] But what is the 'natural' territory of a (by definition 'de-territorial') ethnic group? The conclusion is clear—in the end it is again a territorial entity that is seceding, not the ethnic group. But why ascribe the 'subjectivity' of self-determination to an ethnic group, and not to the political entity which attempts to separate? There are two reasons why parties on the ground have a preference for a 'nationalist', group-based construction of self-determination, and not a territorial understanding. First, a territorial understanding would raise the issue that, regularly, the population of a certain territory is not homogeneous; rather, there will be different ethnic, linguistic, and religious groups living in the territory. But who decides on the fate of the territory? This should not be monopolized by one group alone. The 'secessionist' group will either have to build a consensus with the other parts of the population, which will often prove difficult, or must at least demonstrate in a referendum that an overwhelming majority wants secession—and, as a consequence, then must find a compromise on minority protection for the other segments of the population. Second, secession in terms of a predetermined political entity brings *uti possidetis* into play, thus foreclosing from the beginning any territorial claims going beyond the established boundaries of the given historical entity.[69]

If one thus concludes that not ethnic groups (or minorities) but only territorial entities of a predetermined, historical nature can claim rights of self-determination, this does not mean that the issue of secession is completely closed. In exceptional cases of brute oppression, there might be reasonable grounds for political entities to strive for secession. Ongoing or pending genocide may be such a case, but so would gross and consistent patterns of (discriminatory) crimes against humanity,

[66] See eg Saxer (n 15) 394–400; in addition Welhengama (n 59) 255–87; Kohen (n 26) 10; A Tancredi, 'A Normative "Due Process" in the Creation of States through Secession' in MG Kohen (ed), *Secession: International Law Perspectives* (CUP 2006) 171–207.

[67] See TM Franck, 'Postmodern Tribalism and the Right to Secession' in C Brölmann et al. (eds), *Peoples and Minorities in International Law* (Nijhoff 1993) 3–27.

[68] See L Brilmayer, 'Secession and Self-Determination: A Territorial Interpretation' (1991) 16 YJIL 177–202, as well as Crawford (n 14) 127 and M Moore, 'The Territorial Dimension of Self-Determination' in M Moore (ed), *National Self-Determination and Secession* (OUP 1998) 134–56.

[69] See Saxer (n 15) 772–5; see in addition Beaudouin (n 44); M Bothe, 'Drawing Borders as a Means to Restore and Maintain Peace: From Palestine to Kosovo and Back' in P Hilpold (ed), *Kosovo and International Law. The ICJ Advisory Opinion of 22 July 2010* (Brill 2012) 181–96; Raić (n 17) 293–304.

targeted massacres among an oppressed population, and large-scale 'ethnic cleansing'.[70] Whether such (exceptional) circumstances, however, can lead to a clear 'right' to secession is open to doubt. Ultimately it is up to the international community to judge the legitimacy of such attempts at secession.[71] There will always exist opposing strands of argument, resulting in a large margin of appreciation for external actors. Despite the brute violence characterizing a specific situation, the international actors still might prefer a solution of 'internal self-determination', ie a solution of autonomy. Overriding concerns of international policy might demand such a situation—and a clear legal entitlement, a 'right' to secession, would create obstacles for all attempts at international mediation. It is thus better to conceive such situations of (exceptional) legitimacy of secession not in terms of a clear-cut (collective) right, but in broader terms of legitimacy open to international moderation and judgement.[72]

Do the cases of Kosovo, Abkhazia, and South Ossetia, where some practice of recognition was observable, fit into the doctrine of remedial secession? In the cases of Abkhazia and South Ossetia, a very small number of states felt it appropriate to recognize these new entities,[73] and even in the case of Kosovo, a large part of the state community perceived recognition as an independent state to be inappropriate.[74] It is thus difficult to argue that these cases create a new practice that has established a different custom, departing in principle from traditional state practice. One might even argue the opposite. Using a proverbial saying of lawyers, one might say that 'hard cases make bad law'—and such bad law is not made any better by stressing the 'uniqueness' of the cases concerned.[75] The cases of Kosovo, Abkhazia, and South Ossetia will not help to establish a doctrine of remedial secession in state practice, as they show too much of an ad hoc character and are plagued by problems of moral hazard.[76]

Why do I argue that the cases of Kosovo, Abkhazia, and South Ossetia constitute 'hard cases' that make 'bad law'? Even if one supports the doctrine of remedial secession in principle as a recipe for cases of extreme emergency, the

[70] See Oeter (n 63) 759–60. [71] See Saxer (n 15) 362–8.

[72] See also L Seshagiri, 'Democratic Disobedience: Reconceiving Self-Determination and Secession at International Law' (2010) 51 HILJ 553–98, as well as RS Beiner, 'National Self-Determination: Some Cautionary Remarks Concerning the Rhetoric of Rights' in M Moore (ed), *National Self-Determination and Secession* (OUP 1998) 158–79.

[73] See Ker-Lindsay (n 13) 47–53; Geldenhuys (n 36) 69–86; S Wolff, 'The Limits of International Conflict Management in the Case of Abkhazia and South Ossetia' in N Caspersen and GR Stansfield (eds), *Unrecognized States in the International System* (Palgrave Macmillan 2011) 147–64; see also the papers by C Waters (175 et seq.) and F Mirzayev (191 et seq.) in this volume.

[74] See eg DI Efevwerhan, 'Kosovo's Chances of UN Membership: A Prognosis' (2012) 4 GJIL 93, 120–7, as well as—critical of the 'law talk' of most western powers—C Borgen, 'The Language of Law and the Practice of Politics: Great Powers and the Rhetoric of Self-Determination in the Cases of Kosovo and South Ossetia' (2009) 10 Chicago JIL 1, 10–16.

[75] See in particular R Mullerson, 'Precedents in the Mountains: On the Parallels and Uniqueness of the Cases of Kosovo, South Ossetia and Abkhazia' (2009) 8 Chinese JIL 2–25; see also Borgen (n 74) 10–28; A Tancredi, 'Neither Authorized nor Prohibited? Secession and International Law after Kosovo, South Ossetia and Abkhazia' (2008) 18 IYIL 37–62.

[76] For an explicit argument in this direction see N Kemoklidze, 'The Kosovo Precedent and the "Moral Hazard" of Secession' (2009) 5 JILIR 117–40.

above-mentioned cases do not provide solid grounds for arguing for the necessity of secession, as instances of an 'external right of self-determination'. As mentioned already, remedial secession is a tool for genuine cases of extreme emergency where the very survival of specific population groups is at stake.[77] But was this the case in the mentioned situations? I do not think so. In the case of Kosovo, the military intervention of NATO states had relieved the Kosovar Albanians, which might have been under severe menace in the last phase of the Milosevic regime, from the conditions of emergency.[78] Kosovar elites did not head towards independence because they still felt threatened, but because they had obviously been promised that independence might be an option—and the relevant outside powers were not raising principled objections against such a path (despite the continued applicability of Res. 1244). And what about Abkhazia and South Ossetia? The titular nations of these autonomous entities inside the Georgian Republic probably had reasons to feel threatened in the civil war situation under the late President Gamsachurdia, but with the Russian intervention they gained security, and it is difficult to argue that around 2010, when they declared independence, they were still under a situation of 'extreme urgency'.[79]

As a result, established doctrine has good cause to argue for the precedence of territorial integrity.[80] This does not say anything about the legitimacy of claims for internal self-determination. In all three cases, there were convincing grounds that called for extended autonomy of the territories, with institutionalized international guarantees for the stability of such autonomy. Serbia as well as Georgia were rather late in recognizing that such autonomy would be needed, but it was evident that such a construction might not only make sense in political terms, but was also a realistic political option in terms of international negotiations. Recognition of independent statehood by third states in such situations tends to lend support to the hardliners that go for maximum goals, and tends to consolidate a maximalist strategy oriented towards separate statehood where—in terms of mediation—the situation would be better kept fluid in order to preserve enough stakes for both sides to strike a compromise at the end.

In a more principled perspective of international legality, there are solid arguments speaking against recognition of secessionist entities in such situations. These are:

> In a principled perspective taking into consideration the preferences of the state community as it found its expression in traditional doctrine and practice, territorial integrity should take priority over claims of separate statehood.

[77] See Oeter (n 63) 753–5; but see also, arguing against a customary status of the doctrine of 'remedial secession', Jaber (n 4) 936–41.

[78] See eg Jaber (n 4) 941–2, and G Wilson, 'Self-Determination, Recognition and the Problem of Kosovo' (2009) 56 Netherlands ILR 455–81; but see also for the opposite position Cismas (n 4) 567–72; Fierstein (n 4) 437–8; K Paeameswaran, 'Der Rechtssstatus des Kosovo im Lichte der aktuellen Entwicklungen' (2008) 46 Archiv des Völkerrechts 172–204.

[79] See Kemoklidze (n 76) 128–33.

[80] See eg R Trisotto, 'Seceding in the Twenty-First Century: A Paradigm for the Ages' (2010) 35 BJIL 419, 422–5; A Gioia, 'Kosovo's Statehood and the Role of Recognition' (2008) 18 IYIL 3–35; Kohen (n 26) 6–8; WE Butler, 'Territorial Integrity and Secession: The Dialectics of International Order' in Dahlitz (n 40).

This does not speak against a certain consolidation of the (de facto separate) political entities as 'de facto regimes'.

Such a stabilization of the de facto situation is important in order to preserve the primordial value of international law, the non-use of force.

A final and lasting settlement usually needs quite a long time for negotiations to go ahead; such international negotiations should be supported, in the interest of finding an equitable solution, and should not be sabotaged by a premature legal entrenchment of the factual status quo.

For such negotiations, the question of incentives is decisive: the situation must remain fluid enough to promise both sides potential gains from a final settlement.

It must be made clear to factual holders of power that there is no way towards sovereign statehood, except as a result of negotiations.

At the same time, the former sovereign must be aware that any change of the situation in the direction of restitution of sovereign rights requires considerable concessions, typically in the form of extended autonomy with international guarantees.

Any final settlement needs a strong (and continued) involvement of outside powers—the parties to the conflict will not have enough trust to believe in a loyal implementation of the settlement and will need credible and reliable reassurances and guarantees from the outside world in order to be able to rely on the settlement.

IV. Patterns of Collective Recognition

As a consequence of such embedding of recognition in a pattern of international negotiations, recognition practice tends to lose its nature as a unilateral mode of action of a purely political nature and develops strong traits of a collective pattern of action. This is not a new insight, but has been quite clearly observed in some more recent studies.[81] As an instrument of conflict management, recognition (or non-recognition) only develops certain leverage if it is exercised collectively, leaving the parties to the conflict no choice (in terms of playing out third states against each other).

Such a trend towards a collective mode of action became obvious for the first time in the case of the dissolution of former Yugoslavia, where recognition by the member states of the neighbouring European Union was made dependent upon a catalogue of legal criteria going way beyond the traditional criteria of effectiveness of the classical declaratory theory.[82] The catalogue, drafted by the famous Badinter Commission, contained the magic triangle of EU values laid down now in Article 2 EU Treaty, namely the values of democracy, human rights, and the

[81] See eg Ker-Lindsay (n 13) 10–11; Dugard (n 14) 57–69; Crawford (n 14) 501; Grant (n 14) 128–40, 213–19; Hillgruber (n 25) 492–5.

[82] See Saxer (n 15) 264–8, and in addition Dugard and Raič (n 14) 126–30.

rule of law, complemented by the protection of minorities[83]—the same criteria used in a more or less identical form as the so-called 'Copenhagen criteria' in the context of accession to the EU.[84] These values constitute criteria of homogeneity of a value-based order of states. As a set of criteria for newly independent states to be recognized as new members of the state community, they are probably going a bit too far—although it must be admitted that politically it made sense to remind the (would-be) successor states of Yugoslavia that in order to fit into the new, post-1990 European environment, they should conform to certain basic values laid down in Council of Europe documents as basic requirements to become a member of the club of European states.[85]

What is important in our context here is less the justification of the substance of the criteria that are set up than the collective element that deeply characterized the recognition process with regard to the new states resulting from the dissolution of the Yugoslav Federation. The community of states—here in the particular emanation of the regional community of European states—took the role of a regulator of self-determination conflicts, in the result judging less the justification of the self-determination claims raised by the various republics than the political quality of the proclaimed new states.[86] There is again a side question of precedent: how does the recognition practice in the case of former Yugoslavia fit the traditional patterns of recognition (and non-recognition) with regard to secession? At first sight, not that well! At least from the perspective of Belgrade—and this term comprises not only the clique around Serbian President Milosevic, but also the remnants of the former federal bureaucracy and the federal army—the declarations of independence first of Slovenia and Croatia, then of Bosnia and Macedonia, constituted attempts at secession from the Yugoslav state.[87] Some of the western powers, such as France and Great Britain, initially had strong reservations about supporting such secession. It was political pressure from Germany and some smaller Central European states, in combination with the legal assessments of the Badinter Commission, that paved the way for recognition.[88] In order not to count the recognition of Slovenia

[83] Conference on Yugoslavia Arbitration Commission, *Opinions on Questions Arising from the Dissolution of Yugoslavia* (1992) 31 ILM 1488 ('Badinter Commission Opinions'). For arduous criticisms of the Badinter Commission's opinions see eg Roth (n 15) 409–15; TW Waters, 'Contemplating Failure and Creating Alternatives in the Balkans: Bosnia's Peoples, Democracy, and the Shape of Self-Determination' (2004) 29 YJIL 423, 438–44; M Jovanovic, *Constitutionalizing Secession in Federalized States: A Procedural Approach* (Eleven International Publishing, 2007) 83–114; P Radan, 'Yugoslavia's Internal Borders as International Borders: A Question of Appropriateness' (1999) 33 EEQ 137, 137; Radan (n 11) 204–42.

[84] See eg E Faucompret and J Konings, *Turkish Accession to the EU: Satisfying the Copenhagen Criteria* (Routledge 2008).

[85] See as an argument in this direction A Buyse and R Lawson, 'State Recognition: Admission (Im) Possible' (2007) 20 LJIL 785–95.

[86] See Saxer (n 15) 715–18, but also S Oeter, 'Yugoslavia, Dissolution of' in *Max Planck Encyclopedia of Public International Law* (OUP online 2012), paras 27–33.

[87] For an argument in this direction see A Pavković, 'Recursive Secessions in Former Yugoslavia: too Hard a Case for Theories of Secession?' (2000) 48 PS 485–502.

[88] See chapter 2 in M Weller, *Twenty Years of Crisis: The Violent Dissolution of Yugoslavia* (OUP 2013), but also KP Zeitler, *Deutschlands Rolle bei der völkerrechtlichen Anerkennung der Republik Kroatien unter besonderer Berücksichtigung des deutschen Außenministers Genscher* (Tectum 2000).

and Croatia as unhappy precedents, the Badinter Commission's finding that the Yugoslav Federation was in a process of dissolution played a central role.[89] Such legal categorization helped in saying: stop, this is a special case—Slovenia and Croatia (and later Bosnia-Herzegovina and Macedonia) did not secede, but the federation fell apart and the constitutive republics of the federation gained full statehood as a result.[90]

The background of such a collective pattern of recognition is obvious. Delicate normative issues such as a people's entitlement to its own statehood, the creation of new states and the settlement of territorial conflicts and boundary issues—issues that are extremely disputed in international law, but also in normative political theory[91]—cannot be left to the unilateral decision of the warring parties. The international community has an important role in moderating such conflicts and judging the validity of competing claims.[92] This is particularly true for secessionist conflicts where a self-proclaimed people or a sub-entity of an established state claims its own statehood while the government of the previous territorial sovereign claims respect of its territorial sovereignty and integrity.[93] There is an urgent need for the international community to exert moderating pressure upon both sides of the conflict, bringing them to a table in order to negotiate.[94] But if the international community wants to have a decisive influence upon the parties, it must do its best to speak with one voice. Only when there is no possibility of playing the different international actors against each other will international efforts directed towards moderating the conflict have the chance of success.[95] There is nothing worse than unilateral action in such cases, giving malign parties hope of achieving their objectives without any moderation or compromise. [96]

In this perspective, the old rule of non-recognition of attempts at secession, as long as the former territorial sovereign has not accepted such secession, has a very

[89] See Roth (n 15) 411–15; Sterio (n 59) 34–6; Vidmar, (n 17) 723–9; Fierstein (n 4) 432; Crawford (n 14), 397; S Tierney, 'In a State of Flux: Self-Determination and the Collapse of Yugoslavia' (1999) 6 IJMGR 197, 211–14; Grant (n 14) 153–68; MCR Craven, 'The European Union Arbitration Commission on Yugoslavia' (1995) 66 British YIL 333, 389–90.

[90] See as a critical account of such practice RJ Delahunty and A Florido Pérez, 'The Kosovo Crisis: A Dostoievskian Dialogue on International Law, Statecraft, and Soulcraft' (2009) 42 VJTL 15, 72–85.

[91] See as a critical survey of the various normative theories J McGarry and M Moore, 'Secession and Domination' in A Pavković and P Radan (eds), *The Ashgate Research Companion to Secession* (Ashgate 2011) 427–39; M Moore, 'The Ethics of Secession and a Normative Theory of Nationalism', (2000) CJLJ 225–50; M Freeman, 'The Right to Self-Determination in International Politics: Six Theories in Search of a Policy' (1999) 25 RIS 355–70; A Buchanan, 'Theories of Secession' (1997) 26 PPA 31–61; A Buchanan, *Secession: The Morality of Political Divorce from Fort Sumter to Lithuania and Quebec* (Westview 1991) 27–125.

[92] See Saxer (n 15) 362–8, as well as MN Shaw, 'The Role of Recognition and Non-Recognition with Respect to Secession: Notes on Some Relevant Issues' in Dahlitz (n 40) 243–57.

[93] See in particular R Müllerson, 'Sovereignty and Secession: Then and Now, Here and There' in Dahlitz (n 40) 125–65.

[94] See Saxer (n 15) 410–12.

[95] As to the strategic implications of attempts to secede see BF Walter, 'Information, Uncertainty, and the Decision to Secede' (2006) 60 IO 105–35.

[96] See also B Coggins, 'Friends in High Places: International Politics and the Emergence of States from Secessionism' (2011) 65 IO 433–67.

good rationale.[97] There is—as was stressed above—a principled presumption in favour of territorial sovereignty. Secessions may have legitimate causes in some exceptional cases—but whether this is the case should be sorted out in negotiations, and if this is not possible the third states should at least try to come to a concerted answer and should recognize the secessionist entity as a sovereign state only when more or less all agree that there is no alternative. Recognition in these cases gains a more or less 'constitutive' character since it is the concerted recognition of the international community that makes the entity claiming a right of self-determination a full-fledged state, becoming a member of the community of states.[98] The constitutive character of recognition is becoming even more obvious as recognition is linked to certain substantial criteria of constitutional and political structure in order to secure a degree of structural homogeneity of states.[99]

As long as such a collective procedure of concerted recognition is not achieved through diplomatic efforts, recognition of secessionist entities is 'premature', which under traditional terms means that it is a violation of the principle of territorial integrity and of the prohibition of intervention.[100] States should continue to respect these rules—otherwise they damage their political leverage over the parties to the conflict and risk ending up in open conflict with other third states.

In other words: the pattern of collective action in recognition stressed so much in this chapter is needed in order to gain political leverage over the parties—leverage that is needed in order to broker a peace arrangement.[101] As a result of such a collective approach, recognition becomes a tool in political conflict management—and such a tool works only if recognition is organized as a collective process.[102] This leads to an important political lesson. Collective recognition policy as an instrument of political management (and steering) ends up in an arrangement where recognition structures the accession of new political entities to the community of states. In order to achieve collective action, a group of states must agree in principle on a set of normative criteria concerning the required quality of statehood as a guideline for such common action. As a result, however, it is less effectiveness than some (normative) criteria of legitimacy that matters.

Put differently: the new state must fit into the normative framework of the existing community, and the process of state formation must have been compatible with normative underpinnings of the international community. This mechanism can be explained best through the example of the Turkish Republic of Northern Cyprus (TRNC). The TRNC fulfils all the classical criteria of statehood: it has a clearly circumscribed territory and people and it clearly rests on the democratic

[97] See Raić (n 41) 89–170; S Talmon, *Kollektive Nichtanerkennung illegaler Staaten* (Mohr Siebeck 2006).

[98] See Saxer (n 15) 718–35, as well as Vidmar (n 17) 734–42.

[99] Saxer (n 15) 725–30.

[100] See eg Raić (n 41) 92–104, and O Corten, 'Déclarations unilatérales d'indépendance et reconnaissance prématurées' (2008) 112 Revue générale de droit international public 721–60.

[101] For the resulting argument that the United Nations should play a central role 'as regulator of state creation' see Grant (n 39) 52–7; but see also, with a particular emphasis on the influence of great powers on the process of state creation in current practice, Sterio (n 59) 57–70.

[102] See J Vidmar, 'Kosovo: Unilateral Secession and Multilateral State-Making' in J Summers (ed), *Kosovo: A Precedent?* (Nijhoff 2011) 143–77.

consent of its inhabitants, which regularly elect a parliament and a president.[103] There are some Turkish troops stationed in Northern Cyprus, but they do not dominate the political process in Northern Cyprus, as was the case in the first years after the Turkish invasion of 1974. There is one original deficiency, however, that plagues the TRNC to this day—its process of state-building in the 1970s. The Turkish invasion of Cyprus in 1974 clearly constituted a breach of Article 2 (4) of the UN Charter, all rights from the Guarantee Treaty notwithstanding.[104] The Turkish army engaged in an exercise of 'ethnic cleansing' and expulsed more or less all Greek Cypriots from the North with brute force. These violations of *jus cogens* norms tend to obscure the strong Greek responsibility for the dead-end situation which resulted from the 1974 attempt at *enosis* and the resulting Turkish invasion.[105] In a way, the original faults of the process of state creation hide the normative weaknesses of the Greek Cypriot position—a position that claims that the current 'Republic of Cyprus' represents the entire Cypriot state and is identical to the state founded in 1959. But the original Republic of Cyprus had a bicommunal constitution, guaranteed by the United Kingdom, Greece, and Turkey, and it was the Greek Cypriot side that brushed aside the original constitutional arrangement and—in a kind of coup d'état—transformed Cyprus into a majoritarian democracy that marginalized its Turkish population segment.[106] It was the Greek side that commenced massacres and attempts at ethnic cleansing, and it was the Greek 'putsch' government that declared *enosis* and instigated Turkey's military intervention. The way in which the invasion occurred, however, was clearly illegal—and this deficiency prevents the TRNC from recognition even nowadays, decades after the original events.[107] Here, again, we find a pattern of collective non-recognition based on normative reasons[108]—and the same might be said for the collective pattern of non-recognition for Transnistria and for Nagorno-Karabakh.[109] Separate statehood as a recognized member of the community is no option for these entities—at least as long as the other side does not consent to it.[110] Negotiations must be held on federative arrangements or extended constructs of autonomy. In political terms, only this makes sense; options of separate statehood as a mini-statelet in the middle of nowhere do not.

V. Conclusions

The result is of far-reaching importance: recognition transforms from an instrument of bilateral diplomacy which governs state-to-state relations into a legal act

[103] See Talmon (n 17) 37–41 and B Ercan, *Zypern, die Türkei und die EU* (Nomos 2012) 203–6.
[104] See Talmon (n 17) 20–6; Ker-Lindsay (n 13) 41–2; Ercan (n 103) 35–44, 79–95.
[105] See Ercan (n 103) 30–40, 79.
[106] See Ercan (n 103) 30–5, 76–9.
[107] See Talmon (n 17) 78–81.
[108] See Ker-Lindsay (n 13) 42, and very much in detail Talmon (n 17) 48–78.
[109] See Ker-Lindsay (n 13) 53–7, and the papers of Bill Bowring (157 et seq.) and Heiko Krüger (214 et seq.) in this volume.
[110] Concerning the drastic consequences of such collective 'non-recognition' see Grant (n 39) 49–52 and Ker-Lindsay (n 13) 12–14.

of a collective nature, based on a normative value judgement regarding whether a new political entity conforms to basic normative underpinnings of the international legal order (and the international community). It becomes a collective tool deciding upon the position of political entities in the structures of the community of states.

If this tool of collective management is to work, the nature of recognition as a collective process is of utmost importance. Collective action, however, requires processes of collective formation of will—and a spirit of seeking compromise, because otherwise the collective becomes fragmented into various factions, pulling in opposite directions. Alas, there are policy reasons why I find the Kosovo case so unfortunate as a precedent—so unfortunate that international lawyers should do everything in order to prevent it from becoming a precedent in a genuine sense—and these are:

> First, it is extremely unfortunate as a precedent because there was no justified claim of 'remedial secession'. There simply did not exist any normative argument that could override Serbia's legitimate interest in territorial integrity (and the corresponding statements in Res. 1244 stressing the continuing territorial sovereignty of Serbia over Kosovo).
>
> Second, unilateral recognition dividing the international community into opposing factions tends to erode the potential of collective patterns of recognition, and thus aborts any chance to use collective recognition as a tool of (collective) conflict management. Such a traditional form of unilateral recognition strengthens the stubbornness and intransigence of the parties to the conflict and leaves international negotiators with empty hands, without clear incentives to enter into compromise.
>
> Third, it sets the wrong type of precedent in substance. It tells actors that intransigence in international negotiations, insisting stubbornly upon maximalist positions, is ultimately successful. But if such lessons are disseminated, radicals can easily avoid a moderated solution in self-determination conflicts, based on compromise, and can in the end impose maximalist claims on international negotiators as long as they can credibly threaten to cause trouble. The task of the international community, however, should be just the opposite: moderating the extremes and forcing parties to compromise on a middle-of-the-road solution—a solution which, in most cases, will consist of constructions of autonomy or federative arrangements.

The fact that such a bad precedent was immediately taken up by Russia in a (revenge-style) repetition by unilaterally recognizing Abkhazia and South Ossetia as independent states does not make the precedent better, but worse. Fortunately, the overwhelming majority of the members of the community of states have not applauded such a precedent. Despite strong political pressure from the US and the bigger EU states, a majority resisted following the 'friends of Kosovo' and refrained from recognition of Kosovo as an independent state. In the cases of Abkhazia and South Ossetia, even fewer states joined in—only a tiny group of states followed Russia in recognition. The argument of this chapter is that an overwhelming number of states had strong policy reasons, as well as principled grounds based on international law, to remain sceptical of these 'precedents'. And in the cases of Transnistria and Nagorno-Karabakh, even Russia resisted the temptation to appease the secessionist regimes by recognition—obviously for more or less the same principled reasons that caused the majority of the states community to avoid any step towards recognition of secessionist entities in general. As already said above, 'hard cases make bad law'—and international lawyers should not allow the cases of Kosovo, Abkhazia, and South Ossetia to finally succeed in making bad law.

5

Secession and Use of Force

Antonello Tancredi

I. Introduction

The ban on the use of force established by Article 2, para 4 of the UN Charter—along with the parallel rule of customary international law—might seem totally unrelated to the problem of secession, since it applies only to 'international relations' between the member states. In other words, in principle it does not affect the use of force *within* the state.[1] Since secessionist struggles have traditionally been regarded as an internal matter of sovereign states, it would be logical to conclude that the international ban on the use of force prohibits neither secession nor its forceful repression.[2] International law, rather, stays 'neutral' in this field, ie it does not prohibit nor authorize events of secession while, by contrast, wars of self-determination are fought in the name of a legal entitlement recognized and to some extent guaranteed by the international legal system.[3]

However, different factors can intervene to 'internationalize' secessionist conflicts. As a result of their occurrence, the principle of the non-use of force becomes applicable also in these contexts.

If, for instance, the conflict leads to the creation of a new state or state-like entity (including de facto regimes),[4] the customary prohibition applies automatically in its relationship with the state that has suffered the partition and with third states. Another case in point is a third-party state's direct or indirect military intervention in civil strife in another state. Finally, for those who support the existence of a right to remedial secession, severe persecution to the detriment of an infra-state group (ie gross violations of human rights and internal self-determination) would activate interventionist rules and protection that traditionally came along with the right of peoples to self-determination, and that were considered, even if only by a part of the international community, as legally entrenched in the *ius ad bellum*.

[1] See O Corten, *Le droit contre la guerre* (Pedone 2008) 174.

[2] For this view, see for instance G Abi-Saab, 'Conclusions' in M Kohen (ed), *Secession: International Law Perspectives* (CUP 2006) 474, and M Kohen, 'Introduction' in Kohen, *Secession*, 8.

[3] A Cassese, *Self-Determination of Peoples. A Legal Reappraisal* (CUP 1995) 153.

[4] JA Frowein, 'De Facto Regime', *Max Planck Encyclopedia of Public International Law* (OUP 2009) para 4.

The method chosen for this contribution is to combine the analysis of the sociolegal relations between the different actors normally involved in secessionist conflicts (incumbent state/secessionist group; incumbent state/third-party international subjects; secessionist group/third-party international subjects) with the possible factors of internationalization mentioned above. As will be seen, for each bundle of relationships, one or more factors become relevant and are therefore suited to bringing the principle of the non-use of force into the general picture.

Eventually, it will be shown that the international prohibition of the use of force is often very helpful in disentangling the complexities of these conflicts, since secessionist struggles almost never remain a purely internal matter. In this regard, the traditional neutrality kept by the international legal order will turn out to be not so neutral after all. However, it would be simplistic to consider this only as a manifestation of an old-fashioned international legal order, benevolent towards the *raison d'état*. As will be seen, in line with the contemporary evolution of the paradigm of sovereignty, today the protection of territorial integrity—at least when collective interests are also at stake—is increasingly seen as a responsibility of the state towards its civilian population and the international community, rather than as a simple sovereign right.

II. The State/Secessionist Relationship: a Matter of (Which?) Effectiveness

As has been said, the traditional view holds that neither the contractual nor the customary prohibition of the use of force in international relations applies *within* the state, ie in the relationship between the state undergoing a secessionist conflict and rebels. In other words, the state is not prevented from using the monopoly of legitimate force to restore its constitutional order, and rebels—in turn—are not prohibited from using violence to achieve their ends.

Indeed—as mentioned—some international treaties go so far as to give the state the responsibility, indeed the duty, to preserve its national unity and territorial integrity 'by all legitimate means'.[5] The existence of a positive obligation to recapture control of breakaway regions has also been repeatedly affirmed by the European Court of Human Rights. In the *Ilaşcu* case,[6] for instance, as well as in the subsequent case law,[7] the Strasbourg Court has recognized—pursuant to Article 1 of the ECHR (that is, as an exercise of jurisdiction)—that Moldova was under a

[5] See Article 3, para 1 of the 1977 Additional Protocol II, and Article 8, para 3 of the International Criminal Court's Rome Statute. According to D Akande, 'Classification of Armed Conflicts: Relevant Legal Concepts' in E Wilmshurst (ed), *International Law and the Classification of Conflicts* (OUP 2012) 37–8, the inclusion of these provisions witnesses the concern of the states not to abolish the distinction between international and non-international conflicts, since this would encourage secessionist struggles and restrain the hand of States in putting down a rebellion.

[6] *Ilaşcu and Others* v *Moldova and Russia* (App no 48787/99) ECHR 8 July 2004, paras 331–333.

[7] *Ivanţoc and Others* v *Moldova and Russia* (App no 23687/05) ECHR 15 November 2011, paras 105–106; *Catan and Others* v *Moldova and Russia* (App no 43370/04, 8252/05 and 18454/06) ECHR 19 October 2012, paras 109–10.

positive obligation to 're-establish control over Transnistria',[8] a secessionist region that is recognized under public international law as part of Moldova's territory although Moldova is prevented by a separatist regime from exercising its authority and control.

Over the past few years, however, an increasing number of authors have been maintaining that the international ban on the use of force may be applicable also in secessionist conflicts as a result of post-Cold War practice. We shall come back to this later.

Let me set out here some difficulties with the traditional approach. It assumes a static view of the breakaway phenomenon whereby everything remains an internal matter until a new statehood is produced. However, phenomena of secession are better understandable as dynamic, historical *processes* that go through different stages, each of which may create a legal relationship with different content.

1. First hypothesis: the 'internal disturbances and tensions' stage

The process can come to a stop at the 'internal disturbances and tensions' stage, a situation that—according to Article 1, para 2 of the 1977 Additional Protocol II to the Geneva Conventions, but also Article 8(2)(f) of the Statute of the ICC—remains below the threshold of a non-international armed conflict and is therefore not regulated by the relevant rules of humanitarian law. At this stage, the government normally has not yet adopted exceptional measures, such as dispatching the army instead of police forces or declaring martial law. In any respect, the secessionist group as such is *not* considered a subject of international law. Therefore its relationship with the central authorities is regulated by internal, not international, norms. In this regard, one can think of the examples of the Basque region, or Padania some years ago.

The only legal relations governed by international law in this phase are those between the state from which secession is sought and third states, and between the 'incumbent' state and individuals under its jurisdiction (the two relationships coincide if one believes that individuals are not subjects of international law, and that the obligations concerning human rights are owed *only* to other states). Accordingly, third-party states must refrain from any direct or indirect intervention against the sovereignty and territorial integrity of the incumbent state, while the latter can adopt forcible means to subdue the rebellion, provided that human rights are respected. For the rest, the question essentially remains an internal affair, which is regulated neither by *ius in bello* nor *ius ad bellum*.

2. Second hypothesis: the non-international armed conflict

The conflict may reach the threshold of a non-international armed conflict. According to the international jurisprudence and especially the case law of the

[8] *Ilaşcu* (n 6) para 340.

International Criminal Tribunal for the former Yugoslavia, which has made a major contribution in this field, a non-international armed conflict regulated by common Article 3 to the 1949 Geneva Conventions on humanitarian law occurs when a situation can be defined as 'protracted armed violence between governmental authorities and organized armed groups or between such groups within a State',[9] a test which also is codified by Article 8(2)(f) of the ICC Statute. The threshold in question is assessed on the basis of two criteria: the *intensity* of the violence and the *organization* of the parties.[10] With regard to intensity, criteria to be taken into account include resorting to the army because police forces are no longer able to deal with the situation on their own, the duration of the conflict, the frequency of violence, the nature of the weapons, displacement of civilians, territorial control of forces, etc. Another criterion is that non-governmental armed groups must show a minimum level of organization. As observed by the Trial Chamber of the ICTY in the *Limaj* case[11]—when considering the nature of the fighting that took place in 1998 between Serbian forces and the Kosovo Liberation Army (KLA)—the organization must inter alia display the capacity to coordinate and implement a unified military strategy through a chain of command, the ability to recruit and train new combatants, or the existence of internal rules.

While these two criteria are sufficient to define the field of application of common Article 3, the applicability of Additional Protocol II to an internal conflict involving a party's governmental forces depends on the recurrence of an additional element, established by Article 1, para 1[12] of that Protocol, namely control over part of the territory by the dissident armed forces. If this condition is met, then the whole body of rules of *ius in bello* designed for non-international armed conflicts may be applied.[13] This means that insurgents are recognized as international subjects, at least with reference to humanitarian law.

Then, the question arises of whether *ius ad bellum* also becomes applicable in this phase.

The answer can be positive when the matter is regulated through an agreement. A state, for instance, can contractually accept extension of the rules of *ius ad bellum* to the regulation of a secessionist conflict in which it is involved. A case in point is the Sochi Agreement, concluded in 1992 between the Republic of Georgia and the Russian Federation, which reaffirms in its preamble the 'commitment to

[9] ICTY Appeals Chamber, *Prosecutor* v *Tadic,* Decision on the Defence Motion for Interlocutory Appeal on Jurisdiction, ICTY-94-1-T, 2 October 1995, para 70.

[10] ICTY Trial Chamber, *Prosecutor* v *Tadic,* Judgment, ICTY-94-1-T, 7 May 1997, para 562. See also ICTY Trial Chamber, *Prosecutor* v *Limaj,* Judgment, ICTY-03-66-T, 30 November 2005, paras 84 and 90, and ICTY Trial Chamber, *Prosecutor* v *Haradinaj,* Judgment, ICTY-04-84-T, 3 April 2008, paras 37 et seq.

[11] *Limaj,* paras 94–134. See also *Prosecutor* v *Haradinaj,* para 60, and ICTY Trial Chamber, *Prosecutor* v *Boskoski,* Judgment, ICTY-04-82, 10 July 2008, paras 199–203.

[12] '...organized armed groups which, under responsible command, exercise such control over a part of its territory as to enable them to carry out sustained and concerted military operations and to implement this protocol'.

[13] See on this topic S Vité, 'Typology of Armed Conflicts in International Humanitarian Law: Legal Concepts and Actual Situations' (2009) 91 IR Red Cross 69.

the principles of the UN Charter and the Helsinki Final Act'.[14] In the *Tagliavini* report on the 2008 'five-day war' in Georgia, this reference—read also in the light of subsequent agreements—has been interpreted as meaning that Georgia accepted the applicability of the non-use of force in the conflict with the breakaway region of South Ossetia.[15] Another example is provided by agreements that establish lines of armistice.[16] As provided for by the UN General Assembly's 1970 Friendly Relations Declaration, in fact, every state has the duty to refrain from the use of force 'to violate international lines of demarcation, such as armistice lines, established by or pursuant to an international agreement to which it is a party or which it is otherwise bound to respect'.

What, however, if no contractual limitation to the use of force is established? Here we come back to the argument touched upon before, ie the idea that the scope of the customary ban on the use of force today is actually broader than the contractual one enshrined in the UN Charter, so that it would extend to non-international relations and thus apply also in instances of secessionist struggles. This argument is predicated on two elements: post-1990 practice and the ICJ's 2010 Kosovo Advisory Opinion.

3. Towards a wider customary ban on the use of force in non-international relations? Post-1990 practice

As regards practice, the stand taken by the international community on the secessionist conflicts fought in the former Yugoslavia, in Georgia/Abkhazia, and in Kosovo is often mentioned. As regards the conflict in Georgia, for instance, the Security Council demanded in Res. 876 (1993) that 'all parties refrain from the use of force'.[17] In regard to the former Yugoslavia, the Security Council demanded in Res. 959 (1994) of 19 November 1994 that 'all parties and others concerned,

[14] Text at <http://peacemaker.un.org/sites/peacemaker.un.org/files/GE%20RU_920624_Agreemen On PrinciplesOfSettlementGeorgianOssetianConflict.pdf>. The same can be said of the 1996 Memorandum on Measures to Provide Security and Strengthen Mutual Trust between the Parties to the Georgian-Ossetian Conflict, signed in Moscow. According to this agreement, the use of force was to be excluded as a means of conflict resolution (see A Nußberger, 'South Ossetia', *Max Planck Encyclopedia of Public International Law* (OUP 2013), paras 13 and 24).

[15] *Independent International Fact-Finding Mission on the Conflict in Georgia*, Report of September 2009, vol. II, chapter VI, 240 at <www.ceiig.ch/Report.html>.

[16] According to Heiko Krüger's contribution in this book, 'Nagorno-Karabakh', 230, lines of ceasefire would also be protected by the ban on the use of force. Actually, pursuant to Article 36 of the Hague Regulations Respecting The Laws and Customs of War on Land annexed to the 1889 Convention with Respect to the Laws and Customs of War on Land and the 1907 Convention concerning the Laws and Customs of War on Land—a rule that is considered as corresponding to customary international law, and that although nominally directed to regulating armistices, together with the following articles 37–41, has 'to be read today as applicable to ceasefire, rather than to armistice' (see Y Dinstein, 'Armistice', *Max Planck Encyclopedia of Public International Law* (OUP 2009), para 3)—if '... the duration is not fixed, the belligerent parties can resume operations at any time, provided always that the enemy is warned within the time agreed upon'.

[17] See UNSC Res 876 (19 October 1993) UN Doc S/RES/876. The same demand was then reiterated in UNSC Res 881 (4 November 1993) UN Doc S/RES/881; UNSC Res 1225 (28 January 1999) UN Doc S/RES/1225; UNSC Res 1311 (28 July 2000) UN Doc S/RES/1311.

and in particular the so-called Krajina Serb forces, fully respect the border and refrain from hostile acts across it'. In Kosovo, the Council emphasized that 'all elements in the Kosovo Albanian Community should pursue their goals by peaceful means only'.[18] Again in the framework of the conflict in the former Yugoslavia, the Council repeatedly proclaimed the principle of the inadmissibility of territorial gains obtained through the use of force.[19] In addition, in the former Yugoslavia[20] and in Kosovo,[21] the Security Council, but also the European Union, has adopted comprehensive military embargoes (including arms, munitions, vehicles, etc.) which have deprived the central authorities of external military assistance (a corollary of a righteous resort to force aimed at restoring order). Furthermore, the UN General Assembly, in its Res. 48/88 of 20 December 1993, qualified the violence used by Bosnian–Croat forces against Bosnia-Herzegovina as 'aggression'. Finally, in Res. 2056 (2012) of 5 July 2012, the UN Security Council demanded the 'full, immediate and unconditional cessation of hostilities by rebel groups in the North of Mali', a call reiterated in para 4 of Res. 2100 (2013).

What assessment can be given of this practice? First, in interpreting the UN resolutions, one must never forget that these acts are adopted by political bodies that pursue political objectives. The solutions they propose would be seriously weakened if not addressed to all actors involved in an internal conflict. It is not necessarily the case, however, that diplomatic terms can be translated into legal rights and obligations.

Second, no explicit reference to the prohibition of the use of force or to Article 2 para 4 of the UN Charter can be found in the resolutions mentioned above. The impression rather is that the call on the parties to refrain from using force was prompted by the will of the international community to ensure respect for *other* international principles, such as those protecting fundamental human rights, the territorial integrity of states, that of *uti possidetis iuris* and, according to some authors, the right of peoples to self-determination.

Third, if the ban on the use of force may apply in civil wars, it should apply to both parties involved in them, ie the central government as well as the rebels. How is it possible to reconcile this with the fact that—as already noted—Article 3 of the 1977 Protocol regulating internal armed conflicts states that 'Nothing in this Protocol shall be invoked for the purposes of affecting the responsibility of the government... to defend the national unity and territorial integrity of the State'?

It is true that the UN Security Council's *exceptionalism*, when it is exercised under the authority of Chapter VII of the UN Charter and through Article 103 of the UN Charter, prevails over every other contractual provision in specific cases. But this can only apply to ad hoc internal situations deemed to constitute a threat

[18] UNSC Res 1203 (24 October 1998) UN Doc S/RES/1203.

[19] See for instance: UNSC Res 713 (25 September 1991) UN Doc S/RES/713; UNSC Res 752 (15 May 1992) UN Doc S/RES/752; UNSC Res 757 (30 May 1992) UN Doc S/RES/757; UNSC Res 820 (17 April 1993) UN Doc S/RES/820; UNSC Res 824 (6 May 1993) UN Doc S/RES/824; UNSC Res 859 (25 August 1993) UN Doc S/RES/859.

[20] See UNSC Res 713 (25 September 1991) UN Doc S/RES/713.

[21] UNSC Res 1160 (31 March 1998) UN Doc S/RES/1160.

to international peace and security. If, on the other hand, the argument is that the post-1990 UN practice is contributing to broaden the scope of the *customary* rule on the non-use of force, one should verify whether this practice is sufficiently uniform, constant, and protracted to achieve that effect. In this regard, it must be highlighted that the international recognition of the responsibility of a state to preserve its territorial integrity is not a historical relic buried along with the climate of the Cold War.

In Chechnya, for instance, the international community regarded the two secessionist conflicts fought in 1994–5 and 1999–2000 as an internal matter of the Russian Federation, recognizing its right to preserve territorial integrity and to restore constitutional order and condemning only the disproportionate character of the internal use of force that resulted in violations of human rights and of humanitarian law.[22] The limit did not concern the *ius ad bellum*, but only rules of *ius in bello* and human rights. The same kind of response was given more recently, in January 2009, when the government of Sri Lanka resorted to forceful means to recapture control of the Tamil capital.[23]

In the midst of the conflict in Kosovo, in 1998, the UN Secretary-General went so far to recognize that '[t]he authorities of the Federal Republic of Yugoslavia have the inherent right, as well as the *duty*, to maintain public order and security and to respond to violent acts of provocation'.[24] The problem in that context was rather that the use of force against civilians was 'excessive' (as stated in the preamble of Res. 1160 (1998)). The limit, once again, concerned the modalities of repression and their impact on the humanitarian situation.

Also in the framework of the secessionist conflict that occurred in the FYROM in 2001, the Security Council affirmed in Res. 1345 (2001) that it would 'support the government of the FYROM in its efforts to end the violence in a manner consistent with the rule of law'. The only limit, again, was respect for the rule of law.

More recently, when on 14 March 2005 the Third Session of the Tenth National People's Congress of the People's Republic of China adopted the Anti-Secession Law,[25] whose Article 8 provides the use of 'non-peaceful means' against the

[22] In 1995, the French Ministry of Foreign Affairs observed: 'La Tchétchénie fait partie de la Fédération de Russie. Le respect du principe de souveraineté et d'integrité territoriale est une des règles de base de la vie internationale', reason for which 'le rétablissement de l'ordre en Tchétchénie relève, sur le plan juridique, des affaires intérieures de la Fédération de Russie'. Notwithstanding this, 'les méthodes et les moyens militaires employés vont bien au-delà des règles générales fixeés pour l'usage des forces armées dans les conflits internes' (J Charpentier, 'Pratique des faits internationaux' (1995) 41 Annuaire français de droit international 911). For an analogous position held by the German Bundestag, see (1995) 65 Archiv der Gegenwart 39657–8. On 17 February 1995, the UN Commission on Human Rights deplored 'the disproportionate use of force by the Russian armed forces' and the breaches of human rights committed by both parties in the conflict (UN Doc E/CN.4/1995/Sr.44, of 3 March 1995, 18–19). See also the European Council's Declaration of 11 December 1999: 'The European Council does not question the right of Russia to preserve its territorial integrity nor its right to fight against terrorism. However this fight cannot, under any circumstance, warrant the destruction of cities, nor that they be emptied of their inhabitants'.

[23] See *International Herald Tribune*, 3–4 January 2009, 3.

[24] UNSC, *Report of the Secretary-General Prepared Pursuant to Resolutions 1160 (1998) and 1199 (1998) of the Security Council* (3 October 1998) UN Doc S/1998/912, para 29 (emphasis added).

[25] The text is reproduced in (2005) 4 Chinese JIL 461.

'Taiwan independence' secessionist forces,[26] mixed reactions followed at the international level. Grave 'concern' was expressed in the US Congress[27] and by the European Parliament[28] while, on the other hand, many other states expressed 'support' or 'understanding'.[29] The US White House spokesman called the adoption of the Anti-Secession Law 'unfortunate',[30] while the French Prime Minister Raffarin described it as 'completely compatible with the position of France'.[31]

Finally, with reference to the secessionist crisis that began in Mali in early 2012 (to which we will return shortly), the UN Security Council, in Res. 2071 (2012) of 12 October 2012, stressed 'the primary responsibility of the Malian authorities for ensuring... the unity in its territory'.

4. (Sequitur) The 2010 ICJ's Kosovo Advisory Opinion

More recently, some authors[32] have inferred from the ICJ's Kosovo Advisory Opinion some elements that seem to militate in favour of the applicability of the non-use of force within states. Indeed, it has been observed that with regard to the non-use of force, the ICJ did not repeat in para 81 of the Kosovo Advisory Opinion the same statement made in the above para on the principle of territorial integrity, namely that its application is limited 'to the sphere of relations between states'. As a consequence, the existence of a customary rule on the use of force with a broader extension than the contractual prohibition could be envisaged.

[26] More precisely, Article 8 provides for the use of 'non-peaceful means and other necessary measures to protect China's sovereignty and territorial integrity' in three instances: in the event that Taiwan's secessionist forces 'should act under any name or by any means to cause the fact of Taiwan's secession from China', or that 'major incidents entailing Taiwan's secession from China should occur', or, finally, that 'possibilities for a peaceful reunification should be completely exhausted'. The Law—whose aim is to oppose a potential secession, and not to impose re-unification between 'the mainland and Taiwan' (see CN Wei, 'China's Anti-Secession Law and Hu Jintao's Taiwan Policy' (2010) 5 YJIA 124–125)—has been regarded by several commentators as substantially 'maintaining the *status quo*' of the *de facto* existence of Taiwan, while opposing any scenario of *de jure* independence (see K Zou, 'Governing the Taiwan Issue in Accordance with Law: An Essay on China's Anti-Secession Law' (2005) 4 Chinese JIL 455, 459).

[27] 109th Congress, 1st Session H. Con. Res. 70.

[28] European Parliament resolution on the annual report from the Council to the European Parliament on the main aspects and basic choices of CFSP, including the financial implications for the general budget of the European Communities, P6_TA(2005)0132, 14 April 2005, para 33. See also the Declaration by the Presidency on Behalf of the European Union concerning the adoption of the 'anti-secession law' by the National People's Congress of the People's Republic of China (<http://www.eu-un.europa.eu/articles/en/article_4470_en.htm>).

[29] Among them, CIS countries such as Russia, Belarus, Uzbekistan, Azerbaijan, Tajikistan, plus Georgia; Latin American countries such as Venezuela, Cuba, and Dominica; Asian countries such as Indonesia, Cambodia, Sri Lanka, Pakistan, Vietnam, and Bangladesh; Arab countries, like Jordan, Bahrain, Iraq, Kuwait, Yemen, and Syria; and several African countries such as Nigeria, Tunisia, Zimbabwe, Mauritania, the Democratic Republic of Congo, Ethiopia, Namibia, Burundi, Gabon Republic of Central Africa, Guinea, Zambia, Uganda, Niger (see <http://www.fmprc.gov.cn/eng/topics/AntiSecession/default.shtml>).

[30] See <http://www.washingtonpost.com/wp-dyn/articles/A33702-2005Mar14.html>.

[31] See <http://www.dw.de/france-backs-china-on-taiwan/a-1559253>.

[32] A Peters, 'Does Kosovo Lie in the Lotus-Land of Freedom?' (2011) 24 LJIL 95, 106–7.

Some doubts may be cast on the view just mentioned. In fact, affirmation of the interstate scope of the non-use of force might be considered as already being contained in the part of the reasoning concerning the interstate character of the principle of territorial integrity. To reach the latter conclusion, in fact, in para 80 the Court makes reference not only to the contractual obligation enshrined in Article 2 (4) of the UN Charter, but also to General Assembly Res. 2625 (XXV) 'which reflects customary international law', as recognized by the ICJ in the *Nicaragua* case.[33] This instrument provides precisely 'that *States* shall refrain in their international relations from the threat or use of force against the territorial integrity or political independence of any *State*' (emphasis added).

Furthermore, it is rather difficult to reconcile the idea that the Court positively considers the non-use of force applicable also to insurgents with the broader statement that declarations of independence, and thus the secession they purport to bring about, are not prohibited by international law. If the first proposition were true, then any secession obtained by resorting to the use of forcible means (separations obtained with the consent of central authorities, in fact, are qualified as instances of devolution more than secession)[34] would be internationally prohibited. The parallelism drawn by the Court between the scope of the principle of territorial integrity and that of the prohibition of the use of force also militates in support of this consideration.[35]

For all these reasons, one cannot but share the view that tendencies in favour of the customary extension of the non-use of force to internal conflicts have not yet matured into law and practice.[36]

If this is true, then the degree of effectiveness required by Additional Protocol II to activate the whole body of the *ius in bello* designed for non-international armed conflicts might not prove sufficient to reach the same result with the *ius ad bellum*. The threshold beyond which these latter set of norms becomes applicable is higher. If, in fact, Additional Protocol II makes do with an *operational effectiveness*, namely a control which must be 'such... as to enable to carry out sustained and concerted military operations and to implement this Protocol', the type of control requested to render the *ius ad bellum* applicable is better defined by the doctrine of 'ultimate success', as is widely implemented in adjudicative and diplomatic international practice. Accordingly, secessionist control must acquire stability, in the sense that 'the parent State must in fact have ceased to make efforts, promising success, to reassert its authority'[37]. This type of control goes along with the capacity of 'maintaining law and order, instituting and maintaining courts

[33] *Military and Paramilitary Activities in and Against Nicaragua (Nicaragua* v *United States of America), Merits,* ICJ Reports 1986, 101–3.

[34] See Kohen (n 2) 3.

[35] See O Corten, 'Territorial Integrity Narrowly Interpreted: Reasserting the Classical Inter-State Paradigm of International Law' (2011) 24 LJIL 90–1.

[36] G Nolte, 'Secession and External Intervention' in Kohen (n 2) 80. See also O Dörr, 'Use of Force, Prohibition of', *Max Planck Encyclopedia of Public International Law* (OUP 2011), paras 21 and 26.

[37] H Lauterpacht, *Recognition in International Law* (CUP 1947) 8.

of justice, adopting or imposing laws regulating the relations of the inhabitant of the territory to one another and to the government'.[38] Only then will secession be regarded as productive of a new state-like entity, or at least a de facto (though not recognized) regime, so that the relations will become 'international' and therefore covered by the ban on the use of force.

III. The Relationship Between the 'Incumbent' State and Third States: The Riddle of the Intervention by Invitation. Preliminary Remarks

As has been seen, the only legal relationship which exists independently of the nature, type, and intensity of the secessionist conflict is between the state that undergoes a separatist threat and third states. Any direct or indirect military intervention carried out by third-party subjects to threaten or violate the territorial integrity and national unity of another state falls squarely under the prohibition of the use of force in international relations.

More intricate to assess is the opposite scenario, namely whether third states may lawfully intervene to help preserve the territorial integrity of another state. In this regard, the most interesting question is whether foreign military intervention upon invitation is permitted. This is one of the most thoroughly examined issues in this field. To approach it, some preliminary methodological remarks are necessary.

First, with many authors—in the wake of the resolutions adopted by the *Institut de droit international* on this topic[39]—there is a tendency to deny autonomy to the practice concerning secessionist conflicts.[40] The analyses of these conflicts often end up being absorbed into the much wider practice regarding civil wars *in general*, with the result that the indications derived from the general category are automatically considered valid in cases of secession. In the present writer's view, however (for reasons that will be shown below), it would be advisable to 'unpack' the category of 'civil wars': secessionist conflicts have special characteristics that suggest assessing them on their own basis,[41] even if the relevant practice

[38] As famously stated by Lord Atkin in *Government of the Republic of Spain* v *SS 'Arantzazu Mendi'* [1939] AC 256, 264–5 (HL).

[39] See in particular the Resolution on 'The Principle of Non-Intervention in Civil Wars', adopted by the *Institut* at its session of Wiesbaden in 1975 (especially Article 1, on the concept of civil war), (1975) 56 Annuaire de l'Institut de Droit International 544–9. See also the Resolution on 'Military Assistance on Request', adopted at the session of Rhodes, in 2011 (text at <http://www.idi-iil.org/idiE/resolutionsE/2011_rhodes_10_C_en.pdf>). The scope of this latter Resolution is limited to 'situations of internal disturbances, and tensions', below the threshold of non-international armed conflict (Article 2).

[40] See for instance O Schachter, 'The Right of States to Use Armed Force' (1984) 82 MLR 1642, according to whom the prohibition to intervene on either side in a civil war applies regardless of 'whether the insurgency was directed at overthrow of the government or at secession (or autonomy) of a territorial unit'.

[41] In favour of this approach, see T Christakis and K Bannelier, '*Volenti non Fit Injuria?* Les effets du consentement à l'intervention militaire' (2004) 50 Annuaire français de droit international 133–4.

is relatively scant. Indeed, the balance between legal principles and substantive values may vary considerably depending on the type of internal conflict that is taken into account (ie a political struggle for power, an attempt at secession, a fight against terrorist organizations, or a combination of these hypotheses among themselves or with other instances in which the protection of collective interests is at stake). This cannot but affect the permissibility or otherwise of an intervention by invitation.

Second, the scholarship is divided between those who believe that the lawfulness of an intervention upon invitation should be analysed on the basis of the secondary rule *volenti non fit iniuria*[42] and those who think that it is a matter of primary rules, in the sense that one must determine whether there are principles whereby intervention is *ab origine* lawful.[43] The question is interesting for theoretical rather than practical reasons. In both cases, in fact, lawfulness eventually depends on the interplay between well-established, and in some cases peremptory, principles of international law. Whether they are considered as primary rules or as a limit to the operation of circumstances precluding wrongfulness (such as consent), the final assessment does not change radically.

Having said that, let us now focus on the parameters to be employed in order to respond to the question concerning the lawfulness of intervention in secessionist conflicts on the invitation of central governments. The issue will be analysed under three headings: issues of political/legal expediency, applicable principles of international law, and practice.

1. Issues of political/legal expediency

In this area, one immediately perceives the importance of giving autonomous consideration to secessionist conflicts. Indeed, one of the main reasons why part of the scholarship denies the lawfulness of interventions on invitation in civil wars is linked to the difficulty of identifying who represents the will of the state at the international level.[44] In particular, this happens in three circumstances: duality or plurality of governments, total anarchy, and divergence between effectiveness and international legitimacy (in the sense that the authority that has effective control is not internationally recognized or democratically legitimated, and vice versa). These scenarios are less frequent in cases of secession. In fact, by definition,

[42] See for instance N Ronzitti, 'Use of Force, Jus Cogens and State Consent' in A Cassese (ed), *The Current Legal Regulation of the Use of Force* (Martinus Nijhoff 1986) 148; A Tanca, *Foreign Armed Intervention in Internal Conflict* (Martinus Nijhoff 1993) 13–16; AB Mansour, 'Circumstances Precluding Wrongfulness in the ILC Articles on State Responsibility: Consent' in J Crawford, A Pellet and S Olleson (eds), *The Law of International Responsibility* (OUP 2010) 439, all substantially endorsing the approach adopted by the International Law Commission's Special *Rapporteur* on State Responsibility Roberto Ago (Eight Report on State Responsibility (1980), *Yearbook of the International Law Commission* vol. II, Part 1, 31), and by the Commission itself (*Yearbook of the International Law Commission* vol. II, Part 2, 100).

[43] See Christakis and Bannelier (n 41) 102.

[44] See on this topic CJ Le Mon, 'Unilateral Intervention by Invitation in Civil Wars: The Effective Control Test Tested' (2003) 35 New York University JILP 741.

secession does not put into question the continuing existence of the state as an international legal person. The only possible *deminutio* concerns its geographical extension. Furthermore, as has already been said, the doctrine of the 'ultimate success' creates a strong presumption, not easily rebuttable, in favour of the incumbent state's effectiveness. Accordingly, the international community is normally well aware of who is speaking on behalf of the state from which secession is sought, and therefore is entitled to issue a legally valid invitation.

2. Applicable principles of international law

These are essentially three: non-use of force, non-intervention, and the self-determination of peoples.

(a) *Non-use of force.* According to the Friendly Relations Declaration, every state has the duty to refrain from '...assisting or participating in acts of civil strife...in another State'. This prohibits both direct and indirect military intervention, namely the sending of troops as well as the supply of weapons, munitions, etc.

While it is not seriously contested that this prohibition covers any form of assistance given to rebels, it is open to question whether these forms of military intervention are still prohibited by the ban on the use of force if they are carried out upon the invitation of the central government in order to help preserve its territorial integrity. Some authors give a negative response since in these cases military assistance would be given in an internal context.[45] Therefore, the criterion of the use of force in 'international relations' would not be met. Furthermore, the force that is prohibited must be directed against the territorial integrity and sovereignty of a state, while exactly the opposite is true here. On the other hand, it has been argued that 'any possible kind of transfrontier use of armed force'[46] is covered by the ban. If this is true, then any use of armed force in the sovereign spaces of another subject would be illegal, and the question would become whether and to what extent such illegality may be considered as excluded because of the recurrence of circumstances precluding wrongfulness.[47]

(b) *Non-intervention.* This principle is relevant to our purposes because, in some cases, its scope tends to overlap with the prohibition of the use of force, as was observed by the ICJ in the *Nicaragua* judgment[48] with reference to the hypothesis of the supply of arms and other support given by a state to rebels in another state.

The first argument which is traditionally put forward in order to deny that the principle at issue here prohibits external intervention at the request of the incumbent government is that when consent is given, it eliminates the element which

[45] Christakis and Bannelier (n 41) 112.

[46] A Randelzhofer, 'Article 2(4)' in B Simma (ed), *The Charter of the United Nations. A Commentary* (2nd edn, vol I, OUP 2002) 123.

[47] In this perspective, A Abass, 'Consent Precluding State Responsibility: A Critical Analysis' (2004) 53 ICLQ 211.

[48] *Military and Paramilitary Activities* (n 33) 117, para 247.

'forms the very essence' of prohibited intervention,[49] ie coercion. In other words, there is no 'dictatorial interference'.[50]

Notwithstanding this, some declarations of principles adopted by the UN General Assembly—as, for instance the *Declaration on the Inadmissibility of Intervention in the Domestic Affairs of States and the Protection of Their Independence and Sovereignty*, adopted by Res. 2131 (XX) of 21 December 1965, and the 1970 Friendly Relations Declaration—seem to enshrine a general prohibition of intervention in civil wars occurring in another state ('...no State shall...interfere in civil strife in another State'). Here again the secessionist conflicts' *exceptionalism* becomes relevant. The authors[51] who have examined the *travaux* of these UN Declarations in fact invariably emphasize that the prohibition in question was codified having in mind not secession but another type of internal strife, namely struggles for power over the central government. Only these latter conflicts were in fact seen as a form of choice over political status that should remain unimpaired by outside intervention. This leads us to examine the third principle that is relevant here, that of self-determination.

(c) *Self-determination*. The traditional, unqualified right of the incumbent government to demand external military aid has been eroded by the increasing relevance of the principle of internal self-determination, whereby—as recognized in common Article 1 of the 1966 UN Covenants on human rights and in the *Friendly Relations* Declaration—'all peoples have the right freely to determine, without external interference, their political status'. This includes the right to choose and to modify the political regime. If the purpose of foreign intervention upon invitation is to crush a political rebellion aimed at overturning the local government, the intervention will run contrary to self-determination and, therefore, will not be considered as allowed under international law.[52] The question at this point is whether the principle of self-determination generally includes a right to secession—and the response is negative. As for *opinio iuris*, the need to strike a balance between self-determination and territorial integrity has traditionally led to a parallel affirmation of both principles in many UN documents adopted over the past 50 years. As regards practice, secession is a matter of external (not internal) self-determination, and it is well known that the external dimension of the principle of self-determination has been confined to cases of colonial, foreign, or racist domination.

Concerning the hypothesis of 'remedial secession' mentioned above, it is safe to share the position taken by the Canadian Supreme Court in the *Québec* case and affirm that today it remains 'unclear' whether it corresponds to 'an established

[49] *Military and Paramilitary Activities* (n 33) 108, para 205.

[50] L Oppenheim (ed), *International Law: A Treatise* (8th edn, Longmans, 1955) 305.

[51] Nolte (n 36) 82.

[52] This argument has been sustained by many authors. See, for instance, M Bennouna, *Le consentement à l'ingérence militaire dans les conflits internes* (LGDJ 1974) 213; Schachter (n 40) 1641; L Doswald-Beck, 'The Legal Validity of Military Intervention by Invitation of the Government' (1985) 56 BYIL 251.

international law standard';[53] a conclusion which, in terms of *opinio iuris*, is further reinforced by the reference made by the ICJ in the Kosovo Advisory Opinion to the 'radically different views'[54] maintained on this issue by the states participating in that procedure and which, concerning practice, is confirmed by the negative diagnosis contained in the 2009 *Tagliavini* report.[55]

3. The practice of secessionist conflicts

Often the government involved in a secessionist conflict asks for and receives military assistance from abroad in the form of the supply of weapons, military equipment, vehicles, training, infrastructure, etc. (Nigeria from the UK/USSR; Papua New Guinea from Australia; Ethiopia from Iran/Israel; Georgia from Russia). One is confronted here with a phenomenon—the military cooperation between states—that is largely unregulated by general international law[56] except for the ban on the supply of military material to a government that represses a struggle for self-determination. During the *travaux* of the Special Committee on Friendly Relations, states such as the US[57] and the UK[58] repeatedly affirmed that nothing prevented military assistance in favour of a legitimate government. The same position was defended by the British Secretary of State to justify the supply of arms to Nigeria during the conflict against the breakaway region of Biafra.[59]

Turning now to the practice concerning *direct* military interventions, the first remark to be made is that it is rather scant. Nonetheless, in a few cases, foreign military interventions have been carried out upon the invitation of governments involved in secessionist conflicts and directed against rebels without meeting with international condemnation. The three clearest examples—though not the only ones—are: the UN intervention in the conflict fought by the Congolese forces against the secessionist attempt of Katanga in 1960–1; the intervention of India in Sri Lanka in 1987; and the recent intervention of France and the African-led International Support Mission in Mali (AFISMA) in 2013.

As regards the first case, it is often observed that the military intervention carried out by the UN force in Congo at the request of the local government was essentially aimed at repelling the external intervention of the former colonial power, Belgium, in support of the secessionists. The UN Secretary-General declined demands for direct action against Katanga, arguing that such intervention would have violated the principle of non-intervention in internal matters enshrined in Article 2, para 7, of the UN Charter. His position was backed by the majority of

[53] (1998) 37 ILM 1372–1373.

[54] *Accordance with International Law of the Unilateral Declaration of Independence in Respect of Kosovo* (Advisory Opinion) ICJ Reports 2010, 438, para 82.

[55] Vol. II 141 (at <www.ceiig.ch>).

[56] See Bennouna (n 52) 81; Corten (n 1) 461.

[57] *Report of the Special Committee on Principles of International Law Concerning Friendly Relations and Co-operation among States*, (1970) UN Doc GAOR Suppl. No. 18, A/8018, 120, para 259.

[58] UN Doc A/AC125/SR.57.

[59] See C Rousseau, 'Chronique des faits internationaux' (1970) 74 Revue générale de droit international public 497.

the states sitting in the Security Council, as witnessed by SC Res. 146 of 9 August 1960, according to which the UN force in the Congo 'will not be a party to or in any way intervene in or be used to influence the outcome of any internal conflict'. Consequently, the contention is often made that this practice only shows the permissibility of counter-intervention, namely that the central government can invite external military intervention *only* in response to a prior foreign intervention in support of the rebels which does not meet the threshold of the 'armed attack' (and therefore does not authorize collective self-defence), and only with a view to securing the withdrawal of foreign military forces from the country.[60]

In a later phase of the conflict, however, the UN's attitude changed. This is clearly reflected in the wording of SC Res. 169 of 29 November 1969, which describes the purposes of the UN intervention in the Congo as including the necessity '[t]o maintain the territorial integrity and the political independence of the Republic of Congo'. In the same resolution, the Council completely rejected the claim that Katanga was a 'sovereign and independent nation'.

As concerns the intervention carried out by India in 1987 upon the invitation of the central government of Sri Lanka, which was involved in a large-scale conflict against the Tamil secessionist groups, it was carried out in execution of a treaty of military assistance between the two states (concluded the day immediately preceding the request for intervention). The intervention was mentioned as part of the Security Council's proceedings concerning the situation in Northern Cyprus. Both India and Sri Lanka cited the invitation as the sole legal justification for the Indian intervention against the breakaway groups and clarified that one of the prime objectives of that intervention had been 'to preserve the unity, sovereignty, and territorial integrity of Sri Lanka',[61] so that no analogy could possibly be drawn with the Turkish intervention in Cyprus. At any rate, the intervention was never criticized by other states.[62]

4. (Sequitur) the French and African-led intervention in Mali

Interesting indications also derive from the recent—complex and multilayered—crisis in Mali.

In mid-January 2012, Mali experienced an armed insurgency in the northern part of the country, followed, on 22 March, by a military coup d'état in Bamako. The coup accelerated the collapse of the state in the north, allowing a Tuareg movement known as the National Movement for the Liberation of Azawad (MNLA)—along with Islamic armed groups including Al-Qaida in the Islamic Maghreb (AQIM), Ansar Eddine, and the Movement of Unity and Jihad in Western Africa

[60] See for instance Corten (n 1) 480.

[61] UN Doc S/19355 (17 December 1987). See also UN Doc S/19354 (17 December 1987) and UNSC Verbatim Record (14 December 1987) UN Doc S/PV.2771 for the intervention of the Turkish representative.

[62] G Nolte, *Eingreifen auf Einladung: Zur völkerrechtlichen Zulässigkeit des Einsatzes fremder Truppen im internen Konflikt auf Einladung der Regierung* (Springer 1999) 529.

(MUJWA)[63]—to easily overrun government forces in the northern regions of Kidal, Gao, and Timbuctu. An independent State of Azawad was proclaimed on 6 April. By 18 November, Ansar Eddine and MUJWA had driven MNLA out of the main towns in the north.

The immediate response of the international community to these events has identified the defence of Mali's territorial integrity as the 'central priority'.[64] In reaction to the coup, on 27 March, the Heads of State and Government of the Economic Community of West African States (ECOWAS) declared that they had 'decided to take all necessary measures to end the rebellion and ensure the territorial integrity of Mali, including the use of force'.[65] In response to the proclaimed independence of Azawad, the Peace and Security Council of the African Union declared that it rejected the declaration, 'which is null and void'.[66] The same position was taken by the UN Security Council. In Res. 2056 (2012) of 5 July 2012, the Council reiterated its 'categorical rejection of statements . . . regarding the so-called "independence" of Northern Mali', considering such announcements 'as null and void'.

From words to deeds. Taking note, expressly or indirectly, of three requests—one made by the Transitional Government of Mali to ECOWAS on 1 September 2012 to obtain military assistance in order, inter alia, to restore the territorial integrity of Mali ('la priorité des priorités'),[67] which was also quoted in a similar letter addressed by the same transitional authorities to the UN Secretary-General, requesting the authorization of deployment through a Security Council resolution of an international military force acting under Chapter VII of the UN Charter 'in order to assist the Malian Army in recapturing the occupied northern regions',[68] as well as ECOWAS' request regarding a Security Council resolution with the same mandate[69]—on 20 December 2012, in Res. 2085, the UN Security Council—acting under Chapter VII of the UN Charter—finally (and unanimously) authorized the deployment of an African-led Mission (AFISMA), inter alia '[t]o support the Malian authorities in recovering the areas in the north' (Article 9, lit. (b)).

With reference to this first phase of the crisis, it may therefore be said that the consent of the Transitional Government of Mali has been considered as a necessary, albeit not a sufficient, condition for authorizing outside military intervention in defence of that country's territorial integrity—[70]a case of cumulative, mutually

[63] As recalled in the preamble of UNSC Res 2100 (2013), the three organizations are on the sanctions list established by the Committee pursuant to Resolutions 1267 (1999) and 1989 (2011).

[64] UN Doc S/2013/189, para 33.

[65] See UN Doc S/2012/237, Annex.

[66] UN Doc S/2012/298, Communiqué on the situation in Mali, para 7.

[67] For the text of the letter, see <http://medias.lemonde.fr/mmpub/edt/doc/20120907/1757276_0337_requete_dioncounda_traore_cedeao_1er_septembre_2012.pdf>.

[68] UN Doc S/2012/727.

[69] UN Doc S/2012/739. Among the objectives of the ECOWAS stabilization force was 'Helping the Government to restore the territorial integrity of Mali by extending State authority to the north'.

[70] See, in this same vein, V Hadzi-Vidanovic, 'France intervenes in Mali Invoking both SC Resolution 2085 and the Invitation of the Malian Government–Redundancy or Legal Necessity?' (<http://www.ejiltalk.org/france-intervenes-in-mali-invoking-both-sc-resolution-2085-and-the-invitation-of-the-malian-government-redundancy-or-legal-necessity/>). One can only speculate on the reasons

reinforcing legal bases. It is also important to note, for our purposes, that the demand for foreign intervention in Mali never concerned the internal struggle for power triggered by the military coup of March 2013, but only the restoration of the territorial integrity of the country[71] in order to avoid the creation of a 'terrorist state' in West Africa.

The second part of the crisis erupted in early January 2013, with the sudden deterioration of the security situation in Mali. Elements of the three Islamist extremist groups mentioned above advanced southwards, capturing the town of Konna, not far from Mopti, which is a key access point to the south of the country and the capital, Bamako. The capture of Konna led the Malian authorities to request the assistance of France 'to defend Mali's sovereignty and restore its territorial integrity'.[72] In response, on 11 January 2013, France launched 'Operation Serval'. The deployment of AFISMA—originally scheduled for the second half of the year—was also accelerated, allowing some contingents to move to northern Mali in February. In any case, by the end of January, state control had been restored in most of the larger cities in the north. This effort to restore 'the territorial integrity of Mali' was commended by the UN Security Council in the preamble of Res. 2100 of 25 April 2013.

With reference to this second phase of the Malian crisis, the first element to be taken into account for our purposes is that, legally speaking and with exceptions made regarding some sporadic condemnations,[73] France's military intervention seems not to have raised widespread protests at the international level.[74] The UN Secretary-General went so far as to 'applaud' it,[75] while the UN Security Council, in its subsequent Res. 2100 (2013)—whereby authority was transferred from AFISMA to the United Nations Multidimensional Integrated Stabilization Mission (MINUSMA)—welcomed swift action by the French forces.

This brings us to a second important aspect: having established that the legality of the intervention of the African-led support mission is firmly rooted in UNSC Res. 2085 (2012), what is the legal basis justifying French military intervention in Mali? In the aftermath of the intervention, the French government provided the press with two distinct grounds: first, collective self-defence triggered 'by the

why the UN Security Council wished to be authorized in order to authorize: the need to ensure the non-hostility of all the components of the local political scene (since it was known that the military perpetrators of the coup were not entirely in agreement with an outside intervention), or the need to remove any doubt as to whether the conditions that trigger the powers conferred by Chapter VII had actually been met.

[71] See, on this, MB Metou, 'Mali, aide militaire ou intervention sollicitée?', in 316 Sentinelle, 23 September 2012, at <http://www.sentinelle-droit-international.fr/bulletins/a2012/20120923_bull_316/bulletin_sentinelle_316.php#291>.

[72] UN Doc S/2013/189, para 4.

[73] Such as that of the Turkish Ministry of Foreign Affairs, available at <http://www.todayszaman.com/news-304399-turkey-says-against-unilateral-intervention-in-mali.html>.

[74] In the words of the French Ministry for Foreign Affairs, Laurent Fabius, addressing the *Sénat* on 16 January 2013: 'Son opportunité et sa légalité sont incontestées' (<http://basedoc.diplomatie.gouv.fr/vues/Kiosque/FranceDiplomatie/kiosque.php?fichier=bafr2013-0117.html#Chapitre3>).

[75] UN Doc S/2013/37.

appeal and the request made by Mali's legitimate government'; second, 'all the United Nations resolutions'.[76] In subsequent statements, this second argument quickly evaporated,[77] leaving the first to the fore.

Accordingly, the demand for French military intervention by the Transitional Government of Mali would not provide a justification *in itself*, but would only represent one element of a broader scenario of collective self-defence based on Article 51 of the UN Charter. As subsequently stated by the French government: 'France reacts to an invitation by the Malian authorities which have issued a request for help; this falls within the framework of Art. 51 UN Charter'.[78]

However, there are other elements regarding this practice, as well as theoretical reasons, that seem to show how, in the case at hand, the consent of the sovereign played a role independent of collective self-defence, namely as an autonomous justification anchored in general international law. First, in the identical letters informing the UN Secretary-General and the Security Council of the launch of 'Operation Serval', one reads that the French government 'has responded today to a request for assistance',[79] while no mention is made of Article 51 of the UN Charter. Secondly, in her comments to the press before the start of the French military intervention, Susan Rice, the US Permanent Representative to the United Nations, observed that 'there was clear-cut consensus about... the right of the Malian authorities to seek what assistance they can receive'.[80] Here, too, there is no reference to collective self-defence or Article 51 of the UN Charter; such a reference is also nowhere to be found in the conclusions of the EU Foreign Affairs Council of 17 January 2013,[81] nor in the G8 Political Directors' Statement on Mali of 15 January 2013.[82] Third, as already mentioned, in the preamble of Res. 2100 (2013), adopted on 25 April 2013, the UN Security Council welcomes 'the swift

[76] At http://basedoc.diplomatie.gouv.fr/vues/Kiosque/FranceDiplomatie/kiosque.php?fichier=baen2013-01-14.html#Chapitre2.

[77] Indeed, in para 9 of Res 2085, the African-led International Support Mission in Mali (not France) appeared to be the only addressee of the authorization of direct use of force, contained in the standard formula 'all necessary measures'. On the other hand, in para 7, Member States were requested to provide 'assistance, expertise, training... and capacity-building support' to the Malian army, which suggests, at most, forms of support that constitute an indirect use of force. Nor could this situation be changed by the press statement (UN Doc SC/10878) whereby, on 10 January 2013, the Security Council responded to the capture of Konna by terrorists, reiterating its call to member states 'to provide assistance' to the Malian Defence and Security Forces, and calling, at the same time, for a rapid deployment of AFISMA. A press statement can, at best, contribute to an authentic interpretation of a Security Council Resolution, but it has no legal force to amend or supplement its normative content. For further discussion, see M Starita, 'L'intervento francese in Mali si basa su un'autorizzazione del Consiglio di sicurezza?' (2013) 96 Rivista di diritto internazionale 561.

[78] 'La France agit à la demande des autorités du Mali qui ont lancé un appel à l'aide; elle s'inscrit dans le cadre de l'article 51 de la Charte des Nations Unies', Déclaration du government et débat au Sénat–Intervention du ministre des affaires étrangères, M. Laurent Fabius, Paris, 16/01/2013 (http://basedoc.diplomatie.gouv.fr/vues/Kiosque/FranceDiplomatie/kiosque.php?fichier=bafr2013-01-17.html#Chapitre3; translation by the author).

[79] UN Doc S/2013/17.

[80] Text available at <http://usun.state.gov/briefing/statements/202714.htm>.

[81] Text available at <http://www.consilium.europa.eu/uedocs/cms_Data/docs/pressdata/EN/foraff/134770.pdf>.

[82] Text available at <http://www.g8.utoronto.ca/political_directors/130115-poldirs.html>.

action by the French forces, at the request of the transitional authorities of Mali', without making reference to Article 51 or to a right to collective self-defence. All things considered, it seems that the position expressed by the French government on the legal basis of its intervention in Mali has been characterized by a certain degree of ambivalence or ambiguity. Unlike the arguments sustained during press conferences and the domestic debates in the *Sénat*, in fact, the official communication to the UN and its reception at international level indicate consent as a legal basis in itself.[83]

From a theoretical viewpoint, then, it has been observed that self-defence is a 'curious' argument in the case at issue here[84]—first, because the invocation of Article 51 of the UN Charter presupposes a violation of Article 2 (4) of the same instrument, a norm which—as has been seen—applies 'in international relations', not in conflicts taking place within the state. Private individuals or terrorist groups '...may be the objects of policing or law enforcement operations, but not the addressees of legitimate acts of self-defence'.[85] Second, one might wonder why it is necessary to distort the category of self-defence, extending the applicability of Article 51 of the UN Charter to a hypothesis of attacks by private parties from *within* the territory of the state being attacked (a case that—even assuming, without conceding,[86] that Article 51 can be invoked to respond to armed attacks from non-state entities—would still be different from the '9/11' or the 'Israel/ Hizbollah' scenario, ie the hypothesis of attacks of terrorists or non-state militias *from abroad*, since of the three radical Islamic groups only AQIM seems to operate from bases located mainly outside Mali).[87] Such an argument is rather curious, especially if one thinks that the same conduct that was authorized in this way for collective self-defence (use of force to counter the rebels and the invitation to foreign aid) is already authorized under general international law.[88]

Finally, if the invitation of the government of Mali has represented an independent justification of a military action whose legality has not been challenged at the international level, there is a final question to be addressed: why has this intervention been considered legal while, for instance, according to the resolution on 'The Principle of Non-Intervention in Civil Wars' adopted by the *Institut de*

[83] For this argument, see Pierre D'Argent, at <http://www.ejiltalk.org/french-military-intervention-in-mali-its-legal-but-why-part-2-consent-and-unsc-authorisation/>, and L Magi, 'Sulla liceità dell'intervento militare francese in Mali' (2013) 96 Rivista di diritto internazionale 551.

[84] Thus, the comments of Olivier Corten, at <http://www.ejiltalk.org/french-military-intervention-in-mali-its-legal-but-why-part-i/>.

[85] Dörr (n 36) para 30.

[86] I have expressed my doubts on this issue, along with an alternative analysis concerning the legal basis, in A Tancredi, 'Il problema della legittima difesa nei confronti di milizie non statali alla luce dell'ultima crisi tra Israele e Libano' (2007) 90 Rivista di diritto internazionale 969.

[87] See, on this, Magi (n 83) 556–557.

[88] Thus, T Christakis and K Bannelier, 'French Military Intervention in Mali: It's Legal but...Why? Part I', at <http://www.ejiltalk.org/french-military-intervention-in-mali-its-legal-but-why-part-i/>; see also P Weckel, 'Mali: l'intervention française et la gestion africaine de la crise', 331 Sentinelle 20 January 2013, at <http://www.sentinelle-droit-international.fr/bulletins/a2013/20130120_ bull_331/bulletin_sentinelle_331.php#408>.

droit international at its session of Wiesbaden in 1975, foreign military intervention aimed at substantially influencing the final outcome of a civil war in favour of one of the struggling parties should *never* be considered permissible under general international law? This question, of course, presupposes a preliminary qualification of the conflict in Mali as a civil war. In this regard, the recurrence of at least some of the requirements necessary for the determination of a civil war (as mentioned above) seems to be evidenced by the resolutions adopted by the Security Council during the crisis—see, for example, resolutions 2085 (2012), and 2100 (2013), in which the Islamist rebel groups active in Mali are qualified as 'organizations'. The recurrence of the additional element of the acquisition of control over part of the territory by the insurgents also seems to be proven, since they had actually wrested control of the northern part of the country from the state authorities for about a year.

Having said that, it is noteworthy that according to the initial comments in the scholarship, 'Operation Serval' would have been characterized by an absorbing anti-terrorist end, so that an intervention upon invitation would be allowed 'when a State assists another during a joint fight against terrorism'.[89] From this reading of the Malian case, it might be inferred that intervention upon invitation remains generally inadmissible in cases of civil war (a category that—as we have seen—is normally considered also to encompass secessionist struggles). In line with the approach that we have adopted, however, we deem it necessary to distinguish—within the general category of the civil wars—between power struggles and conflicts of secession, since the obstacles (mainly the respect due to the principle of self-determination of peoples) that hinder the legality of an outside intervention upon invitation in the first case are absent in the second. This approach seems to be somewhat confirmed by the practice regarding Mali. In this context, in fact, if one reads the relevant UN documents (for instance, the fifth recital in the preamble of UNSC Res. 2100 (2013)),[90] the demands of the Malian government, and the positions adopted by France (especially those concerning the objectives of its armed intervention),[91] and finally takes into account operational practice, it becomes immediately clear that the anti-terrorist purpose never came to be

[89] T Christakis and K Bannelier, 'French Military Intervention in Mali: It's Legal but… Why? Part II: Consent and UNSC Authorisation', at <http://www.ejiltalk.org/french-military-intervention-in-mali-its-legal-but-why-part-2-consent-and-unsc-authorisation/>. However—as already mentioned (n 41)—according to these authors in '*Volenti non Fit Injuria?*', the prohibition to intervene upon request in civil wars does not extend to secessionist struggles.

[90] '*Welcoming* the swift action by the French forces, at the request of the transitional authorities of Mali, to stop the offensive of terrorist, extremist and armed groups towards the south of Mali and *commending* the efforts to restore the territorial integrity of Mali by the Malian Defence and Security Forces, with the support of French forces and the troops of the African-led International Support Mission in Mali (AFISMA)'.

[91] '…la France poursuit des objectifs clairs: arrêter l'avancée terroriste; préserver l'État malien et l'aider à recouvrer son integrité territorial; favoriser l'application des résolutions internationales avec le deployment de la force africaine et appui aux forces maliennes dans la reconquête du nord du Mali', Declaration of the French Government during the debate held at the *Sénat* on 16 January 2013, text available at <http://basedoc.diplomatie.gouv.fr/vues/Kiosque/FranceDiplomatie/kiosque.php?fichier=bafr2013-01>.

separated from what has always been defined as the 'top priority', ie the restoration of the territorial integrity of Mali. Consequently, the case of Mali can be taken as a confirmation that—in principle—a government may request external military help, either directly and/or indirectly, in order to fulfil its responsibility to defend the territorial integrity of the country it represents, especially or at least when collective interests such as the protection of international peace and security and/or fundamental human rights are also at stake.

Furthermore, in a normative perspective, if the defence of territorial integrity may also be a responsibility in pursuit of the protection of collective interests (and not only a right) and if a state is unable to guarantee its unity autonomously, it is submitted that the international legal order should leave open the possibility of sending a request for military aid as an *extrema ratio*. The legality/legitimacy of this demand, of course, will only be strengthened by the terrorist character of the armed rebel groups to be countered.

5. (Sequitur) Remaining practice

Other episodes have less evidentiary value.

Some of them concern the former Yugoslavia. We refer here to the 'essential harvest' operation carried out by NATO in Macedonia in 2001 to disarm Albanian insurgents, after a request for NATO's assistance was issued by the President of the FYROM.[92] The mission was preceded by the Ohrid Peace Agreement, whereby the Albanian side undertook to put down weapons on a voluntary basis. Another case in point is the Split Declaration of July 1995, whereby Bosnian authorities invited Croatia to provide military assistance in the Bihac safe area.[93] In this case, intervention was mostly grounded in humanitarian reasons.

Practice also records minor external interventions on the invitation of the governments of micro-states involved in secessionist struggles. In 1979 the government of St. Vincent and the Grenadines invited troops from Barbados to counter the attempted breakaway of Union Island.[94] Similarly, Vanuatu (New Hebrides), when facing the independentist struggle of the island of Santo, called in first British and French troops, and then troops from Papua New Guinea.[95] In both cases, however, the operations undertaken by foreign troops were essentially aimed at restoring internal security rather than crushing separatist operations and did not provoke significant international reaction.[96]

Finally, concerning the CIS area, peacekeeping forces have been deployed, for instance, in Abkhazia and South Ossetia at the request of both parties involved in the conflict.[97] These forces were primarily responsible for ensuring compliance

[92] Statement by the North Atlantic Council, NATO Press Release (2001)093, 20 June 2001 (at <http://www.nato.int/docu/pr/2001/p01-093e.htm>).

[93] UN Doc S/1995/666.

[94] (1980) *Keesing's Contemporary Archives*, 30180.

[95] (1980) *Keesing's Contemporary Archives*, 30641.

[96] See, on this practice, Nolte (n 36) 86–7.

[97] See, respectively, Farhad Mirzayev's (191–293) and Christopher Waters' (175–190) contributions in this book.

with the ceasefire and stabilizing the situation. As is usual in these cases (with some notable exceptions, such as MONUC in the Congo), this implied the obligation to remain neutral. However, the existence of a limited mandate and the neutrality it implies do not mean that the peacekeeping operations took place in a legal vacuum. Quite to the contrary, the principles that should have guided an international resolution of these crises had been established, respectively, by the UN and the OSCE.[98] In both cases these principles included a commitment to respect the territorial integrity of Georgia, also as a basis for future negotiations aimed at a political settlement. Furthermore, the actions of the peacekeeping forces became the object of an international control entrusted to missions of observers deployed by the UN and the OSCE. From this it might be inferred that the peacekeepers were requested at least to hinder attempts to impose a fait accompli unilaterally, in violation of Georgia's territorial unity.

To summarize, even though the practice regarding secessionist conflicts is scant, sometimes chaotic and not easy to interpret (given the conflation between different grounds of justification), it nonetheless shows that foreign military interventions carried out upon the invitation of the central authorities with a view to repelling a secessionist attempt are, generally speaking, well tolerated, especially if additionally motivated by reasons of counter-intervention or reaction to threats/violations of collective interests. The traditional thesis of the asymmetry observed by international law in favour of the state from which secession is sought therefore remains preferable to that of the 'negative equality' between parties to a civil conflict (according to which external intervention on invitation in civil wars would be always prohibited).

IV. The Relationship Between Secessionist Groups and Third States: The Prohibition of Military Intervention in Support of Secessionist Struggles Fought in Another State

Below the threshold of effectiveness that is required to consider a state-like entity as formed, there is no standing legal relationship between secessionist groups and third states. Such a relation was typically created by recognitions of insurgency or belligerency, acts which today have fallen into desuetude.

The only 'international relations' are those between third states and the state under civil war. Therefore—as stated by the Friendly Relations Declaration and repeated in many other UN instruments (the 1965 Declaration of Intervention; UNGA Res. 36/103 of 1981)—the ban on the use of force prohibits third states

[98] See, respectively, UNSC Res 937 (21 July 1994) UN Doc S/RES/937, CSCE and the New Europe. Our Security is Indivisible, Decisions of the Rome Council Meeting, 1993, Regional Issues, para 2.1 (text at <http://www.osce.org/mc/40401>); Towards a Genuine Partnership in a New Era, CSCE Budapest Document 1994, Decisions, Regional Issues, Georgia, para 1 (text at <http://www.osce.org/mc/39554?download=true>); Istanbul Summit Declaration, in Istanbul Document 1999, para 15 (text at <http://www.osce.org/mc/39569?download=true>).

from participating or providing military assistance, either direct or indirect, to secessionist groups active in other states.

Direct use of force largely corresponds, either directly or indirectly, to the notion of aggression enshrined in UN General Assembly Res. 3314 (XXIX). It therefore encompasses the deployment of regular troops or armed bands, irregulars, and mercenaries, as well as substantial involvement in their acts. Indeed, according to the *travaux* of the Declaration on the Definition of Aggression,[99] the hypothesis of 'indirect aggression' (*sub* Article 3, lit. g) applies also if the sending of armed bands takes place in the framework of a civil war.

On the other hand, the supply of weapons, munitions, military vehicles, logistical support, etc., represents a use of *indirect* force equally prohibited by Article 2, para. 4—as recognized by the ICJ in the Nicaragua case[100]—even if these hypotheses remain below the threshold of aggression defined for the purposes of Article 39 (but used also with reference to Article 51) of the UN Charter. In such cases, therefore, no right to self-defence can be invoked. The only reactions which are permitted are a request for counter-intervention and resort to peaceful countermeasures on the part of the state that has been the victim of this indirect use of force.

Furthermore, the international ban also extends beyond direct or indirect military assistance by including any other form of assistance (financial, political) deemed to contravene the principle of non-intervention, considered independently.[101]

To the prohibition to assist rebels in any form as imposed on third states by Article 2, para 4 of the UN Charter corresponds the lack of any right for the rebels to seek and receive external support, a prerogative which therefore remains confined to national liberation movements struggling for self-determination (pursuant to the Friendly Relations Declaration and UNGA Res. 3314 (XXIX)). In this regard, the citation of the ICJ's *Nicaragua* judgment is of key significance, in which the Court affirmed that it was difficult to see 'what would remain of the principle of non-intervention in international law if intervention, which is already allowable at the request of the government of a state, were also to be allowed at the request of the opposition'.[102]

1. Relevant practice

Practice is entirely supportive of these conclusions, so that the 'positive equality' thesis—according to which third states may, upon request, intervene on either

[99] For a reconstruction in this sense, see V Grado, *Guerre civili e terzi Stati* (CEDAM 1998) 78–81.

[100] *Military and Paramilitary Activities* (n 33) 117, para 247.

[101] As is clearly stated in the General Assembly's 'Declaration on the Inadmissibility of Intervention and Interference in the Internal Affairs of States', UNGA Res 36/103 (9 December 1981) UN Doc A/RES/36/103, which affirms 'The duty of the State to refrain from the promotion, encouragement or support, direct or indirect, of rebellious or secessionist activities within other States, under any pretext whatsoever, or any action which seeks to disrupt the unity or undermine or subvert the political order of other States'.

[102] *Military and Paramilitary Activities* (n 33) 116, para 246.

side of a civil war—is to be considered as 'limited to a mere description of reality'.[103]

In this regard, one may start with two cases recalled by the ICJ in the Kosovo Advisory Opinion,[104] namely the condemnation expressed by the UN Security Council regarding the independence proclaimed in 1983 by the Turkish Republic of Northern Cyprus owing to the decisive military support of Turkey[105] and the warning addressed by the UN Security Council in Res. 787 (1992) to all parties involved in the conflict in Bosnia-Herzegovina (and in particular the Republika Srpska, whose secessionist attempt was backed by Belgrade) that 'any entities unilaterally declared . . . will not be accepted'.

As for Kosovo itself, it is more problematic to assess whether, and to what extent, the secession of Kosovo is a consequence of the illegal bombing carried out by NATO, invoking humanitarian justification, against Serbian forces in the spring of 1999. The negative stand taken by the Court in its Advisory Opinion seems to support those commentators who have argued that—in contrast to the case of Northern Cyprus—no direct causal link may be established, after nine years of UN administration whose legality is firmly anchored in Res. 1244 (1999), between NATO's illegal military intervention of 1999 and Kosovo's proclamation of independence.[106] Having said that, the fact remains that the reason why Serbian forces had to leave control of Kosovo to the international community lies precisely in that unlawful military intervention, and in the fact that the international commitment to allow a limited return of Serb military and police forces in the province, provided for in para 4 of Res. 1244 (1999), has never been honoured by the United Nations Mission in Kosovo.

An inescapable precedent is the secession obtained by Bangladesh from Pakistan in 1971, thanks to India's decisive armed intervention against Pakistan. Although the intervention was legally justified on grounds of self-defence and humanitarian intervention,[107] it was mostly condemned, both in the Security Council[108] and in the UN General Assembly,[109] where many states re-affirmed their adherence to the principle that nothing can justify armed action against the territorial integrity of a member state. Moreover, Bangladesh was admitted to the United Nations only in 1974, after recognition was given by Pakistan.

103 Randelzhofer (n 46) 122. 104 *Accordance with International Law* 437 (n 54), para 81.

105 See UNGA Res 37/253 (13 May 1983) UN Doc A/RES/37/253. For the position of the UN Security Council see UNSC Res 541 (18 November 1983) UN Doc S/RES/541. See also UNSC Res 550 (11 May 1984) UN Doc S/RES/550, in response to the exchange of ambassadors between Turkey and the Turkish Republic of Northern Cyprus.

106 For this argument, see O Corten, 'Déclarations unilatérales d'indépendence et reconnaissance prématurées: du Kosovo à l'Ossétie du sud et à l'Abkhazie' (2008) 112 Revue générale de droit international public 721, 748.

107 See the remarks made by the Indian representative at the debate of the UN Security Council held on 4 December 1971, UNSC Verbatim Record (4 December 1971) UN Doc S/PV.1606, 17 and 32.

108 See, in this regard, the statements of China (UNSC Verbatim Record (4 December 1971) UN Doc S/PV.1606, 23) and the United States (UNSC Verbatim Record (4 December 1971) UN Doc S/PV.1606, 19).

109 In this sense, see the statement of the representative of Iran, in GAOR, 26th Session 2003rd Plenary Meeting (7 December 1971), 5; of Jordan (GAOR, 26th Session 2003rd Plenary Meeting

2. The practice in the CIS area

Concerning practice relating to the Commonwealth of Independent States, some confirmative indications derive from the 'five-day war' fought in Georgia in 2008. In response to Russia's direct military intervention in Georgia in support of South Ossetia and Abkhazia and the following recognition of the two breakaway entities as independent Republics, states intervening during the debate at the UN Security Council on 28 August 2008 spoke of 'a unilateral attempt to redraw the borders of a neighbouring country through the use of force'.[110] Indeed, as observed by Canada,[111] it was hardly possible to imagine a clearer example of the use of force against the territorial integrity of another state and, thus, a more evident breach of Article 2, para 4, of the UN Charter and the corresponding norm of general international law. According to the *Tagliavini* report, the Russian military reaction was clearly disproportionate in relation to a purely defensive purpose[112] and directly aimed at supporting the secessionists in Abkhazia and South Ossetia, thus violating the territorial integrity of another state.[113] On this basis, condemnation was also manifested by the Council of the European Union,[114] the Secretary-General, and the Council of NATO.[115]

As regards the conflict in Abkhazia more particularly, as early as 1993 the UN Security Council, in Res. 876 (1993), called on all states 'to prevent the provision from their territories of all assistance to the Abkhaz side and in particular to prevent the supply of any weapons and munitions'.

On the conflict in Nagorno-Karabakh, the UN Security Council has repeatedly regarded the external direct and indirect military support given by Armenia to the breakaway region of Azerbaijan as unlawful. In its Res. 853 (1993), for instance, that body reaffirmed its call 'to refrain from supplying any weapons and munitions'. In the subsequent Res. 884 (1993), the Council called upon the Government of Armenia to use its influence to ensure that the forces involved in the conflict 'are not provided with the means to extend their military campaign further'. The same call not to 'render aid or assistance in maintaining' the situation in the 'occupied territories' of Azerbaijan has been repeated by the UN General Assembly in its Res.

(7 December 1971), 12); of Sweden (GAOR, 26th Session 2003rd Plenary Meeting (7 December 1971), 27); of Mauritania (GAOR, 26th Session 2003rd Plenary Meeting (7 December 1971), 28).

[110] Thus the statement of the United Kingdom, UNSC Verbatim Record (28 August 2008) UN Doc S/PV.5969, 12. A similar view was held by Costa Rica (UNSC Verbatim Record (28 August 2008) UN Doc S/PV.5969).

[111] See the Statement on Georgia by the Delegation of Canada to the OSCE, 729th meeting of the Permanent Council, 28 August 2008, PC.DEL/717/08, at <http://www.osce.org/search>.

[112] *Independent International Fact-Finding Mission* (n 13) 275.

[113] *Independent International Fact-Finding Mission* (n 13) 293. On the illegality of Russia's intervention in the 'five-day war', see also Farhad Mirzayev's contribution to this book, 'Abkhazia', 205–206.

[114] See the Conclusion of the Extraordinary European Council meeting held at Brussels on 1 September 2008, para 2 (text available at <http://www.consilium.europa.eu/ueDocs/cms_Data/docs/pressData/en/ec/102545.pdf>).

[115] See, respectively, NATO Press Release (2008)107, of 26 August 2008 (text available at <http://www.nato.int/docu/pr/2008/p08-107e.html>), and NATO Press Release (2008)108, of 27 August 2008 (text available at <http://www.nato.int/docu/pr/2008/p08-108e.html>).

62/243, of 25th April 2008. Today, this situation remains characterized by the Parliamentary Assembly of the Council of Europe as 'de facto annexation'[116] and as illegal occupation by Armenia of a region which is still internationally regarded as part of Azerbaijan.

A final word on the separatist struggle fought by Transnistrians in Moldova. According to the European Court of Human Rights in the *Ilaşcu* case, this breakaway entity was 'set up in 1991–1992 with the support of the Russian Federation'[117] and 'remains under the effective authority, or at least the decisive influence'[118] of Moscow. The government of Moldova has repeatedly protested against the presence of Russia's 14th army in the east of its territory, qualifying that presence as 'flagrant and violent interference into the internal affairs' and the territory of Moldova on the left bank of the Nisdru river as 'occupied' in an act of military aggression.[119] Russia has been accused of 'supply[ing]' the secessionists 'with military equipment'[120] and supporting them in violent acts directed against legal state bodies. Paradoxically enough, as recalled in Bowring's contribution to this book,[121] Russia has (at least formally) always been in favour of Moldovan sovereignty and territorial integrity, proposing a special status for Transnistria within Moldova. Accordingly, Moscow itself has never recognized Transnistria as an independent state.

Theoretically, the regime thus far described might be reversed only by proving the existence of a right to secessionist self-determination. In fact, according to the UN General Assembly's Resolutions 1514 (XV) and 2625 (XV), in instances of classic self-determination states are prohibited from resorting to repressive force or asking for external aid, while peoples are entitled to forcibly resist colonial or foreign oppression, seeking and receiving external support.[122] Correspondingly, third states have been deemed authorized to provide financial, political and, in some instances of apartheid regimes (Namibia, Zimbabwe, South Africa),[123] indirect military assistance to national liberation movements.

According to the position defended by socialist and non-aligned states, these guarantees were based on the *ius ad bellum*, since colonial oppression or foreign occupation had to be considered as an ongoing armed attack authorizing collective self-defence.[124] On the other hand, western states have always opposed this view.[125]

[116] See Res 1416 (2005). [117] *Ilaşcu* (n 6) para 392. [118] *Ilaşcu* (n 6) 392.

[119] UN Doc S/24041, 30th May 1992. [120] UN Doc S/24041, 30th May 1992.

[121] B Bowring, 'Transnistria', 167.

[122] On this, see also para 7 of UNGA Res 3314 (XXIX) on the 'definition of aggression'.

[123] See, for instance, the resolutions in which the UN Security Council '*commends* the front-line States' for the aid given to peoples fighting against racist domination, aid consisting mainly in allowing the use of their territories by national liberation movements to install training bases, shelters, weapons depots, and also as a launchpad for attacks against oppressing governments – eg UNSC Res 393 (1976); Res 411 (1977), Res 424 (1978), and 428 (1978) (adopted unanimously); Res 445 (1977) and 447 (1979), Res 455 (1979) (adopted by consensus), Res 577 (1985) (adopted unanimously), Res 581 (1986). These resolutions were adopted with diminishing reluctance by western states (and indeed, sometimes, unanimously). In the legal scholarship, see L-A Sicilianos, *Les réactions décentralisées à l'illicite: des contre-mesures à la légitime défense* (LGDJ 1990) 444, and Grado (n 99) 142.

[124] On the relevant debate, see Sicilianos (n 123) 432 et seqq.

[125] See RE Gorelick, 'Wars of National Liberation: Jus ad Bellum' (1979) 11 CWRJIL 84 et seqq.

For this reason, some authors prefer to speak of a *sui generis* primary regime,[126] rather than admitting the existence of new exceptions to the non-use of force. Be that as it may, for the reasons given above, we remain rather sceptical about the existence today—at least *de lege lata*—of a general or remedial right to secessionist self-determination.

V. Conclusion

The research conducted on the relationships binding each of the actors potentially involved in a secessionist conflict confirms that the traditionally alleged neutrality of international law in this context is still showing significant *favour* towards the state.[127] The high threshold of effectiveness below which the state continues to enjoy the monopoly of internal force, the presumption in favour of its effectiveness, the prerogative to invite support from third parties that is denied to secessionists, are all elements that from the perspective at issue here would seem to confirm that, to use a rather trite expression,[128] the community of nations is not a 'suicide club'. However—as mentioned in the introduction—this final diagnosis would be misleading. The favour in question here, in fact, today is less and less a mere concession to state sovereignty and more and more a reflection of the idea that—at least when collective interests are threatened and/or violated as a consequence of secessionist conflicts—preservation of the unity of the state, rather than being merely a right, is a state's responsibility towards its citizens and their fundamental rights on the one hand, and the international community and other collective interests concerning peace, security, and stability on the other. Precisely because of this functional link, however, a state can be condemned and/or sanctioned internationally, or in extreme cases (as the precedent of Serbia/Kosovo seems to indicate) even be considered devoid of the full prerogatives relating to the use of internal force, ie if it is deemed responsible for crimes/gross violations of human rights or humanitarian law against civilians or rebels, or threatens or violates (other) collective interests of the international community.

[126] Corten (n 1) 186.

[127] See in this sense O Corten, 'Are There Gaps in the International Law of Secession?' in Kohen (n 2) 231, 254.

[128] HLA Hart, *The Concept of Law* (OUP 1961) 188.

6

The Principle of *Uti Possidetis Juris*

How Relevant is it for Issues of Secession?

Anne Peters[1]

Dans ses écrits, un sage Italien
Dit que le mieux est l'ennemi du bien.
Voltaire, *La Bégueule: Conte moral* (Grasset et Comp. 1772).

I. Problématique

'Borders have always been drawn with blood.' This dictum is ascribed to the former Bosnian Serb military leader, Ratko Mladic, who is accused of being responsible for the massacre in Srebrenica and is currently being tried for war crimes, crimes against humanity, and genocide by the International Criminal Tribunal for the Former Yugoslavia (ICTY).[2] Obviously, the use of military force and bloodshed as an instrument to define state boundaries is outlawed by contemporary international law.[3] Instead, the principle of *uti possidetis* was (selectively) applied to the dissolution of the Soviet Union and Yugoslavia in 1991 and 1992, namely to upgrade the boundaries of first-level territorial entities (Republics) of the former multilevel federal states to international boundaries of new states. The subsequent establishment of Kosovo in 2008 did not respect the boundary of the former Yugoslav Republic, Serbia.

[1] The author thanks Tigran Beknazar and Olivier Corten for valuable comments on the draft of this chapter.

[2] Spiegel online (2011), 'Portrait of a Man Possessed: A Search for the Real Ratko Mladic': 'Mladic could still play the charmer when the cameras were on him. In his headquarters north-east of Sarajevo, he wined and dined with SPIEGEL correspondent Renate Flottau. He answered her critical questions and his protests were muted when she spoke of human rights abuses: "Borders have always been drawn with blood."' <http://www.spiegel.de/international/europe/portrait-of-a-man-possessed-a-search-for-the-real-ratko-mladic-a-784851-3.html> accessed 18 August 2013. Mladic is also quoted by Steven Ratner in 'Drawing a Better Line: Uti Possidetis and the Borders of New States' (1990) 90 AJIL 590.

[3] For example, the preamble of the United Nations Security Council Resolution (UN SC Res) 713 (1991) para 8 states: 'No territorial gains or changes within Yugoslavia brought about by violence are acceptable.' See on Georgia UN SC Res 1065 (1996), para 3; Res 1808 (2008), para 1.

The question is what these events mean in law for territorial entities, such as Abkhazia, South Ossetia, Transdniestria (PMR), and Nagorno-Karabakh, claiming independence from their respective mother states, which are former Soviet Republics and all of which—except Georgia—are member states of the Commonwealth of Independent States (CIS). Does the international legal principle of *uti possidetis* apply to their boundaries? If yes, what would this principle demand?

In the current debate on contested territories in the CIS, commentators pointing to *uti possidetis* disagree on whether the principle is applicable or not. If it is applicable, it is unclear to *which* boundaries and to which not. Finally, observers draw quite different conclusions from any application or non-application of the principle. A first group (observers and interested parties alike) maintains that *uti possidetis* is inapplicable to current CIS member states (and was probably not even applicable to the dissolution of the Soviet Union). They draw the conclusion that a secession of territorial entities within former Soviet Union Republics is *not* hindered by that principle.[4] The opposing view is that *uti possidetis* was and is applicable to all levels of territorial units of the former Soviet Union, which would mean that both the former Republics and sub-units within them could and can rely on that principle to upgrade their boundaries, transforming the former administrative lines into international boundaries.[5] Importantly, with regard to the admissibility of the secession of territories within CIS member states, the application or non-application of *uti possidetis* does not make a difference under those two views: either *uti possidetis* may also privilege the boundaries of breakaway territories once secession has become effective, or it is not applicable at all.

A third group of observers favours the application of *uti possidetis*, but only with regard to the former Soviet Union's first level of administration. Farhad Mirzayev, in his chapter in this volume (ch 10) on Abkhazia, a breakaway region in Georgia, notably highlights that the constitutive parts of the former Soviet Union agreed to apply the principle of *uti possidetis* with regard to their boundaries and territories. According to Mirzayev, the main intention of the former Soviet Republics was to approve and strengthen the principle of *uti possidetis* but to use it only as an instrument to stabilize the newly independent states and to prevent further

[4] This seems to be Armenia's position on the region of Nagorno-Karabakh, which is situated within Azerbaijan but ethnically and politically affiliated with Armenia. See Krüger, ch 11 (in this volume) 226: 'The Armenian side... questions the application of the *uti possidetis* principle. It is said that the affiliation of Nagorno-Karabakh to Azerbaijan was conditioned exclusively by the formation and existence of the Soviet Union'. See against the application of *uti possidetis* also the written statement of the USA on Kosovo in the Advisory Opinion Proceedings, note 128.

[5] MG Kohen, 'Le problème des frontières en cas de dissolution et de séparation d'Etats: Quelles alternatives?' in O Corten et al. (eds), *Démembrements d'Etats et délimitations territoriales: L'uti possidetis en question(s)* (Bruylant 1999) 365, 383. For a contextualized discussion of whether *uti possidetis* is transferable at all to the boundaries in the former Soviet Union see O Luchterhandt, 'Grenzen in Mittelasien und uti possidetis-Prinzip: der Fall „Fergana-Tal"' in A Nußberger and C von Gall (eds), *Bewusstes Erinnern und bewusstes Vergessen* (Mohr Siebeck 2011) 51, 58–60, 105–106. The author concludes that despite differences between classical colonialism and the Soviet Empire, and despite the quite uneven and variable status and legitimacy of internal Soviet boundaries, *uti possidetis* is applicable to the territory of the former Soviet Union.

fragmentation.[6] The argument, hence, is that the former Republics' boundaries were upgraded by virtue of *uti possidetis*, and that this principle now sanctifies the new states' boundaries and prevents the secession of territories from them. This view is also endorsed by Krüger with regard to Azerbaijan (ch 11 in this volume).[7] According to that view, neither Abkhazia in Georgia nor Nagorno-Karabakh in Azerbaijan can draw any support from *uti possidetis* for their claims to independence—quite to the contrary, *uti possidetis* works only in favour of the mother state. The result would be the same for a territory such as Transdniestria (PMR),[8] which did not enjoy any specific administrative status within the former Soviet Republic of Moldova. Therefore, *uti possidetis* would not privilege its boundaries in any case. Nevertheless, in this volume, Bill Bowring seems to assume a right to self-determination by a kind of consolidation through 20 years of separation and predicts that the exercise of this right will lead to a special status within Moldova (ch 8). As far as South Ossetia (in Georgia) is concerned, Christopher Waters (ch 9) tends towards a denial of a right to secession of South Ossetia and records that the parties' positions on status are irreconcilable for the time being. He does not rely on *uti possidetis* but suggests abandoning the focus on status and rather concentrating on improvements for humans' lives, on human rights, and on internally displaced persons.

In order to answer the question of the applicability of *uti possidetis* to secessions, we must first determine whether the past application of *uti possidetis* to the territorial realignments (or some of them) in the course of those two dissolutions (Soviet Union and Yugoslavia) was correct in legal terms or whether it violated international law. A third possibility is that the application was not fully covered by international law of the time (at the beginning of the 1990s), but that it constituted a practice which legitimately developed the law further. In that case, contemporary law as it stands now might hold a new and refined answer to the question of applying *uti possidetis* to the current territorial problems within the CIS.

II. A Brief Introduction to *Uti Possidetis*

Uti possidetis in international law is—in the words of the ICJ—'a principle which upgraded former administrative delimitations, established during the colonial period, to international frontiers. . .'.[9] The term *uti possidetis* stems from Roman law, which knew an interdict of the Praetor by which the disturbance of the

[6] Mirzayev, ch 10 (in this volume) 203. [7] Krüger (n 4) 225–227.

[8] See on this territory ch 8 in this volume by Bowring.

[9] *Case Concerning the Frontier Dispute (Burkina Faso* v *Republic of Mali)* [1986] ICJ Rep 554 para 23. See for monographical treatments in scholarship G Nesi, *L'uti possidetis iuris nel diritto internazionale* (CEDAM 1996); C Simmler, *Das uti possidetis-Prinzip: Zur Grenzziehung zwischen neu entstehenden Staaten* (Duncker & Humblot 1999); S Lalonde, *Determining Boundaries in a Conflicted World: The Role of Uti Possidetis* (McGill-Queen's University Press 2002); A Beaudouin, *Uti possidetis et sécession* (Dalloz 2011).

existing state of possession of immovables, as between two individuals, was forbidden. The interdict evolved into an ancillary mechanism for the purpose of deciding which of the parties, as a possessor, should have the advantage of standing in the defensive in a litigation to determine ownership. The formula employed by the Praetor was: 'Uti eas aedes, quibus de agitur, nec vi nec clam nec precario alter ab altero possidetis, quominus ita possideatis, vim fieri veto'. The literal translation is: 'As you possess the house in question, the one not having obtained by force, clandestinely, or by permission from the other, I forbid force to be used to the end that you may not continue to possess it'.[10] The core is: '*uti possidetis*, ita possideatis' ('as you possess, so you may possess').

When transferred to international relations in the nineteenth century, the meaning of *uti possidetis* was changed in two respects. First, it was no longer applied to private actors but to states, not to private immovable property but to state territory. Second, *uti possidetis* no longer operated as a merely procedural and provisional shift of the burden of proof or a mechanism of standing, but denoted a definitive status.[11] The creative adaptation of the principle is just one example of the transfer of Roman (private) law concepts to interstate law which gave rise to the characterization of classical international law as 'private law writ large', to use the words of Thomas Holland.[12] The curious aspect is that *uti possidetis* entered international law at a time when its 'fundamental object, in private law, of preventing and invalidating the use of force, no longer existed' in international law.[13] In contemporary international law, however, *uti possidetis* once again has the purpose of securing the fundamental international prohibition of forcible transfers of territory. In our times, *uti possidetis* has reverted to its primary purpose, so that international *uti possidetis* is currently closer to its Roman original than when it was first transferred to international law.

The first important application of the internationalized *uti possidetis* occurred in Latin America. In the second half of the nineteenth century, when the Spanish colonies declared themselves independent, they adopted a principle which they called *uti possidetis juris* of 1810. It denoted the upgrading of colonial boundaries to international boundaries. One arbitral award on *uti possidetis* was handed down in 1922 by the Swiss Federal Council (the Swiss government), called upon as an arbiter in a boundary dispute between Columbia and Venezuela.[14] This award qualified *uti possidetis* as a 'principle of constitutional and South American international law'.[15]

[10] This exposition of the Roman origin is based on John Bassett Moore, *Memorandum on Uti Possidetis: Costa-Rica Panama Arbitration* (Bancroft Library 1911) 5–8, who also gives the formula and the translation.

[11] JC Bluntschli, *Das moderne Völkerrecht der civilisierten Staaten als Rechtsbuch dargestellt* (Beck'sche Buchhandlung 1868), para 715.

[12] T Holland, *Studies in International Law* (Clarendon Press 1898) 152.

[13] Moore (n 10) 8.

[14] Swiss Federal Council (Bundesrat), *Affaire des frontières Colombo-Vénézuéliennes* (24 March 1922) 1 RIAA 223.

[15] Bundesrat, *Affaire des frontières Colombo-Vénézuéliennes* 248.

In Africa, *uti possidetis* has been applied since around 1960.[16] The leading case is the ICJ Chamber Judgment of 1986 concerning Burkina Faso and Mali, two former French colonies.[17] Here the Court stated that *uti possidetis* meant to upgrade former colonial delineations to international boundaries.[18] The meaning of *uti possidetis*, according to the ICJ, is 'pre-eminence accorded to legal title over effective possession as a basis of sovereignty... The essence of the principle lies in its primary aim of securing respect for the territorial boundaries at the moment when independence is achieved'.[19] The function of *uti possidetis* is to secure '[t]he essential requirement of stability in order to survive, to develop and gradually to consolidate their [the new states'] independence in all fields'.[20] That judgment was confirmed by the plenary Court in 2007 in a boundary dispute between Nicaragua and Honduras which involved two former Spanish colonies.[21]

In 1991 and 1992, the Badinter Commission pronounced itself on *uti possidetis* in the context of the dissolution of Yugoslavia. Opinions No. 2 and 3 expressed that the prime principle to define a boundary is the agreement between the involved states, thus the consent principle. *Uti possidetis* applies, according to the Badinter Commission, only as a fallback rule. The wording of these Opinions is quoted at p. 131, where the residual character of *uti possidetis* will be discussed.

III. The Normative Quality of *Uti Possidetis*

1. Customary and contractual *uti possidetis*

We must first identify the legal source of the principle of *uti possidetis*. In which legal shape can it be applied? Both the ICJ Chamber and the Badinter Commission have called *uti possidetis* a 'general principle'.[22] *Uti possidetis* cannot be a 'general principle of law recognized by civilized nations' in the sense of Art. 38 (1) lit c) ICJ Statute because *uti possidetis* has not been transferred from domestic to international law. *Uti possidetis* is a genuine international law concept, although it is

[16] Organization of African Unity (Assembly of Heads of State and Government) 'Border disputes among African states' (Cairo 17–21 July 1964) Res AHG/RES 16 (I) para 2: 'The Assembly of Heads of State and Government meeting in its First Ordinary Session in Cairo... solemnly declares that all Member States pledge themselves to respect the borders existing on their achievement of national independence.' The Decolonization Resolution did not expressly stipulate *uti possidetis* but rather its twin principle of territorial integrity: UN General Assembly Res 1514 (XV) (14 December 1960) para 6: 'Any attempt aimed at the partial or total disruption of the national unity and the territorial integrity of a country is incompatible with the purposes and principles of the Charter of the United Nations'.

[17] *Frontier Dispute case (Burkina Faso* v *Mali)* (n 9) notably paras 20–6.

[18] See the Court's definition of *uti possidetis* at p. 97, with n 9.

[19] *Frontier Dispute Case (Burkina Faso* v *Mali)* (n 9) para 23.

[20] *Frontier Dispute Case (Burkina Faso* v *Mali)* (n 9) para 26.

[21] *Case concerning Territorial and Maritime Dispute between Nicaragua and Honduras in the Caribbean Sea* [2007] ICJ Rep 659 paras 151 ff.

[22] *Frontier Dispute Case (Burkina Faso* v *Mali)* (note 9) para 20; Badinter Commission, Opinion No. 3 (11 January 1992) para 3, third principle.

also enshrined in some national constitutions of Latin America. This means that *uti possidetis* might be, first, applicable as a customary law principle. Second, it could be applied to a given territorial rearrangement by virtue of an agreement. The first type of application is general, whereas the second type of application is specific: the agreement relates to a concrete case and it is only opposable to an actor who agrees. The two types of applicability can coexist, because the agreement to apply *uti possidetis* to a situation does not need to be constitutive but can also be merely declaratory. In the latter case, it simply manifests an *opinio juris* concerning an already existing customary norm.

The agreement to apply *uti possidetis* can be explicit or implicit. An implicit agreement can lie in the simple act of applying the principle.[23] Historically, in Spanish America and in Africa, both the colonial powers and the colonies among themselves *agreed* to apply *uti possidetis*. In the words of the ICJ: 'Indeed it was by deliberate choice that African states selected, among all the classic principles, that of *uti possidetis*'.[24] An agreement to allow for the application of *uti possidetis* can also be embodied in an agreement to submit the drawing of the boundary to adjudication or arbitration because the parties must then reckon with the arbiters' reliance on that principle. This will be especially the case if the mandate allows for adjudication *ex aequo et bono*. In that sense, the application of *uti possidetis* by the Badinter Commission can be said to flow from an agreement, too.

If an arbitral tribunal is authorized (explicitly or implicitly) to apply *uti possidetis*, the relevance of that principle for the determination of the boundary ends once the award has been issued. If the award is binding (which was not the case with the 'opinions' of the Badinter Commission), then it becomes the legal basis of the definition of the boundary. In that case, it is the award that is legally decisive (even if it is based on a view of the *uti possidetis* position). Then the award's view on the *uti possidetis juris* prevails and cannot later be questioned juridically.[25]

The customary law quality of *colonial uti possidetis* is uncontroversial and has been affirmed by case law. The open question is only whether a *non-colonial uti possidetis* exists as a matter of customary law (on this question, see section V of this chapter). However, even if a general and automatic application of *uti possidetis* to cases of non-colonial secession is rejected, *uti possidetis* can always be applied, also in the context of secession, by virtue of an agreement which refers to it. But then, the actual legal basis of its application is (only) the agreement: 'C'est l'accord, et non le mode d'accession à l'indépendance, qui représente le titre juridique qui fondera la délimitation'.[26]

[23] O Corten, 'Droit des peuples à disposer d'eux-mêmes et uti possidetis: deux faces d'une même medaille?' in O Corten et al. (eds), *Démembrements d'Etats et délimitations territoriales: L'uti possidetis en question(s)* (Bruylant 1999) 403, 432.

[24] *Frontier Dispute Case (Burkina Faso* v *Mali)* (n 9) para 26.

[25] *Case concerning the Land, Island and Maritime Frontier Dispute (El Salvador* v *Honduras, Nicaragua intervening)* [1992] ICJ Rep 351 para 67.

[26] Corten (n 23) 430.

2. Independence of the legal basis of the state and its boundary

The creation of a new boundary normally coincides with the emergence of a new state (as opposed to the situation of shifting a boundary due to cession of a piece of territory). How does *uti possidetis* relate to the legal qualification of statehood and to the process leading to the creation of a state? This relationship can be formulated either in a facticist or a normativist way: the question of whether a state boundary exists is synonymous with the question of whether a given entity is a state or not. The question of whether there should be a state boundary is concomitant to the question of whether the entity has lawfully become a state. The traditional and still widespread view is that in this context, only the factual question should be asked, because 'lawful' or 'not lawful' is no relevant category for the emergence and existence of states.[27] From that perspective, the emergence of a new state happens in an international legal vacuum, which means that no international rules govern this process.

Only if—alternatively—we assume that states do have (and need) some kind of legal basis might the applicability of *uti possidetis* depend on that legal basis. Importantly, even *arguendo* that a state needs a legal basis, in any case *uti possidetis* itself does not furnish such a basis. The legal basis must be found elsewhere, in international law or in domestic law. Possible international legal bases for the emergence of a new state are consent (an interstate treaty or other type of agreement on the creation of the state); self-determination (decolonization or—controversially—remedial secession); effectiveness (understood as a legal principle or title); or historical titles. However, tying the application of *uti possidetis* to the new state's legal basis does not seem to be warranted by state practice and does not make much sense, last but not least because the mentioned legal bases often overlap. For example, decolonization was mostly based both on the exercise of colonial self-determination and—often in a later stage—on the consent by the former administrative power.

Therefore, the better view seems to be that *uti possidetis* is indifferent to the (legal) grounds of statehood as such.[28] That view can also be framed in temporal terms: the question of boundaries arises only once independence has been acquired. *Uti possidetis* enters the scene only after independence has been acquired and 'ne vise pas à donner une justification quelconque à l'existence de l'Etat'.[29]

Second, what is the meaning of *uti possidetis* for the legal validity (the existence in law) of a boundary, and how does this relate to title?[30] In the Frontier Dispute

[27] G Abi-Saab, *Cours général de droit international public*, Vol 207 (Recueil de Cours: Collected Courses of the Hague Academy of International Law, Martinus Nijhoff Publishers 1987) 9, 68. Cf. Badinter Commission Opinion No. 1 (29 November 1991): 'the existence or disappearance of a state is a question of fact.' (Reprinted in Alain Pellet, 'The Opinions of the Badinter Arbitration Committee: A Second Breath for the Self-Determination of Peoples' (1992) 3 EJIL 178, 182).

[28] Kohen (1999) (n 5) 375. See generally on the critical date O Corten, 'Réflexions sur l'applicabilité de l'uti possidetis dans un conflit sécessionniste: le cas du Kosovo' in *Le procès international: Liber Amicorum Jean-Pierre Cot* (Bruylant 2009) 29–50.

[29] Kohen (n 5) 375.

[30] 'Title' in this context means first the source of a right to territory and second the evidence which might establish the existence of that right (*Frontier Dispute Case (El Salvador* v *Honduras, Nicaragua intervening)* (n 25) para 45).

between El Salvador and Honduras, the ICJ stated, somewhat confusingly: 'the principle of *uti possidetis juris* is concerned as much with title to territory as with the location of boundaries'.[31] However, it is generally accepted that the validity of a boundary is independent of the validity and legality of any title to territory. So the boundary's validity is legally independent of the legal instrument which has created that boundary. For example, with regard to the establishment of a boundary by treaty, the ICJ held in the territorial dispute between Libya and Chad that, once agreed upon, the boundary stands in law, irrespective of the nature and status of the treaty. The treaty can cease to be in force without affecting the legal continuance of the boundary in any way.[32]

The ICJ also said, for example, that in Latin American decolonization the *source* of the right to territory was succession of the new state to the Spanish Crown, whereas 'the *extent* of territory to which each State succeeded [was] being determined by the *uti possidetis* juris of 1821'.[33] Put differently yet again, '*uti possidetis* guarantees an objective situation *erga omnes*', the existence of a certain border, 'and not the legal validity of the underlying instrument'.[34] *Uti possidetis* protects a boundary, independently of the title; 'quel que soit le titre juridique qui le fonde'.[35]

3. The universality of *uti possidetis*

With a view to potential applications to territorial problems in the CIS, we must also rule out that *uti possidetis* is a merely regional—as opposed to a universal—principle. At the beginning of the twentieth century (before African decolonization), *uti possidetis* was probably only a principle of regional international law, a 'principe fondamental du droit public et international *sud-américain*', as the Swiss government, acting as an arbiter in a Latin American boundary dispute, put it.[36] Meanwhile, an ICJ Chamber clearly stated that *uti possidetis* is not only a regional principle of Latin American international law: '...the principle is *not* a special rule which pertains solely *to one specific system* of international law. It is a general principle, which is logically connected with the phenomenon of the obtaining of independence, *wherever* it occurs'.[37] The African practice 'must be seen *not* as a mere practice contributing to the gradual emergence of a principle of customary

[31] *Frontier Dispute Case (El Salvador* v *Honduras, Nicaragua intervening)* (n 25) para 42.

[32] *Territorial Dispute (Libyan Arab Jamahiriya* v *Chad)* [1994] ICJ Rep 6 para 73.

[33] *Frontier Dispute (El Salvador* v *Honduras, Nicaragua intervening)* (n 25) para 45 (emphasis added). The ICJ did not mention self-determination as a 'source' of the right to territory. This makes sense, because self-determination was not part of international law in the nineteenth century.

[34] E Milano, *Unlawful Territorial Situations in International Law: Reconciling Effectiveness, Legality and Legitimacy* (Martinus Nijhoff Publishers 2006) 111. Milano calls this the 'factual' existence of the border, but it would seem that what is meant is its existence in law.

[35] G Abi-Saab, 'Le principe de l'uti possidetis: son rôle et ses limites dans le contentieux territorial international' in MG Kohen (ed), *Promoting Justice, Human Rights and Conflict Resolution through International Law/La promotion de la justice, des droits de l'homme et du règlement des conflits par le droit international: Liber Amicorum Lucius Caflisch* (Martinus Nijhoff Publishers 2007) 657, 659.

[36] *Swiss Federal Council* (1922) (n 14) 248 (emphasis added).

[37] *Frontier Dispute Case (Burkina Faso* v *Mali)* (note 9) para 20 (emphases added).

international law, *limited in its impact to the African continent as it had previously been to Spanish America*, but as the application in Africa of a rule of *general scope*'.[38]

IV. *Uti Possidetis* in the Dissolution of the Soviet Union and Yugoslavia

1. The legal qualification of the dissolution processes of the Soviet Union and of Yugoslavia

The propriety and lawfulness of the past application of *uti possidetis* to the dissolution of Yugoslavia and the Soviet Union do not depend on the legal qualification of those processes as continued *secessions* or as *dismemberments*.[39] This dichotomy is relevant for the legal status of the successor states, notably to answer the question of whether in the CIS Russia is the sole successor to the former Soviet Union, and in Central Eastern Europe whether Serbia is the sole successor to the Socialist Federal Republic of Yugoslavia (SFRY). These matters had been controversial, but an *opinio communis* has formed.

With regard to the dissolution of the Soviet Union, the best legal view seems to be that the Soviet Union was dismembered, rather than that the Republics seceded from Russia. This means that Russia is not identical to the Soviet Union as a state and as a subject of international law, but merely one of various successor states.[40] Russia (in contrast to the other former Soviet Republics) had never declared its independence, and had in various international fora claimed to be identical with or 'continuous' to the USSR. Indeed, continuity was, for practical reasons, admitted with regard to the state's membership in the UN. However, third states' statements and their legal qualification of Russia's legal relation to the USSR were erratic.[41] Most importantly, the CIS formally dissolved the USSR.[42]

[38] *Frontier Dispute Case (Burkina Faso* v *Mali)* (n 9) para 21 (emphases added).

[39] These terms are used here to denote the difference as to whether the previous state persists with a reduced territory (as identical to the former state or as its sole successor state, as in the case of the Soviet Union and Russia) or whether the predecessor state is completely dissolved and disappears (as in the case of Yugoslavia). A different usage of the dichotomy is to call a consented territorial re-arrangement a 'dismemberment' and the non-consented re-arrangement a 'secession'.

[40] See for a good discussion of the problem U Saxer, *Die internationale Steuerung der Selbstbestimmung und der Staatsentstehung* (Springer 2010) 802–6 with numerous further references; with regard to the succession into treaties A Zimmermann, *Staatennachfolge in völkerrechtliche Verträge* (Springer 2000) 372–421. See in favour of discontinuity T Schweisfurth, 'Soviet Union, Dissolution' in R Bernhardt (ed), *Encyclopedia of Public International Law* (vol. 4, Elsevier 2000) 529, 539–46; T Schweisfurth, 'Vom Einheitsstaat (UdSSR) zum Staatenbund (GUS)' (1992) 52 ZaöRV 541, esp 669–91. But see *Case Concerning Application of the International Convention on the Elimination of All Forms of Racial Discrimination* (*Georgia* v *Russian Federation*), *Order of 15 October 2008* [2008] ICJ Rep 353 para 105. Here the ICJ speaks of the 'Russian Federation, as the State continuing the legal personality of the Union of Soviet Socialist Republics'. See also in favour of Russia as 'Etat continuateur de l'ex-URSS' the note of the Swiss Federal Directorate of Public International Law, (1996) 6 SZIER 618–19.

[41] See the references in B Stern, *La succession d'Etats*, Vol 262 (Recueil des Cours: Collected Courses of the Hague Academy of International Law, Martinus Nijhoff Publishers 1996) 9, 48–51.

[42] Cf. the Agreement Establishing the Commonwealth of Independent States of Minsk of 8 December 1991, in which the heads of state of Belarus, the RSFSR, and the Ukraine 'declare that

So in legal terms, Russia is not identical with or 'continuous' to the USSR—only for reasons of political expediency has the Russian claim of continuity come to be accepted by the international community.[43]

The dissolution of Yugoslavia is best qualified as a prolonged secession of the Republics of the SFRY which began in 1991. The domestic law of the SFRY was ambiguous on the internal lawfulness of secession. While the preamble of the Constitution of Socialist Federal Republic of Yugoslavia of 21 February 1974 mentioned a right to secession, its Art. 5 prohibited internal territorial changes. Notwithstanding that internal illegality, the Republics proclaimed their independence, often backed by territorial referendums, and were then recognized as sovereign states and later acceded to the United Nations. The SFRY ceased to exist. Serbia (until 2006 united with Montenegro) initially tried to interpret these facts differently from other observers. Serbia first claimed to be identical or the sole successor state to the former SFRY. This claim of identity or sole succession by Serbia–Montenegro was refuted, inter alia, in Opinion No. 9 of the Badinter Commission of July 1992.[44] Ultimately, all Republics are successor states to the extinct state, the SFRY. This legal difference—Russia being a 'continuer' of the Soviet Union, Serbia not being the only successor to the SFRY—does not play a role for the applicability of *uti possidetis*. It is correct to qualify both dissolution processes, in a simplified *façon de parler*, as secessions as opposed to decolonization. What matters is the difference between those processes and decolonization (as will be discussed further in this chapter).

2. The legal source of the application of *uti possidetis* to the Soviet Union and Yugoslavia in 1991/2: consent-based, customary, or purely political?

The precise analysis of the historical application of *uti possidetis* to the Soviet Union and to Yugoslavia in 1991 and 1992 helps to determine—in an abstract fashion and prospectively—whether the principle of *uti possidetis* is at all applicable (as a matter of positive analysis) and whether it reasonably should be applied (normative analysis) to pending situations and future scenarios of secession (as opposed to the classical field of application of the principle: decolonization). With regard to the Soviet Union and Yugoslavia, the application of *uti possidetis* has been construed and explained in the literature in two different ways, pointing to the two different sources (customary law or treaty) mentioned in section III.1 (pp. 99–100).

A look at the relevant documents on the dissolution of the Soviet Union shows that all of them relied on *uti possidetis* only implicitly by insisting on territorial integrity and on the intangibility of borders (in detail and on the relationship

the USSR as a subject of international law and a geopolitical reality no longer exists' (reproduced in (1992) 31 ILM 143).

[43] Saxer (n 40) 805–6. For Stern (n 41) the conclusion to draw from the non-existence of the USSR must be that all Republics, including Russia, are successor states. It amounts to an 'illogisme' to qualify Russia as the continuing state.

[44] Badinter Commission, Opinion No. 9 (4 July 1992) (1993) 4 EJIL 88–90, para 1.

between those principles and *uti possidetis* see pp. 127–29). One group of authors qualifies the application of *uti possidetis* to the Soviet Union (as to Yugoslavia and Czechoslovakia) as a purely *consensual one* (on the basis of agreements or parallel unilateral declarations by all interested sides). For example, Santiago Torres Bernárdez has argued that *uti possidetis* could only be applied to the Yugoslavian situation through a 'contracting-in' consent of the parties concerned, not by the mere operation of the principle *qua norm* of international law. *Uti possidetis juris qua norm* of international law is, according to Torrez Bernárdez and others, not directly applicable to territorial problems arising in relations between new states which were formerly constituent territorial units of a given sovereign state.[45]

A related view is that in the case of Yugoslavia, *uti possidetis* was applied not even as a matter of law (based on international treaties) but purely as a political device, outside the realm of international law: 'In short, the territorial solution adopted in Yugoslavia was the result of a policy decision that was quite possibly justified. It was not, however, required by international law'.[46]

The 'contractual' or 'political' explanation of the application of *uti possidetis* to the Soviet Union has its deeper foundation in the conviction that the ultimate foundation and source of the applicability of *uti possidetis* as a customary law principle is its correlation to the principle of self-determination. From that perspective, self-determination provides a kind of legal basis for (customary) *uti possidetis*, too. This means that where territorial claims are raised which cannot (or cannot uncontroversially) be based on self-determination, *uti possidetis* has no (automatic) place but can—if at all—come in through a space opened by agreement on its application to the specific case. In combination with the restrictive view on self-determination, which holds that any exercise of that right which would lead to the establishment of a new state is basically allowed only in the context of decolonization, this construction leads to the general applicability of *uti possidetis* being limited to decolonization and thus makes *customary uti possidetis* a matter of the past, not of the future.

A third, opposing, view is that in the course of the breakup of the Soviet Union and of Yugoslavia, the explicit or implicit acceptance of the upgrading of administrative boundaries to international frontiers by the various interested actors was purely 'declaratory'. The agreement to apply *uti possidetis* was—from that perspective—a manifestation of an extant *opinio juris* on the (general) applicability of that pre-existing principle to the situation: 'It is difficult not to see in this practice the expression of a conviction of a compulsory character of the respect of existing frontiers in the moment of independence, that is to say the ancient administrative

[45] S Torres Bernárdez, 'The "Uti Possidetis Juris Principle" in Historical Perspective' in K Ginther (ed), *Völkerrecht zwischen normativem Anspruch und politischer Realität: Festschrift für Karl Zemanek zum 65. Geburtstag* (Duncker & Humblot 1994) 417, 435–6; Corten (n 23) 428–9.

[46] Lalonde (n 9) 240. The same author considers the application of *uti possidetis* to the Soviet Union as a political result, not legally determined (Lalonde at 233). See in this sense on Yugoslavia also Barbara Delcourt, 'L'application de l'*uti possidetis juris* au démembrement de la Yougoslavie—règle coutumière ou impérative politique' in Olivier Corten et al. (eds), *Démembrements d'Etats et délimitations territoriales: L'uti possidetis en question(s)* (Bruylant 1999) 35–78.

delineations. The formal acts declaring the respect of existing frontiers thus have a value which declares the law in force, recognizing an existing rule.'[47]

These three different legal constructions of the application of *uti possidetis* to the Soviet Union and to Yugoslavia make a difference for its possible future application to the CIS. If the legal basis was (only) a contractual or a purely political one, *uti possidetis* cannot lawfully and correctly be relied upon by the current metropolitan states against the will of breakaway territories. If, in contrast, *uti possidetis* is applicable as a matter of customary law, then it is also applicable to the pending territorial controversies. However, the exact meaning and consequences of this application must be further examined anyway (see p. 119).

A fourth interpretation of the historical situation is that the relevant actors' decisions to apply *uti possidetis* to the Soviet Union and to Yugoslavia, even if it furnished the necessary contractual basis for applying the principle to that case, can play the role of practice and *opinio juris* needed as elements for the formation of an emerging customary rule of *uti possidetis*. This construction raises the question of whether treaties and the practice of concluding treaties can count as practice formative of customary law or whether practice must rather be understood as the opposite: as a negation of a customary rule.

The divergent legal interpretations of the historical use of *uti possidetis* in the course of the dissolution of the Soviet Union call for a closer doctrinal examination of the scope of *uti possidetis ratione materiae*, to which we now turn.

V. Customary *Uti Possidetis* Limited to Decolonization?

Uti possidetis could play no role *qua* customary law for current territorial issues in the CIS or elsewhere if the scope of application of the customary principle were, from the outset, limited to decolonization. The divergent legal qualifications of the practice of the 1990s concerning the Soviet Union and Yugoslavia have failed to settle that matter, as we have seen. In scholarship, both views have been espoused. One side rejects the applicability of customary *uti possidetis* beyond (historical) decolonization.[48] Under that view, the application of the *uti possidetis* guarantee as a pre-independence guarantee of administrative boundaries within states is a matter of politics, but not a pre-existing requirement of international law.[49] The opposing camp supports a more general scope of the principle which stretches beyond decolonization.[50] No dominant opinion has emerged so far.

[47] 'Il est alors difficile de ne pas déceler dans cette pratique l'expression de la conviction du caractère obligatoire du respect des frontières existantes au moment de l'indépendance, c'est-à-dire des anciennes limites administratives. Les actes formelles proclamant le respect des frontières existantes ont donc une valeur déclaratives du droit en vigueur, reconnaissant une règle existante'. Kohen (1999) (n 5) 378 (translation by the author); see also 379. Recent international practice is witness to the existence of a belief in the compulsory character of *uti possidetis* in cases of separation or dissolution.

[48] See for an excellent exposition of that view Corten (n 23); see also Bernárdez (n 45); Lalonde (n 9).

[49] Lalonde (n 9) 240.

[50] See comprehensively Kohen (1999) (n 5); Beaudouin (n 9); G Nesi, 'Uti Possidetis Doctrine' in R Wolfrum (ed), *The Max Planck Encyclopedia of Public International Law* (Oxford University Press online 2013) para 8.

The question of whether *uti possidetis* is also a customary law principle outside the context of decolonization must be examined both with regard to the underlying rationales of the principle itself and with a view to other principles of international law (on its purposes see pp. 115 ff.; on the legal context see pp. 125 ff.). Most arguments against the applicability of customary *uti possidetis* beyond the colonial context rest on the view that decolonization and non-colonial secession differ in crucial respects which outweigh the similarities of both scenarios. The relevant principles and policy considerations must be examined one by one.

The first is legitimacy/legality as opposed to effectiveness. A doctrinal argument—elegantly made by Olivier Corten—is that decolonization and non-colonial secession are two different modes of acquiring independence which have differing legal bases and which follow 'distinct logics'.[51] Decolonization was an exercise of self-determination, and therefore the attainment of independence was based on 'legitimacy.' In contrast, in the situation of secession, independence is attained on the basis of 'effectiveness' (as opposed to legitimacy).[52] Because of these differences, so the argument runs, *uti possidetis* cannot be reasonably transferred from one context to the other, at least not without any specific agreement—it is in no way 'logically' linked to acquiring independence, as the ICJ put it in the *Frontier Dispute Case*.[53]

The premise of this bifurcated view is that there is no right to secession, that secession occurs in an international law-free realm. Therefore, there is no space for any legal principle relating to the territorial delimitation. Due to the principle of effectiveness, secession is a fact which imposes itself over the law. The same must be true not only for the fact but for the spatial extension of that secession. Therefore, there is no 'right' to have certain boundaries.[54] The territorial title and the delineation of the boundaries cannot be separated from the mode in which the new state came into existence. Therefore, the legal regime concerning the existence must also apply to the (geographical) extension of the state. The new state is a matter of fact,[55] and its existence depends on effectiveness without any room for reliance on the pre-existing boundaries in the predecessor state.

The purported distinction between decolonization and secession may also be framed in terms of lawfulness. Decolonization was allowed and even mandated by international law. Colonization had, by the 1950s, come to be seen as an internationally wrongful act, and there was an international legal obligation to decolonize. Jörg Fisch has pointed out that decolonization started from a

[51] Corten (n 23) 432.

[52] Corten (n 23) 407. A remark on 'effectiveness' seems in order: Historically, notably in Latin America, *uti possidetis* was designed to replace the idea of effectiveness. It did so by defining territories in disregard of the fact that much of the territory was not effectively occupied or governed by the colonial state. But the relationship between *uti possidetis* and effectiveness is ambivalent. *Uti possidetis* can also be considered as an interpretation of the legal principle of effectiveness which is at work in the instance of a secession. There is no necessary contradiction between the principle of effectiveness and *uti possidetis*; the principle of *uti possidetis* rather confirms the normative dimension of effectiveness. *Uti possidetis* gives effectiveness its 'spatial dimension'. Beaudouin (n 9) notably 610–13.

[53] *Frontier Dispute Case (Burkina Faso* v *Mali)* (n 9) para 20.

[54] Corten (n 23) 408.

[55] See on this facticist view p. 101.

perception of the illegitimacy and, eventually, illegal and even criminal character of colonial rule. In contrast, federations, including the defunct Soviet Union, did not have a comparably criminal character. Nobody maintained that the Soviet Union or Socialist Yugoslavia were as such contrary to international law. The dissolution of the Eastern European federations therefore had a legal basis different from decolonization.[56]

However, the seeming difference between decolonization and secession fades if we take into account that in nineteenth-century Latin America, the establishment of the first Republics was not supported by contemporary international law. On the contrary, the Latin American states' independence was perceived by contemporary observers as what we would now call secession (for detail see p. 114). The distinction between decolonization and secession is further undermined by the insight that its underlying claim, namely that secession is outside international law, rests on controversial premises. Many commentators think that secession is regulated by international law but do not agree on when it is allowed and when not. Maybe it can be safely said that the lawfulness of secession is controversial, and that it in any case depends on the context. The complete dissolution of the Soviet Union and of Yugoslavia was not justifiable in regard to all Republics as an exercise of a right to self-determination, and it was surely not mandated by international law. Overall, recent state practice, notably Kosovo's acquisition of independence in 2008, bolsters the view that, under exceptional circumstances, secession can be tolerated, justified, or exculpated as an *ultima ratio* in cases where 'internal' self-determination is persistently denied to a people.[57]

In addition, Corten's entire paradigm of 'effectiveness' as a legal basis of non-colonial state formation can be questioned. The emergence of a state does not happen in a law-free zone but is embedded in international prescriptions, beginning with the right to self-determination and the prohibition of the use of force.[58] The facticist view of statehood (considering states as pure matters of fact) glorifies the *fait accompli*,[59] implies an abdication of international law, and has as a result that the 'law' of the more powerful governs and determines whether

[56] J Fisch, *Das Selbstbestimmungsrecht der Völker: die Domestizierung einer Illusion* (Beck 2010) 284.

[57] See for the classical exposition LC Buchheit, *The Legitimacy of Self-determination* (Yale University Press 1978) 220–3. Diagnosing and supporting remedial secession (as a rule of positive international law derived from the savings clause of the Friendly Relations Declaration) see C Tomuschat, 'Secession and Self-determination' in M Kohen (ed), *Secession—International Law Perspectives* (Cambridge University Press 2006) 23, 42: '[R]emedial secession should be acknowledged as part and parcel of positive law, notwithstanding the fact that its empirical basis is fairly thin. But not totally lacking…'. But see K del Mar, 'The Myth of Remedial Secession' in D French (ed), *Statehood and Self-determination: Reconciling Tradition and Modernity in International Law* (Cambridge University Press 2013) 79. On Kosovo see A Peters, 'Does Kosovo Lie in the *Lotus*-Land of Freedom?' (2011) 24 LJIL 95.

[58] I leave aside the question of under which circumstances the prohibition may apply in internal situations; it is in any case directed at bystander states to a territorial conflict.

[59] T Christakis, 'The State as "Primary Fact": Some Thoughts on the Principle of Effectiveness' in M Kohen (ed), *Secession—International Law Perspectives* (Cambridge University Press 2006) 138, 157.

there is a state or not. Statehood needs a factual basis, but lawyers ascribe a legal significance to these facts. The facts are and must be—for a legal evaluation—'conceptualized'.[60] To conclude, the argument that *uti possidetis* can play no role in non-colonial secession because that phenomenon is outside the law appears too schematic to capture the messy political and legal processes leading to the creation of new states, and also disregards the emerging views on remedial secession.

The second factor distinguishing between decolonization and secession which might prevent the transfer of customary *uti possidetis* from the colonial context to the non-colonial one is the implication for territorial integrity. In decolonization, peoples rose against distant powers; territories outside the territory of the colonial power formed new sovereign states; independence did not affect the ordinary territory of the metropolitan state (the 'salt water test'). For example, the independence of Mali (from France) did not involve the neighbouring state or the people of Burkina Faso.

In contrast, in a secession conflict, independence and territorial integrity are at stake simultaneously.[61] In fact, the breaking away of territories from the Soviet Union and from the SFRY led to a full dismemberment of the former state in the case of Yugoslavia, and to a significant shrinking of the state in the case of the Soviet Union/Russia. As far as current conflicts are concerned, the creation of a state of Abkhazia, for example, could only come about at the cost of the territorial integrity of Georgia.

The third issue is extension over time. Decolonization happened step by step over decades. In that situation, the principle of *uti possidetis* secured the *equal treatment* of all geographical entities. Other criteria could have been applied even-handedly only if all boundaries had been drawn at once, which was not the case. So only *uti possidetis* allowed treating all colonies equally, even if all were treated equally badly.

The fourth argument is that colonial delimitations (often) had a *semi-international status* (unlike domestic administrative lines). Neighbouring colonies often had a different legal position vis-à-vis the metropolitan state, and therefore the lines dividing them resembled international boundaries.[62] While it is acceptable to upgrade such semi-international boundaries to international ones, such upgrading is far-fetched with regard to administrative lines, which are normally ignored altogether by international law.

The fifth argument against the applicability of *uti possidetis* outside decolonization is that such a rule would *not* be *universalizable*. It cannot work as a general rule for all cases of secession, because it does not provide any solution to secessions involving unitary states which do not possess any internal administrative dividing lines.[63]

[60] A Peters, 'Statehood after 1989: "Effectivités" between Legality and Virtuality' in J Crawford and S Nouwen (eds), *Select Proceedings of the European Society of International Law*, Vol 3 (Hart Publishing 2012) 171.

[61] Cf. Corten (n 23), 'Débats', 446; Lalonde (n 9) 234.

[62] Ratner (n 2) 609; Lalonde (n 9) 234.

[63] P Radan, 'Post-Secession International Borders: A Critical Analysis of the Opinions of the Badinter Arbitration Commission' (2000) 24 MULR 50, 71.

The sixth issue is the legal policy consideration that a state would be penalized for devolution and federalization because the establishment of sub-units with political autonomy (which necessarily possess internal boundaries) would carry the risk of being prone to upgrading. This 'danger' is not present if the state is maintained as a fully centralized state without any internal boundary.[64] This incentive against federalization is an undesirable policy outcome, because federal or quasi-federal arrangements seem to be the most promising political strategy for accommodating minority issues.

All in all, these arguments against the application of *uti possidetis* to cases of secession must be taken seriously. However, they are outweighed by doctrinal, contextual, and policy arguments supporting the application of *uti possidetis* to secessions, and these will now be examined.

VI. The Application of Customary *Uti Possidetis* to Secessions

The better view is that today *uti possidetis* has the value of a customary rule which applies to secession beyond the colonial context.[65]

1. Case law

This view can first of all rely on two international rulings, namely the ICJ Chamber Judgment in the *Frontier Dispute Case* (*Burkina Faso* v *Mali)* and on the Opinions of the Badinter Commission on the dissolution of Yugoslavia. Taken together with the absence of a prior rule of international law clearly precluding the application of *uti possidetis* to non-colonial or postcolonial situations, the burden of argument seems to fall on those who claim that the principle's material scope is limited to decolonization and who seek to deny, against those dispute settlement bodies' findings, the applicability of *uti possidetis* to all modes of creation of states.

The ICJ Chamber's leading judgment of 1986, the *Frontier Dispute Case*, is ambiguous. On the one hand, it contains sentences referring solely to decolonization;[66] on the other, it contains general statements on *uti possidetis* which sound as if *uti possidetis* were applicable outside the context of decolonization as well. The Chamber notably stated that *uti possidetis* 'is a general principle, which is logically connected with *the phenomenon of the obtaining of independence*, wherever it

[64] Lalonde (n 9) 237.

[65] MN Shaw, 'Peoples, Territorialism and Boundaries' (1997) 3 EJIL 478; Kohen (1999) (n 5); Beaudouin (n 9); Nesi (2013) (n 50) paras 6, 15–16. See in support of the existence of a principle of regional customary law in Eastern and Central Europe and of a universal customary principle after 1989 Simmler (n 9) 280–4 and 293.

[66] *Frontier Dispute Case (Burkina Faso* v *Mali)* (n 9) para 20: 'a firmly established principle of international law where decolonization is concerned.'; also para 23: '*Uti possidetis*, as a principle which upgraded former administrative delimitations, established during the colonial period, to international frontiers, is therefore a principle of a general kind which is logically *connected with this form of decolonization* wherever it occurs' (emphasis added).

occurs' (emphasis added).[67] The Chamber also said: 'There is no doubt that the obligation to respect pre-existing international frontiers in the event of a *State succession* derives from a general rule of international law, *whether or not the rule is expressed in the formula uti possidetis*' (emphasis added).[68] Overall, the ICJ did not give an unequivocal answer to the question of whether *uti possidetis* applies to all kinds of state succession, but seemed to lean more towards a general scope *ratione materiae.*

The Badinter Commission applied the principle outside the context of colonization. Opinion No. 3 stated: '*Uti possidetis,* though initially applied in settling decolonization issues in America and Africa, is today recognized as a general principle...'. Malcolm Shaw pointed out that two types of criticism have been directed at that decision.[69] The first critique is that the decision did not correctly depict the law as it stands and was not in conformity with pre-existing international law.[70] The second is that the opinion offended other principles of international law and was in systemic violation of those more general principles which form the context. That context will be examined in section IX of this chapter.

The first critique is unfounded. In particular, the reproach that the Badinter opinion misrepresented or distorted the 1986 Chamber Judgment of the ICJ in the *Frontier Dispute Case (Burkina Faso* v *Mali)* is unwarranted. In fact, as we have seen, that Chamber Judgment was ambiguous. The Badinter Commission quoted only that sentence of the Chamber Judgment which qualified *uti possidetis* as 'a general principle, which is logically connected with the phenomenon of the obtaining of independence'.[71] It thereby produced a legitimate interpretation of the Chamber's statement and was not acting in legal error.[72] Given the openness of the ICJ judgment, the Badinter Commission was entitled to develop further the law in one particular direction which was already—albeit in a rudimentary form—encapsulated in the ICJ's case law.

It is conceded that the awards of both bodies have no formal *erga omnes* value as binding precedents. The ICJ's statements were, in strict terms, *obiter dicta*, and are in any case binding only *inter partes*. The Badinter Awards were not binding judgments but only advisory opinions. However, despite the weak formal status of these decisions, they have high authority in substance.

[67] *Frontier Dispute Case (Burkina Faso* v *Mali)* (n 9) para 20. However, the preceding sentences of para 20 refer only to decolonization.

[68] *Frontier Dispute Case (Burkina Faso* v *Mali)* (n 9) para 24.

[69] Shaw (n 65) 496.

[70] See for this type of critique eg H Hannum, 'Self-Determination, Yugoslavia, and Europe: Old Wine in New Bottles?' (1993) 57 TLCP 57, 66: 'This opinion is dubious if it purports to identify a rule of international law which requires the maintenance of existing administrative borders outside the colonial context...'; Radan (n 63) esp at 62: 'The principle is not, as claimed by the Badinter Commission, recognised as a general principle applicable to all cases of independence'.

[71] From para 20 of the ICJ Chamber judgment, *Frontier Dispute Case (Burkina Faso* v *Mali)* (n 9).

[72] See notably the careful analysis by Shaw (n 65) 498–9.

2. State practice in the *Kosovo Advisory Opinion* proceedings

The customary law status of *uti possidetis* beyond the colonial context, and notably in the situation of secession, was put to the test in the *Kosovo Advisory Opinion* proceedings. First of all, the ICJ itself did *not* mention *uti possidetis* here.[73] The Court pronounced itself only on the corollary principle of territorial integrity[74] and found that this principle was applicable only among states and thus had no role to play as a legal yardstick for the declaration of independence's conformity or non-conformity with international law.[75] The written statements filed by 37 states are important indicators of the prevailing *opinio juris* on this matter. Only eight states mentioned *uti possidetis* at all.

Of the eight states which did mention *uti possidetis*,[76] only five (Cyprus, Ireland,[77] Romania,[78] Serbia, and the Netherlands) explicitly or implicitly considered the principle of *uti possidetis* to be applicable to the Kosovo case. Of those five, only three states espoused the legal position that the declaration of independence was not in accordance with international law. Only two of those three states (Serbia[79] and Cyprus) explicitly said that this illegality resulted (inter alia) out of a violation of *uti possidetis*. In contrast, the Netherlands considered *uti possidetis* to be applicable, but nevertheless found the declaration of independence to be lawful and *uti possidetis* not violated in the present case.[80] In the end, leaving out Serbia, which was obviously a self-interested party, only one single state (Cyprus[81]) out of the entire international community found the Kosovo secession to be in violation of *uti possidetis*.

In contrast, two states (the United States and Finland) clearly opined that *uti possidetis* was *not* applicable to the Kosovo case (and both states also found the declaration of independence to be in accordance with international law). The

[73] *Accordance with International Law of the Unilateral Declaration of Independence in Respect of Kosovo, Advisory Opinion of 22 July 2010* [2010] ICJ Rep 403.

[74] See p. 127.

[75] *Unilateral Declaration of Independence in Respect of Kosovo* (n 73) para 80.

[76] For example, Slovenia mentioned *uti possidetis*, but it remained unclear whether the state deemed the principle applicable to the Kosovo case (Written Comment (17 July 2009) <http://www.icj-cij.org/docket/files/141/15696.pdf> 4, accessed 18 September 2013).

[77] Ireland's statement was inconclusive in that point; it mentioned *uti possidetis* only in a literature quote. Written Statement of Ireland (17 April 2009) <http://www.icj-cij.org/docket/files/141/15662.pdf> para 20 accessed 18 September 2013. Ireland concluded that the declaration of independence was not unlawful.

[78] Written Statement of Romania (14 April 2009) <http://www.icj-cij.org/docket/files/141/15616.pdf> paras 85–7 accessed 18 September 2013. The overall conclusion was that the declaration of independence was not in accordance with international law.

[79] Written Statement of Serbia (17 April 2009) <http://www.icj-cij.org/docket/files/141/15642.pdf> paras 499, 575, 577 accessed 18 September 2013.

[80] Written statements of the Kingdom of the Netherlands (17 April 2009) <http://www.icj-cij.org/docket/files/141/15652.pdf> para 3.8 accessed 18 September 2013 and 17 July 2009 <http://www.icj-cij.org/docket/files/141/15692.pdf> para 3.8: 'The proclamation of independence is linked to this territorial basis, follows existing international boundaries and former internal boundaries, and respects the principle of uti possidetis juris' accessed 18 September 2013.

[81] Written Statement of the Republic of Cyprus (3 April 2009) A.G. File No: 37/1969N.4/8 <http://www.icj-cij.org/docket/files/141/15609.pdf> paras 85–6, 118, 156 accessed 18 September 2013.

United States deemed *uti possidetis* not addressable to non-state actors.[82] The most substantive and best-reasoned statement has been made by Finland, which argued that applying *uti possidetis* 'would be to put the cart before the horse'. The state deemed *uti possidetis* not applicable in an 'abnormal case' in which the question of who possesses the territory and which boundary is valid is itself the controversy. Finland also forwarded the teleological argument that the rule's rationale could not be respected because there was no stability to protect.[83]

In conclusion, *uti possidetis* has been quite conspicuously marginalized in the Kosovo proceedings. The explanation for non-reliance on that principle (by the Court and by most states) might be the genuine legal belief that this principle has no role to play. It might, however, also be motivated by legal tactics. It is therefore difficult to extract the international community's *opinio juris* from these proceedings. Moreover, in most if not all of the governmental statements which do mention *uti possidetis*, the exact consequences of an application of *uti possidetis* to the Kosovo case remain unclear. Two issues deserve to be highlighted. First, *uti possidetis*, even if applicable, would not have prohibited Kosovo's declaration of its independence because it is agnostic regarding that question (see p. 115). Second, *uti possidetis* privileges not only the boundary of the former Socialist Republic of Serbia (which would amount to stating that the declaration of independence violated *that uti possidetis*), but in principle also other types of internal administrative boundaries, notably the provincial one (see pp. 119 ff.). *Uti possidetis* (if deemed applicable to Kosovo and to its provincial boundary) only came into play *once* Kosovo had declared its independence. The legal consequence is only that the provincial boundary had to be *provisionally* accepted as the new international boundary until and unless a different arrangement had been brought about by peaceful means, notably a territorial free and fair referendum. With this limited substantial scope, *uti possidetis* had indeed been respected.

3. The analogy between decolonization and secession

The following arguments, drawing on the analogy between decolonization and secession, can be made in support of the transfer of *uti possidetis* from

[82] See n 132. This resembles the reasoning which the Court later adopted, couching it in terms of territorial integrity, not in terms of *uti possidetis*.

[83] Written Statement of Finland (16 April 2009) Verbal Note/Embassy of Finland HM5013-31 <http://www.icj-cij.org/docket/files/141/15630.pdf> paras 5 and 9 accessed 18 September 2013. Para 9: 'The rationale invoked in these cases points to a distinction between normal situations and those of abnormality, or rupture, situations of revolution, war, alien subjugation or the absence of a meaningful prospect for a functioning internal self-determination regime. The First World War and the ensuing revolutions constituted such an "abnormality" in the Aaland Islands case, just like "colonialism" in the 1950s and 1960s, or the prolonged war in the territory of the former Yugoslavia in the 1990s. In such situations, to rely on the principle of "stability and finality of boundaries", for example, or *uti possidetis*, would be to put the cart before the horse: there is little or no stability of boundaries to be protected. Instead, the very question "who possesses" or "which boundary" has become part of the controversy and cannot therefore be used as a criterion for resolving it.'

decolonization to secession. First, both decolonization and secession have the same result, namely the attainment of independence. Both are cases of state succession. Second, in both contexts *uti possidetis* can deploy the same function, namely securing stability, all the while admitting that the stabilization of a territorial entity-in-the-making whose boundaries are not precisely recognized is somewhat difficult.[84] Third, the restrictive camp's observation that the two situations of attaining independence have a different legal basis is misconceived (see pp. 107 ff.). Fourth, the non-determination of the territorial basis of the new state would mean that important legal principles, such as prohibition of the use of force and territorial integrity,[85] could not be applied to it—which is an undesirable result.

In addition, some similarities between decolonization and the dissolution of the Soviet Union further support the extension of *uti possidetis* to the latter case. First of all, the Soviet Union has often been characterized as a modern quasi-colonial empire. In fact, Russia pursued a policy of hegemony and transfer of populations in order to secure Russian domination. Soviet rule, dominated by Russia, over non-Russian Republics was a mix of direct and indirect rule, of economic exploitation accompanied by a civilizing mission, and to that extent displayed the same characteristics as the classic colonial rule of European powers over overseas territories.[86] In that analysis, the boundaries of Soviet Republics were comparable in functional terms to the Latin American inner-Spanish boundaries, and the dissolution of the Soviet Union was a kind of decolonization, too. At least in part, the pending secession attempts are still a reaction to the Soviet *divide et impera* politics. If the breakup of the Soviet Union was in functional terms an instance of decolonization, and if the current unresolved issues can be seen as incomplete decolonization, then the application of colonial *uti possidetis* to the dismemberment of that empire is functionally adequate.

Next, we must remember that in the nineteenth century, no concept of decolonization existed. The colonies' declarations of independence were considered to be illegal secession from Spain. At that time, the proclamation of independent American states was potentially illegal, just as some if not all secessions are today. Independence was the result of internal conflicts between the political leaders of the dominated territories and the colonial powers; conflicts which might be considered as civil wars. '*Uti possidetis* is thus born for being applied to cases of secession', is the conclusion drawn by Marcelo Kohen.[87]

To sum up, while *uti possidetis* cannot simply be transferred from decolonization to secession, its applicability to that novel context is warranted by the case law, by state practice, and by doctrinal and policy considerations. Most importantly, applying *uti possidetis* to cases of secession in no way prohibits

[84] Corten (n 23) 433. [85] Kohen (n 5) 380.

[86] Some use the term 'internal colonialism' to qualify colonial-type relationships between the centre and the peripheries within one single state—cf. J Osterhammel, *Colonialism* (Markus Wiener Publishing 1997) 17.

[87] 'L'*uti possidetis* est ainsi né pour être appliqué à des cas de sécessions', Kohen (n 5) 376 (translation by the author).

or condones secessions. The principle is agnostic as to the question of *whether* there should be a new state with its own territory and new boundaries in the first place.[88] It 'only refers to a rule for the identification of boundaries following the proclamation of independence and is without prejudice to the existence of a right to proclaim independence', as the Netherlands put it in its written statement in the Kosovo proceedings.[89] *Uti possidetis* is, as Marcelo Kohen has pointed out, only the response of the law to a given reality, the existence of a state. It is no means of secession, no encouragement of secession, and no justification of secession.[90]

VII. The Purposes of *Uti Possidetis*

The overall underdetermined state of the law should encourage legal scholars to reflect about the reasonableness of applying *uti possidetis* to secession. Does *uti possidetis* give a satisfactory answer; does it offer a reasonable tool which is—in legal policy terms—superior to other potential mechanisms for resolving the specific boundary problem raised by secession?

From the perspective of normative individualism which underpins modern international law, the ultimate objective of drawing boundaries should always be human wellbeing and flourishing (as opposed to any *raison d'état*).[91] The generally acknowledged function of *uti possidetis* is to secure the stability and finality of borders. Concomitantly, *uti possidetis* has the latent function to reinforce the political entity called the state, whose constituent and definitional element is its territory, by assigning a clearly defined territory to it and by stabilizing its boundaries.[92]

Jörg Fisch has recently argued that reliance on the principle of *uti possidetis* in Latin America meant determining a boundary in a purely formal and hence 'neutral' fashion. The Spanish officials who defined colonial lines (without even really knowing the terrain) did not know that they thereby fixed future state boundaries and can therefore not be reproached for having been partial.[93] This analysis seems to allude to the existence of a kind of veil of ignorance (in a Rawlsian sense) which guarantees fairness. But is this adequate? I submit not, because the overall context was one of violence. The occupation and subordination of South America was

[88] Ratner (n 2) 601: 'Thus, *uti possidetis* is agnostic on whether or not secessions or breakups should occur and is not simply the legal embodiment of a policy condemning them'.

[89] Accordance with International Law of the Unilateral Declaration of Independence in Respect of Kosovo, Advisory Opinion Proceedings (Written Statement of the Kingdom of the Netherlands of 17 April 2009) <http://www.icj-cij.org/docket/files/141/15652.pdf> para 3.8 accessed 18 September 2013.

[90] Kohen (n 5) 400.

[91] Cf. A Margalit and J Raz, 'National Self-determination' (1990) 87 J Philosophy 439 *passim*.

[92] P Klein, 'Les glissements sémantiques et fonctionnels de l'uti possidetis' in O Corten et al. (eds), *Démembrements d'Etats et délimitations territoriales: L'uti possidetis en question(s)* (Bruylant 1999) 299, 316.

[93] Fisch (n 56) 92.

brought about by war, extermination policies, and forced labour. The exact lines may have been coincidental and owed to chance, but the entire enterprise was tainted by blood, as it was in Africa. The concept of a veil of ignorance presumes a non-violent decision-making procedure which is normally not given in the situation of territorial realignments. Ignorance of geography, of ethnic divisions, and of other features of the territories and its inhabitants cannot, in such a context, bring about fairness.

The stability of states and boundaries, and legal certainty with regard to these institutions, are not only secondary virtues. This holds true notwithstanding the fact that the application of *uti possidetis* means to legalize the *fait accompli*.[94] Indeed, the 'freeze' of territorial demarcations which are for the most part the result of violence and of historical coincidence may perpetuate the outcomes of past injustice. So does not the application of *uti possidetis* risk violating the principle of *ex iniuria jus non oritur* (no right should arise from unlawful situations)? This might indeed be the case. However, it is normally—in practical terms—impossible to return to a state of innocence in territorial matters. Any attempt to rectify historical territorial wrongs risks creating new injustices. It may be the most pragmatic course to renounce, in territorial matters, the application of distributive justice.[95]

Stability is a postulate of a different type of justice. It is one aspect of legal certainty, and forms part of the international rule of law. Stability and legal certainty are from that perspective legitimate ends in themselves. More importantly, the stability of boundaries and of states normally helps to safeguard peace. Especially with regard to territorial issues, stability tends to prevent war. This connection between territorial status quo and peace underpins the reasonable belief that international boundaries should be changed as little as possible.[96] The maintenance of the territorial status quo is desirable because all modifications carry the danger of interstate violence and of creating a domino effect. This runs counter to the objective of international law—the maintenance of international peace and security, which has as its ultimate goal human security. Against the background that the establishment of states has been the single most important historical achievement leading to a relative decrease of interpersonal violence and bloodshed,[97] it is justified to privilege the territorial status quo as a plausible contribution to secure human flourishing.

As an aside, it is worth recalling that, besides adjusting and changing boundary lines, other strategies have been tried throughout history to establish stable and peaceful political–territorial units. One tool was the forcible transfer of population, as occurred in the Greco–Turkish exchange of populations after the peace

[94] Cf. A Rivier, *Principes du Droit des Gens*, Vol. I (Alphonse Rouesseau 1896) 55 on *uti possidetis*: 'Le fait accompli . . . est générateur du droit.'

[95] Kohen (n 5) 400.

[96] MC Johanson, 'Kosovo: Boundaries and the Liberal Dilemma' (2004) 73 NJIL 535, 539.

[97] S Pinker, *The Better Angels of Our Nature: Why Violence Has Declined* (Viking 2011) 680: 'A state that uses a monopoly on force to protect its citizens from one another may be the most consistent violence-reducer. . .'.

treaty of Lausanne in 1923. Another tool was exchanges of territory, such as the exchange of Zanzibar against Helgoland between Germany and the United Kingdom in 1890. But these were possible only as colonial relics. Finally, numerous international peace and boundary treaties and domestic laws have granted populations affected by a boundary change the right to choose their nationality within a certain period (right of option).[98] Besides, individuals always have the right to emigrate (*jus emigrandi*) under customary international law as it stands. Neither of these strategies works well, and the forced transfer of populations is unlawful under contemporary law.

Uti possidetis furthermore intends to prevent boundary disputes arising from *outside* threats. During decolonization, the principle prevented other European powers, under the pretext of a lack of factual occupation of territory, from claiming these as *terra nullius*. The Swiss Federal Council in 1922 clearly explained this function: 'This general principle offered the advantage of positing as an absolute rule that there is not, in ancient Spanish America, any territory without master, although there existed numerous regions which had not been occupied by the Spanish and numerous unexplored regions... Finally, this principle precluded any attempt by the European colonizing States over territories which they could have tried to proclaim as *terra nullius*.[99] Along that line it has been observed that in Latin America, *uti possidetis* was a defensive principle very much inspired by considerations of self-preservation.[100] The ICJ highlighted this function of the principle in Spanish America in several decisions: 'Its purpose, at the time of the achievement of independence by the former Spanish colonies of America, was to scotch any designs which non-American colonizing powers might have on regions'.[101] '[C]ertainly a key aspect of the principle is the denial of the possibility of *terra nullius*.'[102]

[98] Y Ronen, 'Option of Nationality' in R Wolfrum (ed), *Max Planck Encyclopedia of Public International Law* (OUP online 2012). No right of option was granted in the Laws on Citizenship of Azerbaijan and Belarus. Some of the newly independent States provided for a right of option to acquire the citizenship of the State concerned (positive option), for example the Citizenship Law of Uzbekistan of 2 July 1992 (Art. 4(1)) and the Citizenship Law of Armenia of 6 Nov. 1995 (Art. 10 I(2)). Many CIS countries granted a negative right of option, ie a right to refuse the citizenship concerned. Examples are Turkmenistan (Art. 49(1) of the Citizenship Law of 30 Oct. 1992); Georgia (Art. 3a of the Citizenship Law of 25 March 1993); Russia (Law N 1948-I of 28 Nov. 1991 as amended by the Law N 5206-I of 17 June 1993); Ukraine (Art. 2(1) of the Law on Citizenship of 8 Oct. 1991); Kazakhstan (position 3 of the Resolution by the Parliament introducing the 1991 Citizenship Law). Art. 1(1) of the Kyrgyz Citizenship Law of 18 Dec. 1993 provided for a qualified negative option: refusal of Kyrgyz citizenship required a declaration about the possession of a foreign citizenship. In certain cases no genuine right of option was granted, but rather a right to privileged naturalization, for example by the Law on Citizenship of the Republic of Moldova of 5 June 1991 (Art. 2(4)), and by the Law on Citizenship of the Azerbaijan Republic of 30 Sept. 1998 (Art. 5(2)). I thank Tigran Beknazar for this information.

[99] 'Ce principe général offrait l'avantage de poser en règle absolu qu il n'y a pas, en droit, dans l' Ancienne Amérique espagnole, de territoire sans maîre; bien qu il n'existât de nombreuses régions qui n'avaient pas été occupées par les Espagnoles et de nombreuses régions inexplorées.... Enfin, ce principe excluait des tentatives d'Etats colonisateurs européens sur des territoires qu'ils auraient pu chercher à proclamer res nullius', *Swiss Federal Council (Bundesrat), Affaire des frontières Colombo-Vénézuéliennes* (n 14) 228 (translation by the author).

[100] Bernárdez (n 45) 437.

[101] *Frontier Dispute Case (Burkina Faso* v *Mali)* (n 9) para 23.

[102] *Frontier Dispute Case (El Salvador* v *Honduras, Nicaragua intervening)* (n 25) para 42.

Today, the application of *uti possidetis* (beyond Latin America) has the related external function of forestalling irredentism, ie claims of (neighbouring) states advocating the recovery of territories administered by another state on the grounds of common ethnicity or actual or alleged prior historical possession. In post-socialist Eastern Europe, this is an important policy issue. The reign of *uti possidetis* would, for example, give a clear signal against any attempt of recovery of parts of Romania by Hungary.

With regard to the subject matter of this chapter, a core question is whether *uti possidetis* has the additional function, besides protecting boundaries from threats from the *outside*, of protecting the boundaries from *internal threats* which stem from secessionist movements. The ICJ Chamber Judgment is ambiguous on this point: 'Its obvious purpose is to prevent the independence and *stability of new States* being endangered *by fratricidal struggles* provoked by the challenging of frontiers following the withdrawal of the administering power'.[103] The term 'fratricidal struggles' suggests, more than aggression from the outside, civil wars inside a given state. Parts of contemporary scholars affirm the inward-looking rationale of *uti possidetis*: it 'deters the local exploitation of weaknesses and disorders in newly created States, which are often vulnerable to secessionist actions', writes Giuseppe Nesi.[104]

Another functional advantage of *uti possidetis* is its clarity and unambiguity. All alternative rules for identifying the boundary of a secessionist entity are at worst not in conformity with international law; at best, each of them points to different boundary lines, and consequently to dispute over them. What would be the alternative criteria? Ethnicity of those groups settling in a given territory? Criteria such as language, culture, or religion will never result in congruent human communities and will therefore never result in an undisputedly 'proper' territory for such groups. What about geography, such as rivers and mountains? As early as 1882, Ernest Renan, in his famous lecture 'Quest-ce qu'une nation?',[105] showed the absurdity of relying on so-called 'natural boundaries', an idea which was fashionable in Europe at that time. He had the disputed territory of Alsace in mind. If the Rhine is considered as the natural boundary, then the Alsace must be French; if the Vosges are seen as the natural boundary, then the Alsace must be German.[106] That type of thinking had contributed to a series of wars over that territory. No substantive criterion for drawing a boundary is unquestionably decisive and legitimate.

Finally, *uti possidetis* is in line with the fundamental achievement of modern international law no longer being 'constitution-blind'. Minority protection, human rights protection, and even democracy are international legal prescriptions which governments are obliged to respect when organizing and running their states. If a state is organized in conformity with these international precepts, then it

[103] *Frontier Dispute Case (Burkina Faso* v *Mali)* (n 9) para 20 (emphasis added).

[104] Nesi (2013) (n 50) para 8.

[105] E Renan, 'Qu'est-ce qu'une nation?' (Lecture at the Sorbonne of 1 March 1882) in *Ernest Renan, Oeuvres Complètes*, Vol. 1 (Calman-Lévy 1947) 887, 902.

[106] See on the German–French boundary in the Alsace area and on the idea of 'natural boundaries' D-E Khan, *Die deutschen Staatsgrenzen* (Mohr Siebeck 2004) 524–68.

can—in theory—function within whatever boundaries. This would mean that *uti possidetis* can and should be applied, because the exact lines of the boundary do not matter anyway. It does not matter whether a boundary 'makes sense' or not, because the well-functioning state does not need a specific ethnic composition or a specific territory.

The objection against this line of argument is that it is utopian. A boundary based on *uti possidetis* will often lead to states which harbour ethnic minorities. As just said, modern international law obliges states to respect minority rights and to guarantee equal political participation to all (ethnic) groups, but to place all bets on minority protection and democracy as a guarantee of stable states means to stretch the power of international law, maybe to overstretch it. If the normative requirements are too strict, international law (as any law) will defeat itself. In order to avoid utopianism, a contextualized drawing of boundaries has been suggested. The delineations should not be orientated to an illusionary ideal of a liberal state, but should take into account the real problems on the ground.[107] Contextualized boundary-drawing would have to deviate from *uti possidetis*, because *uti possidetis* is not exactly contextualized, but artificial, abstract, and coincidental.

However, this suggestion seems both backwards-looking and unfeasible. A legal principle of 'contextualized' boundaries, which notably takes into account ethnicity, culture, and language, seems problematic exactly because it draws on factors which are suspect under international law and are in potential conflict with the international legal prohibitions on discrimination.

To conclude, besides being based on the case law (see p. 110), the crucial argument in favour of applying *uti possidetis* to secessions is that this is most in conformity with the ensemble of the international legal system. According to Ian Brownlie, the general principle '... is in accordance with good policy'.[108]

VIII. The Scope of *Uti Possidetis*

1. Applicability *ratione materiae*: which frontiers?

A salient question in the context of secession is which type of boundary is privileged by *uti possidetis* so that it may (or must) be upgraded to an international boundary. One question is whether the internal constitutional status of the boundary and its intangibility (or flexibility) under domestic constitutional law matters. This question was particularly relevant for the Soviet Union and Yugoslavia. The Soviet Union was a five-level state consisting of the entire state, the Union Republics (such as Georgia),[109] the Autonomous Soviet Socialist Republics (ASSR, such as

[107] Johanson (n 96).

[108] J Crawford, *Brownlie's Principles of Public International Law* (8th edn, OUP 2012) 239.

[109] The Union Republics were enumerated in Art. 71 of the Constitution of the Soviet Union of 7 October 1977. Art. 72 awarded them a right to secede from the Soviet Union.

Abkhazia),[110] the Autonomous Provinces (*Oblasts,* such as South Ossetia),[111] and the Autonomous Areas (*Okrug*).[112] Yugoslavia was a three-level state composed of the Federal State, Socialist Republics, and Autonomous or non-Autonomous Provinces (such as Kosovo).

With regard to Yugoslavia, Badinter Opinion No. 3 stated: 'The principle [of *uti possidetis*] applies all the more readily to the Republics since the second and fourth paragraphs of Article 5 of the Constitution of the SFRY stipulated that the Republics' territories and boundaries could not be altered without their consent'. In a similar fashion, with regard to the CIS, importance has sometimes been ascribed to the fact that (only) the first-level entities, the former Soviet Republics (Art. 71), had a constitutional right to secede under Art. 72 of the 1977 Constitution. This right arguably implied a somewhat different constitutional status to their boundaries (as opposed to the boundaries of lower-level federal entities). The Tagliavini Report of 2009 on the Georgian–Russian conflict of 2008 applied *uti possidetis* only to the internal frontiers between Union Republics, but not to boundaries between Union Republics and Autonomous Republics, and not between Union Republics and Autonomous Regions.[113] Along that line, Malcolm Shaw has argued that the presumption of *uti possidetis* is weaker the more unitary the state is. The presumption is stronger the more entrenched the administrative lines are. He goes on to claim that if secession is proclaimed constitutionally, then the presumption is at its least assailable.[114] This would mean that the former Soviet Union Republics' boundaries could 'unassailably' benefit from *uti possidetis*, while territories within the successor states of the Soviet Union cannot (or can only to a lesser extent).

To flesh out the debate on the significance of domestic law for the application of *uti possidetis,* we might cite the case of South Ossetia (ch. 9 in this volume). In the Soviet Union South Ossetia was, within the Georgian Soviet Socialist Republic (SSR), only an Autonomous Region (*Oblast*)[115]—a fourth-level entity within the Soviet Union. It was one more step farther removed from Union Republic status than Abkhazia, which was for the most of the Soviet period an Autonomous Republic (Art. 85(3)). Domestic law, both in the Soviet era and after the dissolution of the Soviet Union, quite clearly prohibited and continues to prohibit South Ossetia's secession from Georgia. *Oblasts* did not enjoy a right to secede under

[110] Arts 82–5 of the Soviet Constitution of 7 Oct. 1977 defined the status of 'Autonomous Soviet Socialist Republics'. Under Art. 85(3) '[t]he Georgian Soviet Socialist Republic includes the Abkhazian and Adzhar Autonomous Soviet Socialist Republics'. In 1989, the Soviet Union had 20 ASSR, 16 of which were in the Russian SFSR.

[111] Arts 86–7 dealt with 'Autonomous Provinces' (*Oblasts,'* sometimes translated as 'regions'). In 1989, the SU had eight autonomous provinces, five of which were in the Russian SFSR.

[112] Art. 88 dealt with 'Autonomous Areas' (*Okrug*). In 1989, the Soviet Union had ten Autonomous Areas, all of which were in the Russian SFSR.

[113] Independent International Fact-Finding Mission on the Conflict in Georgia (Report of September 2009) <http://www.ceiig.ch/Report.html> ch 3, 143, accessed 18 September 2013.

[114] Shaw (n 65) 504.

[115] See Art. 87(2) of the Soviet Union Constitution (7 October 1977): 'The Georgian Soviet Socialist Republic includes the South Ossetian Autonomous Region'. Art 86: 'An Autonomous Region is part of a Union Republic or a Territory'.

the Soviet Constitution. Additionally, within the Soviet Union still, the 1978 Constitution of the Socialist Soviet Republic of Georgia (as other Union Republics) denied the right to secede to any of its sub-entities.[116] Article 1 of the post-Soviet Georgian Constitution of 24 August 1995 states: 'Georgia shall be an independent, unified and indivisible state, as confirmed by the Referendum of 31 March 1991, held throughout the territory of the country, including the Autonomous Soviet Socialist Republic of Abkhazia and the Former Autonomous Region of South Ossetia and by the Act of Restoration of the State Independence of Georgia of 9 April 1991'. Additionally, Art. 26(3) of that post-Soviet Georgian Constitution states that '[t]he formation and activity of such public and political associations aiming at overthrowing or forcibly changing the constitutional structure of Georgia, infringing upon the independence and territorial integrity of the country or propagandising war or violence, provoking national, local, religious or social animosity, shall be impermissible'. Nevertheless, South Ossetia declared its 'sovereignty' on 20 September 1990, before the dissolution of the Soviet Union, and before Georgia's Declaration of Independence. The territory then declared its independence on 21 December 1991 (the date of the dissolution of the Soviet Union). Also, it held referendums on independence in 1991 and in 2006.

To sum up the historical practice, *uti possidetis* in the Soviet Union and in Yugoslavia has only been applied to the boundaries of first-order sub-units (in the Soviet Union to the Union Republics). In practice, no 'new' *uti possidetis* has emerged so far which would protect second- or third-level entities within the Soviet Union, ranging from Abkhazia to Chechnya. So the fiction was upheld that below that level, no ethnic or social differences exist which would demand the further fragmentation of territories. This fiction was and is empirically false, but, according to Jörg Fisch, is useful in order to avoid endless fragmentation.[117]

But should it—in terms of legal doctrine and stringency—matter which boundary is affected? In particular, should *uti possidetis* from the outset be inapplicable to boundaries belonging to former entities below the former Soviet Union Republic status (such as South Ossetia and Abkhazia in Georgia, and other breakaway territories of CIS members)? The discussion should start from the insight that normally, domestic law (or colonial law) is considered simply as a *fact* under international law. The whole idea of *uti possidetis* is in itself an exception to that principle, because it attaches international legal consequences to delineation acts under domestic (or colonial) law.[118] But the ordinary agnosticism of international

[116] Art. 70 of the Georgian SSR Constitution of 15 April 1978 stipulated: 'The territory of Georgia shall not be altered without its consent'. See extracts of the constitutional text in English at <http://www.rrc.ge/law/Gkon_1978_04_15_e.htm> accessed 18 September 2013. Identical provisions were contained in all other Soviet Union Republics' constitutions.

[117] Fisch (n 56) 264–5.

[118] It does not seem convincing to depict *uti possidetis* as some kind of 'factual element', as the ICJ had: 'The principle of *uti possidetis* freezes the territorial title; it stops the clock, but does not put back the hands. Hence, international law does not effectuate any *renvoi* to the law established by the colonizing State, nor indeed to any legal rule unilaterally established by any State whatever; French law—especially legislation enacted by France for its colonies and *territoires d'outre-mer*—may *play a role not in itself* (as if there were a sort of continuum juris, a legal relay between such law and

law concerning domestic law arrangements (as long as they respect international law) would normally suggest that, in principle, *any internal boundary* might benefit from *uti possidetis.*

This is all the more compelling as the internal status of administrative boundaries often changed over time, both within the Soviet Union and within Socialist Yugoslavia. The most conscious examples are of course the up- and downgrading of Abkhazia (short-lived as a Socialist Soviet Republic from 1921 to 1931, thereafter downgraded to an Autonomous Republic within the Soviet Union Republic of Georgia) and Kosovo (upgraded 1974, downgraded 1989), and the concomitant change of the status of those territories' boundaries.

Historically, in Latin America, quite diverse types of territorial entities existed: provinces, *vice-royautés, alcaldìas mayores, corregimientos, intenencias*, and the jurisdictions of a higher court (*audiencias*).[119] Importantly for this chapter, in Latin America *uti possidetis juris* was not only applied to the boundaries between *vice-royautés* (vice-kingdoms), but was likewise applied to administrative subdivisions (called *audiencia* or *intendencia*) within a single vice-kingdom. It was also applied to subordinate entities of different types within one Captaincy-General. For example, until 1803 the Captaincy-General of Guatemala encompassed the Government of Honduras and the General Command of Nicaragua, which later became sovereign states.[120] *Uti possidetis* was applied to the different types of boundaries without regard for the differences in status.

Most importantly, the *constitutional guarantees of secession* to Union Republics or Socialist Republics in the Soviet and Yugoslav constitutions should be irrelevant for the application of *uti possidetis*. First, it is unpersuasive to ascribe any importance to a constitutional guarantee when its effect only becomes relevant after a breakdown of the constitutional order.[121] Second, it is not in line with the historical practice of colonial *uti possidetis* to limit the application of the principle to entities with a right (in domestic law) to secede, because of course the former overseas colonies had *no* right to secede under the domestic constitutional law of their time, and still their frontiers were upgraded by *uti possidetis*.

A different argument has been made by Marcelo Kohen, who asserts that the internal boundaries must have been lawfully established according to the domestic law of the state in order to be eligible to be upgraded to international boundaries.[122]

international law), *but only as one factual element among others,* or as evidence indicative of what has been called the "colonial heritage", ie, the "photograph of the territory" at the critical date'—*Frontier Dispute case (Burkina Faso* v *Mali)* (n 9) para 30, emphasis modified. Rather, one might say that reliance on *uti possidetis* does not mean to apply the law of the predecessor state but to use it as a proof of the territorial title of the new state.

[119] Cf. *Frontier Dispute Case (El Salvador* v *Honduras, Nicaragua intervening)* (n 25) para 43.

[120] *Territorial and Maritime Dispute between Nicaragua and Honduras in the Caribbean Sea* (n 21) para 161. To give another example: The new states of Paraguay and Bolivia within their international boundaries emerged from the province of Paraguay on the one hand and on the other hand from the *audiencia* of Charcas. Both had been part of the vice-kingdom of Rio de la Plata, but were not assigned to the 'United Provinces of Rio de la Plata' (which later became Argentina). Kohen (1999) (n 5) 372 n 14.

[121] Lalonde (n 9) 235. [122] Kohen (n 5) 394.

Along this line, South Ossetians sometimes rely on the 'illegality' of South Ossetia's inclusion in Georgia following the breakup of the Russian Empire after the 1917 revolutions to avoid the application of the *uti possidetis* principle. Their argument is that *uti possidetis* (in favour of Georgia) cannot override a prior illegality. Christopher Waters, in chapter 9, finds this claim weak.[123] Indeed, it is difficult to find support (in practice or as a matter of legal reasoning) for the claim that prior 'illegality' precludes *uti possidetis*. It is exactly the function of *uti possidetis* to terminate arguments about prior territorial illegality.

The general scope of the principle (independent of the precise internal status and meaning of the boundary) is covered by case law. The Swiss Federal Council mentioned 'anciennes ordonnances royales de la mère patrie espagnole'.[124] Badinter Opinion No. 2 spoke of 'existing frontiers at the time of independence'. Badinter Opinion No. 3 spoke of 'the former boundaries', while the opinion's context (the question asked) shows that this referred to boundaries between Croatia and Serbia and between Bosnia-Herzegovina and Serbia.

Finally, several states commented in their written statements in the *Kosovo* Advisory Opinion proceedings on the type of boundaries suitable for upgrading through *uti possidetis*. The Netherlands named all 'former internal boundaries'.[125] Slovenia[126] seemed to insinuate that all kinds of 'administrative boundaries' could be taken into account, including the borders of 'municipalities'. But the Slovenian statement did not clearly say whether *uti possidetis* was then applicable against or in favour of Kosovo's claim.

A related salient question is whether a new international boundary could be based on *uti possidetis* pointing to informal displays of territorial jurisdiction (as opposed to internal colonial or administrative boundaries). If that were true, then a territory such as Abkhazia, which is under the rather firm control of a separatist Abkhaz leadership and hardly controlled by Georgia, could rely on *uti possidetis*. State practice does not support such an extended version of *uti possidetis*. Although in some instances 'not only were formal data considered, but also conduct from which the existence of territorial divisions at the critical date could be inferred',[127] these were never displays of territorial control after a secession of a territory within a metropolitan state.

To sum up, *uti possidetis* is applicable (if its preconditions are met) to all kinds of internal boundary lines, independent of the precise domestic law status and meaning of the boundary. *Uti possidetis*, 'in and of itself, does not identify which administrative divisions and lines are to be preserved' and which are not.[128] *Uti possidetis* is, in particular, not restricted to upgrading lines which delineate entities with a right to secession based on domestic law. Still, it remains a challenge to

[123] Waters, ch 9 (in this volume) 182. [124] *Swiss Federal Council Award 1922* (n 14) 228.

[125] Written Statement of 17 July 2009 <http://www.icj-cij.org/docket/files/141/15692.pdf> para 3.8 accessed 18 September 2013.

[126] Written Comment of 17 July 2009 http://www.icj-cij.org/docket/files/141/15696.pdf, 4, accessed 18 September 2013.

[127] Nesi (2013) (n 50) para 10. [128] Lalonde (n 9) 237.

consistently apply the principle to multilevel political entities which possess numerous layers of different types of boundaries—although as we have seen, starting in nineteenth-century America, this has always been done.

The conclusion for the breakaway territories in states that were former Soviet Union Republics is that it is neither consistent as a matter of doctrine and logic nor in line with the broad statements in the case law to limit the application of *uti possidetis* to first-level boundaries (boundaries of former Union Republics) and to deny the application of the principle to former second-level boundaries. If *uti possidetis* is applicable in Eastern and Central Europe at all, then it can also play a role (if the conditions are met) for former administrative boundaries between former Soviet *Oblasts*, or between former Yugoslav provinces.[129]

2. Applicability *ratione personae*

With regard to the pending territorial issues in the CIS, there arises the question of who is bound to respect the principle of *uti possidetis* and who can lawfully rely on it. The question is, in other words, the principle's scope *ratione personae*. If breakaway territories were the beneficiaries of *uti possidetis*, then the obligees or addressees would be the metropolitan states or previous mother states.

The colonial *uti possidetis* benefited non-self-governing territories (colonies) in the moment of proclaiming their independence as states. The principle here had different addressees. The principle was first of all operative in the new states' (former colonies') relationships among each other.[130] Second, it was addressed against competing dominant states (other colonial powers), notably in situations in which the new states' effective governmental control was rather weak, in order to forestall those competitors' assertions that there existed *terra nullius* susceptible to occupation.[131] The (previous) colonial powers were not, in practical terms, the most important addressees of that norm, although these states were bound by the principle, too.

It has been argued, for example by the United States in the Kosovo Advisory Proceedings, that non-state actors (eg independence movements) can never benefit from *uti possidetis*, because these entities are outside the personal scope of the principle.[132] However, colonial *uti possidetis* in its classical form did at least indirectly benefit independence movements and similar types of non-state actors. To assert that non-state actors not relying on colonial self-determination are not within the scope of the principle raises the question of whether *uti possidetis* is applicable outside the colonial context or not. Moreover, much hinges on the relevant point in time (see p. 125). It is generally assumed that the critical date for applying *uti possidetis* is the moment of declaring independence. At that point

[129] Luchterhandt (n 5) 59. [130] Cf. *Frontier Dispute case (Burkina Faso* v *Mali)* (n 9) para 20.

[131] *Swiss Federal Council Award* 1922 (n 14) 228. See also p. 117.

[132] United States of America, Written Comment (17 July 2009) 20 n 60: 'Arguments about the principles of stability of boundaries and *uti possidetis*... also are unavailing, as those principles do not operate on non-state actors', only against states. http://www.icj-cij.org/docket/files/141/15704.pdf, 9, accessed 18 September 2013.

in time, the beneficiaries already purport to be a state. It seems reasonable not to exclude them in a purely definitional fashion from the principle's scope.

3. Applicability *ratione temporis*

It is usually said that *uti possidetis* is not applicable during the process of acquiring independence, but only afterwards.[133] For example, the Badinter Commission stated that '*once* the process in the SFRY *leads to the creation* of one or more independent states' the principle of *uti possidetis* would apply.[134] '*Uti possidetis*, as a customary rule providing for the respect of territorial limits as they exist at the moment of independence, does not come into issue during the process of secession.'[135] But these and similar statements do not provide clear guidance, because the actual moment at which independent statehood is acquired is typically controversial, and a central international institution to authoritatively determine the completion of the state-forming process does not exist. For example, the breakaway territories in the CIS have for the most part proclaimed their independence several times already, but to date are generally not recognized as independent states. Even when independence is acknowledged by an agreement or a unilateral declaration by other involved political actors, formal recognition of statehood has only declarative value. What matters for statehood is a certain measure of effectiveness acquired by the territorial–political entity. Because 'effectiveness' is a matter of degree and not an all-or-nothing concept, it cannot be pinpointed easily. This also means that the moment from which *uti possidetis* will apply might often be quite unclear.

IX. *Uti Possidetis* within the International Legal Order

The question of whether *uti possidetis* is generally applicable also to secessions must take into account the overall legal context. Would application of *uti possidetis* to secessions be in harmony with the overall system of international law? It has been claimed that 'application of *uti possidetis* to the breakup of states today... is profoundly at odds with current trends in international law and politics'.[136] This section examines the international legal principles which usually come into play in the context of secession,[137] in order to identify a substantive scope which is in conformity with both the principle's purposes (see section VII) and its overall legal context. A contextualized interpretation of *uti possidetis* can help answer the question of its general applicability.

[133] See Kohen (1999) (n 5) 375.
[134] Conference on Yugoslavia Arbitration Commission, Opinion 3, para 2 (1992) 3 EJIL 184, 195.
[135] M Kohen, 'Introduction' in M Kohen (ed), *Secession: International Law Perspectives* (CUP 2006) 1, 14–15.
[136] Ratner (n 2) 591.
[137] On the relationship between *uti possidetis* and effectiveness, see n 52.

1. *Uti possidetis* and self-determination

Roughly speaking, *uti possidetis* normally stands in an antagonistic relationship to the principle of self-determination. In the *Frontier Dispute Case* of *Burkina Faso* v *Mali*, the ICJ Chamber stated: 'At first sight this principle conflicts outright with another one, the right of peoples to self-determination'.[138] Badinter Opinion No. 2 depicted *uti possidetis* as trumping or at least limiting the possible consequences of the exercise of a right to self-determination: 'whatever the circumstances, the right to self-determination must not involve changes to existing frontiers at the time of independence (*uti possidetis* juris)'.[139] Along this line, several authors in this volume consider *uti possidetis* and self-determination to be in opposition to each other. From that perspective, any South Ossetian claim to secession would have to, according to Christopher Waters (ch. 9), be based on Soviet law, on Georgian law or on a separate international legal principle 'capable of overcoming the application of the *uti possidetis* principle'.[140] The same view is espoused by Farhad Mirzayev with regard to Abkhazia (ch. 10). According to him, *uti possidetis* trumps the right to self-determination, 'meaning the principle was a prevailing force over the right of such newly independent states to external self-determination'.[141] '[I]n the conflict between the right to self-determination and the principle of territorial integrity and *uti possidetis*, the former is *limited* in favour of the latter. External self-determination in the form of secession is not recognized in international law and *primacy* has been given to the principle of territorial integrity.[142]

It must however be noted that there is no inevitable or irreconcilable conflict between the two principles; *uti possidetis* is not a simple counter-principle to self-determination. The two norms have different functions and goals, different beneficiaries; they cover different subject matters, and have a different temporal scope.[143] Self-determination means a people's right to choose its political, economic, and social status (not inevitably linked to domination over territory). *Uti possidetis* refers to territorial boundaries of states. Self-determination applies before independence, and *uti possidetis* only after.

Still, there normally is a tension because the group claiming self-determination typically has some territorial basis (the people live somewhere), and even internal self-determination usually includes some territorial aspect. Moreover, colonial self-determination in particular had a very strong territorial component, and its prime content was to award a territory to a group of persons.[144] Article 73 UN Charter mentions 'Non self-governing *territories*'. The provision also mentions 'self-government' of 'peoples', not self-determination, but in substance concerned decolonization—which has (partly in hindsight) been conceptualized as an exercise of the colonial peoples' right to self-determination.

[138] *Frontier Dispute case (Burkina Faso* v *Mali)* (n 9) para 25.
[139] Badinter Commission, Opinion No. 2 (11 January 1992) para 1.
[140] Waters (n 123) 182. [141] Mirzayev (n 6) 203.
[142] Mirzayev (n 6) 212, emphases added.
[143] Kohen (1999) (n 5) 375 and 380; Nesi (n 50) para 20.
[144] Cf. Corten (n 23) 417 and 419.

On the other hand, *uti possidetis* can—depending on the concrete case—also point in the same direction as the principle of self-determination for a particular group, and then both principles are mutually supportive.[145] Along that line, self-determination has even been considered as one legal component of *uti possidetis*: '*Uti possidetis juris*, as it stands at the present, is based on two ideas: self-determination and the non-interference....'.[146] As the ICJ Chamber argued in the *Frontier Dispute Case, uti possidetis* brings about the territorial stability which the different African peoples need in order to develop. If they waste energy with fighting over boundaries, they cannot develop, and this in turn endangers their independence.[147] From that perspective, *uti possidetis* can at times serve self-determination.

2. *Uti possidetis*, non-intervention, territorial integrity, and the intangibility of frontiers

Historically, the principle of *uti possidetis* is older than the prohibition of intervention. The latter was indeed shaped not least on the basis of *uti possidetis* in Latin America. In contemporary international law, a state's territory, as demarcated by the state's boundaries, is first protected by the international legal principle of non-intervention. Second, it is protected by the principle of territorial integrity: 'Once the new state is established, the principle of *uti possidetis* will give way to the principle of territorial integrity, which provides for the protection of the new state so created'.[148] Third, *uti possidetis* points in the same direction as the principles of inviolability or intangibility of frontiers as enshrined, for example, in Article III of the Helsinki Final Act of 1 August 1975.[149] In the Kosovo Advisory Proceedings, Romania qualified *uti possidetis* as a 'counterpart' to the principle of inviolability.[150] The ICJ described the functional relation as follows: 'the Chamber cannot disregard the principle of *uti possidetis juris*, the application of which gives rise to this respect for intangibility of frontiers'.[151]

[145] Cf. Mirzayev (n 6) 212.

[146] E Hasani, 'Uti Possidetis Iuris: From Rome to Kosovo' (2003) 27 FLFWA 285, 286.

[147] 'In fact, however, the maintenance of the territorial status quo in Africa is often seen as the wisest course, to preserve what has been achieved by peoples who have struggled for their independence, and to avoid a disruption which would deprive the continent of the gains achieved by much sacrifice. The essential requirement of stability in order to survive, to develop and gradually to consolidate their independence in all fields, has induced African States judiciously to consent to the respecting of colonial frontiers, and to take account of it in the interpretation of the principle of self-determination of peoples.' (*Frontier Dispute case (Burkina Faso* v *Mali)* (n 9) para 25).

[148] Shaw (n 65) 495.

[149] Helsinki Final Act 1975: III. Inviolability of frontiers. 'The participating States regard as inviolable all one another's frontiers as well as the frontiers of all States in Europe and therefore they will refrain now and in the future from assaulting these frontiers. Accordingly, they will also refrain from any demand for, or act of, seizure and usurpation of part or all of the territory of any participating State.'

[150] Written Statement of Romania (14 April 2009) <http://www.icj-cij.org/docket/files/141/15616.pdf> para 87 accessed 18 September 2013.

[151] *Frontier Dispute case (Burkina Faso* v *Mali)* (n 9) para 20.

The documents relating to the dissolution of the Soviet Union do not explicitly endorse *uti possidetis*, but rather the intangibility of borders and territorial integrity. First is the *Agreement Establishing the Commonwealth of Independent States of Minsk* of 8 December 1991, concluded between the three states of Belarus, the Russian Soviet Federative Socialist Republic (RSFSR), and the Ukraine. In its preamble, the three states 'declare that the Union of Soviet Socialist Republics as a subject of international law and a geopolitical reality is ceasing its existence'. In Art. 5, the High Contracting Parties 'acknowledge and respect each other's territorial integrity and inviolability of existing borders within the Commonwealth'.[152] Second is the *Declaration of Alma Ata* of 21 December 1991, proclaimed by 11 former Republics of the Soviet Union, 'recognizing and respecting each other's territorial integrity and the inviolability of existing borders'.[153] Third, Art. 3 of the *Charter of the Commonwealth of Independent States* (CIS) of 22 June 1993 enshrined the principle of the 'inviolability of frontiers'.[154] Finally, in the *Declaration on Observance of the Sovereignty, Territorial Integrity and Immunity of Borders of the States-Members of the Commonwealth of Independent States* of 15 April 1994, the 'Heads of states-participants of the Commonwealth of Independent States... *confirming territorial integrity, inviolability of borders of each other, refusal of illegal territorial acquisitions and of any actions directed on the partition of another's territory*... 1. Provide accomplishment in the relations of principles of the sovereignty, territorial integrity and *inviolability of frontiers*. 2. Confirm that, building the relations as friendly, the *states will abstain from* military, political, economic or any other uniform of pressure, including blockade, and also *supports and uses of separatism against territorial integrity* and immunity, and also political independence any of the states-members of Commonwealth'.[155]

Given the functional similarity between the principles, the explicit mention of territorial integrity and inviolability of frontiers in the documents relating to the dissolution of the Soviet Union has been interpreted by many as amounting to an indirect endorsement of *uti possidetis* with regard to the boundaries of the Soviet Republics.[156] However, there are no logical links between those principles which would warrant such inference. It is true that once *uti possidetis* has been applied, one consequence is the intangibility of the boundary. While *uti possidetis* refers to the creation of boundaries, intangibility/inviolability refers to their preservation.[157] Also, the principle of territorial integrity can only be applied once we know where the boundaries lie. In that sense, application of the principles of territorial integrity, intangibility, and non-intervention necessarily comes *after uti possidetis* (in a temporal sense); however, their application is not conditioned upon

[152] Agreement Establishing the Commonwealth of Independent States of Minsk (8 December 1991), reproduced in (1992) 31 ILM 143.

[153] Alma Ata Declaration, Preamble (21 December 1991) 2nd para, reproduced in ILM 31 (1992) 148.

[154] (1995) 34 ILM 1282, 1283.

[155] <http://cis-legislation.com/document.fwx?rgn=3921> accessed 18 September 2013; English translation provided on Russian website, emphases added.

[156] For example by Mirzayev (n 6), ch 10 in this volume.

[157] Corten (n 23) 432.

having used *uti possidetis*. Their application presupposes the prior determination of a boundary, but this can take place through various principles or procedures; either *uti possidetis* or, for example, a territorial referendum. Therefore, just endorsing the inviolability of boundaries in international legal texts does not in itself manifest the legal opinion that these borders must be defined on the basis of *uti possidetis*; intangibility is no veiled substitute for *uti possidetis*.

X. *Uti Possidetis* as a Provisional Starting Point in Secession Processes

Uti possidetis is dispositive in three different senses. First, it does not belong to the small body of *jus cogens*. Second, states can agree from the outset not to apply *uti possidetis* to a given situation, but may draw a boundary line based on different considerations.[158] Third, a boundary first drawn on the basis of *uti possidetis* can still be *changed later by mutual consent* among the parties concerned.[159] That third aspect is probably the most important one in practice.

1. Deviations from the principle and concomitant revision of a boundary

The dispositive quality of *uti possidetis*, taken together with its normal temporal scope (application in the moment of establishing a state), leads to the qualification of *uti possidetis* as a fallback rule or as a 'presumption'.[160] The fallback rule means that *uti possidetis* is applied only *unless* and only *until* a different boundary line is established peacefully. Put differently, the normative quality of customary *uti possidetis* as a fallback rule means that a 'contracting-out'[161] is required in order to lawfully deviate from it.

On a timeline, *uti possidetis* is a starting point. It will govern the boundary only *as long as* no agreement on the boundary (or/and on the application of a different principle to define it) is reached. It is a 'transitional mechanism' only,[162] a 'valuable point of departure' [163] for future territorial negotiations—but no more. Giuseppe Nesi well explains this function through time: '*Uti possidetis* is a norm operating particularly in the first phase of the relationships established between

[158] 'It must be emphasized that the principle is by no means mandatory and the states concerned are free to adopt other principles as the basis of settlement'—Brownlie (n 108) 130. It is 'nullement un principe absolu'—Corten (n 23) 416.

[159] Romania, Written statement, Kosovo Advisory Opinion Proceedings, para 87: 'this principle does not entail that the frontiers are immutable, but that they can only be changed by agreement between or among the parties concerned and without the use of force.' See in scholarship Nesi (n 50) paras 7, 12, 17, 18.

[160] Shaw (n 65) 492 and 504. Cf. Ratner (n 2) 590: 'states emerging from decolonisation shall *presumptively* inherit the colonial administrative borders' (emphasis added).

[161] Cf. for this term Bernárdez (n 45) 421 (who also considers contracting-in possible).

[162] Shaw (n 65) 495. See also Ratner (n 2) 617–18; Saxer (n 40) 774.

[163] Lalonde (n 9) 235.

newly independent States.... [W]ith the passage of time *uti possidetis* as a norm autonomously defining the territory of newly independent States is "overridden" (rectius "specified") by the delimitations set by these very States. In this context, *uti possidetis* tends to act as a norm that "retires" ....'[164] This provisional function of the principle is actually in line with the Roman origins of the principle.[165]

Although *uti possidetis* may thus turn out to be applied merely provisionally, it is not superfluous. Using *uti possidetis* (only) as a rebuttable presumption corresponds to the overall objective of international law, which is to achieve (territorial and legal) stability, but not rigidity. Some options for adaptations must be left open. Then the dual follow-up question is which *substantive* considerations play a role for the 'rebuttal' (maybe better conceptualized as a departure from the fall-back rule), and in which *procedures* this might happen. 'Departure' here means both the decision not (or no longer) to use the rule of *uti possidetis* (ie to discard or to deviate from it in the concrete case) and—at the same time—the revision of the boundary line that was provisionally assumed to be at the place of the former administrative line.

2. Material and procedural factors for deviating from *uti possidetis*

In this section, I examine material considerations that justify a deviation from the starting point of *uti possidetis*. Which considerations, through which procedures, can lead to a revision of the line provisionally drawn on the basis of *uti possidetis*? The guiding concern must be the wellbeing of human beings affected by drawing a boundary. That concern is reflected in international law through the principles of international human rights, international standards of minority protection, and the principle of self-determination of peoples. In this context, 'people' would appear to be the sum of those affected by drawing a boundary line. The follow-up question is into which procedures the observation of these substantive principles translates, as I will discuss (see also pp. 133 ff.).

Besides the mentioned international legal principles, which further factors might be taken into account? One factor might be the age of a boundary. The older it is, the higher the probability that humans have adjusted to it. Another factor might be the viability of the state resulting from a particular delimination. For example, the separatist region of South Ossetia in Georgia seems hardly viable, as opposed to the region of Abkhazia which can thrive on tourism and agriculture. But the criterion of 'viability' which was used during the times of the League of Nations to group the mandates into three categories was (or was perceived as) a pretext to delay independence and decolonization. Since World War II, the idea of viability has been thoroughly discredited—but maybe we now pay the price for ignoring it.

In which procedures should boundary lines provisionally or presumptively established on the basis of *uti possidetis* be revised? One option would be a

[164] Nesi (n 50) para 18. [165] See pp. 97–98.

determination by the Security Council. Such a determination would seem to fall within the Council's general mandate (cf. Art. 24 UN Charter) because the determination of a boundary is a means to maintain international peace and security. The problem with such a procedure is that it has the taste of a dictate of the Great Powers, which is charged with negative historical connotations. Another option would be arbitral proceedings. History offers numerous examples, such as the Arbitral Awards of the Swiss Federal Council of 1922 or of the Badinter Commission of 1991–92, which have already been mentioned. Arguably, the procedures applied should not contradict the substantive principles of human rights, minority protection, and self-determination mentioned above, and this means that any procedure that does not at least seek to accommodate the opinions of affected populations is not admissible as a matter of international law as it stands.

3. Deviations based on interstate consent

It is generally accepted that a boundary line that deviates from the starting point provided by *uti possidetis* can only be adopted upon an *agreement*, but not unilaterally. As the Badinter Commission put it: 'it is well established that, whatever the circumstances, the right to self-determination must not involve changes to existing frontiers at the time of independence (*uti possidetis juris*) *except where the States concerned agree otherwise*.'[166] '*Except where otherwise agreed*, the former boundaries become frontiers protected by international law. This conclusion follows from the principle of respect for the territorial status quo and, in particular, from the principle of *uti possidetis*.'[167]

Normally, 'agreement' (consent) in this context is understood as an agreement between the involved political–territorial entities: states and seceding groups. That intergovernmental (or state–group) agreement can be made explicit in a boundary treaty. It can also, according to the ICJ, come about through mere acquiescence.[168] Consent can moreover be embodied in an agreement to outsource the delimitation of a boundary to an arbitrator. It is my claim that consent should preferably be sought from the involved *populations* (on this see pp. 133–35).

Furthermore, speaking of 'consent' in this context not only masks *who* must consent, but also risks conflating different objects to which an agreement relates.

[166] Badinter Opinion No. 2 (20 November 1991), in which the Badinter Commission advocates the internal right to self-determination of the Serbian population in Croatia and Bosnia-Herzegovina but does not grant a right to secession, reprinted in EJIL 3 (1992) 182 et seq., emphasis added.

[167] Badinter Opinion No. 3 (11 January 1992).

[168] In the *El Salvador* v *Honduras* dispute, the ICJ discussed whether a boundary line (originally based on *uti possidetis*) could be changed later, after the acquisition of independence by acquiescence and recognition. The Court saw no reason to preclude the possibility of such a change, 'where there is sufficient evidence to show that *the parties have in effect clearly accepted* a variation, or at least an interpretation, of the *uti possidetis juris* position' (*Frontier Dispute Case (El Salvador* v *Honduras, Nicaragua intervening)* (n 25) para. 67, emphasis added). Nesi (n 50) para 13 draws from *Land and Maritime Boundary between Cameroon and Nigeria* (*Cameroon* v *Nigeria, Equatorial Guinea Intervening*) [2002] ICJ Rep 303 that a consolidated acquiescence can overcome *uti possidetis*. But this was not explicitly stated by the Court.

In all processes of state formation, the primary question is *whether* there should be a boundary at all; the second question is *where* the boundary is supposed to run, and a third question can be which principles ought to be applied in order to answer the first two questions. Consent/agreement of interested political actors can relate to all of those three questions. First, it can relate to whether a new interstate boundary shall be established at all; second, it can relate to the geographical position of that boundary; third, it can relate to the application (or non-application) of *uti possidetis* to the territorial issue.

Secession is defined as a territorial disruption against the will of the state. There is (at least initially) no consent on the 'whether'. Put differently, in the event of a secession, the very right to existence of the seceding entity is contested (and this is in fact the definition of secession). The issue is not *where* the boundary should run but *whether* it exists *at all*. But once the secession has succeeded, the affected state will and must come to terms with it. From thereon, there is consent on the 'whether', albeit not necessarily a freely determined one. This was also the course of events in post-1989 Eastern and Central Europe. The declarations of independence pronounced by Soviet Union Republics and by Slovenia, Croatia, and Bosnia basically occurred against the will of the respective metropolitan states. The successive breakaway of sub-national territories met with resistance of varying degrees. But at some point, agreements were negotiated.

It may well be that in twentieth-century decolonization, that moment of acceptance on the part of the dominating states occurred earlier. Typically, the colonial administering powers had accepted at an early stage that the colonies had a right to self-determination. From then on, the right to existence of two political–geographical entities—eg of Burkina Faso and Mali—as internationally relevant entities, as subjects of international law, was no longer contested. The question was only *where* to draw the line. But, as argued above, the dividing line (in law and in fact) between decolonization and non-colonial secession seems to be blurry, not at least because of the applicability of the principle of self-determination to both situations (see pp. 113–15). The two scenarios are therefore not radically distinct, and the consent of the affected territorial entity can play a similar role in both contexts.

One minor problem with consent is that it implies a territorial *settlement on a case-by-case basis*. The boundary in that case results from a negotiation process. However, in such settlements, the parties will always have unequal bargaining power. This inequality necessarily taints the material justice of such a settlement. In reality, the case-by-case settlement approach is an abdication of the law at that precise point. The settlement solution is no fully legalized solution because it precisely fails to do the job of the law, which is to posit *general* rules ex ante and to neutralize unequal power. Interestingly, in historical practice, there is no case in which the line of a boundary has been modified by interstate consensus to deviate from a previous internal administrative delimitation. No subsequent bargaining actually took place on the exact position of the line. The involved entities consented at some point to the boundary provisionally drawn on the basis of *uti possidetis*; there was (implicit) agreement that it should not be modified.

The prevailing view that interstate consent is a necessary but sufficient condition to deviate from *uti possidetis* is often accompanied by the claim that the overall function of *uti possidetis* is quite modest. It has been pointed out that the actual stabilizing factor is not *uti possidetis*, but consent on using it as a starting point: 'History teaches that when *uti possidetis* is contested by one party and no alternative to *uti possidetis* is provided (such as the conclusion of a delimitation agreement or the deferral of the delimitation to a judicial or arbitral award) the risk of instability and clashes increases enormously'.[169] *Uti possidetis* has (historically) only ever provided a peaceful solution to boundary disputes in cases where its application has been based on consent—on the agreement of the parties to apply it. To use '[u]ti possidetis "as law"—without consent—is... dangerous.'[170] Along that line, the customary law value of *uti possidetis* has been questioned with the legal policy argument that this would constitute a disincentive for negotiations: *uti possidetis* can only unfold its useful role if its application is founded on the consent of the parties. If *uti possidetis* were applied automatically, then the seceding territory would automatically have resolved in its favour the most important issue in its bid for independence: the determination of its boundaries.[171] To sum up this point, even if *uti possidetis* were applicable to secessions as a matter of contemporary customary international law (as argued in section VI of this chapter), it would only work as a stabilizer when the parties agree on its application (which means that its actual source in the concrete case may well be called a contractual one).

4. Deviations based on consent of the populations: territorial referendums

It is submitted that focus should be shifted from the desirable consent between the affected territorial state and the 'representatives' of the breakaway territory to the consent of individuals. Importantly, this involves a move away from a *unanimous* contract-like decision (in a bilateral treaty or implicit agreement) to a *majoritarian* decision taken in a vote. So 'consent' on the individual level means something other than consent on the interstate level.

From a purely normative perspective, the best procedure for establishing a state boundary is a referendum conducted among the interested populations under international supervision.[172] The consent of the populations of the concerned territories can also be ascertained indirectly. A democratic justification of the creation of a new state and of its boundaries can be brought about through the democratic election of a government whose political programme is clearly directed at a specific territorial rearrangement. In order to function as a legitimating factor, a territorial referendum or election must satisfy the international standards of a free and fair vote—which is often lacking in practice.

[169] Nesi (n 50) para 21. [170] Johanson (n 96) 545. [171] Lalonde (n 9) 235.

[172] See in scholarship in favour of referendums A Peters, *Das Gebietsreferendum im Völkerrecht* (Nomos 1995); A Cassese, *Self-Determination of Peoples* (Grotius/CUP 1995) 180; Ratner (n

Historically, referendums have often been used to justify boundaries, mostly in combination with *uti possidetis*. Widespread use was made during decolonization in Africa and the breakup of Yugoslavia was accompanied by territorial referendums, too. Notably, the Badinter Commission specifically demanded a referendum for Bosnia as a precondition for recognition by the then European Community.[173] In 2006, the creation and the boundary of the State of Montenegro were agreed upon by Serbia and additionally bolstered with a referendum.[174] In Kosovo, numerous referendums have been held since 1991, but their fairness is dubious. Recent examples all over the world include the vote on the autonomy of Greenland (2008), the vote on Curaçao's partial autonomy from the Netherlands (2009), the independence referendum in South Sudan (2011), and the 'sovereignty referendum' on the Falkland Islands/Malvinas (2013).[175] A difficult case is the projected UN-supervised referendum on the status of Western Sahara, which has been repeatedly delayed.

When the Soviet Union started to falter, a Soviet Secession Act was adopted in April 1990[176] which prescribed referendums (in Art. 2(2)). The application of that law would have arguably furnished additional procedural justification for the ongoing secessions of the Republics, even if its primary political objective was to slow down the dissolution by building up procedural barriers. However, that law was not really applied and remained a dead letter. Most of the disputed territories now located in the CIS and in Georgia[177] have conducted one or several referendums on independence, and the results have always been clear. One example is Nagorno-Karabakh (see also ch. 11 in this volume). As early as 1988, the local Soviet of Nagorno-Karabakh had called for the territory's separation from the Azerbaijan SSR and unification with Armenia. On 30 August 1991, Azerbaijan declared the re-establishment of its statehood of 1918–1920. Nagorno-Karabakh then renounced reunification with Armenia, because Armenia no longer supported

2) 622–3; A Tancredi, 'A Normative "Due Process" in the Creation of States through Secession' in M Kohen (ed), *Secession—International Law Perspectives* (CUP 2006) 171, 190–1; Saxer (n 40) 777.

[173] Opinion No. 4 of the Badinter Commission on Bosnia-Herzegovina, reproduced in (1992) 31 ILM 1501–3.

[174] The referendum was held on 3 June 2006. Upon a proposal of the EU, voter turn-out of 50% and approval of 55% were required to reach a valid decision on independence. The referendum had a turnout of 85%, and 55% of the participants voted in favour of independence. Montenegro acceded the United Nations on 28 June 2008.

[175] A referendum on the political status of the Falkland Islands/Malvinas was held on 10–11 March 2013. The inhabitants were asked whether or not they supported the continuation of their status as an Overseas Territory of the United Kingdom. On a turnout of 92%, 99.8% voted overwhelmingly to remain a British territory. For a critique of this referendum (which was conducted without UN involvement) as irrelevant for the international legal status of the islands, see the Argentinean scholar MG Kohen, 'El reférendum en Malvinas o la autosatisfacción británica', (5 March 2013) El País 12.

[176] *Law on the Procedure on the Decision of Questions Connected with the Secession of a Union Republic from the USSR of 4 April 1990* (Vedomosti S'ezda narodnyh deputatov SSSR i Verhovnogo Soveta SSSR 1990 No. 15, 252).

[177] For example, South Ossetia conducted a referendum on independence on 19 January 1992 which did not satisfy international standards of fair and free voting.

this plan. On 2 September 1991, the local Soviet of Nagorno-Karabakh declared a 'Republic of Nagorno-Karabakh', relying on Art. 70 of the Soviet Union Constitution.[178] On 18 October 1991, the Supreme Council of Azerbaijan adopted a Declaration of Independence of Azerbaijan. In November 1991, Azerbaijan abolished the autonomous status of Nagorno-Karabakh. On 10 December 1991, the region then organized a referendum.[179] On a turnout of around 85%, 98% of the voters, or 82% of those eligible, voted in favour of Nagorno-Karabakh's independence.[180] That referendum was organized without the involvement of the Azerbaijan SSR, as required by the Soviet Secession Act of April 1990.[181] Overall, it did not follow the cumbersome procedure prescribed by that Act.

A problem of territorial referendums is that they are decided by the majority. If, as is mostly the case, the proponents of a new state (and of a new boundary) belong to a specific ethnic group, the result of the vote simply reflects the ethnic composition of a territory. So even if 'ethnicity' is not used as a formal criterion for drawing the boundary line, it pops up and becomes decisive through the referendum. Does this mean that a referendum is precisely the wrong tool to safeguard minority rights? Is, therefore, a referendum genuinely and in structural terms unsuitable for legitimizing territorial rearrangements?

This is not the case, as the successful referendums on the Jura territory in Switzerland demonstrate. In that case, a truly democratic decision on the establishment of a new canton and on the exact location of its boundaries was reached in a process which lasted eight years (from 1970 to 1978). This was done by a series of votes asking all affected populations on the various governmental levels (ranging from the local community to the Swiss Federation) whether and where boundaries should be drawn.[182] The boundary line in the end satisfied the needs of the local population. Such a procedure can only function if it is rooted in a strong democratic culture embedded in the rule of law. These indispensable preconditions have been lacking in many areas where territorial rearrangements have been effectuated in the recent past. Therefore, many recent territorial referendums did not—although they are, under ideal conditions, superior to *uti possidetis* from the point of view of normative theory—in the real world provide a strong justification for the drawing of territorial boundaries. To conclude, despite obvious practical difficulties in organizing fair territorial referendums, they still provide the best normative basis for territorial rearrangements in contemporary international law. *Uti possidetis*, understood as a residual preliminary rule, can provide a useful function here, because any vote put to the population needs a starting point for the position of the boundary.

[178] Peters (n 172) 195–6 with references. [179] Peters (n 172) 194–8.

[180] Peters (n 172) 196 with further references; A Manutscharjan, 'Nagornyj Karabach im Kampf um das Selbstbestimmungsrecht: Eine Darstellung aus armenischer Sicht' (1992) 42 Osteuropa 951, 962.

[181] Cf. n 176.

[182] U Häfelin and W Haller, *Schweizerisches Bundesstaatsrecht* (5th edn, Schulthess 2001) paras 1004–7. The more recent editions of the book do not give any details on that procedure.

XI. Conclusions and Outlook

Frontiers are no longer 'the razor's edge on which hang suspended the modern issues of war and peace, of life or death to nations', as Lord Curzon had put it in his 1907 Romanes lecture.[183] But even in the era of globalization—only seemingly an age of boundlessness—state boundaries continue to matter. The physical boundaries of states have become porous with the transnational mobility of persons, goods, services, data, and finance flows. Still, states continue to be the most powerful international legal subjects, and their physical delineation remains relevant for the application of their domestic law, for their jurisdiction to enforce, and for their responsibility under international law. Because most people are neither willing nor able to migrate and thus to 'vote with their feet' against the laws they live under, the side of the state boundary on which they live is crucially important to their lives.

This chapter has sought to demonstrate that *uti possidetis* is, as a matter of positive law and practice, applicable to non-colonial secessions. This extended scope is reconcilable with other relevant international legal principles, and defensible as a matter of legal policy.

Importantly, *uti possidetis* can potentially transform *any type* of internal territorial demarcation that has been established in domestic law in the period of time before secession into an international one once secession has been successful. Generally speaking, older administrative lines stemming from the pre-independence era (eg Soviet era) cannot be opposed against the currently existing 'mother' states (eg CIS states) if they are not acknowledged in *their* domestic law as it stands, too. Neither does *uti possidetis* apply on the basis of factual control over a territory, in the absence of a formal administrative line.

A core question for the resolution of CIS matters is therefore whether the successor states of the Soviet Union do possess clearly defined internal administrative territorial demarcations. This seems to be true in many, but not in all cases. Although those CIS member states which are affected by secessionist attempts are not constituted as federation-type states but rather unitary states, they still have internal domestic administrative boundaries which in some instances correspond with former Soviet administrative boundaries, in others not. For example, Georgia is divided into nine regions, two autonomous Republics, and the capital, Tbilisi. Chechnya's administration was reformed between 2006 and 2009, and the Republic is now divided into 15 rajons and two cities. However, the exact boundary lines of these administrative units in Chechnya have not been exactly defined for the most part.

Therefore, the overall conclusion for the CIS *problématique* is that all depends on the existence of internal territorial demarcations. Where administrative boundaries exist, breakaway territories defined by such boundaries *can* lawfully

[183] Lord Curzon of Kedleston, 'Frontiers' in *Oxford Lectures on History, 1904–1923* (Clarendon Press 1924) Vol 1, 1, 7.

rely on *uti possidetis* for their case. Although this finding might estrange international lawyers because it means that details of domestic law determine the international legal situation, this anomaly is inbuilt in the concept of *uti possidetis*. More seriously, the finding seems to provide a wrong incentive: in order to avoid the potential application of *uti possidetis*, a state is well advised not to federalize and decentralize its territory, and this is a course which does not well accommodate the needs of minority populations.

The real issue in the CIS is *whether* there should be new boundaries, and not *where* these should run. Although *uti possidetis* is often invoked as a battle slogan by defenders of national and territorial unity (and sometimes by proponents of secession), the principle does not offer any answer to the question of the 'whether'.

In any event, *uti possidetis*, far from being a perfect solution to define an international boundary, is only the prima facie least bad, and it should only constitute the starting point, the fallback rule, for the final determination of a boundary unless and until consent on the boundary is reached. Ideally, this consent should not be limited to intergovernmental level but should assure the support of the majority, ideally a qualified majority, of the population.

Reliance on *uti possidetis* is a purely formal device; it respects a former administrative line independent of any material factor. The application of *uti possidetis* can however be set aside on the basis of material considerations, notably respect for a concerned people's right to self-determination, exercised in proper procedures. If a fair procedure (eg in a referendum) results in boundary lines which circumscribe a territory whose residents form an ethnically more or less uniform group, this should be tolerated. Obviously, the establishment of a state boundary in an 'ethnicity-conscious' fashion will not resolve the inevitable problem of conflicting cultures in a globalizing world.

Uti possidetis is a suitable mechanism for (provisionally) determining a boundary line also in the event of a secession. But in the end, any drawing or shifting of a state boundary has to grapple with the tension between satisfying demands of formal stability/legal security and material justice. Both the formal and the substantive criteria to determine boundaries have their drawbacks, but the worst is to mix formal and material criteria, because then all regularity is lost.[184] Some chance of securing stability exists when a formal criterion (namely *uti possidetis*) is implemented consistently and without regard to material questions. This means renouncing substantive justice. But this renunciation is in turn irreconcilable with the promise given by the Human Rights Covenants proclaiming the principle of self-determination. The relevant actors continue to ruminate about self-determination, and this undermines all attempts to reach stability through pure formality.[185] Therefore, the tension will persist. It is an open question which principle—the formal *uti possidetis* principle, or the material principle of democratic self-determination, ideally expressed in a fair and free referendum—offers the best opportunity to minimize conflict and bloodshed in the long run.

[184] Fisch (n 56) 266. [185] Fisch (n 56) 266–7.

7

Secession in the CIS

Causes, Consequences, and Emerging Principles

Thomas Burri[1]

Whoever is a Serb and of Serb birth
And of Serb blood and heritage
And comes not to fight at Kosovo
May he never have the progeny his heart desires!
Neither son nor daughter
May nothing grow that his hand sows!
Neither dark wine nor white wheat!
And let him be cursed from all ages to all ages!

I. Introduction

The above was engraved[2] on the monument of Gazimestan on the *Amselfeld*, just north of Pristina in Kosovo, to commemorate the famous existential battle between the Serbian and Ottoman forces in 1389. Ever since then—but in particular in our times—the *Amselfeld* has been one of the bones of contention between Serbia and Kosovo. A visit to the memorial of Gazimestan in 2010 saw it fortified and guarded by the NATO forces in Kosovo. The memorial was surrounded by fortification and the KFOR controlled everyone who sought to approach closer

[1] Assistant Professor of International and European Law at University of Saint Gallen, Switzerland; Dr iur. (Zurich), LLM (College of Europe, Bruges), lic. iur. (Basel), admitted to the Zurich Bar; <thomas.burri@unisg.ch> or <www.thomas-burri.com>. My thanks go to: Professor Christian Walter, Dr Antje von Ungern-Sternberg, and their team for organizing the wonderful conference in Munich in January 2012 and for hosting me at LMU Munich; the participants in the conference for thought provoking comments and discussions; Professor Hans-Peter Folz for fruitful discussions and for hosting me at LMU Munich—the community of public and international lawyers in Munich has indeed been a source of true inspiration. Finally, I would like to thank Ambassador Jenö Stähelin and Professor Bill Alford for hosting me at Harvard Law School from May to September 2012. Much of this article was written during that time.

[2] The author of this article saw the inscription of the battlefield curse at the monument on the *Amselfeld* when visiting it. The translation of the inscription from Serbian to English is from Wikipedia (<http://en.wikipedia.org/wiki/Gazimestan> accessed 4 August 2012); the accuracy of the translation was confirmed by a Serbian native speaker.

than 50 metres. A soldier was placed on top of the tower that had been erected as a monument. The task of the soldier was to constantly scan the horizon with binoculars.

Something like a state[3] has been unilaterally established in Kosovo as a sort of retribution for the hostile acts committed by the Milošević regime at the turn of the millennium. However, the new 'state' has left many of the ancient problems unresolved. NATO forces may no longer be needed to guard the memorial of Gazimestan (apparently it is guarded by the Kosovar police today), but they are still indispensable slightly to the north of it. The part of Kosovo beyond the River Ibar, including the city of Mitrovica, has become the hot ground. 'The situation in the north remains extremely sensitive to any political developments between Pristina and Belgrade', as the UN Secretary General reports.[4] While the 'state' of Kosovo has undoubtedly come to a point where it is inconceivable to go back to the status quo ante,[5] talk of re-adjusting the borders of Kosovo lingers.[6]

The international community has been longing for clarification and tasked the International Court of Justice to opine on the legality of Kosovo's declaration of independence of early 2008. But the community remains as discombobulated as it had been before the opinion.[7] Thus, the song of Kosovo is still being composed.[8]

[3] For the whole gamut of subjects, actors, and entities in international law, see C Walter, 'Subjects of International Law' in Rüdiger Wolfrum (ed), *Max Planck Encyclopedia of Public International Law* (Vol IX, OUP 2012) 634–43.

[4] UN Secretary General, Report of the Secretary-General on the United Nations Interim Administration Mission in Kosovo (S/2012/275) 27 April 2012, para 11. Note also the referendum organized by the Serb community in Northern Kosovo on whether they accept the institutions of the Republic of Kosovo, para 8. The Commission of the European Union continues to push for a solution for northern Kosovo. See Commission of the European Union, Kosovo 2011 Progress Report (SEC(2011) 1207) 12 October 2011, 5, and the conclusions in Commission of the European Union, Communication from the Commission to the European Parliament and the Council: Enlargement Strategy and Main Challenges 2011–2012 (COM(2011) 666) 12 October 2011, 17. The European Union meanwhile has upgraded Serbia to the status of an accession candidate and contemplates an Association Agreement with Kosovo. The latest document adopted under the Framework Convention (Council of Europe, Framework Convention for the Protection of National Minorities (CETS no. 157) 1 February 1995) does not yet reflect the problems in northern Kosovo (see Committee of Ministers, Resolution on the implementation of the Framework Convention for the Protection of National Minorities in Kosovo (CM/ResCMN(2011)14) 6 July 2011).

[5] V Epping, 'Völkerrechtliche Aspekte der Wiederherstellung von Staatlichkeit in Nachkonfliktgesellschaften' (2008) 83 Die Friedens-Warte 1, 25, 35.

[6] See 'The border question' *The Economist* (London, 5 June 2010); A Ernst, 'Nord-Kosovo: Die Krise als Chance—Steckt im Zankapfel der Keim für eine serbisch-albanische Aussöhnung?' (2011) 51 Südosteuropa Mitteilungen 5–6, 26.

[7] International Court of Justice, *Accordance with International Law of the Unilateral Declaration of Independence in respect of Kosovo* [2010] Advisory Opinion, General List No. 141.

[8] The latest note for once did not concern a problem linked to the secession. Instead, it concerned the sometimes peculiar political manoeuvres in Kosovo. The President of Kosovo (Ms Atifete Jahjaga) had been elected as an 'interim' solution after the election of the previous President was invalidated. Her election was based on a deal by political parties providing that the constitution would be amended so that the President would be elected by the people (instead of the parliament, as with Ms. Jahjaga). The Constitutional Court of Kosovo held on 12 July 2012 that Ms. Jahjaga had to serve the full constitutional term of five years, although the constitutional amendment was accepted and the President, according to the new rule, would henceforth be elected by the people (Constitutional Court of Kosovo, *Proposed Amendments of the Constitution submitted by the President of the Assembly of*

Is it a siren song? Is the song of secession being heard around the world? Are other peoples ineluctably drawn to what it promises? Are perhaps the Caucasus—South Ossetia, Abkhazia, and Nagorno-Karabakh—and Transdniestria quietly humming along?

This chapter serves to cut across the case studies on South Ossetia, Abkhazia, Nagorno-Karabakh, and Transdniestria provided in this volume and to perceive them in the context of the developments in Kosovo. Overarching issues in terms of secession are to be identified. First, we ask the most pressing question: whether the situation in the Caucasus, generally, gives rise to a right to secession. Not much space is needed to answer it (section II). Then, in section III, we take a look at the common traits of the conflicts in South Ossetia, Abkhazia, Nagorno-Karabakh, and Transdniestria. Section IV briefly adopts a critical perspective. Section V examines whether the case studies confirm certain 'soft ideas' that are often floated with regard to secession. Section VI then examines the pledges of federalism. It does so by means of a judgment of the European Court of Human Rights as to Bosnia and Herzegovina. The conclusion in section VII finally questions whether international law is based on the right approach—'right', that is, in terms of forestalling and solving conflicts such as those that have plagued the Caucasus.

The chapter does not go into the details of the Kosovo Opinion and its implications for secession again. We have done that already[9] and chapter 2 provides further insight. The reader is also referred to our analyses of the legal intricacies of

the Republic of Kosovo on 23 March 2012 and 4 May 2012 [2012] K.O. 29/12 and K.O. 48/12 (Ref. No: AGJ 284/12) <http://www.gjk-ks.org/?cid=2,4> accessed 4 August 2012, paras 248–71).

[9] We analysed one aspect of it in T Burri, 'The Kosovo Opinion and Secession: The Sounds of Silence and Missing Links' (2010) 11 GLJ 8, 881. Aspects of secession had been extensively analysed before the opinion had been handed down, for instance in MG Kohen (ed), *Secession—International Law Perspectives* (CUP 2006) (with contributions by Christian Tomuschat, Andrew Clapham, Georg Nolte, John Dugard and David Raić, Théodore Christakis, Antonello Tancredi, Andreas Zimmermann, Olivier Corten, Fatsah Ougouergouz and Djacoba Liva Tehindrazanarivelo, Li-Ann Thio, Photini Pazartzis, Frida Armas Pfirter and Silvina González Napolitano, Patrick Dumberry, Christian Dominicé, Georges Abi-Saab); P Hilpold, 'Die Sezession—zum Versuch der Verrechtlichung eines faktischen Phänomens' (2008) 63 ZöR 117—and, of course, thereafter, eg (2010) 24 LJIL (1) with contributions by Theodore Christakis, Oliver Corten, Anne Peters, Marcelo G Kohen and Katherine Del Mar, Marc Weller, Ralph Wilde, Hurst Hannum and (2) with contributions by Dov Jacobs and Yannick Radi and Jure Vidmar; K Odendahl, 'The Scope of Application of the Principle of Territorial Integrity' (2010) 53 GYIL 512; R Tricot and B Sander, 'Recent Developments: The Broader Consequences of the International Court of Justice's Advisory Opinion on the Unilateral Declaration of Independence in Respect of Kosovo' (2011) 49 CJTL 2, 321; JR Ablan, 'Signal and Affirm: How the United Nations Should Articulate the Right to Remedial Secession' (2012) 45 VJTL 1, 211 (arguing that the UN General Assembly should regulate the right to secession); EM Brewer, 'To Break Free from Tyranny and Oppression: Proposing a Model for a Remedial Right to Secession in the Wake of the Kosovo Advisory Opinion' (2012) 45 VJTL 1, 245 (proposing a way to make remedial secession operable); P Hilpold (ed), *Das Kosovo-Gutachten des IGH vom 22. Juli 2010* (Nijhoff 2012) (with contributions by Peter Hilpold, Christian Tomuschat, Stefan Oeter, Matthias Niedobitek, Isabel Lirola Delgado, Michael Bothe, Andrea Gioia, Helmut Philipp Aust, Andrea Gattini, Anne Peters, Gerhard Hafner and Nadia Kalb). At least in terms of scholarship—if only—the Kosovo Opinion did not amount to 'deferral, denial, disappointment'—a formula used by David Kennedy to describe the Nuclear Weapons opinion: D Kennedy, 'The Nuclear Weapons Case', in L Boisson De Chazournes and P Sands (eds), *International Law, the International Court of Justice and Nuclear Weapons* (CUP 1999) 462–72, 466.

secession (including remedial secession) and self-determination in *the Max Planck Encyclopaedia of Public International Law*.[10]

II. The Core Question: The Right to Secession

We have to answer one core question: do any of the entities discussed in the four case studies have a right to secession? If we answered that question in the affirmative, another question would inevitably arise: do we now have to assume that the right to secession is *general*? Is there a body of law that gives us a clear indication of *when* a people can sever its links with an existing state?

The answer seems simple. The authors of the case studies all agree: none of the entities have a right, based on international law, to secede from the state to which they have traditionally belonged. Christopher Waters, at least implicitly, comes to this conclusion for South Ossetia: it belongs to Georgia;[11] Farhad Mirzayev is very explicit: he repeatedly states that there are no grounds for Abkhazia to secede from Georgia;[12] Heiko Krüger reasons in the same vein for Nagorno-Karabakh: no secession from Azerbaijan;[13] and Bill Bowring finds Transdniestria cannot secede from Moldova. Only Bowring implicitly clears some room for secession: in the unlikely event that Moldova joined Romania, Transdniestria would be allowed to create a separate state.[14]

So it is simple: none of the entities have a right to secession. We do not even have to bother with the larger issue, ie whether a right to secession emerges from the four conflicts in general. Obviously, the authors of the case studies concur, Kosovo (and the Kosovo Opinion) has had little impact in that regard on the situations under scrutiny.

But is it really that simple? Why have the conflicts then been frozen for almost 20 years? Should not, a cynic might suggest, unison among lawyers automatically arouse suspicion? Where is the critical perspective, Koskenniemi's goggles, which taught us that there were *always* different ways of looking at situations, legally? And how do the authors all come to the very same conclusion?

It is therefore necessary to dig a little deeper, if only for the sake of argument, and take a look at some common traits of the four conflicts—call them causes or call them consequences of the conflicts; one is as usual difficult to distinguish from the other. In doing so, this article heavily relies on the case studies in this volume.[15]

[10] D Thürer and T Burri, 'Self-determination', in Wolfrum (n 3) 113–28; D Thürer and T Burri, 'Secession' in Wolfrum (n 3) 53–65.

[11] C Waters, 'South Ossetia' (ch 9 in this volume) 188, 212, and 213. Waters thereby joins the *Independent International Fact-Finding Mission on the Conflict in Georgia* (Tagliavini Report) (2009) I–III, vol. I, 17.

[12] F Mirzayev, 'Abkhazia' (ch 10 in this volume) 195 et seq.

[13] H Krüger, 'Nagorno-Karabakh' (ch 11 in this volume) 223 and 224.

[14] B Bowring, 'Transnistria' (ch 8 in this volume) 171 and 174.

[15] See also C Frei, 'Summary Report of the Global Leadership Seminar on The Economics and Politics of the Eurasian Region', 2008, <http://fletcher.tufts.edu/global/~/media/Fletcher/Microsites/Globe%20Seminar/1_GS_pdfs/Summary_Report_2008.ashx> accessed 4 August 2012.

III. Common Traits of the Four Frozen Conflicts

It is clear that all four cases became conflict zones when the Soviet empire began to crumble. The ensuing power vacuum opened the scene for new, sometimes renewed, claims of oppressed populations. In this sense the four conflicts are typical consequences of a dying empire, well known from the demise of the colonial empires. Think only of France in Algeria. The relatively calm escape from Soviet rule in *Central* Europe was the exception in that regard, and certainly one of the biggest achievements of the European Union. Only the arm of the European Union did not reach as far as the Caucasus, or beyond the Dniester. Thus, the early 1990s saw violent conflicts arise in each of the four cases—some of them longer, some of them shorter: between South Ossetia/Russia and Georgia, between Abkhazia/Russia and Georgia, between Armenia and Azerbaijan over Nagorno-Karabakh, and between Transdniestria/Russia and Moldova. These conflicts had arisen at a time when the Soviet republics themselves, in a '*vague de déclarations unilatérales d'indépendance*',[16] were making use of their *constitutional* right to secede from the Soviet Union. Georgia, Armenia, Azerbajian, and Moldova then became independent. It was while those republics were still young (and weak) that some parts of those republics saw what they considered their only chance and tried to break away. The misfortune of each—South Ossetia, Abkhazia, Nagorno-Karabakh, and Transdniestria—has been their status. None of them had been a 'proper' Soviet republic, but some sort of 'inferior' unit, much like Kosovo within Yugoslavia: autonomous entities that did not enjoy the same rank as the republics. Such entities had no *constitutional* right to secede. And the procedure of the Soviet Law of Secession was too cumbersome and slow for them to achieve independence, as Heiko Krüger shows in his study.[17] So they each trod the path of violent conflict to achieve independence in the 1990s—with mixed success, to say the least. In the case of South Ossetia, it is well known that violent conflict flared up again in 2008 for five days. After the violence had ended several international bodies sprang into action: an independent international commission issued a report,[18] the ICJ delivered a judgment[19]—in which it ducked out on grounds of jurisdiction[20]—and the European Court of Human Rights has been

[16] O Corten, 'Déclarations unilatérales d'indépendance et reconnaissances prématurées: du Kosovo à l'Ossétie du sud et à l'Abkhazie' (2008) 112 Revue général de droit international public 4, 721, 721 [emphasis added]; see the criticism of this article in P Weckel, 'Plaidoyer pour le processus d'indépendance du Kosovo: réponse à Olivier Corten' (2009) 113 Revue général de droit international public 2, 257.

[17] H Krüger, 'Nagorno-Karabakh' (ch 11 in this volume) 217.

[18] 'Tagliavini Report' (n 11). Out of the voluminous literature covering the 2008 war, see eg F Dubuisson and A Lagerwall, 'Le conflit en Géorgie de 2008 au regard du jus contra bellum et à la lumière du rapport de la mission d'enquête internationale de 2009' (2009) 42 Revue belge de droit international (2) 448.

[19] International Court of Justice, *Case concerning the Application of the International Convention on the Elimination of All Forms of Racial Discrimination (Georgia* v *Russian Federation)* [2011] General List no. 140.

[20] Compare with the separate opinion of Judge Bruno Simma to the ICJ judgment.

dealing with two cases.[21] Yet it seems that the tensions underlying the conflict have not been eased permanently.

It is true that history and ethnicity fuelled the conflicts around South Ossetia, Abkhazia, Nagorno-Karabakh, and Transdniestria; however, as is usual in such situations, history and ethnicity were interpreted to suit the needs of the nationalistic cause of each side. Yet it seems that one player looms large over these interpretations and clearly stands out: Russia. The empire undone is involved in all four conflicts. In South Ossetia and Abkhazia, Russia is directly implicated, as Christopher Waters and Farhad Mirzayev show:[22] Russia fought on behalf of South Ossetia again in 2008, retains de facto control over both territories, distributes passports,[23] recognizes the territories as states based on a creative interpretation of Kosovo,[24] makes others do so, and watches over the UN Security Council. In Transdniestria, Russia exercises effective control, if one adheres to the human rights perspective from Strasbourg.[25] Here, in contrast, Russia apparently does not support secession, as Bill Bowring shows.[26] In Nagorno-Karabakh, Russia seems to exercise influence on both sides, Azerbaijan and Armenia. It maintains 'controlled instability', as Heiko Krüger puts it.[27]

Why is Russia so involved in these conflicts? Is it just the flickering embers of the empire? Is it strategic interests—energy interests—in the region? Undoubtedly, both play a role; yet two further aspects all too easily escape attention and should therefore be raised here. One of them is Chechnya, which was another one of those autonomous units.[28] Russia has fought two cruel wars with Chechen separatists in

[21] European Court of Human Rights, *Georgia* v *Russia (I)* [2011] Application no. 13255/07, decision on admissibility (the case has been relinquished to the Grand Chamber on 15 December 2009; the Chamber of the Court had held the case *prima facie* admissible); and European Court of Human Rights, *Georgia* v *Russia (II)* [2011] Application no. 38263/08 decision on admissibility (the Court held the case *prima facie* admissible).

[22] C Waters, 'South Ossetia' (ch 9 in this volume), inter alia 179; F Mirzayev, 'Abkhazia' (ch 10 in this volume) 204.

[23] 'Passportization': 'Tagliavini Report' (n 11) I–III, 18. See the legal assessment: A Peters, 'Extraterritorial Naturalizations: Between the Human Right to Nationality, State Sovereignty and Fair Principles of Jurisdiction' (2010) 53 GYIL 623.

[24] Note the interesting argument by Jure Vidmar: based on Kosovo the argument can be made that in cases of unilateral secession, collective recognition has a constitutive effect for statehood: J Vidmar, 'Explaining the Legal Effects of Recognition' (2012) 61 ICLQ 2, 361. In a similar vein: C Ryngaert and S Sobrie, 'Recognition of States: International Law or Realpolitik? The Practice of Recognition in the Wake of Kosovo, South Ossetia, and Abkhazia' (2011) 24 LJIL 2, 467.

[25] European Court of Human Rights, *Ilaşcu and Others* v *Moldova and Russia* [2004] Application no. 48787/99, and European Court of Human Rights, *Ivanţoc and Others* v *Moldova and Russia* [2011] Application no. 23687/05. See for a perspective of conflict resolution HM Sieg, 'Der Transnistrien-Konflikt: Voraussetzungen für eine Konfliktlösung' (2011) 51 Südosteuropa Mitteilungen 3, 62; M Renner, 'Krisenstaat Republik Moldau: Anzeichen einer demokratischen Konsolidierung' (2011) 51 Südosteuropa Mitteilungen 2, 60.

[26] B Bowring, "Transnistria" (ch 8 in this volume) 158, 165, and 167.

[27] H Krüger, 'Nagorno-Karabakh' (ch 11 in this volume) 232.

[28] See R Schaefer, *The Insurgency in Chechnya and the North Caucasus: From Gazavat to Jihad* (Praeger Security International 2010), on the conflict in Chechnya from the military perspective of counter-insurgency; see also J Lapitskaya, 'ECHR, Russia, and Chechnya: Two is not Company and Three is Definitely a Crowd' (2011) 43 NYUJILP 2, 479, as to Russia's record before the European Court of Human Rights with regard to Chechnya.

the past 20 years. It conceded in the first war, after the hostage crisis in the hospital in Budyonnovsk in 1996; it did not surrender to separatists in the Moscow theatre hostage crisis in 2002 or in the Beslan school siege in 2004. Even after the war, since 2009, Russia has remained extremely wary of ripple effects into Chechnya from other attempts at secession, especially from within the Southern Caucasus. The other important element that drives Russia is a person: Vladimir Putin. The man stands for a new Russian assertiveness after a period of relative weakness that followed the collapse of the Soviet Union. A separate study would, of course, be needed to assess his impact. Even without such a study one can say, though, that his own personal approach steers much of what Russia does in the region. And he is unlikely to go away soon.

IV. The Critical Perspective and Remedial Secession

Does the law have any role in this? In particular, is the law of self-determination relevant in this power play? It is tempting to adopt Martti Koskenniemi's view, presented in his article in the *International and Comparative Law Quarterly* in 1994:[29] in this critical perspective Georgia would play the role of the state-centrist in the quarrel over South Ossetia and Abkhazia, while Russia would be the romantic; Azerbaijan would play state-centrist in Nagorno-Karabakh, while Armenia would play romantic; Moldova would argue as a state-centrist in Transdniestria, while the romantic role would fall to Transdniestria. Whether and when the right to secession arose would be a matter of competing claims about the existence of an exceptional situation, an emergency. No one would be 'right' and endless squabbles over the meaning of the saving clause in the Friendly Relations Declaration would ensue.

However, with respect, we part company with Martti Koskenniemi on this—and so, it seems, do the authors of the four case studies presented in this volume. In fact, the message from the case studies, as I read it, is not that there is *no* right to secession at all. Rather, my reading of the case studies is that there could indeed be a remedial right to secession, at least in principle. The hitch is only that the requirements for such a right to arise are not met in any of the four cases. Put simply, the threshold beyond which the internal right to self-determination becomes external is not crossed.[30] It seems to me—misunderstandings excepted—the

[29] M Koskenniemi, 'National Self-Determination Today: Problems of Legal Theory and Practice' (1994) 43 ICLQ 2, 241.

[30] I am, of course, aware that this view does not square with the finding in Tagliavini Report (n 11) I–III, 17, para 11, which is worth quoting in full: 'It is true that a number of contentious legal issues resulting from the break-up of the Soviet Union also played their part in setting the stage for the armed conflict that was to follow in August 2008. The issue of self-determination of South Ossetians and Abkhaz as well as their right to unilateral secession from Georgia are two legal issues related to the conflict. Both South Ossetians and Abkhaz consider their right to self-determination as the legal basis for their quest for sovereignty and independence of the respective territories. However,

authors, by concluding that none of the entities can secede, implicitly make room for the possibility that a remedial right to secession could arise in the future. They thus conclude in a similar vein as the Supreme Court of Canada in relation to Quebec on the basis of international law,[31] and they allow for the same free space that the ICJ created with the Kosovo Opinion.

So, it comes down to the basics: human rights. They must not be sacrificed over status and state issues, no matter how important these issues may seem to the actors involved. That is the message Strasbourg sent in *Ilaşcu*.[32] My reading of the four cases studied in this volume is that massive and widespread violations of human rights could still command the ultimate punishment: the loss of sovereignty over a part of a territory. Before following this train of thought further in the perspective of conflict resolution, some soft ideas are run past the case studies.

international law does not recognize a right to unilaterally create a new state based on the principle of self-determination outside the colonial context and apartheid. An extraordinary acceptance to secede under extreme conditions such as genocide has so far not found general acceptance. As will be shown later, in the case of the conflict in August 2008 and the ensuing recognition of South Ossetia and Abkhazia, the Mission has found that genocide did not take place. Furthermore, much of international state practice and the explicit views of major powers such as Russia in the Kosovo case stand against it. This applies also to a process of dismemberment of a state, as might be discussed with regard to Georgia after the dissolution of the Soviet Union. According to the overwhelmingly accepted *uti possidetis* principle, only former constituent republics such as Georgia but not territorial sub-units such as South Ossetia or Abkhazia are granted independence in case of dismemberment of a larger entity such as the former Soviet Union. Hence, South Ossetia did not have a right to secede from Georgia, and the same holds true for Abkhazia for much of the same reasons. Recognition of breakaway entities such as Abkhazia and South Ossetia by a third country is consequently contrary to international law in terms of an unlawful interference in the sovereignty and territorial integrity of the affected country, which is Georgia. It runs against Principle I of the Helsinki Final Act, which states 'the participating States will respect each other's sovereign equality and individuality as well as all the rights inherent in and encompassed by its sovereignty, including in particular the right of every State to juridical equality, to territorial integrity and to freedom and political independence." ' I rather concur with Olivier Corten, who concludes (based on other parts of the Tagliavini Report): 'On aurait pu s'attendre à ce que la Mission, un peu à la manière de la Court supreme du Canada dans son avis sur la secession du Québec, se contente d'affirmer qu'aucune violation grave des droits de l'homme n'était susceptible de fonder cet argument, sans se prononcer sur la validité de principe de celui-ci. [footnote omitted] Mais elle a fait bien davantage, en condamnant de manière générale tout droit à la «secession-remède»'—O Corten, 'Le rapport de la mission d'enquête internationale indépendante sur le conflit en Géorgie: quell apport au jus contra bellum?' (2010) 114 Revue général de droit international public 1, 35, 42–43. See also the further critique, which I share, on p 44 where Corten finds that the Mission takes some liberties with regard to existing positive international law, since it is normally considered that international law neither grants a right to nor prohibits secession; the finding of the Mission is therefore 'dans sa prétention généraliste, excessive'.

31 Supreme Court of Canada, *Reference re Secession of Quebec* [1998] 2 SCR 217: 'Clearly, such a circumstance [when a people is blocked from the meaningful exercise of its right to self-determination internally] parallels the other two recognized situations [those of colonial peoples and of peoples subject to alien subjugation, domination or exploitation] in that the ability of a people to exercise its right to self-determination internally is somehow being totally frustrated. While it remains unclear whether this third proposition actually reflects an established international law standard, it is unnecessary for present purposes to make that determination. Even assuming that the third circumstance is sufficient to create a right to unilateral secession under international law, the current Quebec context cannot be said to approach such a threshold' (para 134).

32 See n 24.

V. The Soft Ideas

Some ideas, which may be called 'soft' for the purposes of this paper, have been put forward on a regular basis in contexts of secession. Do they hold water in the four case studies? The question is important, because if they do, such soft ideas might just as well condense into something like principles.

One of the most common ideas is that of the viral nature of a secession: if one secession is allowed to happen, secessionist tendencies will spread, and other secessions will unavoidably follow. Secession is, in short, contagious. That idea was clearly at work when the (former) president of Transdniestria invoked the secession of Kosovo—'Both legally and historically, Transdniestria has a better claim to independence than Kosovo'[33]—or when Russia recognized South Ossetia and Abkhazia as independent states in the wake of Kosovo, and perhaps will be again when the population of Chechnya in the future—if ever—raise a mirror to the face of Russia and claim the very same right to be recognized as an independent state.[34] However, these instances show the true nature of the idea of contagion: it is an argument invoked for a specific purpose. One can just as easily argue against a contagious effect, typically by claiming that the situation at hand is so unique that it can *never* possibly serve as a yardstick in other cases. Other cases, the counter-argument goes, necessarily differ in a myriad of aspects from the case under consideration. Surely, then, no harm can be done by secession in this one clearly defined case. Obviously, that is the line of argument of most of the governments that chose to recognize Kosovo. Ultimately, the contagious nature of secession therefore boils down to precedent. As all lawyers know, however, the nature of precedent is such that it hardly ever quenches further arguments; the haggling usually just continues in terms of similarity and analogy. That the argument for treating Kosovo as a binding precedent is fragile can be seen by another 'precedent': to argue that the Security Council is bound by its resolutions regarding Libya[35] (where it activated the responsibility to protect)[36] to act in the same way in the situation in Syria surely stretches international law a bit too far.

[33] B Bowring, 'Transnistria' (ch 8 in this volume) 157.

[34] R Schaefer (n 27) 4–5: 'Now that the Russian government has so vociferously supported the rights of the North [sic] Ossetians and Abkhazians for independence, it will be difficult to claim that the Chechens, the Circassians, and the rest of the North Caucasus peoples should be denied those same rights. Presently, the Kremlin avoids the inconsistency by saying that the Chechen Republic is happy with its status within the Russian Federation, and as long as current President Ramzan Kadyrov continues to speak for the Chechen people, that will remain the case. However, when President Kadyrov begins to lose control of the Chechen majority and they publicly state their desire to be independent again, Russia will be in a difficult spot'.

[35] UNSC Res 1970 (26 February 2011) UN Doc. S/Res/1970 (2011), and notably UNSC Res 1973 (17 March 2011) UN Doc. S/Res/1973 (2011) (fourth indent of the preamble and para 4).

[36] Contra R Geiß and M Kashgar, 'UN-Maßnahmen gegen Libyen—Eine völkerrechtliche Betrachtung' (2011) 59 *Vereinte Nationen* 3, 99, 100 (for the sake of clarity: Geiß and Kashgar did *not* argue that the Security Council was bound by its Libya resolutions with regard to Syria).

Another soft idea is that of the runaway nature of autonomy: you grant autonomy and, the idea goes, more autonomy will be demanded. Ultimately, you invite secession. Autonomy is the stepping stone towards secession; it, by nature, snowballs.[37] Interestingly, the idea can be made to work the other way around as well: autonomy contains secession.[38] You grant it to forestall secession. Once groups have autonomy, the idea goes, they will see that no secession is needed. If anything, the four case studies support the first line of thinking. All four of the breakaway territories had some sort of autonomous status and now vie for secession. The autonomy they had did not prevent them from striving for secession. Rather, the entities' autonomous status deprived them of the right to secession in the Soviet constitution and thereby set them on the pathway of revolution. The idea is all the more tempting since the situation in Kosovo, too, came about because Kosovo had no right to secede, in contrast to the other constituent republics of Yugoslavia. There is undoubtedly a grain of truth in that idea. However, it is almost certainly flawed. It is an oversimplification to say that the status of autonomy of the four regions propelled forward their claims for secession. Perhaps the clarion call for secession resounded not because of autonomy, but *despite* it. Be that as it may, it was undoubtedly the collapse of the Soviet Union that led to the rally for independence by the constituent republics of the Union. The autonomous entities merely joined the rally and claimed what in fact the Soviet republics had a right to claim. While autonomy might have been one factor in their calculation,

[37] See the description of the argument in S Oeter, 'Minderheiten zwischen Segregation, Integration und Assimilation—Zur Entstehung und Entwicklung des Modells der Kulturautonomie' in D Blumenwitz, G Gornig and D Murswiek (eds), *Ein Jahrhundert Minderheiten- und Volksgruppenschutz* (Verlag Wissenschaft und Politik 2001) 63–82, 80–1: 'Keine Regierung gibt gerne Macht ab, es sei denn aus besserer Einsicht. Die Einsicht aber wird vielfach noch durch die Perhorreszierung jeder Form von Autonomiegewährung blockiert. In zentralen Bürokratien ist der Gedanke nicht auszurotten, dass Autonomie nicht nur zu Kontrollverlusten führt, sondern dass sie den Keim der Auflösung ins sich trägt sowie unweigerlich Ansätze zu Verselbständigung und Sezession fördert.' [No government likes to give up power, unless out of deeper insight. Such insight, however, is often blocked by the repulsion to grant any form of autonomy. In central bureaucracies the thought cannot be eradicated that autonomy does not only lead to a loss of control, but that the nucleus of disintegration is inherent in it and that it inevitably furthers the beginnings of independence and secession.—my translation] See also YT Jabareen, 'Redefining Minority Rights: Successes and Shortcomings of the U.N. Declaration on the Rights of Indigenous Peoples' (2011) 18 UCDJILP 1, 119, 137, with further references in n 107 (the paper also elaborates on the new right to autonomy of indigenous people in the UN General Assembly, United Nations Declaration on the Rights of Indigenous Peoples (UN Doc. A/RES/61/295, GAOR 61th session supp 49, vol 3, 15) 13 September 2007; on the rights of indigenous peoples, see 15 UCLAJILFA 1 (2010), with articles by Robert T Coulter, Ariel E Dulitzky, Lorie M Graham, Catherine J Iorns Magallanes, Rebecca Tsosie, and Siegfried Wiessner, all issuing from a symposium entitled 'Indigenous Peoples' Rights in the International Human Rights Framework: A Comfortable Fit?'). See CR Majinge, 'Southern Sudan and the Struggle for Self-Determination in Contemporary Africa: Examining its Basis Under International Law' (2010) 53 GYIL 541 (who on p. 577 concludes that claims for secession in most African cases, including Southern Sudan, only arose *after* claims for autonomy had not been heeded and the members of the peoples concerned had not been treated as equal citizens).

[38] In that sense: J Lluch, 'Autonomism and Federalism' (2012) 42 Publius 1, 134, 154: 'Most autonomists are nationalists. However, most mainstream autonomists reject the independence alternative, and wish to work within existing state structures.'

it was most probably a minor one, which was outweighed by other factual and political considerations.

The last soft idea was probably best captured by Martti Koskenniemi, who called it the 'onion problem of nationalism'.[39] Minority–majority conflicts can hardly be solved by means of territorial approaches such as secession. Usually, a secession merely reverses the minority–majority position, and the same problems between the two groups involved re-emerge, if only in an inverse constellation on a 'lower level'. The late Thomas Franck discussed a similar idea under the 'ripple effect of postmodern tribalism'.[40] The idea is first of all evident in Kosovo. Kosovars were a minority within Serbia; now the Serbs are a minority within Kosovo as a whole—though not in the north, in Mitrovica, where they are again a majority—and the position would probably be reversed again further down the scale.[41] It is clear that the situation in northern Kosovo, beyond the River Ibar, has become the key challenge after Kosovo's declaration of independence. Undoubtedly, the 'onion problem' is at work here: what was originally an issue between Kosovo and Serbia has been pushed down with the secession to become an issue between Kosovo and Mitrovica (while it continues to simmer between Kosovo and Serbia). While the phenomenon is not very obvious in the case studies in this volume, nonetheless there is indirect evidence. The idea seems to have been at work when the constituent republics that had seceded from the Soviet Union denied the very same benefit (secession) to the four regions that sought to break away from the republics. Consequently, the conflicts were frozen. The population movements which seemingly occurred in some of the four regions—however forceful they may have been—are also testimony to the idea: individual groups moved away from the breakaway regions where a 'new' majority had taken over towards their homeland, notably in South Ossetia and in Nagorno-Karabakh, according to the case studies.

[39] M Koskenniemi (n 28) 260.

[40] TM Franck, 'Postmodern Tribalism and the Right to Secession' in C Brölmann, R Lefeber and M Zieck (eds), *Peoples and Minorities in International Law* (Martinus Nijhoff 1993) 3–27, 19.

[41] It is worth noting again that the 'onion problem' is not always a problem. Quite the contrary, it sometimes can be a key factor contributing to the success of a territorial regime. Joseph Marko pinpointed that aspect for the case of South Tyrol, where the majority/minority position of the Italian and German-speaking population is reversed on each level of the state: in Italy as a whole the Italian-speaking population is the majority; in Alto Adige/Südtirol the German-speaking population is the majority; in Bolzano/Bozen the Italian-speaking population is again the majority. J Marko, 'Südtirol: Zur Frage des Exports einer Konfliktlösung' in J Marko, S Ortino, F Palermo, L Voltmer, and J Woelk (eds), *Die Verfassung der Südtiroler Autonomie* (Nomos 2005) 511–25, 519; see my discussion in T Burri, *Models of Autonomy? Case Studies of Minority Regimes in Hungary and French Polynesia* (Schulthess 2010) 49–50, and in particular n 141. (The book is available in full on <www.thomas-burri.com>.)

VI. And Federalism?

The histories of the United States of America, Germany, Switzerland, and the European Union—indeed, possibly of any federation—bear witness to the fact that federalism is not a simple thing. However, given the (occasional) success of federalism in integrating populations with very different backgrounds, it is tempting to ask the question: would the four cases under scrutiny in this volume benefit if federal arrangements were adopted? Would federalism have the power to tame the quarrelling parties in Abkhazia, Nagorno-Karabakh, South Ossetia, and Transdniestria? Only the real test could, of course, provide a certain answer. However, some indicative evidence already exists. The most recent comes from Bosnia and Herzegovina. The European Court of Human Rights has had the occasion to review the federalism *à la Dayton* in *Sejdić and Finci*.[42] The judgment warrants a closer look as it is a landmark decision with possible implications for the Caucasus.

The Dayton Peace Agreement of December 1995[43] had established the foundations of Bosnia and Herzegovina.[44] It essentially ended years of warfare in Bosnia, the nadir of which had been the massacre in Srebrenica. The Dayton Agreement attempted to bring back together the three constituent communities (Bosniacs, Croats, and Serbs) under one umbrella. At least in restoring peace, the Dayton Agreement has been a success.[45] The Dayton Agreement, which had been brokered by the United States and the other members of the contact group, is 'an extremely complex instrument'.[46] It provided the constitution for the successor state of Bosnia and Herzegovina in annex 4. With the territorial integrity of Bosnia carved in stone,[47] Dayton essentially validated the federation agreed between Bosniacs and Croats in 1994[48] and put it next to the Republika Srpska, which encompassed most of the Bosnian Serb population (at least since the end of the war). The two entities were endowed with extensive powers while the overarching roof, the *Mantelstaat*[49] of Bosnia and Herzegovina, was kept to a

[42] European Court of Human Rights (Grand Chamber), *Sejdić and Finci* v *Bosnia and Herzegovina* [2009] Applications nos. 27996/06 and 34836/06.

[43] General Framework Agreement for Peace in Bosnia and Herzegovina with Annexes [Dayton Agreement] (35 ILM 75 (1996)) 14 December 1995.

[44] For an overview of the 15 years since Dayton: V Džihić, 'Bosnien und Herzegowina in der Sackgasse? Struktur und Dynamik der Krise fünfzehn Jahre nach Dayton' (2011) 59 Südosteuropa 1, 50.

[45] PC McMahon and J Western, 'The Death of Dayton—How to Stop Bosnia From Falling Apart' (2009) Foreign Affairs (September/October) 69, 72: 'The Dayton framework had many advantages. It stopped the bloodshed, and it created the conditions for life to return to normal—at least on the surface'.

[46] PC Szasz, 'Introductory Note [to the Dayton Peace Agreement]' (1996) 35 ILM 75, 77.

[47] PC Szasz (n 45) 75: '[...] in a way that respected the international personality and territorial integrity of Bosnia-Herzegovina, which was an important condition set by the international community'.

[48] PC Szasz (n 45) 76.

[49] V Epping (n 5) 25, 34.

minimum. In the institutions of this overarching state, strict parity between the three constituent communities has been the rule. In particular, the office of the president has been tripled. Representatives of each of the three communities act together as the presidency of Bosnia and Herzegovina. Ethnical *Proporz* has also been the rule for one chamber of the parliament (the House of the Peoples), where a third of the members are appointed by each of the three communities on an ethnic basis (while the House of Representatives, the other chamber, is constituted through elections in each community, resulting only in a de facto ethnic *Proporz*). Essentially, when a community considers a matter to be of vital interest, it has the power to veto a decision (arts IV(3)e–f and V(2)c–d of the constitution of Bosnia and Herzegovina).[50]

The central state has become largely inoperable.[51] Obstruction by either the Serb, Croat, or Bosniac community has become more the rule than the exception it had initially been intended as.[52] The High Representative of the international community, designated pursuant to Art. 1(2) annex 10 of the Dayton Agreement, quickly had to intervene to substitute for the blocked organs of Bosnia and Herzegovina, and use of this safeguard mechanism has become common: as of April 2009, Wählisch had counted 860 acts in which the High Representative substituted for the local powers.[53]

However, not only Serbs, Croats, and Bosniacs have been living in Bosnia and Herzegovina. 'Others', mentioned as such by the preamble of the constitution, have always been present in the territory of Bosnia, too. However, if these 'others' for some reason fail to affiliate themselves with either the Serb, the Croat, or the Bosniac community, they are not eligible in elections to the House of Peoples or the presidency. The declaration of affiliation is based on self-identification.

Mr Dervo Sejdić was of Roma origin. Mr Jakob Finci was of Jewish belief. They both held a number of highly respected positions on behalf of their communities in Bosnia and Herzegovina. Since they refused to affiliate with one of the constituent peoples of Bosnia, they were not eligible to the House of Peoples nor to the tripartite presidency. They went to the European Court of Human Rights alleging that the ethnic *Proporz* system violated their rights under the European Convention of Human Rights[54] and, 14 years after the Dayton Peace Agreement

[50] This construction is commonly seen as an ethnic federation. For a differentiated view highlighting territorial elements, see S Keil, 'Mythos und Realität eines ethnischen Föderalismus in Bosnien und Herzegowina' (2010) 50 Südosteuropa Mitteilungen 1, 76.

[51] See OJ Rolofs, 'Bosnien-Herzegowina: Kein Licht am Ende des Tunnels' (2010) 50 Südosteuropa Mitteilungen 1, 42, who pointed to the fact that for the first time since Dayton, media and politicians have spoken of 'war' again (43); he also discussed the looming secession of Republika Srpska (48).

[52] D Sarajlić-Maglić, 'Bosnia and Herzegovina: Will Europe Make Democracy Work?' (2009) 57 Südosteuropa 2/3, 168, 173 and 185 (pointing at the 'lack of a consensual political culture').

[53] M Wählisch, 'Internationale Organisationen als Staatsersatz? Bosnien-Herzegowina als Modell der Relativierung von Staatlichkeit' in C Tomuschat (ed), *Weltordnungsmodelle für das 21. Jahrhundert* (Nomos 2009) 163–208, 169.

[54] For the preceding judgment of the Constitutional Court of Bosnia and Herzegovina, see for instance A Engl and B Harzl, 'The Inter-relationship between International and National Minority-Rights Law in Selected Western Balkan States' (2009) 34 RCEEL 307.

had been signed, the European Court of Human Rights acceded to their claim. The applicants' barring from election to the smaller chamber of the parliament violated the prohibition of discrimination (Art. 14 ECHR) in conjunction with the right to free elections (Art. 3 of the first Protocol;[55] paras 39–50). Given that the right to free elections was not applicable to executive elections, the Court found the exclusion from elections to the presidency to violate the independent general prohibition of non-discrimination contained in Art. 1 of Protocol no. 12 (paras 53–56).[56] The justification for the ethnic *Proporz* was probably the most interesting issue. Unfortunately, the judgment of the European Court of Human Rights was tersest here: the Court equated discrimination based on ethnicity with discrimination based on race. Justification of restrictions of fundamental rights based on ethnicity had to be interpreted as strictly as possible (while positive discrimination in principle was not precluded). The Court acknowledged that restoration of peace was an 'aim broadly compatible with the general objectives of the Convention' (para 45) and that the situation at the time at which the Dayton Agreement was signed was difficult: peace between the warring parties had to be restored and the state of affairs had been highly fragile. At that time the situation 'could explain, without necessarily justifying' (para 45) the exclusion from peace negotiations of the groups to which the applicants belonged and the ensuing emphasis on equality focusing exclusively on the constituent peoples (ie Bosniacs, Croats, and Serbs). However, since at the time that the Dayton Agreement was signed Bosnia and Herzegovina had not been a party to the Convention, the Court was not competent *ratione temporis* to rule on the situation at that time. In any case, the existing exclusion of the applicants from the elections was disproportionate (para 46). As alternative proposals for less restrictive electoral systems existed, the restrictions of the rights could not be justified (paras 50, 56).

The ruling of the European Court of Human Rights in *Sejdić and Finci* hardly came as a surprise. It merely confirmed that the constitution of Bosnia and Herzegovina was in need of reconsideration.[57] The Court's human rights

[55] Council of Europe, Protocol to the Convention for the Protection of Human Rights and Fundamental Freedoms (CETS no. 009) 20 March 1952.

[56] Council of Europe, Protocol no. 12 to the Convention for the Protection of Human Rights and Fundamental Freedoms (CETS no. 177) 4 November 2000. The judgment is the first application of the general principle of non-discrimination of Protocol no. 12. See the general remarks in the partly concurring and partly dissenting opinion of judge Mijović, joined by judge Hajiyev, appended to the European Court of Human Rights (Grand Chamber), *Sejdić and Finci* v *Bosnia and Herzegovina* [2009] Application nos 27996/06 and 34836/06. Some member states of the Council of Europe have not yet ratified Protocol no. 12—among them France, Germany, Switzerland, and the United Kingdom.

[57] See for instance Rolofs (n 50) 42, 59, who notes the need to reform the constitution to make the central state operable. On constitutional reform in Bosnia and Herzegovina, see S Gavrić and D Banović, 'Constitutional Reform in Bosnia and Herzegovina—Procedures, Challenges, Recommendations' (2010) 50 Südosteuropa Mitteilungen 1, 60. Note, however, that the judgment was one of the rare occasions, if not the only one, on which the European Court of Human Rights found that a national constitution violated the European Convention of Human Rights: Anne Peters responding to the EJIL talk! blog of M Milanovic, 'Grand Chamber Judgment in Sejdic and Finci v. Bosnia', 22 December 2009, <http://www.ejiltalk.org/grand-chamber-judgment-in-sejdic-and-fi nci-v-bosnia/> accessed 4 August 2012.

perspective, moreover, largely chimes with more security-oriented assessments.[58] However, the European Court of Human Rights avoided the toughest nut to crack—the question of whether structures based on ethnic/national affiliation are permissible from a human rights perspective in the phase *immediately after violent conflict*. The debate on whether an 'accommodationist' or an 'integrationist' approach[59] (based on group characteristics such as ethnicity or on a civil, 'French' understanding of the nation, respectively) is better suited to address post-conflict challenges therefore continues. While the development under the Dayton Agreement and the current status quo in Bosnia and Herzegovina suggest that the accommodationist approach has failed because it has further entrenched ethnicization rather than demobilizing the once warring groups, the integrationist approach fails to present credible alternatives for the immediate post-conflict phase. It would certainly be naïve to believe that truth commissions and reconciliation efforts would do the job of stabilizing peace in the immediate post-conflict phase, during which the stage is often held by 'ethnic entrepreneurs'[60] who draw on resentment. Ethnic demobilization[61] must certainly be the main aim in that phase, but it remains uncertain how this goal is to be achieved without formally separating the warring parties.

In contrast, it follows from the *Sejdić* ruling that *in a later phase*, some time after hostilities have ceased in an ethnically driven conflict, when peace has been consolidated and rebuilding is under way, accommodation of ethnicity must no longer have an exclusive effect. At that point in time, the ethnic argument must recede—though not necessarily vanish altogether[62]—and progressively leave the stage to the forces of free and civil democracy. Of course, those who drafted the

[58] McMahon and Western (n 44) 71, seeing three broader risks in the current situation of Bosnia and Herzegovina (and notably in a short-term exit from Bosnia): the resumption of violence in Bosnia, sending the wrong signal to the worldwide Muslim community (by abandoning Bosniacs) and darkening the prospects of state building in general due to the failure in Bosnia. For an alternative assessment of Bosnia and Herzegovina under the aspect of the war economy (including the related crimes and the judicial means to address them effectively) see J Eichlin, 'Undercutting the Political Economy of Conflict in Bosnia and Herzegovina: A Transitional Justice Approach to Prosecuting Systemic Economic Crimes' (2010) 48 CJTL 2, 353, 353–98.

[59] J Marko, 'Processes of Ethnic Mobilization in the Former Yugoslav Republics Reconsidered' (2010) 34 Southeastern Europe 1, 1, 4.

[60] Marko (n 58) 13.

[61] On ethnic (de)mobilization see also A Mujkic, 'Ethnic Mobilization in the Former Yugoslavia as a Kind of Structural Setting and Framing' (2010) 34 Southeastern Europe 1, 16.

[62] In different circumstances a system based on ethnic or national affiliation could well be reconciled with human rights: when a minority is about to disappear through a process of integration, a system of cultural autonomy is compatible with human rights. The reservation of positive discrimination made by the Court in *Sejdić* (para 44) leaves the necessary room. However, 'special measures' regularly require closer scrutiny, for they often mask particularly elaborate schemes of discrimination, for instance with regard to Roma minorities—see eg H-P Folz, 'Ethnische Diskriminierung im Bildungswesen—Das Urteil der Grossen Kammer des Europäischen Gerichtshofs für Menschenrechte in der Sache D.H./Tschechische Republik vom 13. November 2007' (2009) Recht der Jugend und des Bildungswesens 3, 395, 395–405, regarding segregation of Roma children in Czech schools; compare with T Pilvi, 'Segregated Education and Texts: A Challenge to Peace in Bosnia and Herzegovina' (2009) 26 IJWP 2, 65, for schools in Bosnia and Herzegovina.

Dayton Agreement had also given thought to such a phasing out. They therefore included a directly effective, overriding human rights clause in the constitution of Bosnia and Herzegovina via the Dayton Agreement. That clause has now been given fresh content by the Court.

Unfortunately, *Sejdić* does not provide clear guidance on whether federalism is an option to be pursued in the Caucasus. The judgment was about the inclusion of those minorities in the post-conflict phases that were not involved as principal, larger parties (ie Bosniacs, Croats, or Serbs) in a conflict, but were rather smaller groups that had also suffered from the conflict (people of Jewish and Roma origin). However, the tone underlying the judgment is that exclusive ethnic federalism is no option in the long run. That is confirmed by the current fragile state of Bosnia and Herzegovina. The lesson from Dayton seems to be that federalism is not the key to unlock a bright future in a situation of deep division, but rather a key to lock up the past for the time being. There are other such keys, such as federalism, autonomy, or even secession. However, whether deep divisions can be overcome does not depend so much on which key is chosen as on other factors.

VII. Conclusion

What if secession is not a solution per se? What if a secession—remedial or not—does not solve the underlying problem, but is part of it? What if the law of self-determination, and international law more generally, feeds the problem instead of solving it? The recent developments in South Sudan, the latest product of secession, certainly do not dispel these suspicions.[63] They also come to the fore in Christopher Water's last sentence, where he mentions an 'obsession with status'[64] as one root of the problems in South Ossetia. Arguably, such obsession with status is not just a problem of Ossetia. It might well be ingrained in all of international law. Most privileges in international law are attached to the status of a state. Is it surprising then that so many strive for that status?

The situation for a state is like that of any binary good: you either have it or you do not. Think only of the nuclear weapon.[65] One has it and is inside the club or one does not and is outside. To prevent endless struggles, and definitely to settle a problem involving binary goods, two options are available: everyone gets it or no one does. For nuclear weapons, this means either distributing them to all or disarming everyone. For statehood, this either means opening it up to all players, making it available to everyone who desires it, or rethinking the concept as such (if not abolishing it altogether). The situation for statehood, moreover, is

[63] See only the newspaper reporting, such as 'Clinton pocht auf Friedensvertrag' *Süddeutsche (online)* (München, 3 August 2012), <http://www.sueddeutsche.de/politik/frieden-im-sudan-clinton-mahnt-zur-eile-1.1430740> accessed 3 August 2012.

[64] C Waters, 'South Ossetia' (ch 9 in this volume) 190.

[65] On the latest in this regard, see DH Joyner, 'Recent Developments in International Law Regarding Nuclear Weapons' (2011) 60 ICLQ 1, 209.

comparatively favourable because fewer collective action problems are involved than is the case with nuclear weapons (and it is harder to hide statehood). Of course, these perspectives are utopian—though only to some extent.[66] On the one hand, would it not have defused, perhaps even prevented in the first place, conflicts such as those in South Ossetia, Abkhazia, Nagorno-Karabakh, and Transdniestria if at the pivotal moment a state had been a freely available option for *all*, including those within these regions? A step towards such a solution would be smaller than it may now seem. The solution proposed by the Supreme Court of Canada in *Reference re Secession*, when it answered the first question in the light of the Canadian constitution, would probably suffice:[67] when there is a clear will to secede, good faith negotiations must be undertaken to work towards that aim. On the other hand, would it not defuse conflicts if a third option was available, a *tertium* with an official international status similar to that of the state?

[66] In a similar sense: L Sheshagiri, 'Democratic Disobedience: Reconceiving Self-Determination and Secession at International Law' (2010) 51 HILJ 2, 553, 598: 'Where consensual separation or full-scale revolution (in the Arendtian sense) is unlikely, a disobedience approach stressing non-violence and leading to a negotiated solution may be the preferable way forward. The goal, no doubt optimistic, is a fuller measure of self-determination for all'. For a positive note on recent developments in the Balkan that, in a sense, put statehood in a different perspective, too, see I Ristić, 'Rapprochement as a Paradigm Shift: Does the Wheel Come Full Circle in Former Yugoslavia?' (2011) 59 Südosteuropa 3, 286, arguing that bottom-up processes are underway that tend towards convergence in the Balkans.

[67] Supreme Court of Canada, *Reference re Secession of Quebec* [1998] (n 30), first question, paras 32 et seq.

PART II

CASE STUDIES FROM THE COMMONWEALTH OF INDEPENDENT STATES

8

Transnistria

Bill Bowring

I. Introduction

This case study concerns an unrecognized entity which, having been a paradigm of 'frozen conflict', may soon start to thaw. There is no consensus as to its name. Most of the scholarly literature refers to it as 'Transnistria'; however, in its judgments in 2004 in *Ilaşcu and Others* v *Moldova and Russia*[1] and in 2011 in *Ivanţoc and Others* v *Moldova and Russia*[2] the European Court of Human Rights (ECHR) refers to it as the 'Moldavian Republic of Transdniestria (MRT)', while in 2012 in *Catan* v *Moldova and Russia*[3] the ECHR refers to it as both 'Transdniestria' and 'the MRT'. The entity in question calls itself in Russian the 'Pridnestrovskaya Moldavskaya Respublika (PMR)' or 'Pridnestrovie', or in English 'Transdniestria'. The New York Bar mission, mentioned below, referred to it as the 'Transnistrian Moldovan Republic' (TMR). I will stick to 'the PMR'.

On 28 December 2007, Igor Smirnov, president of the PMR from its declaration of independence on 2 September 1990 to his fall on 16 December 2011, said that '[b]oth legally and historically, Transdniestria has a better claim to independence than Kosovo'.[4] This case study will examine that claim.

In this case study I refer to a wide range of scholarly material. In February 2004 I participated in a Mission to Moldova including the PMR on behalf of the International Commission of Jurists. We spent a week in Moldova, and our Report, entitled 'Attacks on Justice: The Rule of Law in Moldova', was published on 30 November 2004.[5] I also draw from the legal assessment report published in 2005 by the New York Bar Association, which considered in depth one of the

[1] Application no. 48787/99, judgment of 8 July 2004.

[2] Application no. 23687/05, judgment of 15 November 2011.

[3] Application nos. 43370/04, 8252/05 and 18454/06, judgment of 19 October 2012.

[4] This appeared on former President Smirnov's official website as late as 9 December 2011. This has of course now vanished.

[5] B Bowring, C L'Heureux-Dubé and L Besharaty-Movaed, *Attacks on Justice: The Rule of Law in Moldova* (International Commission of Jurists 2005) at <http://www.icj.org/attacks-on-justice-2005-moldova/> accessed 4 February 2014.

central issues for this collection: whether the PMR has a right under international law to autonomy or possibly sovereignty.[6]

This is not a report on human rights violations in Transnistria; there have been many egregious violations, aptly summed up in the US State Department's Report on Human Rights in Moldova in 2011:

> Transnistrian authorities restricted political activity and interfered with the ability of Moldovan citizens living in Transnistria to vote in Moldovan elections. Torture, arbitrary arrests, and unlawful detentions were regularly reported. Transnistrian authorities harassed independent media and opposition lawmakers, restricted freedom of association, movement, and religion, and discriminated against Romanian speakers.[7]

The Report gives details of grave violations under every heading. The human rights situation in Moldova is bad; that in the PMR is worse.

The structure of this case study is as follows. First, I describe the geographical location of the PMR, and its population. Second, I analyse the history of this territory. It is generally agreed that the left, east, bank of the Dnester river has an identity quite different from that of the right, west, bank, previously known as Bessarabia. Third, I describe the institutions of the PMR, and its industrial base. Fourth, I analyse the ethnic composition and identity of the population of the PMR. Fifth, I consider whether the PMR could have a claim to self-determination, internal or external. I conclude on a note of optimism.

Two aspects of the history of the PMR since 1990 are of particular significance. First, not only is its territory separated from Moldova by the river, but its history has followed a very different course from that of the 'right bank'. Its population is ethnically and linguistically distinct from that of the rest of Moldova. Second, Russia, which has been found by the European Court of Human Rights to exercise effective control over its territory, has consistently insisted that the PMR must remain part of Moldova, albeit with guarantees and a special status. Russia does not and has not supported independence for the PMR, or any kind of closer association with Russia.

II. Location and Population

The territory in question lies mostly to the left (eastern) bank of a river which changes its name several times as it flows to the Black Sea. It is called Dnister at its beginning in Ukraine, Nistru in Moldova, and in its final passage to the Black Sea becomes the Dnester.[8] So 'Transnistria' is the Moldovan (Romanian) name of the territory. I will refer to the Dnester river.

[6] At <www.nycbar.org/pdf/report/NYCity%20BarTransnistriaReport.pdf>.

[7] At <http://www.state.gov/j/drl/rls/hrrpt/humanrightsreport/index.htm#wrapper> accessed 24 November 2012.

[8] <http://www.european-waterways.eu/e/info/moldova/nistru_dnester_dniestr_dnistr.php>.

The population of Moldova was estimated by the CIA to be 3,656,843 as at July 2012 and was 3,938,679 in the 2004 census.[9] The 2004 census gave Moldova's ethnic composition as Moldovan/Romanian 78.2%, Ukrainian 8.4%, Russian 5.8%, Gagauz (a Turkic minority) 4.4%, Bulgarian 1.9%, other 1.3%. The PMR held its own census simultaneously, showing a population of 555,347 people (a fall from 679,000 in 1989), including Moldovan 32.10%, Russian 30.35%, Ukrainian 28.81%, Bulgarian 2.50%, Gagauz 0.74%, Roma 0.09%, Jewish 0.23%, Polish 0.32% and other 4.94%.[10]

III. History

In his dissenting opinion in *Ilaşcu*, the Russian Judge Anatoly Kovler sought to remedy the fact that the majority of the Court failed to consider the history of the left (east) bank of the Dniester (Nistru) river.

1. History prior to 1991

The only reference by the ECHR to pre-1991 history in *Ilaşcu* was the following:

> 28. The Moldavian Soviet Socialist Republic, which was set up by a decision of the Supreme Soviet of the USSR on 2 August 1940, was formed from a part of Bessarabia taken from Romania on 28 June 1940 following the Molotov-Ribbentrop Pact between the USSR and Germany, where the majority of the population were Romanian speakers, and a strip of land on the left bank of the Dniester in Ukraine (USSR), Transdniestria, which was transferred to it in 1940, and is inhabited by a population whose linguistic composition in 1989, according to publicly available information, was 40% Moldavian, 28% Ukrainian, 24% Russian and 8% others.

That is, in population terms, Moldovans were a minority on the left (east) bank.

Judge Kovler asserted[11] that the Court should have started its historical account considerably earlier. On his account, prior to 1360 the territory of Moldova was part of Hungary. In that year the principality of Moldova was created. In 1456 the principality was conquered by the Ottoman empire, and remained under Ottoman rule for several centuries. In 1711 Prince Dmitri Kantemir of Moldova and Peter the Great agreed that Russia should protect Moldova, and in 1791, following the war between Russia and Turkey, their peace treaty ceded control of the left (east) bank of the Dnester, where a high proportion of the population were Slavs, to Russia. The Treaty of Bucharest of 1812, concluded following further conflict between Russia and Turkey, incorporated the territory of Moldova between the Prut and the Dnester. This was named Bessarabia.

[9] <https://www.cia.gov/library/publications/the-world-factbook/geos/md.html> accessed 24 November 2012.

[10] <http://www.olvia.idknet.com/ol37-09-05.htm>.

[11] *Ilaşcu* 144–5.

Having lost the Crimean War (1854–6), Russia was obliged to cede Bessarabia, which was included in the Kingdom of Romania, created in 1859. However, in 1878 the Treaty of Berlin returned Bessarabia to Russia, and Romania obtained Dobruja in compensation. In January 1918 Romania occupied Bessarabia and secured a vote from the local assembly in favour of its attachment to the Kingdom. At the same time, the Directory of Ukraine (at that time independent) proclaimed its sovereignty over the left (east) bank of the Dnester. At that time 48% of the population was Ukrainian, 30% Moldavian, 9% Russian, and 8.5% Jewish. In 1924 a Moldavian autonomous republic was created there. After 1924 the USSR compelled Romania to hold a plebiscite in Bessarabia, before occupying Bessarabia on 28 June 1940.

It is therefore the case that the left (east) bank of the Dnester has had a distinct, Slavic, identity since the late eighteenth century. Kolstø and Malgin confirmed this in 1998:

> The right and left banks of the Dnestr are regional entities with rather different historical fates. In contrast to Bessarabia, the left bank has never been a part of the Romanian state. The Moldovan settlements here are newer than in Bessarabia and from the outset have been heavily exposed to Slavic culture.[12]

Another account is given by Andreas Johanssen.[13] He also explains how in the period following the Napoleonic wars, that is from 1812 to 1917, the eastern half of Romanian Moldavia, the territory between the rivers Prut and Dnester, was a part of the Russian empire and was known as Bessarabia. Bessarabia declared its independence following World War I, and shortly afterwards the Moldova Republic (minus Bessarabia) voted to join Romania. The USSR considered Bessarabia still part of its territory and, following the Molotov–Ribbentrop Pact invaded Bessarabia and the remaining parts of Moldova, despite Romanian protests.[14] He also points out that even as a joint republic, the Transnistrian part of the MSSR was deemed more trustworthy by Moscow. It was from Transnistria that much of the political leadership came, and the bulk of heavy industry was accordingly based there. Examples of the latter category are the metallurgical plant in Rıbnitsa and the hydroelectric plant in Dubasari.[15]

The 2005 New York Bar Report also addressed the question of history, citing Charles King for the proposition that Transnistria was not part of traditional Romanian territory and was a classic borderland.[16] From the ninth to the fourteenth centuries it was part of Kievan Rus;[17] it then fell under Ottoman rule and, from 1812, was part of Russia.

[12] P Kolstø and A Malgin, 'The Transnistrian Republic: A Case of Politicized Regionalism' (1998) 26 NP 103–27, 106.

[13] A Johansson, 'The Transnistrian Conflict after the 2005 Moldovan Parliamentary Elections' (2006) 22 JCSTP 507–16.

[14] Johansson (n 13) 508.

[15] Johansson (n 13) 509.

[16] C King, *The Moldovans: Romania, Russia, and the Politics of Culture* (Studies of Nationalities) (Hoover Institution Press 2000) 181.

[17] King (n 16) 179.

It seems clear, taking these sources together, that the territory of the PMR has a very different history from the territory, formerly Bessarabia, to the west of the Dnester river. The fact that in the USSR it became part of the Moldovan SSR, and hence part of independent Moldova after 1991, is one of many historical anomalies thrown up by the rather arbitrary Soviet territorial organization.

2. History after 1991[18]

According to the 1978 Constitution of the Moldavian SSR, there were two official languages in Moldova: Russian and 'Moldavian' (Moldovan/Romanian written with the Cyrillic alphabet). In August–September 1989 the Latin alphabet was reintroduced in Moldova for written Moldovan/Romanian, which became the first official language.

On 23 June 1990 Moldova proclaimed its sovereignty, along with many other autonomous subjects of the USSR; on 23 May 1991 it changed its name to the Republic of Moldova, and on 27 August 1991 the Moldovan parliament adopted the Declaration of Independence of the Republic of Moldova, whose territory included Transdniestria. The USSR finally collapsed in December 1991.

From 1989 onwards, ethnic Russians and Ukrainians in Transdniestria began to organize a movement of resistance to incorporation in a new Republic of Moldova. On 2 September 1990, shortly after the Moldovan Declaration of Independence, these Transdniestrian separatists announced the creation of the PMR. On 25 August 1991 the 'Supreme Council of the PMR' adopted the Declaration of Independence of the PMR. On 1 December 1991 a presidential election was organized in the Transdniestrian provinces and Mr Igor Smirnov was elected president of the PMR. The Moldovan authorities declared this election to be illegal.

At the time of Moldova's declaration of independence, it did not have its own army. The USSR's 14th Army, whose headquarters had been in Chişinău since 1956, remained on Moldovan territory, although from 1990 onwards equipment and personnel began to be withdrawn. In 1991 the 14th Army in Moldova was composed of several thousand soldiers, infantry units, artillery (notably an anti-aircraft missile system), armoured vehicles, and aircraft (including planes and strike helicopters). It had a number of ammunition stores, including one of the largest in Europe at Colbaşna in Transdniestria.

By Decree no. 234 of 14 November 1991, the President of Moldova declared that ammunition, weapons, military transport, military bases, and other property belonging to the military units of the Soviet armed forces stationed in Moldovan territory were the property of the Republic of Moldova. By his own Decree, dated 5 December 1991, President Smirnov decided to place the military units of the 14th Army deployed in the PMR under the command of 'the National Defence and Security Department of the PMR'. On 1 April 1992 Russia took back control of its forces.

[18] This historical account is drawn from the judgment of the Grand Chamber of the ECHR in *Catan*.

At the end of 1991 and the beginning of 1992 violent clashes broke out between the PMR and Moldovan armed forces, and several hundred people died. On 21 July 1992 Mircea Snegur, President of the Republic of Moldova, and Boris Yeltsin, President of the RSFSR, signed an agreement on the principles for the friendly settlement of the armed conflict in the Transdniestrian region of the Republic of Moldova. This agreement created a security zone from which the forces of the 'parties to the conflict' withdrew (Article 1(2)). Under Article 2 of the agreement, a Joint Control Commission (JCC) was set up, composed of representatives of Moldova, the Russian Federation, and the PMR, with its headquarters in Tighina. The agreement established a peacekeeping force composed of five Russian battalions, three Moldovan battalions, and two PMR battalions subordinate to the JCC. Article 4 required Russian troops stationed in the territory of the Republic of Moldova to remain strictly neutral. Article 5 prohibited sanctions or blockades and laid down the objective of removing all obstacles to the free movement of goods, services, and persons.

Immediately after the ceasefire in 1992, the OSCE became the lead international organization concerned with the PMR. Its current mission was established in February 1993. In April 1993 it opened an office in Chisinau, and it opened an office in Tiraspol in 1995. The OSCE's first intervention was the 1993 'Report No. 13 of the CSCE Mission to Moldova'.[19] This proposed the setting up of a Special Region of Transdniestria with its own regional executive, elective assembly, and court. This status would be established by agreement between both sides and implemented by a Moldovan law, with a guarantee in the new Constitution. The Special Region would be an integral part of the Republic of Moldova but enjoy considerable self-rule. If in future Moldova should choose to give up statehood in order to merge with another country (that is, Romania), the Special Region of Transdniestria would be guaranteed the right of 'external self-determination', ie to determine its own future. This Report referred to 'internal self-determination' in the cases of the Basque Country in Spain and Trentino–South Tyrol in Italy.

On 29 July 1994 Moldova adopted a new Constitution. It provided that Moldova was neutral, that it prohibited the stationing in its territory of troops belonging to other states, and that a form of autonomy might be granted to regions which included some areas on the left bank of the Dnester. According to Article 13 of the Constitution, the national language was Moldovan, to be written using the Latin alphabet.

3. The Primakov Memorandum

On 8 May 1997 in Moscow, President Petru Lucinschi of Moldova and President Smirnov of the PMR signed a memorandum laying down the basis for the normalization of relations between the Republic of Moldova and the PMR. This was known as the Moscow Memorandum (or Primakov Memorandum, after the then Russian Prime Minister).[20]

[19] At <http://www.osce.org/moldova/42307>.

[20] In English at <http://www.osce.org/moldova/42309>.

Decisions concerning the territory of the PMR were to be agreed by both sides, powers were to be shared and delegated, and guarantees were to be secured reciprocally. The PMR had to be allowed to participate in the conduct of the Republic of Moldova's foreign policy on questions concerning its own interests to be defined by mutual agreement. The PMR would have the right unilaterally to establish and maintain international contacts in economic, scientific, technical, cultural, and other fields, to be determined by mutual agreement. The parties undertook to settle conflicts through negotiation, with the assistance where necessary of the Russian Federation and Ukraine, as guarantors of compliance, and of the OSCE and the Commonwealth of Independent States (CIS). The 1997 Memorandum was countersigned by the representatives of the guarantor states, namely President Yeltsin for the Russian Federation and President Kuchma for Ukraine, and by Mr Helveg Petersen, the President of the OSCE.

At the sixth summit of the OSCE in Istanbul in November 1999, 54 Member states signed the Charter for European Security and the Istanbul Summit Declaration and 30 Member states, including Moldova and Russia, signed the Agreement on the Adaptation of the Treaty on Conventional Armed Forces in Europe (CFE). This enshrined the principle that foreign troops should not be stationed in Moldovan territory without Moldovan consent. Russia's agreement to withdraw from the PMR (one of the 'Istanbul Commitments') was set out in an Annex to the adapted CFE Final Act. In addition, the Istanbul Summit Declaration, at paragraph 19, recorded the Russian Federation's commitment to withdraw its forces from Transdniestria by the end of 2002.

4. The Kozak Memorandum

The Communist Party of Moldova won the Moldovan elections in 2001 and the new President of Moldova, Vladimir Voronin, entered into direct negotiation with Russia over the future of the PMR. In November 2003, Russia put forward a settlement proposal, the 'Memorandum on the Basic Principles of the State Structure of the United State'—named the Kozak Memorandum after the Russian civil servant, Dimitry Kozak, who drafted it.[21]

The Kozak Memorandum proposed a new federal structure for Moldova, under which the authorities of the PMR would have a substantial degree of autonomy and guaranteed representation in the new federal legislature. It included transitional provisions under which, until 2015, a three-quarters majority in a newly created second chamber, composed of four representatives from Gagauzia, nine from Transdniestria, and 13 from the new federal legislature's first chamber, would have been required to confirm federal organic laws. This would have given the Transdniestrian representatives in the second chamber an effective veto over any legislation affecting all of Moldova until 2015.

[21] <http://www.regnum.ru/news/458547.html> (in Russian); <http://www.stefanwolff.com/files/Kozak-Memorandum.pdf> (in English).

On 25 November 2003, having previously indicated his willingness to accept these proposals, Mr Voronin decided not to sign the Kozak Memorandum.

There was yet another attempt under the Bulgarian Chairmanship of the OSCE in 2004: the 'Proposals and Recommendations of the Mediators from the OSCE, the Russian Federation, and Ukraine with regard to the Transdniestrian Settlement'.[22] This also proposed a federal state of Moldova, of which Transdniestria would be a subject. However, Steve Roper argues:

> One of the reasons why the federalization plan for Moldova has been so problematic is that there is widespread disagreement among scholars and governmental participants as to the nature and conceptualization of federalism and even what a federal state should look like.[23]

5. The Ukrainian plan

In January 2005, in the 'Orange Revolution', Viktor Yushchenko was elected President of Ukraine. In May 2005 the Ukrainian Government introduced a new proposal for the resolution of the Transdniestrian conflict, 'Towards a Settlement through Democratization'. In July 2005, on the basis of the Ukrainian plan, the Moldovan parliament adopted a law, 'On the Basic Principles of a Special Legal Status of Transdniestria'. Formal negotiations resumed in October 2005, with the European Union and the United States of America participating as observers (referred to as 'the 5+2 talks').

Wolff points out that as required by the 2005 Ukrainian Plan, the Parliament of Moldova passed a law, 'On Fundamental Regulations of the Special Legal Status of Settlements on the Left Bank of the River Nistru (Transnistria)', on 22 July 2005 (the Moldovan Framework Law). But Moldovan thinking is to be found in a 2007 package proposal for a 'Declaration Concerning Principles and Guarantees of the Transnistrian Settlement' and, appended to it, a 'Draft Law on the Special Legal Status of Transnistria'[24] (known as the Moldovan Package Proposal).[25] This proposed that 'Transnistria is an administrative-territorial unit in the form of a republic within the Republic of Moldova…The status of Transnistria within the Republic of Moldova will be determined by Law on the Special Legal Status of Transnistria and will be confirmed accordingly in the Constitution of the Republic of Moldova'.

No doubt in order to strengthen his own bargaining position, President Smirnov organized a referendum in September 2006 in which PMR citizens voted overwhelmingly—with 97% in favour—for independence and 'free association with Russia'.[26]

[22] <http://www.osce.org/moldova/23585> accessed 25 November 2012.

[23] SD Roper, 'Federalization and Constitution-Making as an Instrument of Conflict Resolution' (2004) Demokratizatsiya 527–39, 528.

[24] <http://www.stefanwolff.com/files/Moldovan-Package-Proposals.pdf> accessed 25 November 2012.

[25] Wolff (n 21) 11–12.

[26] E Berg, 'Parent States *versus* Secessionist Entities: Measuring Political Legitimacy in Cyprus, Moldova and Bosnia & Herzegovina' (2012) 64 Europe-Asia Studies 1271–1296, 1282.

Following its victory in the 'Five Day War' against Georgia in August 2008,[27] Russia showed no signs of encouraging the PMR's claim to independence. The commentator Dmitri Trenin wrote in 2009 that in the year of writing, Russian policy focused on revitalizing the peace process in Moldova and closing an agreement between Chisinau and Tiraspol on the modalities of a common Moldovan state.[28] This was despite the fact that following their recognition by Russia, Abkhazia and South Ossetia opened representations in Tiraspol, and the PMR in turn opened representations in Sukhumi (the capital of Abkhazia) and Tskhinvali (the capital of South Ossetia). However, these entities, themselves recognized only by Russia and a handful of other states, will not recognize the PMR. As Maxim Kuzovlev pointed out, Ossetia and Abkhazia would not dare to establish diplomatic relations with the PMR without Russia's consent.[29] Such consent will not be forthcoming.

6. The unexpected fall of President Smirnov

The elections which took place on Sunday 12 December 2011 took all observers by surprise, especially those who considered the PMR to be under strict Russian control, or at any rate believed that the Smirnov regime could not be shaken. After all, in its 2004 judgment in *Ilaşcu* the Strasbourg Court held that:

> 392. All of the above proves that the 'MRT', set up in 1991–92 with the support of the Russian Federation, vested with organs of power and its own administration, remains under the effective authority, or at the very least under the decisive influence, of the Russian Federation, and in any event that it survives by virtue of the military, economic, financial and political support given to it by the Russian Federation.

Stefan Wolff, writing earlier in 2011, did not anticipate such a change.[30] Theodor Tudoroiu, writing in April 2012, regarded Smirnov as a fixed element in the PMR, believing that Smirnov might even contemplate the ignition of small-scale armed conflict to ensure a large-scale mobilization in the PMR to enhance the legitimacy of his regime. However, he added that Smirnov would not have the freedom of deciding such a matter. 'On serious matters, the final decision has always been taken by the Kremlin.'[31]

[27] B Bowring, 'Georgia, Russia and the Crisis of the Council of Europe: Inter-State Applications, Individual Complaints, and the Future of the Strasbourg Model of Human Rights Litigation' in J Green and C Waters (eds), *Conflict in the Caucasus: Implications for International Legal Order* (Palgrave Macmillan 2010) 114–135.

[28] D Trenin, 'The Independence of Kosovo and its Implications' (2009) 5 ESFRES 115–20, <http://www.ceps.be/system/files/book/1855.pdf#page=125> accessed 25 November 2012.

[29] M Kuzovlev, '"Kozak-2 plan" or Recognition of Transnistria?' (2008) Policy Documentation Centre CEU, <http://pdc.ceu.hu/archive/00004198/> accessed 25 November 2012.

[30] S Wolff, 'A Resolvable Frozen Conflict? Designing a Settlement for Transnistria' (2012) 39 NPJNE 863–70.

[31] T Tudoroiu, 'The European Union, Russia, and the Future of the Transnistrian Frozen Conflict' (2012) 26 EPS 135–61, 147.

Indeed, as a comment on *The Economist*'s 'Eastern Approaches' blog on 14 December noted, the outcome of the elections was so surprising that the Central Electoral Commission sat on the results for two days.[32] Mr Smirnov had been expecting to win, as usual. However, he came in third, with just 25% of the vote. The candidate preferred by Russia came second with 26.5%. The winner was Yevgeny Shevchuk, whom Mr Kaminski displaced as chair of the Supreme Soviet, Transdniestria's parliament, in 2009. These results were strong evidence for the fairness of the election. Kálmán Mizsei, who was for five years the European Union's special envoy tasked with settling the frozen conflict between Transdniestria and Moldova, described Mr Shevchuk as 'the candidate of the young of Transdniestria, who are desperate for reform'. In the second round, Shevchuk received about 74% of the vote.

According to Marcin Kosienkowski, writing in August 2012,[33] Shevchuk is seen in Moldova, the west and Russia as a rational and reasonable politician, having proved himself while speaker of parliament in 2005–9 and as leader of the *Obnovleniye* party to 2010. *Obnovleniye* is sponsored by the biggest company in the PMR, *Sheriff*, and won the parliamentary elections in 2005. Kosienkowski presents evidence that having started from a position of demanding independence and integration with Russia, Shevchuk has accepted the idea of reunification with Moldova.[34]

The Russian scholar Andrey Devyatkov confirmed that Russia did not support Shevchuk, and State Duma deputies tried to discredit him, calling him a protégé of the west—the PMR's Saakashvili. Unlike Kaminsky, who presented himself as the Kremlin's candidate, Shevchuk was seen as the bearer of true renewal and a professional governing style. So the Kremlin failed to bring its own protégé to power, but 'completed its mission at the most basic level: Smirnov's regime has been overthrown, and Moscow has recognised the results of the election...'.[35]

Furthermore, by appointing Peter Stepanov, former Minister of Justice, as his Prime Minister in early January 2012, Shevchuk compromised with Russia and with his political opponents in the PMR.[36] This was confirmed in the Russian media.[37] At the same time, Moscow showed its dissatisfaction with the election results on 26 January when it failed to pay a promised sum of $300 million for technical assistance. This was disclosed by none other than Mr Kaminsky, who

[32] <http://www.economist.com/blogs/easternapproaches/2011/12/transdniestrias-election-shock> accessed 24 November 2012.

[33] M Kosienkowski, 'Is Internationally Recognised Independence the Goal of Quasi-States? The Case of Transnistria', Working Paper <http://papers.ssrn.com/sol3/papers.cfm?abstract_id=2132161> accessed 24 November 2012, 5.

[34] Kosienkowski (n 33) 6.

[35] A Devyatkov, 'Russian Policy Toward Transnistria: Between Multilateralism and Marginalization' (2012) 59 Problems of Post-Communism 53–62, at 59.

[36] Devyatkov (n 35).

[37] 'Noviy president Pridnestrovya predstavil soglasovannuyu s Kremlem kandidaturu premyera' (The new president of Pridnestrovia presented his candidate for premier agreed with the Kremlin) 11 January 2012<http://www.newsru.com/world/11jan2012/pridnestr.html> accessed 24 November 2012.

also said that Russia was waiting for the final formation of a new government. At the same time, criminal proceedings had been commenced in Russia against Smirnov's son, Oleg. And Kaminsky obtained from Russia a promise that the 150 roubles per month pension supplement paid by Russia would continue.[38]

Russia has continued to push for a settlement in which the PMR will find its place within Moldova. On 30 July 2012 Grigorii Karasin, the deputy head of the Russian Foreign Ministry, announced in Tiraspol that the conflict between Chisinau and Tiraspol must be settled by way of including the PMR within Moldova with the rights of a special district. This was the first time Moscow's view had been expressed so strongly. Russia's conditions were firm guarantees for Moldova's neutrality and non-membership of NATO, and also for the rights of Russians and the status of the Russian language as second state language in Moldova. The daily *Kommersant* newspaper noted that throughout the years since 1992, Moscow had always considered the PMR to be a part of a united Moldova. However, such an announcement had never previously been made in Tiraspol.[39] The German Chancellor Angela Merkel supported Russia's position when she visited Chisinau in August 2012.[40]

Nonetheless, evidence of continued closeness to Russia was provided first by a parliamentary proposal on 24 October 2012 to bring the PMR's legislation on political parties into line with Russia's,[41] and then by hopes expressed on 25 October 2012 in Tiraspol that Russia would open regular aviation communications with the PMR.[42]

The judgment of the Strasbourg Court on 19 October 2012 in *Catan* v *Moldova and Russia*[43] muddied the water considerably. The complaints were made in 2004–6 by a large group of teachers and parents in three schools in the PMR towns of Benderi, Ribnitsa, and Grigoriopol, where the language of instruction was Moldovan written in Latin script—that is, Romanian. The Court awarded compensation, 'just satisfaction', in the sum of more than one million euros, with 50,000 euros for legal expenses.

[38] 'Rossii ostavila Pridnestrovye bez deneg—vozmozhno, obidelas na svoevolnikh zhitelei' (Russia left Pridnestroviye without money—it is possible that it was upset by its independent-minded inhabitants) 26 January 2012 <http://www.newsru.com/world/26jan2012/pmr.html> accessed 24 November 2012.

[39] 'Rossii zayavila Pridnestrovyu, chto pora vozvrashchatsya v Moldaviyu, i ozvuchila svoi usloviya' (Russia told Pridnestroviya that it is time to return to Moldova, and laid out its conditions) 30 July 2012, <http://www.newsru.com/world/30jul2012/pridnestr.html> accessed 24 November 2012.

[40] See <http://www.newsru.com/world/22aug2012/merkel.html> accessed 24 November 2012.

[41] <http://tiras.ru/jeksperty/36077-partiynaya-sistema-pmr-budet-demokratizirovana.html> accessed 24 November 2012.

[42] <http://www.nr2.ru/pmr/409862.html> accessed 24 November 2012.

[43] Application nos. 43370/04, 8252/05 and 18454/06, judgment of 19 October 2012.

IV. Institutions of the PMR

In 2006 Dov Lynch asserted:

> The amalgam of territory, population and government in the separatist area of Transnistria has produced something that is greater than the sum of these parts—a weak but still determined belief in the separatist region's sovereignty, at least by the region's authorities and elites, if not also by its population. The separatist authorities in Tiraspol maintain that they exist empirically. And, however weak the left bank institutions are, they have the recognisable features of statehood.[44]

Indeed, the PMR has many of the trappings of statehood. Its Constitution was adopted in a referendum held on 24 December 1995 and signed by President Smirnov on 17 January 1996.[45] The Constitution was amended by laws of 15 December 1998, 30 June 2000, 13 July 2005, and 10 February 2006. The Constitutional Court—the first organ of constitutional control in the history of the PMR—was founded on 12 June 2002. On that day a special Session of the Supreme Soviet of the PMR took the oaths of six Judges of the Constitutional Court.[46] On the occasion of my visit to Tiraspol in 2004 I visited the court and met the judges. The Court is closely modelled on the Constitutional Court of the Russian Federation and has—although not often—decided cases against the authorities. Its judgments and other materials are published in three languages.

The Supreme Council ('Soviet' in Russian) of the PMR started work in 1990.[47] The II Extraordinary Congress of People's Deputies of all levels of Pridnestrovie elected an Interim Supreme Council with 50 members. It was authorized to provide organization and efficient government of the republic until 1 December 1990. The Interim Supreme Council was tasked to elect the Chairman of the Supreme Council, the Public Prosecutor, the State Arbitrator, the Minister of Internal Affairs, and the Chairman of the State Security Committee, and also to appoint the Chairman of the Council of Ministers of the Republic and the members of the Presidium. On 3 September 1990 the Presidium of the Supreme Council, comprising 18 persons headed by the Chairman and his three vice-chairmen, was elected.

In March 1990 Igor Nikolaevich Smirnov, director of the Tiraspol factory Electromash, was elected Chairman of Tiraspol City Council of People's Deputies, and also Chairman of the Interim Supreme Council. On 30 January 1991, at the fifth session of the 1st Supreme Council of PMR, the deputies elected at the previous election comprised 25 Russians, 21 Ukrainians, 12 Moldavians, one Bulgarian, one Turkmen, two Gagauzians, and one Jew.

[44] Dov Lynch, 'Peacekeeping in Transnistria: Cooperation or Competition?' (2006) International Spectator <http://www.eu-consent.net/library/deliverables/D82_Lynch.PDF> accessed 25 November 2012.

[45] See <http://pravo.pmr-online.com/View.aspx?id=%2BJvOOkPcRrEMfSv3t80a4w%3D%3D> accessed 25 November 2012.

[46] See the Court's website at <http://www.kspmr.idknet.com/eng/history.htm> accessed 25 November 2012.

[47] See its history in English at <http://www.vspmr.org/?Part=5> accessed 25 November 2012.

Since 1991 the PMR has also had a Supreme Court and an Arbitrazh (Commercial) Court—the latter has now become fully electronic.[48] There is a full set of ministries, each with their own website.[49]

V. The PMR Economy

The main industrial enterprises of the PMR, almost all with their roots in the Soviet period but privatized since 1991, are: the Montazhavtomatika factory in Tiraspol, providing design and construction services in the sphere of water supply, heat supply, and energy supply;[50] the clothes factory Odema, with over 1,000 employees, exporting all over Europe;[51] the textile factory Tirotex, exporting all over the world;[52] the bread factory Tiraspolskiy Khlebokombinat;[53] the Bender factory Elektroapparatura;[54] the footwear factory Floare, with over 1,000 employees;[55] the garment factory Intercenterlux, producing for most of the best-known luxury brands in Europe and elsewhere;[56] the Bendery Starch Products complex, with EU trade preferences;[57] the Rybnitsa Fuel Pump Factory;[58] the Moldovan power station;[59] the Tiraspol factory for metal goods;[60] the Moldavkabel cable factory;[61] the Tiraspol casting machine factory Litmash;[62] the Kvint alcoholic beverages factory;[63] and the giant Moldova Steel Works in Rybnitsa, with an annual turnover of more than $500 million.[64]

This represents, in fact, practically all of the industrial production of Soviet Moldova.[65] And the PMR Federation of Trade Unions has its own website.[66]

In 1998 Kolstø and Malgin confirmed that a significant part of Moldova's industrial potential is concentrated on the east bank of the river, that is, in the PMR. The majority of the urban population—in Tiraspol, Rybnitsa, Dubossary, Slobozia, and Benderi—are engaged in large industrial plants. Like most industrial, urban regions in the former Soviet Union, the population is strongly Russified. They see themselves mostly in the cultural context of Russia, not of 'their own' republic.[67]

48 See <http://arbitr-pmr.org/> accessed 25 November 2012.

49 See the list at <http://president.pmr-gov.org/index.php?option=com_weblinks&catid=60&Itemid=129>.

50 <http://mautomat.com/ in English, accessed 25 November 2012. <http://mautomat.com/index.php?option=com_content&view=article&id=111&Itemid=28&lang=en> accessed 25 November 2012.

51 <http://odema.info/>.

52 <http://www.tirotex.com/index_en.htm>.

53 <http://tirhleb.com/>.

54 <http://www.oaobze.ru/>.

55 <http://www.floare.com/floare/start.aspx> (in English).

56 <http://www.centrelux.com/?lang=en&id=1> (in English).

57 <http://www.zlak.idknet.com/indexen.html> (in English).

58 <http://www.apnasos.idknet.com/> (in English).

59 <http://mgres.org/>.

60 <http://www.tzm.idknet.com/>.

61 <http://www.moldavcable.com/>.

62 <http://www.litmash.com/eng/index.html> (in English).

63 <http://eng.kvint.biz/> (in English).

64 <http://www.aommz.com/pls/webus/webus.main.show> (in English).

65 See also A Gudim (2006), 'Transnistria: Conflicts and Pragmatism of the Economy' *PDC CEU* at <http://pdc.ceu.hu/archive/00003500/01/transnistria.pdf> accessed 25 November 2012.

66 <http://www.fpp-pmr.org/>.

67 Kolstø and Malgin (n 12) 107.

VI. Ethnic Make-up of the PMR—and PMR Identity

It is not contested that the PMR is an ethnically plural society.[68] Ethnic Moldovans, Russians, and Ukrainians each constitute around 30% of the population. Stefan Wolff noted in 2011 that despite or because of this mix, '…there are no significant inter-ethnic tensions in Transnistria itself'. On the contrary, he cited the CSCE Mission to Moldova's Report No. 13 of 1993, which 'asserted a "distinct Transdniestrian feeling of identity" anchored in language (Russian), geography (natural separation from the rest of Moldova by the River Nistru), history (Transnistria as part of the Russian empire, rather than historic Bessarabia), and a perception—rightly or wrongly—to have been at the receiving end of a Moldovan attempt to resolve the dispute by force in 1992'.[69] Wolff referred to further evidence for this shared sense of belonging: the fact that those displaced during the brief spell of violence in 1992 have all been able to return to their homes, regardless of their ethnic identity.[70]

As far back as 1998, Kolstø and Malgin noted that the separate identity of the inhabitants of the PMR had been recognized in Moldova. A draft law on national minorities which was printed in a government newspaper in 1992 stated, inter alia, that '[t]he left bank regions of the Dnestr are distinct in the peculiarities of their history…the national composition of the population, traditions, and mentality, comprise one of the historically defined language zones of the Republic of Moldova.'[71]

In their conclusion, Kolstø and Malgin wrote that 'the idea of Gagauz autonomy can appeal to ethnic Gagauzi only, while the concept of Transnistrian sovereignty is more regional and can find devotees among all ethnic groups in the area'.[72]

Kolstø returned to the topic in 2006. In his view there were cases, of which the PMR was the best example, in which a separate identity for the population of a rebellious region had been achieved without any ethnic cleansing. He emphasized that ethnic Moldovans made up roughly 40% of DMR's population and, while many of them sympathized with the Chisinau regime, a large number shared in the 'common supraethnic Dniester identity fostered by the Tiraspol leadership'. This identity was based not on ethnicity but on a common language, namely Russian; a separate history; and even a certain nostalgia for the Soviet past.[73]

[68] A Skvortsova, 'The Cultural and Social Makeup of Moldova: A Bipolar or Dispersed Society?' in P Kolstø (ed), *National Integration and Violent Conflict in Post-Soviet Societies: The Cases of Estonia and Moldova* (Rowman & Littlefield Publishers 2002) 159–96.

[69] S Wolff, 'The Prospects of a Sustainable Conflict Settlement for Transnistria' <http://www.stefanwolff.com/files/The%20Prospects%20of%20a%20Sustainable%20Conflict%20Settlement%20for%20Transnistria.pdf>.

[70] Wolff (n 69) 5.

[71] P Kolstø and A Malgin, 'The Transnistrian Republic: A Case of Politicized Regionalism' (1998) 26 NP 103–27, 104.

[72] Kolstø and Malgin (n 71) 122.

[73] P Kolstø, 'The Sustainability and Future of Unrecognized Quasi-States' (2006) 43 JPR <http://www.colorado.edu/geography/class_homepages/geog_4712_f07/quasi_states.pdf> 723–40, 731 accessed 25 November 2012.

In 2011 Kolstø, writing with Blakkisrud,[74] argued that '... both the time factor and the quest for recognition have contributed to pushing Transnistria away from being a "black hole" and "racketeer state," and toward developing something akin to full-fledged statehood (minus official recognition)'.[75] They further noted that the new generation of inhabitants of the PMR were officially supposed to be bilingual and fluent in at least two of the three state languages, Moldovan, Russian, and Ukrainian (Article 12 of the Constitution of PMR).[76] In their view, the PMR's official multi-ethnicity made it quite different from Abkhazia, Nagorno-Karabakh, or South Ossetia, and indeed from most recognized states of the former USSR. The willingness to bear the financial cost of official multi-ethnicity was itself remarkable, given the fact that the PMR is not rich.[77] Their conclusion was that although the PMR remained as illegitimate as it was in 1991, the 'parallel processes' of state-building and nation-building had fundamentally changed state and society. In their view, the option of reuniting with Moldova had become increasingly less attractive.[78]

However, as I have shown above, it seems increasingly likely that reunification with Moldova will take place, like it or not.

VII. The Status of the PMR—Self-determination?

The PMR itself declared on its website as late as 9 December 2011—just before the election—that the 2006 referendum, in which 94% of the population voted for sovereign statehood, was a clear sign of a vote for self-determination. That page has now disappeared. However, on 20 November 2012 President Shevchuk signed a Decree on the Conception of Foreign Policy of the PMR.[79] This refers to a 'future model of relations between Pridnestroviye and Moldova' based on firm guarantees.

It should be noted that in 1990 Transdniestria joined some 26 entities of the Russian Socialist Federation of Soviet Republics in declaring sovereignty—that is, seeking the status of a Union Republic within the USSR, with the constitutional right to secede.[80] However, the 2005 New York Bar report stated categorically that '[t]here is no solid basis for a claim of secession under external self-determination. The most basic requirements for a legal claim are not met'.[81]

[74] H Blakkisrud and P Kolstø, 'From Secessionist Conflict Toward a Functioning State: Processes of State- and Nation-Building in Transnistria' (2011) 27 PSA 178–210.

[75] Blakkisrud and Kolstø (n 74) 182.

[76] <http://president.gospmr.ru/ru/news/konstituciya-pridnestrovskoy-moldavskoy-respubliki> accessed 24 November 2012.

[77] Blakkisrud and Kolstø (n 74) 195. [78] Blakkisrud and Kolstø (n 74) 206.

[79] <http://president.gospmr.ru/ru/news/ukaz-prezidenta-pmr-no766-ob-utverzhdenii-koncepcii-vneshney-politiki-pridnestrovskoy> accessed 24 November 2012.

[80] See the table at pages 55–6 of B Bowring, 'The Russian Constitutional System: Complexity and Asymmetry' in M Weller and K Nobbs (eds), *Asymmetric Autonomy and the Settlement of Ethnic Conflicts* (University of Pennsylvania Press 2010) 48–74.

[81] New York Bar (2005) 51, <www.nycbar.org/pdf/report/NYCity%20BarTransnistriaReport.pdf>.

The right of peoples to self-determination in international law is succinctly stated in the first paragraph of common Article 1 of the 1966 (entering into force in 1976) International Covenant on Civil and Political Rights (ICCPR) and International Covenant on Economic, Social and Cultural Rights (ICESCR), as follows:

> 1. All peoples have the right of self-determination. By virtue of that right they freely determine their political status and freely pursue their economic, social and cultural development.

This right, enshrined in Covenants now ratified by almost every state, has now achieved a high status in international law. In its judgment of 30 June 1995 in the *East Timor* case (*Portugal* v *Australia*),[82] the International Court of Justice declared (para 29, p. 102) that it has an *erga omnes* character. Furthermore, in its 9 July 2004 Advisory Opinion in the *Wall in Occupied Palestinian Territory* case,[83] the Court cited those words.

The New York Bar's starting point, upon which all may agree, is that the population of the PMR are not an 'ethnicity'. However, could they qualify as a people? In his classic 1995 text, not referred to by the New York Bar report, Antonio Cassese took the view that:

> ... the general spirit and context of Article 1, combined with the preparatory work, lead to the conclusion that Article 1 applies to: (1) entire populations living in independent and sovereign States, (2) entire populations of territories that have yet to attain independence, and (3) populations living under foreign military occupation. It is thus apparent that the existence of a right to self-determination is not necessarily determined by reference to a territory's international political status.[84]

Richard Kiwanuka, discussing the meaning of 'people' in the African Charter, identified four definitions depending on context, including all persons, or all groups of people with certain common characteristics, within the geographical limits of an entity.[85] Ian Brownlie asserted for the proposition that the principle of self-determination has a 'core of reasonable certainty', namely the 'right of a community which has a distinct character to have this character reflected in the institutions of government under which it lives'. This distinct character may well be determined by matters of culture, language, religion, and group psychology. If purely ethnic criteria were applied exclusively it would mean negating the national identity of, for example, the United States.[86]

The New York Bar rely chiefly on the 1998 judgment of the Supreme Court of Canada.[87] This contained the following:

> In summary, the international law right to self-determination only generates, at best, a right to external self-determination in situations of former colonies; where a people is oppressed,

[82] <http://www.icj-cij.org/docket/index.php?p1=3&p2=3&k=66&case=84&code=pa&p3=4>.

[83] <http://www.icj-cij.org/docket/index.php?p1=3&p2=4&k=5a&case=131&code=mwp&p3=4>.

[84] A Cassese, *Self-Determination of Peoples: A Legal Reappraisal* (Cambridge University Press 1995) 59.

[85] R Kiwanuka, 'The Meaning of "People" in the African Charter on Human and Peoples' Rights' (1988) 82 AJIL 80–101.

[86] I Brownlie, 'The Rights of Peoples in Modern International Law' (1985) 9 BASLP 104–19, 107–8.

[87] *Reference re Secession of Quebec*, 2 SCR 217 at para 123 (1998).

as for example under foreign military occupation; or where a definable group is denied meaningful access to government to pursue their political, economic, social and cultural development. In all three situations, the people in question are entitled to a right to external self-determination because they have been denied their ability to exert internally their right to self-determination.

That would be a conclusive argument if the question in issue were the secession of the PMR from Moldova. The PMR was not a colony; its people were not oppressed except, perhaps, by their own government; and its people have not been denied meaningful access, except, perhaps, by their own government.

But there was no secession from independent, post-Soviet Moldova, but rather a declaration of independence, before the collapse of the USSR in December 1991, from the Moldovan Socialist Soviet Republic. The authors of the New York Bar Report appear to agree with Judge Kovler and others that the left (east) bank of the Dnester had for centuries a quite different history, language, and culture from Bessarabia, the right (west) bank. The fact that several ethnicities and linguistic groups live there cannot be decisive, for the reasons given by Brownlie. If the inhabitants of the territory of the PMR have indeed acquired their own identity, their own 'distinct character'—distinct from the remainder of Moldova—then they may well have a right of self-determination as a 'people'.

Nowadays, the right of peoples to self-determination is generally exercised through varieties of autonomy or even federalism, and it is noteworthy that the various proposals for resolution of Moldova's problems have involved proposals for degrees of autonomy for the PMR territory and for the 160,700-strong Turkic-language Gagauz people of southern Moldova, who now have their own 'national–territorial autonomous unit' with three official languages: Moldovan, Gagauz, and Russian.

Perhaps the strongest point in favour of a right to self-determination is the fact of more than 20 years of separation from Moldova, during which time a strongly state-like, if unrecognized, social and political entity has taken root in the territory demarcated by the Dnester river, with the addition of Bender.

The very firm position taken by Russia gives rise to a reasonably certain prediction that self-determination for the people of the PMR will take the form of a special status within a reunified Moldova.

VIII. Conclusion

Despite all the proposals referred to in the previous section, the status of the PMR has yet to be resolved. Russia has never recognized it as a state and has always maintained that the PMR should have a special status within Moldova, either as the subject of a federation (with Gagauzia as another subject) or as something similar to the Autonomous Republic of Crimea, which has been part of Ukraine, a unitary state.

In 2006 Oleh Protsyk argued that:

Such fundamental characteristics of the Transnistrian conflict as the absence of the deeply entrenched animosity among major ethnic groups, the stabilizing effects of geographic proximity to the EU and strong incentives for economic cooperation across the current political divide favourably distinguish the Transnistrian situation from the conflicts in Abkhazia, South Ossetia, and Nagorno Karabakh. These fundamentals, as well as the great promise of improving economic, social, and political fortunes of people on both sides of the Nistru river that the idea of the country's reintegration contains, should make domestic actors and international mediators keep trying to find a lasting solution for the Transnistrian problem.[88]

Protsyk's fears, expressed in 2009, of intransigence by the PMR leadership[89] have been overtaken by events. International negotiations were restarted on 30 November to 1 December 2011, for the first time since 2005. The OSCE's Lithuanian chairmanship hosted the event in Vilnius in the familiar 5 + 2 format (Russia, Ukraine, OSCE, United States, European Union, Chisinau, Tiraspol). But Russian Foreign Minister Sergei Lavrov, in a number of speeches and lectures in Chisinau, proposed a political settlement 'in the framework of Moldova's sovereignty and territorial integrity, with a guaranteed special status for Transnistria' and with 'Russia as a mediator and guarantor of the settlement', to be negotiated in the relaunched 5 + 2 format. According to Lavrov, the Kozak Memorandum of 2003 should be utilized for 'reference and continuity' of the process. In the opinion of Vladimir Socor, Lavrov's proposal was cynically designed to prevent any progress.[90] However, the talks concluded with agreement to hold further talks in February 2012 in Dublin—a good result, according to the Lithuanian Chairmanship.[91]

In my view, there will, after a hiatus of more than 20 years, be a settlement, with the PMR either as the subject of a federation or with special status in Moldova. Unless, that is, Moldova—the poorest country in Europe—decides to join Romania, which is highly unlikely. So perhaps there are grounds for optimism.[92]

[88] O Protsyk, 'Moldova's Dilemmas in Democratizing and Reintegrating Transnistria' (2006) 53 Problems of Post-Communism 29–41, <http://www.policy.hu/protsyk/Publications/ProtsykMolDilemmainTransnistria April06.pdf> 41.

[89] O Protsyk, 'Representation and Democracy in Eurasia's Unrecognized States: The Case of Transnistria' (2009) 25 PSA 257–81, 277.

[90] V Socor, 'Lavrov Squashes Hope for Constructive Restart of Transnistria Negotiations' (2011) *Eurasia Daily Monitor*, 6 November, <http://www.jamestown.org/programs/edm/single/? tx_ttnews[tt_news]=38709&cHash=8dfd7085624316b3601c676f11e2db6b> accessed 25 November 2012.

[91] <http://www.monstersandcritics.com/news/europe/news/article_1678418.php/Diplomats-see-some-progress-after-restarted-Transnistria-talks> accessed 25 November 2012.

[92] C Urse, 'Solving Transnistria: Any Optimists Left?' (2008) QJ 57–75 <http://kms1.isn.ethz.ch/serviceengine/Files/ISN/57339/ichaptersection_singledocument/7ee8018c-ad17-44b6-8bc2-8171256a7790/en/Chapter_4.pdf> accessed 25 November 2012.

9

South Ossetia

Christopher Waters

> This only resembles one thing: Two men were journeying somewhere along some road; the one who was behind saw the one in front fall into a well. He came up, called down, weeps and cries 'Woe!' Thus he spoke: 'Comrade, stay there, wait for me; I go to bring ropes, I want to pull thee out'.
>
> The man who was beneath laughed, he marvelled greatly, he shouted up: 'Unless I wait, whither can I flee from thee, whither can I go?'
>
> Shota Rustaveli, *The Knight in the Panther's Skin* (Georgian epic poem written *c.* 1196–1207 AD).[1]

I. Introduction

I have written elsewhere that the Georgia–Russia conflict of 2008 provides an example of how international law and international organizations can contribute to peace, stability, and world order.[2] Although realpolitik and the use of hard/coercive power is more than apparent in this violent episode, and the humanitarian suffering tragic, international norms and organizations served to limit the scope, severity, and duration of the war. The conflict was quickly legalized and managed by the European Union, the judicial and political organs of the Council of Europe, and the International Court of Justice, among other institutions (though some, like the UN Security Council, were squeezed out). Further, despite continuing tension, international actors and interventions—including a pre-investigation by the International Criminal Court—played an important role in preventing fresh outbreaks of violence. In no way then is this paper sceptical about the general relevance or importance of international law and organizations to the South Caucasus or the prospects for the international rule of law more generally. However, it is difficult to see at this point in time how international law can play a useful role in the short term in resolving the issues of self-determination and

[1] S Rustaveli, *The Knight in the Panther's Skin* (Marjory Scott Wardrop tr, Abingdon: Royal Asiatic Society 1912) 42.

[2] C Waters, 'The Caucasus Conflict and the Role of Law' in C Waters and JA Green (eds), *Conflict in the Caucasus: Implications for International Legal Order* (Basingstoke: Palgrave 2010) 8–25.

secession in the South Caucasus and, as is the focus of this paper, South Ossetia. The parties have fallen down a well and are relying on (separate) international legal principles to pull them out; unfortunately, it is not clear that international law has sufficient rope with which to haul them out immediately.

II. Competing Facts and Fictions

It would be simplistic to suggest that the conflict between South Ossetia and Georgia is based solely on the manipulation of ethnicity over the span of two decades.[3] However, as most Georgians and Ossetians will say—especially in contrast to the Abkhazia conflict—they have had friendly relations for long periods in history. Ethno-political entrepreneurs, drawing on claims of history and identity, radicalized what had been a largely peaceful coexistence until the late 1980s. All the same, while this account begins in the late Soviet period, it should not be forgotten that the conflicts which led to secession are at least partly rooted in competing cultural historiographies and myths of ethnogenesis (which people were there first) and civilization (which people had the more advanced culture) forged over time.[4] The national 'histories' and myths created by the opposing sides are often mutually exclusive and evoke strong feelings among the people involved. The competing myths make it difficult to sketch a chronology of the conflicts, but a brief account of 'recent' events is attempted here.

During the Soviet Union's *perestroika* years, resurgent nationalism, both among titular ethnicities in each republic (Russians in Russia, Georgians in Georgia, and so forth) and among the ethnic minorities in each republic, began to colour the democratization process.[5] In 1989 the Supreme Soviet of Georgia's semi-autonomous South Ossetian region voted for greater autonomy within Georgia (South Ossetians, together with their ethnic *confrères* in North Ossetia in the Russian Federation, form a distinct ethnic group and have their own language).[6] Georgian authorities, however, purported to annul this vote and strip South Ossetia of the limited autonomy it had before the poll. Violence was triggered by a demonstration of Georgian nationalists in South Ossetia itself, which quickly intensified into full-scale conflict. Roughly 60,000 Ossetians and Georgians were displaced from their homes during the conflict. A ceasefire was signed in 1992, leaving the authorities in Tskhinvali, the South Ossetian capital, with de facto

[3] This factual sketch draws extensively on my chapter in Waters and Green (n 2) *Conflict in the Caucasus* 8–25.

[4] See G Smith et al., *Nation Building in the Post-Soviet Borderlands: The Politics of National Identities* (Cambridge University Press 1998).

[5] See generally RG Suny, *The Making of the Georgian Nation* (Indiana University Press 1994).

[6] Unlike North Ossetia, South Ossetia was integrated into a Georgian administrative unit of the Russian Empire and, from 1924 onwards, successive Soviet constitutions described South Ossetia as an autonomous *oblast* within the Georgian Soviet Socialist Republic. South Ossetia's status under Soviet law is addressed further later in the chapter.

control over a good portion of the territory within the original borders of the region, or *oblast*. Pursuant to the ceasefire agreement signed in 1992 at Sochi, Russian, Georgian, and South Ossetian peacekeeping forces were deployed and international mediation efforts were launched under the auspices of the Conference on Security and Co-operation in Europe (later the Organization for Security and Co-operation in Europe, or OSCE). These mediation efforts were ultimately unsuccessful in solving the conflict. However, they were successful in terms of confidence building, providing roughly a decade of calm between the ceasefire and Georgia's 2003 'Rose Revolution', which saw the removal of Soviet-era leader Eduard Shevardnadze from power and the ascension of Mikheil Saakashvili to the presidency.

Indeed, for anyone who travelled to South Ossetia from the mid-1990s to the early 2000s, the idea that this 'frozen conflict' could have erupted so furiously would have come as a surprise. The Georgian–South Ossetian 'border' was porous, black-market trading between Georgia and Russia via South Ossetia took place in the open, and it was not unusual to hear Georgian spoken in the streets of Tskhinvali.[7] The joint peacekeeping patrols between Georgians, Ossetians, and Russians were successfully coordinated for the most part and there were tentative, small-scale efforts at return for displaced persons forced to flee after the 1991/2 conflict.[8] However, as suggested above, the issues stemming from the conflict of the early 1990s were only frozen and never resolved. Georgia had strenuously insisted on its territorial integrity since the breakup of the Soviet Union and the international community had backed this. Calls for Georgia's reunification—by force if necessary—grew steadily louder after Saakashvili's Rose Revolution ascendancy. At the same time, Saakashvili promised a high degree of autonomy within Georgia for South Ossetia in an effort to bring the latter into the Georgian fold peacefully. In a 2005 initiative, for example, South Ossetians were promised 'broad self-governance' as an autonomous region with power over economic and social matters and guaranteed representation in the levers of government in Tbilisi.[9] Saakashvili also sought to woo ordinary Ossetians through a variety of enticements, from the distribution of farming aids such as fertilizer to the promise of integration into a renewed Georgian democracy and economy.

Yet, over a decade and a half of de facto independence, South Ossetians had built up the institutions of a micro-state—with a legislature, courts, and even at least one relatively (for the region) fair presidential election—as well as a determination not to return to the Georgian fold.[10] Before and during the conflict, President

[7] This assessment is based on fieldwork carried out by the author in Tskhinvali in 2003.

[8] On the challenges facing the return of refugees/internally displaced persons to their homes of origin in the South Caucasus, see A Smit, *The Property Rights of Refugees and Internally Displaced Persons: Beyond Restitution* (Routledge 2012).

[9] See 'Initiative of the Georgian Government with Respect to the Peaceful Resolution of the Conflict in South Ossetia', *Civil.ge* (Georgia, 24 March 2005) <http://www.civil.ge/eng/article.php?id=9426>, accessed 10 May 2012.

[10] See C Waters, 'Rule of Law in the Secessionist States' in C Waters (ed), *The State of Law in the South Caucasus* (Palgrave 2005) 59–80; C Waters, 'Law in Places That Don't Exist' (2006) 34 DJILP 401.

Saakashvili portrayed South Ossetia as simply a stooge of Moscow.[11] This is, like so much of the rhetoric surrounding the conflict, a half-truth. Perhaps the best evidence of this came three years after the war; in November 2011 South Ossetian voters rejected the Kremlin-backed Presidential candidate at the polls, ushering in a political crisis.[12] While it is true that South Ossetians look to Russia for protection—and that in the year or two before the conflict the Russian state, including its security apparatus, absorbed large elements of the South Ossetian government—this was for many the reality of living in an unrecognized and threatened mini-republic. Russian protection—and ultimately absorption into the Russian Federation—is seen as the best available option by the majority of ethnic Ossetians in the Tskhinvali region. This was crystallized after the Rose Revolution, when Saakashvili suggested that if the 'carrots' to reintegration did not work, more bellicose means of restoring Georgia's territory would be tried.[13] Now, to be clear, there may indeed be Russian 'effective control' over most South Ossetian institutions, but this does not mean that the political will of the South Ossetian population is not independent or clear.[14]

One of the still debated facts pertains to who started the 2008 conflict. Both Russia and Georgia blame the other for breaching the decade and a half-old ceasefire on 7 August 2008. It seems the most accurate view is that Georgia launched an attack on the capital of Tskhinvali on 7 August.[15] However, the 'who fired first on 7 August' question in some ways misses the point, as the broader question of causation depends on what frame of time one is looking at. Skirmishes between Georgian and South Ossetian (with Russian support) forces had been occurring for months prior to 7 August, and the latter date simply represents the final breakdown of the ceasefire. During the short war (the main conflict lasted

[11] M Corso, 'Georgia Holds Steady as Moscow Inches Closer To Abkhazia, South Ossetia', *Eurasia Insight* 16 April 2008 <http://www.eurasianet.org/departments/insight/articles/eav041708c.shtml> accessed 17 April 2008.

[12] Authorities annulled the vote, which led to the defeat of the Kremlin-backed candidate. Supporters of the apparent winner, Alla Dzhioeva, protested in the streets of Tskhinvali. See M Schwirtz, 'Political Standoff Escalates in South Ossetia Over Vote', *New York Times* 30 November 2011 <http://www.nytimes.com/2011/12/01/world/europe/political-standoff-escalates-in-south-ossetia-over-disputed-vote.html?_r=2&ref=global-home> accessed 30 November 2011. Most recently, Leonid Tibilov was elected President after winning 54% of the votes. See K Krauthamer, I Caloianu, and J Boissevain, 'South Ossetia elects a new leader on the third attempt', *Transitions Online* 10 April 2012 <http://www.tol.org/client/article/23091-baku-sees-a-rare-legal-protest-albania-catches-the-greek-disease.html?print> accessed 5 May 2012.

[13] See D van der Schriek, 'Georgia Uses Carrot-And-Stick Approach with South Ossetia', *Eurasia Insight* 31 May 2004 <http://dev.eurasianet.org/departments/insight/articles/eav060104.shtml> accessed 1 June 2004.

[14] To use the by now well-known test of the European Court of Human Rights in the *Bankovic* (*Bankovic* v *Belgium*, App. No. 52207/99, Eur. Ct. H.R. (2001), 41 ILM 517) stream of jurisprudence.

[15] See CJ Chivers and E Barry, 'Georgia Claims on Russia War Called into Question', *New York Times* 7 November 2008 <http://www.nytimes.com/2008/11/07/world/europe/07georgia.html?_r=1&hp=&oref=slogin&pagewanted=print> accessed 10 May 2012. This view was adopted by the International Fact-Finding Mission on the Conflict in Georgia (IIFFMCG), which reported on 30 September 2009. See H Tagliavini, *Independent International Fact-Finding Mission on the Conflict in Georgia: Report* (2009) 1, 10 <http://www.ceiig.ch/Index.html> accessed 13 May 2012.

five days) it is clear that violations of international humanitarian law occurred on all sides—though the South Ossetian militia appears to have been particularly brutal—and that ethnic cleansing took place.[16] A ceasefire agreement was negotiated by the EU, through the personal leadership of the French President, and an EU monitoring group was put in place.[17] The EU also established a fact-finding inquiry, the Independent International Fact-Finding Mission on the Conflict in Georgia (IIFFMCG), to look into the August events.[18] The IIFFMCG reported on 30 September 2009 and its findings will be discussed below with respect to the self-determination question.

Following appeals from South Ossetian President Eduard Kokoity to the Russian Federation Council, the Russian President issued a decree recognizing the independence of South Ossetia. In doing so, Russia claimed to be recognizing the international legal claims to self-determination of South Ossetia and Abkhazia (the latter is the subject of another case study in the book and so I note this parallel conflict only in passing):

> A decision needs to be taken based on the situation on the ground. Considering the freely expressed will of the Ossetian and Abkhaz peoples and being guided by the provisions of the UN Charter, the 1970 Declaration on the Principles of International Law Governing Friendly Relations Between States, the CSCE Helsinki Final Act of 1975 and other fundamental international instruments, I signed Decrees on the recognition by the Russian Federation of South Ossetia's and Abkhazia's independence. Russia calls on other states to follow its example. This is not an easy choice to make, but it represents the only possibility to save human lives.[19]

Of course Russia did not act solely to assist South Ossetians. Russian desires to discourage additional oil and gas pipelines transiting through Georgia and regain control over its traditional sphere of influence following a 'humiliating' period of weakness vis-à-vis the west no doubt played a role. So too did Russian resentment over the west's recognition of Kosovo's independence in the face of Serbian opposition. As President Medvedev put it:

> Western countries rushed to recognise Kosovo's illegal declaration of independence from Serbia. We argued consistently that it would be impossible, after that, to tell the Abkhazians and Ossetians (and dozens of other groups around the world) that what was good for the Kosovo Albanians was not good for them. In international relations, you cannot have one rule for some and another rule for others.[20]

Western states, which have recognized the independence of Kosovo, emphasize the *sui generis* nature of the situation—in particular the UN exercised temporary

[16] IIFFMCG (n 15) 1, 10.

[17] See 'European Union Monitoring Mission in Georgia' < http://www.eumm.eu/> accessed 10 May 2012. Unfortunately the EUMM has had restricted access in South Ossetia.

[18] See Tagliavini (n 15), IIFFMCG 1, 10.

[19] 'Medvedev's Statement on South Ossetia and Abkhazia', *New York Times* 26 August 2008) <http://www.nytimes.com/2008/08/27/world/europe/27medvedev.html> accessed 10 May 2012.

[20] D Medvedev, 'Why I Had to Recognise Georgia's Breakaway Regions', *Financial Times* 26 August 2008 <http://www.ft.com/intl/cms/s/0/9c7ad792-7395-11dd-8a66-0000779fd18c.html#axzz1fDVC6nP8> accessed 13 May 2012.

suzerainty over the territory—and consequently do not consider Kosovo to be a precedent for future states in asserting their right to self-determination.[21] However, it is clear from Medvedev's and others' reactions that when we speak about the 'Kosovo precedent' we are not referring solely to legal precedent or the ICJ's Advisory Opinion,[22] but to a new fact in international life.

Besides Russia, the only metropolitan states that have recognized South Ossetia are Nicaragua, Venezuela, Nauru, and Tuvalu, though there has been support from some 'unrecognized peoples'. States and unrecognized peoples alike seem marginally more interested in recognizing Abkhazia than South Ossetia. This may have to do with South Ossetia's small and declining population—there are only slightly more than 30,000 people remaining in the territory—and its lack of economic viability,[23] though it should be remembered that these facts are not fatal to legal statehood. More damaging to South Ossetia's legal claims are its de facto absorption into Russia through administrative and security links and the wholesale passportization of the population (most South Ossetians were given Russian passports prior to the conflict). The International Crisis Group has suggested that South Ossetia is more like a subordinate North Caucasus republic than an independent state.[24] The IIFFMCG itself concluded that while Abkhazia is a state-like entity, South Ossetia lacks effectiveness and is an 'entity short of statehood'.[25]

Georgia has vehemently opposed Russia's 'annexation' of its territories and continues to claim full sovereignty over South Ossetia and its micro-state cousin Abkhazia. A majority of states—most vociferously the United States[26]—have supported the territorial integrity of Georgia and have frequently referred to the numerous pre-conflict UN Security Council Resolutions declaring the same. Indeed, as late as April 2008, the Security Council reaffirmed 'the commitment of all Member States to the sovereignty, independence and territorial integrity of Georgia within its internationally recognized borders'.[27] Similarly, international and regional organizations, most notably the European Union and the Council

[21] N Kemoklidze, 'Kosovo Precedent and the "Moral Hazard" of Secession' (2009) 5 JILIR 117, 125.

[22] *Accordance with International Law on the Unilateral Declaration of Independence in Respect of Kosovo* (Advisory Opinion) 2010 < http://www.icj-cij.org/docket/files/141/15987.pdf > accessed 25 June 2012 [82–83] ('Kosovo Advisory Opinion'). Of course, strictly speaking an Advisory Opinion is inherently incapable of constituting precedent.

[23] International Crisis Group, 'South Ossetia: The Burden of Recognition', 7 June 2010 <http://www.crisisgroup.org/~/media/Files/europe/205%20South%20Ossetia%20-%20The%20Burden%20of%20Recognition.ashx>, accessed 10 May 2012.

[24] International Crisis Group (n 2).

[25] IIFFMCG (n 15) 2, 134.

[26] On the US position, see 'US Statements Responding to Russia's Intervention into Georgia and Recognition of South Ossetia and Abkhazia' (2009) 103 AJIL 138.

[27] UNSC Res 1808 (15 April 2008) UN Doc S/RES/1808, para 1. See also UNSC Res 1781 (15 October 2007) UN Doc S/RES/1781; UNSC Res 1752 (12 April 2007) UN Doc S/RES/1752; UNSC Res 1716 (13 October 2006) UN Doc S/RES/1716; UNSC Res 1666 (31 March 2006) UN Doc S/RES/1666; UNSC Res 1615 (29 July 2005) UN Doc S/RES/1615; UNSC Res 1582 (28 January 2005) UN Doc S/RES/1582.

of Europe, have reaffirmed Georgia's territorial integrity and the inviolability of its borders.[28]

In January 2010, Georgia adopted a strategy regarding the reintegration of Abkhazia and South Ossetia. The strategy is called 'Engagement through Cooperation' and provides for non-violence and engagement of these two regions through educational, social, and economic projects.[29] However, the sides seem as far apart as ever in and outside of the 'Geneva process' put in place as part of the ceasefire and the situation remains tense, though manageable with the assistance of international institutions, notably the European Union. (On this point it is unfortunate that the OSCE has been forced out of its field role as the lead international agency on the ground in South Ossetia at Russia's insistence after the 2008 conflict.)[30]

III. The Self-Determination and Secession Conundrum

South Ossetians base their claim to secession on the principle of self-determination of peoples. Thus South Ossetia's 2001 'Constitution', adopted on the basis of a referendum, states: 'The Republic of South Ossetia is a sovereign democratic rule-of-law-state which has been founded by virtue of the self-determination of South Ossetia's people'.[31] Is this a legally valid claim?

One response to this question arises in the context of South Ossetia's existence within Georgia and the former Soviet Union. The *uti possidetis* principle holds that internal administrative boundaries are inviolable upon independence. As the Badinter commission put it in the Yugoslavian context, 'it is well established that, whatever the circumstances, the right to self-determination must not involve changes to existing frontiers at the time of independence (*uti possidetis juris*) except where the states concerned agree otherwise'.[32] Based on this principle, once Georgia declared its independence from the Soviet Union, its previous 'administrative borders' became international borders within which South Ossetia existed.[33] This was reinforced by the admittance of Georgia by the General Assembly to the UN on 31 July 1992, in accordance with the borders of the former Soviet Georgian Republic which, again, included South Ossetia.[34] Furthermore, various instruments of the

[28] The European Union has reaffirmed its commitment to Georgia's territorial integrity on numerous occasions. Recently, this has included objecting to the installation of fences along the South Ossetian administrative boundary <http://eeas.europa.eu/statements/docs/2013/131001_02_en.pdf> accessed 4 February 2014.

[29] See 'State Strategy on Occupied Territories: Engagement Through Cooperation', *Civil.ge* (Georgia) <http://www.civil.ge/files/files/SMR-Strategy-en.pdf> accessed 18 June 2012.

[30] G Lomsadze, 'South Ossetia vs. the OSCE', *Eurasianet* 12 July 2011 <http://www.eurasianet.org/node/63860> accessed 15 June 2012.

[31] 'Constitution (Fundamental Law) of the Republic of South Ossetia' <http://www.sojcc.ru/zakoniruo/196.html> accessed 20 June 2012.

[32] Arbitration Commission of the European Conference on Yugoslavia (the 'Badinter Commission'), Opinion No. 2, 92 International Law Reports 167, 168.

[33] IIFFMCG (n 15) 2, 143.

[34] Admission of the Republic of Georgia to membership in the United Nations, GA/RES/46/241 (31 July 1992). The vote was unanimous.

Commonwealth of Independent States (CIS) support Georgia's position. Article 5 of the Minsk Agreement signed on 8 December 1991 acknowledges the respect of each member state's territorial integrity, including the inviolability of their existing borders.[35] Additionally, Article 3 of the CIS Charter reaffirms the principles of territorial integrity as well as the recognition of the inviolability of state frontiers.[36] This is further proclaimed in the 15 April 1994 Declaration on the Respect for Sovereignty, Territorial Integrity and Inviolability of Borders signed by CIS members.[37] It should be noted that following the 2008 conflict, Georgia withdrew from the CIS, taking the position that the CIS had failed its own treaty commitments with respect to territorial integrity and sovereignty.[38]

South Ossetians sometimes rely on the 'illegality' of South Ossetia's inclusion in Georgia following the breakup of the Russian empire after the 1917 revolutions to avoid the application of the *uti possidetis* principle. The argument is that *uti possidetis* cannot override a prior illegality. However, this claim is weak; although there were rebellions against the Transcaucasian and then Menshevik Georgian authorities by South Ossetians following the 1917 revolutions, and no doubt atrocities occurred (which the South Ossetians label as genocide at the hands of Georgians), the ethnic lines in these rebellions were blurred (among other things, they had a political Bolshevik-versus-Menshevik flavour) and, importantly, never resulted in the creation of a South Ossetian state, which was subsequently incorporated into Soviet Georgia.[39] Thus if South Ossetia has a legal right to succession, it must be based on Soviet or Georgian law or a separate international legal principle capable of overcoming the application of the *uti possidetis* principle.

1. Right to secession under Soviet and Georgian law

Prior to the dissolution of the Soviet Union, South Ossetia declared its sovereignty on 20 September 1990 and its independence on 21 December 1991.[40] Unilateral secession by South Ossetia under the 1977 Constitution of the Union of Soviet Socialist Republics (USSR) as well as the Constitution of the Soviet Socialist Republic of Georgia was prohibited. South Ossetia was considered an 'autonomous region [*oblast*]' of the Georgian Soviet Socialist Republic.[41] Article 72 of the 1977 USSR Constitution provided that '[e]ach Union Republic retains

[35] Agreements Establishing the Commonwealth of Independent States (1992) 31 ILM 183, 144.

[36] Charter of the Commonwealth of Independent States (1995) 34 ILM 1282.

[37] CIS Declaration on Respect of Sovereignty, Territorial Integrity and Inviolability of Boundaries of Member States (*Embassy of the Republic of Azerbaijan to Canada,* 15 April 1994) <http://www.azembassy.ca/azerbaijan_conflict.php> accessed 10 July 2012.

[38] 'Georgia Finalizes Withdrawal from CIS', Radio Free Europe 18 April 2009 <http://www.rferl.org/content/Georgia_Finalizes_Withdrawal_From_CIS/1802284.html> accessed 10 July 2012.

[39] See generally T Potier, *Conflict in Nagorno Karabakh, Abkhazia and South Ossetia* (Kluwer 2001) 12–13.

[40] A Nuβberger, 'The War between Russia and Georgia—Consequences and Unresolved Questions' (2009) 1 GJIL 343, 353.

[41] 'Constitution (Fundamental Law) of the Union of Soviet Socialist Republics' (1990) 16 RSL 167, art. 87.

the right freely to secede from the USSR'.[42] Accordingly, under the 1977 USSR Constitution, the Georgian Soviet Socialist Republic had a right to declare its independence on 9 April 1991, while South Ossetia, an 'autonomous region', did not. In fact, in the hierarchical scale of Soviet ethno-federalism, South Ossetia was one more step removed from Union Republic status than Abkhazia, which was briefly a Union Republic and then, for most of the Soviet period, an Autonomous Republic within the Georgian SSR.

As an 'autonomous region' of the Georgian SSR, South Ossetia was also subject to the Union Republic's Constitution, as per Article 86 of the 1977 USSR Constitution, which stated:

> An autonomous region is part of a union republic or a territory. A law on an autonomous region is adopted by the Supreme Soviet of a union republic on the recommendation of the Soviet of People's Deputies of an autonomous region.[43]

Article 70 of the Georgian SSR's Constitution held: 'The territory of Georgia shall not be altered without its consent'.[44] In sum, the Soviet legal system did not allow for South Ossetia's unilateral secession.

The post-Soviet Georgian Constitution also prohibited such action. Article 1 of the Constitution provides:

> Georgia shall be an independent, unified and indivisible state, as confirmed by the Referendum of 31 March 1991, held throughout the territory of the country, including the Autonomous Soviet Socialist Republic of Abkhazia and the Former Autonomous Region of South Ossetia and by the Act of Restoration of the State Independence of Georgia of 9 April 1991.[45]

Moreover, Article 2 declares, '[t]he alienation of the territory of Georgia shall be prohibited. The State frontiers shall be changed only by a bilateral agreement concluded with the neighbouring State'.[46] Finally, Article 38(2) states:

> In accordance with universally recognised principles and rules of international law, the exercise of minority rights shall not oppose the sovereignty, state structure, territorial integrity and political independence of Georgia.[47]

Articles 1, 2, and 38(2) clearly prohibit unilateral secession. The referendums held by South Ossetia in 1992 and 2006—where independence was overwhelmingly supported by the remaining ethnic Ossetian population—are also of no legal force according to the Georgian Constitution, intended as they are to alter the

[42] 'Fundamental Law of the USSR' (n 41) art. 72.

[43] 'Fundamental Law of the USSR' (n 41) art. 86. See also art. 76, which holds that a union republic has its own constitution and exercises its own state power in compliance with the Constitution of the USSR.

[44] 'Constitution of the Soviet Socialist Republic of Georgia' (Regionalism Research Center) <http://www.rrc.ge/law/Gkon_1978_04_15_e.htm?lawid=1387&ing_3=en> accessed 15 June 2012.

[45] 'Constitution of Georgia, 1995' (Constitutional Court of Georgia) <http://www.constcourt.ge/index.php?lang_id=ENG&sec_id=19 > accessed 31 August 2012.

[46] 'Constitution of Georgia, 1995' (n 45).

[47] 'Constitution of Georgia, 1995' (n 45).

constitutional structure of the country.[48] Not surprisingly, both the legality and the legitimacy of the 1992 and 2006 referendums were rejected by Georgia and the international community.[49] This leaves international law as the last basis on which South Ossetians have a legal basis for secession and independence. While the ICJ's Kosovo Advisory Opinion tells us little in some respects, one principle that is clear is that peoples of aspirant states may advocate for or declare their independence without automatically being in contravention of an international rule.[50] Beyond that preliminary step, however, does South Ossetia's declaration of independence have any legal impact?

2. Right to secession under international law

The initial stages of an international legal analysis of self-determination and secession are well-worn. UN Charter Article 1(2) states as one of the purposes of the organization 'respect for the principle of equal rights and self-determination of peoples'.[51] The meaning of self-determination has been formulated by several international instruments, among them the Declaration on Principles of International Law 1970, the Helsinki Final Act 1975, the International Covenant on Civil and Political Rights (ICCPR) 1966, and the International Covenant on Economic, Social and Cultural Rights (ICESCR) 1966. For example, common Article 1 of the ICCPR and ICESR (treaties to which Georgia is a party) states: 'All peoples have the right of self-determination. By virtue of that right they freely determine their political status and freely pursue their economic, social and cultural development'.[52] However, the question of what self-determination means for which peoples has created fault lines. It is established that peoples in a colonial context have a right to self-determination, including statehood. Beyond colonialism, it is largely accepted that self-determination applies in cases of peoples subject to 'alien subjugation, domination and exploitation', to use wording from the UN General Assembly's Friendly Relations Declaration.[53] This postcolonial view was adopted by the International Court of Justice in the *Wall* Advisory Opinion with respect

[48] Article 26(3) of the Georgian Constitution (n 45) states, 'The formation and activity of such public and political associations aiming at overthrowing or forcibly changing the constitutional structure of Georgia, infringing upon the independence and territorial integrity of the country or propagandising war or violence, provoking national, local, religious or social animosity, shall be impermissible.'

[49] See for example, 'EU Statement on the Elections in the Breakaway Region of South Ossetia in Georgia' (17 November 2011) PC.DEL/1092/11 whereby the EU declares it 'does not recognize the constitutional and legal framework within which these elections have taken place' and 'reiterates its support to the territorial integrity and sovereignty of Georgia'. See also United States Mission to the Organization for Security and Co-operation in Europe (OSCE) 'Statement on "Presidential Elections" in South Ossetia' (17 November 2011) PC.DEL/1084/11 & Permanent Mission of Georgia to the OSCE and Other International Organizations in Vienna 'Statement by Georgian Delegation' (16 November 2006) PC.DEL/1096/06 whereby Georgia indicates the referendum was held in 'gross violation of the Georgian laws'.

[50] Kosovo Advisory Opinion (n 22).

[51] Charter of the United Nations (1945).

[52] International Covenant on Civil and Political Rights (1966).

[53] *Declaration on Principles of International Law Friendly Relations and Co-operation Among States in Accordance with the Charter of the United Nations* (1970) ['Friendly Relations Declaration'].

to the Palestinian people and described as having an *erga omnes* character.[54] The situation is murkier beyond foreign subjugation.

Internal self-determination by 'peoples' is generally uncontroversial as a principle, if often messy in practice. In order for the right to self-determination to apply, a group must be designated as a 'people'. Juliane Kokott of the European Court of Justice outlined the following objective elements in determining whether a group may be considered as a 'people': 'a separate culture, a separate language or ethnic origins different from the majority population in the State'.[55] Others make reference to a two-part test to be applied in determining when a group is designated as a 'people'. The first prong considers whether the group shares 'a common racial background, ethnicity, language, religion, history, and cultural heritage' including the 'territorial integrity of the area the group is claiming'.[56] The second prong considers 'the extent to which individuals within the group self-consciously perceive themselves collectively as a distinct "people" and the degree to which the group can form a viable political entity'.[57] Under either of these definitions, Ossetians meet the criteria: they form a distinct ethnic community, self-define as a people, and have institutionally expressed their collective will to be recognized as such. They therefore have a right of internal self-determination. Internal self-determination can take various forms, but perhaps the most common is some degree of sub-state recognition such as local autonomy or federal status. However, as suggested above, external self-determination—which often, but not necessarily, means secession—is more contested terrain in the extra-colonial/alien subjugation context.

While some have cautioned that unilateral secession without restraint is 'downright dangerous'[58] and as such a requirement of consent by the territorial state is necessary to ensure peace, others maintain that in certain circumstances the right to secession prevails over a state's right to territorial integrity and unity.[59] Some suggest that 'remedial secession' is possible in extreme circumstances where a government systematically discriminates against peoples and wholly denies them the right to self-determination. The ICJ, in its Kosovo Advisory Opinion, held that it was not necessary to consider the scope of remedial secession in respect of Kosovo, and so we have little guidance from the Court on this important point.[60]

One of the reasons for the reluctance to accept external self-determination outside of the colonial (or colonial-like) context is the competing international legal

[54] *Legal Consequences of the Construction of a Wall in the Occupied Palestinian Territory* (Advisory Opinion) 2004 < http://www.icj-cij.org/docket/files/131/1671.pdf >, accessed 15 June 2012.

[55] J Kokott, 'Human Rights Situation in Kosovo 1989-1999' in C Tomuschat (ed), *Kosovo and the International Community: A Legal Assessment* (Kluwer Law International 2002); R Thomas, 'The Distinct Cases of Kosovo and South Ossetia: Deciding the Question of Independence on the merits and International Law' (2009) 32 FILJ 1990, 2009.

[56] M Sterio, 'On the Right to External Self-Determination: "Selfistans", Secession, and the Great Powers' Rule' (2010) 19 MJIL 137, 142.

[57] Sterio (n 56).

[58] D Horowitz, 'A Right to Secede?' in S Macedo and A Buchanan (eds), *Secession and Self-determination* (New York University Press 2003) 72–3.

[59] Sterio (n 56) 143. [60] Kosovo Advisory Opinion (n 22) 82–3.

principle of territorial integrity of states. The tension between self-determination and territorial integrity is addressed in the General Assembly's Friendly Relations Declaration:

Nothing in the foregoing paragraphs shall be construed as authorising or encouraging any action which would dismember or impair, totally or in part, the territorial integrity or political unity of sovereign and independent States conducting themselves in compliance with the principle of equal rights and self-determination of peoples as described above and thus possessed of a government representing the whole people belonging to the territory without distinction as to race, creed or colour.[61]

Interestingly, this savings clause has itself been viewed by some as a basis for secession; if a state is not conducting itself in compliance with equal rights and the principle of self-determination then there is no right of territorial integrity.[62]

The conservative view—taking into account the 'soft' nature of the Friendly Relations Declaration—is probably that there is no customary law right to secession outside of the colonial/foreign occupation context. This view is challenged by many and it seems these challenges will only gather momentum post-Kosovo independence, no matter how many times the 'Kosovo is *sui generis*' mantra is repeated. Furthermore, among other authorities, the Supreme Court of Canada has admitted to the possibility of extreme exception circumstances in the Quebec reference.[63] In this case, decided one year before NATO's intervention in Kosovo and therefore well before the Kosovo 'precedent', the Court stated:

International law contains neither a right of unilateral secession nor the explicit denial of such a right, although such a denial is, to some extent, implicit in the exceptional circumstances required for secession to be permitted under the right of a people to self-determination, e.g., the right of secession that arises in the exceptional situation of an oppressed or colonial people, discussed below... The recognized sources of international law establish that the right to self-determination of a people is normally fulfilled through *internal* self-determination—a people's pursuit of its political, economic, social and cultural development within the framework of an existing state. A right to *external* self-determination (which in this case potentially takes the form of the assertion of a right to unilateral secession) arises in only the most extreme of cases and, even then, under carefully defined circumstances.[64]

While refusing to decide on the existence of a third exception to the external self-determination rule—since Quebecers were not an oppressed people the issue was moot— the Court did implicitly lean toward recognizing it:[65]

In summary, the international law right to self-determination only generates, at best, a right to external self-determination in situations of former colonies; where a people is oppressed, as for example under foreign military occupation; or where a definable group is denied meaningful access to government to pursue their political, economic, social and cultural

[61] Friendly Relations Declaration (n 53) 9.
[62] Sterio (n 56) 143.
[63] *Reference Re Secession of Quebec* [1998] 2 SCR 217 [112, 126] with emphasis in original.
[64] *Reference Re Secession of Quebec* (n 63) 138.
[65] *Reference Re Secession of Quebec* (n 63).

development. In all three situations, the people in question are entitled to a right to external self-determination because they have been denied the ability to exert internally their right to self-determination.

3. Legal status of South Ossetia

How does all of this pan out in the South Ossetian context? Although recognizing South Ossetians as a people and therefore having a right to self-determination, the IIFFMCG strictly applied the *uti possidetis* principle and took a hard line on the existence of a South Ossetian state and, more generally, the status of self-determination at international law. The Report states that '[a]s evidenced by state practice and United Nations resolutions, the right to secede unilaterally is uncontested for colonial peoples, and peoples subject to foreign occupation. This situation is not present in South Ossetia and Abkhazia'.[66] Even if there had been an additional, remedial secession exception (which, by contrast to the Supreme Court of Canada, the IIFFMCG is very sceptical of) for cases of genocide, the Report concluded that genocide had not taken place in South Ossetia.

Interestingly, there is no real explanation of why genocide is singled out as being the only exceptional circumstance worthy of thorough examination from a remedial secession point of view. As indicated above, some have suggested that a pattern of denial of basic human rights, including in the context of internal armed conflict (such as in the Georgian situation), might also trigger remedial succession.[67] Although the IIFFMCG concluded that genocide had not taken place, it also concluded that Georgia had exercised an unlawful offensive use of force against South Ossetia in August 2008. Briefly put, it held that Georgia breached its obligation not to use force to solve the South Ossetian conflict as pledged in the 1992 Sochi agreement—an agreement ending the first South Ossetian conflict—and related accords.[68] Furthermore, the IIFFMCG report suggested, Georgia's self-defence claims stumbled over its disproportionate response to Russian–South Ossetian actions, including as manifested in the Georgian shelling of Tskhinvali.[69] Moreover, as McCorquodale and Hausler rightly point out, 'the IIFFMCG Report determined that the state of Georgia was responsible for the escalation of the conflict and it must share the responsibilities for the serious human rights violations'.[70] Nonetheless, implicitly at least, the IIFFMCG rejected

[66] IIFFMCG (n 15) 2, 137.

[67] See generally A Cassese, *Self-Determination of Peoples: A Legal Reappraisal* (Cambridge University Press 1995) 359. It should be noted that in vol 2 of the IIFFMCG report (n 15) (vol 1 contains the authoritative findings), a broader discussion of remedial secession is canvassed (139).

[68] For example, a 1994 Agreement *On the further development of the process of the peaceful regulation of the Georgian-Ossetian conflict and on the Joint Control Commission*, which was based on the Sochi Agreement of 1992, stated 'The parties to the conflict reiterate pledged commitments to settle all the issues in dispute exclusively by peaceful means, without resort to force or threat of resort to force'. See IIFFMCG (n 15) 2, 241.

[69] See IIFFMCG (n 15) 2, 252.

[70] R McCorquodale and K Hausler, 'Caucuses in the Caucasus: The Application of the Right of Self-Determination' in C Waters and JA Green (eds), *Conflict in the Caucasus: Implications for International Legal Order* (Palgrave 2010) 41–2.

the possibility that, even if remedial secession as a category existed, Georgia's actions short of genocide did not constitute grounds for reliance on that principle.

For good measure, the Report also considered whether, independent of a 'right' to secession, South Ossetia had nonetheless objectively achieved statehood. It held that South Ossetia was not currently a state using the Montevideo effectiveness criteria; as noted above, South Ossetia was described as being an entity short of statehood. Even if the classic statehood criteria were there, the legitimacy criteria—including minority/human rights protection and return of displaced persons—would presumably militate against post-Badinter claims to statehood.[71] In light of these reasons, the section of the IIFFMCG Report on statehood and self-determination crisply concludes, recognition of South Ossetian statehood by Russia and other states is illegal.

Is the IIFFMCG conclusion paralleled in the scholarship? Some writers have suggested that Kosovo has opened a Pandora's box, or that this box was already open and that there is an expanded space for secession,[72] while others—probably the majority—criticize or distinguish the Kosovo precedent.[73] In my view, the scholarship which presents a more nuanced view poses the best way forward. For example, Robert McCorquodale and Kristen Hausler suggest that there are steps to be taken before external self-determination becomes a right for South Ossetians. However, while they do admit to the latter form of self-determination as an ultimate possibility, they argue that conflict and tensions by themselves do not constitute exceptional circumstances leading to external self-determination:

> In this instance there must be negotiations in good faith between the government of Georgia and representatives of the people of Abkhazia and South Ossetia. This would place a responsibility on Georgia to guarantee in law and practice that the peoples of Abkhazia and South Ossetia will have significant autonomy over their regions... as an exercise of the right of internal self-determination. Where this guarantee is made and fully carried out (preferably with international monitoring) then the right of self-determination does not arise... If, and only if, all negotiations carried out in good faith break down and all avenues of resolution were truly exhausted—which is not yet the situation here—then the peoples may be able to exercise their right of external self-determination.[74]

Furthermore, they suggest that self-determination need not mean only secession and that we should avoid being black and white on this issue. For instance,

> there could be exercise of a free association with Georgia or with Russia in which Abkhazia and South Ossetia have sovereignty over all matters except over their defence and foreign

[71] This is probably implicit from the discussion of the Abkhaz situation: IIFFMCG (n 15) 2, 135.

[72] See for example, A Reding, 'The Georgian and Ukrainian Conflicts: The Limitations of NATO' (2009) 15 BJWA 171. See also McCorquodale and Hausler (n 70) where it is argued that 'the situation in Kosovo can never be *sui generis* as a matter of precedential impact on the development of international law'.

[73] See for example R Thomas, 'The Distinct Cases of Kosovo and South Ossetia: Deciding the Question of Independence on the Merits and International Law' (2009) 32 FILJ 1990.

[74] McCorquodale and Hausler (n 70) 42–3.

affairs, or the possibility of the merging of South and North Ossetia into a single autonomous region within Russia.[75]

As with the excellent work of Marc Weller, who considers a wide range of self-determination settlements beyond a binary secession/no-secession approach,[76] McCorquodale and Hausler are to be commended for creatively exploring options for South Ossetia. As Weller puts it, 'the all-or-nothing game of self-determination has helped to sustain conflicts, rather than resolve them'.[77] Other scholars have similarly settled on the negotiation option as a way forward. Nußberger suggests, for example, that:

Unlike the situation in Kosovo in South Ossetia there were no long-lasting international negotiations with the aim of finding a compromise. Secession and recognition of South Ossetia as a new State therefore cannot be regarded as '*ultima ratio*' in a process without any alternative.[78]

Have negotiations already been exhausted? Negotiations have indeed taken place, but have not been exhausted. In its April 2011 decision in the case brought by Georgia against Russia, the ICJ held that that no real negotiations had taken place with respect to alleged breaches of the Racial Discrimination Convention. It observed however that:

negotiations did take place between Georgia and the Russian Federation before the start of the relevant dispute...These negotiations involved several matters of importance to the relationship between Georgia and the Russian Federation, namely, the status of South Ossetia and Abkhazia, the territorial integrity of Georgia, the threat or use of force, the alleged breaches of international humanitarian law and of human rights law by Abkhaz or South Ossetian authorities and the role of the Russian Federation's peacekeepers.[79]

Although some progress was made under Shevardnadze—a 1996 settlement memorandum gained some traction, for example—since the Rose Revolution there has been no real progress. As indicated above, Saakashvili put forward proposals for regional autonomy (coupled with threats and even at one point a parallel/'puppet' South Ossetian administration), but South Ossetian authorities roundly rejected these proposals. Attitudes on the South Ossetian side were already hard before the 2008 conflict. They are now harder.[80] It is difficult to imagine negotiations on status going anywhere at this time. Although less satisfying than a comprehensive peace deal created within the international law paradigm of self-determination and respect for territorial integrity, probably the best we can hope for the foreseeable future (though the Arab Spring makes clear that 'impossibilities' should not be labelled as

[75] McCorquodale and Hausler (n 70).

[76] See M Weller, 'Settling Self-Determination Conflicts: Recent Developments' (2009) 20 EJIL 111.

[77] Weller (n 76) 114.

[78] Nuβberger (n 40) 341, 360.

[79] *Case Concerning Application of the International Convention on the Elimination of All Forms of Racial Discrimination* (*Georgia* v *Russian Federation*) 2011 <http://www.icj-cij.org/docket/files/140/16398.pdf 170>, accessed 21 June 2012.

[80] See International Crisis Group (n 23) 14.

such without humility) is the continued management of the conflict for the people affected. This will come through insisting on adherence to the Geneva principles, development of confidence-building measures, serious investigation of war crimes and the safe return of displaced persons. As the International Crisis Group put it in its June 2010 report, '[p]ositions on status are irreconcilable for the present and should be set aside' in place of incremental, practical steps to improve the lives of ethnic South Ossetians and Georgians affected by the conflict.'[81] These steps would include improved mechanisms to ensure non-violence, and better freedom of movement for ordinary people across the administrative border.

IV. Conclusion

In 2009 the presidents of Abkhazia and South Ossetia declared in an op ed in *The Guardian* that 'Abkhazia and South Ossetia are free and independent countries, goals sought by our peoples for centuries. We will never again be a part of Georgia'.[82] As much as one might wish otherwise, it is difficult to see these two regions returning to the Georgian fold any time soon, regardless of how high a degree of regional autonomy is offered. At the same time, international law requires that self-determination be permitted in accordance with territorial integrity and that good-faith negotiations are required to resolve this tension. Perhaps some day, with creative leadership in Tbilisi, Tskhinvali, and Moscow, as well as in Brussels and Washington, this will be possible. For now, the best that international law and organizations can offer may be continued management of the conflict—and insistence on respect for protection of minority rights and the return of refugees and IDPs—while holding a space open for real negotiations between the parties on reconciling self-determination and territorial integrity.[83] If this is achieved, it will be a victory of sorts for the role of international norms and institutions in maintaining world order and improving the lives of ordinary people whose leaders' obsession with status have led to a humanitarian catastrophe spanning over two decades.

[81] International Crisis Group (n 23).

[82] S Bagapsh and E Kokoity, 'The West's Moral Failure over Georgia', *The Guardian* 6 August 2009 <http://www.guardian.co.uk/commentisfree/2009/aug/06/georgia-abkhazia-south-ossetia?INTCMP=SRCH> accessed 17 June 2012.

[83] Though even here we must not be naïve. See for example the summary of the debate in the UN General Assembly regarding a July 2012 resolution [Status of Internally Displaced Persons and Refugees from Abkhazia, Georgia, and the Tskhinvali Region/South Ossetia, Georgia, A/RES/66/283] encouraging measures for the return of displaced persons to their homes in Georgia, including in South Ossetia and Abkhazia: <http://www.un.org/News/Press/docs/2012/ga11262.doc.htm >.

10

Abkhazia

Farhad Mirzayev[1]

I. Introduction

The changing of state boundaries has always been a painful process, with serious political impact on the parties involved.[2] Obviously the current issue is more problematic for the newly independent states of Central and Eastern Europe. After the collapse of the USSR, its newly independent states faced significant problems regarding determination of their state boundaries. The collision between states and certain ethnic minorities in the post-Soviet area has led to still unresolved sanguinary conflicts. The aggressive separatism and sanguinary consequences of the conflicts accompanying the secessionist movements in some former USSR republics again raised the problem of correlation of certain international law principles. Some conflicts in the post-Soviet area were peacefully resolved, whereas others led to bloody clashes. One such conflict took place in Abkhazia,[3] of Georgia. Recent developments during the 'Five-Day War' in South Ossetia had complicated the path to the conflict's legal resolution. This article is an attempt to evaluate the Abkhaz conflict and the concerned parties' arguments and positions from an international law perspective.

II. Historical Background of the Conflict

In 1990 Georgia declared its independence and boycotted the Union's referendum on preserving the USSR, while the Abkhazians voted to save the Soviet state.[4]

[1] Farhad Mirzayev, PhD (University of Leicester), LL.M (University of Nottingham), PhD, LL.M and LL.B (Baku State University).

[2] M Shaw, 'Peoples, Territorialism and Boundaries' (1997) 3 EJIL 478.

[3] G Nodia, 'The Conflict in Abkhazia: National Projects and Political Circumstances' in B Coppieters et al. (eds), *Georgians and Abkhazians, The Search for a Peace Settlement* (Cologne, Sonderveröffentlichung des Bundesinstituts für Ostwissenschaftliche und Internationale Studien 1998) 14.

[4] Conciliation Resources, Georgia–Abkhazia Relations Chronology <http://www.c-r.org/our-work/accord/georgia-abkhazia/chronology.php> accessed 12 August 2009.

In the early 1990s Georgia was among the first constitutional units politically fighting for its independence from the USSR. The Abkhazians were among a few minorities that did not support Georgia's referendum on independence held on 31 March 1991.[5] At the end of 1990, nationalistic forces led by Zviyad Gamsakhurdia came to power in Georgia and declared the restoration of the state independence that Georgia had possessed from 1918 to 1921.[6] Finally, on 9 April 1991, based on the results of the referendum held on 31 March 1991, the National Assembly of Georgia adopted the Constitutional Act on Restoration of State Independence of Georgia.[7] Hereunder, Georgia declared itself a legal successor of the Democratic Republic of Georgia and declared the end of the Georgian SSR.[8]

When in 1992 the Georgian authorities announced the restoration of the 1921 Georgian Democratic Republic, minority groups, including Abkhazia, argued that such declaration would infringe their autonomous status, since the 1921 Georgian Constitution did guarantee regional autonomous rights.[9] Simultaneously, the Abkhazian ASSR declared its independence from Georgia. On 25 August 1990 the Abkhazian ASSR adopted the Declaration on State Sovereignty of Abkhazia and the Resolution on Legal Guarantees of State Sovereignty Protection. Therein Abkhazia declared the merger with Georgia in 1931 as void and illegal.[10] Abkhazia used such arguments for the declaration of its independence from Georgia. The declaration of Abkhazia's independence was accompanied by violent actions against the Georgian high officials and civilians. Having been supported by external force, Abkhazia entered into armed clashes with Georgia.[11] Short-term war between the breakaway region and Georgia resulted in the exodus of ethnic Georgians from Abkhazia, and military defeats of the Georgian troops were one of the reasons for Gamsakhurdia's replacement.

The Abkhazian conflict developed in a similar way to the South Ossetian one, but with certain peculiarities. Despite many similarities with the South Ossetian conflict, the Abkhazian conflict had a different nature and history. Having been conquered by certain regional powers at various times in history, Abkhazia always enjoyed a certain autonomous administrative status. Within the Russian empire, it was one of the administrative units, but after the Bolshevik coup d'état it was incorporated into Georgia's territorial frameworks. Abkhazian sources state that after Abkhazia's downgrading to an autonomous republic in 1931 during the period of Stalinism, the Abkhazians were the subject of mass oppression and discrimination.[12] After Stalin's death the Abkhazians regained administrative

[5] B Coppieters et al., *Statehood and Security: Georgia after the Rose Revolution* (American Academy of Arts and Sciences, MIT Press 2005) 384.

[6] D Djaparidze et al., *Democratic Republic of Georgia 1919–1921: Three Historic Documents* (Tbilisi 1991) 109–133.

[7] Djaparidze et al. (n 6) 98–107.

[8] TM Shamba and YA Neproshin, 'Soviet Abkhazia-Sovereign State' in TM Shamba and YA Neproshin, *Legal Grounds of Statehood* < http://abkhazia.narod.ru/SH/chap-44.html> accessed 27 March 2013.

[9] Djaparidze et al. (n 6) 105.

[10] Shamba and Neproshin (n 8).

[11] G Mirsky, *On Ruins of Empire: Ethnicity and Nationalism in the Former Soviet Union* (Greenwood Publishing Group 1997) 72.

[12] Shamba and Neproshin (n 8).

power over the region; this was intentionally supported by the central Moscow authorities as a part of the *divide et empera* policy for loyalty to the Soviet empire by local minorities.

The Bolshevik coup d'état led to the establishment of the independent Georgian state and Abkhazia was incorporated into the Democratic Republic of Georgia. Only after the Red Army's invasion of Georgia was Abkhazia re-established as a Socialist Soviet Republic.[13] However, it did not enjoy full membership status as others did; in contrast, it had the ambiguous status of 'a treaty republic' associated with the Georgian SSR,[14] which in reality meant the high status of autonomy. According to historical documents, on 4 March 1921 Abkhazia was declared as one of the constitutional units of the USSR, ie as one of the Soviet Socialist Republics.[15] In 1931 the Abkhazian SSR was abolished and merged with the Georgian SSR, becoming the Abkhazian Autonomous Soviet Socialist Republic (ASSR) within the latter's territory.[16]

The separatist unit argues that under the 'remedial theory' the Abkhazians, being subject to gross violation of human rights, pursuant to the principle of *uti possidetis juris* have a right to claim independence based on the boundaries of the Abkhazian SSR which existed for several years within the USSR.[17]

Heavy fighting resulted in a short-term ceasefire brokered by the UN and Russia, which was breached by the Abkhazians after their re-capturing of Sukhumi in Autumn 1993.[18] After the ceasefire between Georgia and Abkhazia, the active phase of negotiations started between the parties, which took place under the direct supervision of the UN, the OSCE, and Russia. The Declaration on Measures for a Political Settlement of the Georgian–Abkhaz Conflict was signed on 4 April 1994 between the Parties[19] and was followed by the Proposals Relating to Political

[13] A Neproshin, 'Abkhazia: Problems of International Recognition' (Lecture at the Moscow State Institute of International Relations (MGIMO), 16–17 May 2006) <http://www.abkhaziya.org/server-articles/article-c165f1f9be6ab370d75a0b3d2af71a59.html> (in Russian) accessed 11 September 2009.

[14] A Menteshashvili, *From the History of Georgian Abkhaz and Ossetian Peoples 1918-1921* (Tbilisi 1990) (in Russian) 14–6.

[15] 'Constitution of the USSR'. Adopted on 31 January 1924. Full text in Y Kukushkin and O Chistyakov, *Outline of the Soviet History* (Politizdat 1987) 17–21.

[16] S Lakoba and O Bgajba, *History of Abkhazia* (Alashargaba 2007) (in Russian) 190–210.

[17] S Bagashp, 'Abkhazia is De-facto State', interview with Novoye Vremya in December 2006 <http://www.gazetanv.ru/article/?id=368> (in Russian) accessed 7 February 2010; S Shamba, 'The Right to Independence', *New Politics* (12 May 2005) <http://www.abkhaziya.org/server-articles/article-1297b5ed939b13a5956eef606743750d.html> (in Russian) accessed 12 November 2009; A Cyganok, 'Legal Grounds for Recognition of Abkhazia and South Ossetia' (10 October 2006) <http://www.apn.ru/publications/article10592.htm> (in Russian) accessed 17 October 2009; N Petro, 'What the Tagliavini Report Fails to Consider' OpEdNews (3 October 2009) <http://www.opednews.com/articles/What-the-Tagliavini-Report-by-Nicolai-N-Petro-091002-478.html> accessed 11 February 2010.

[18] Agreement on Ceasefire in Abkhazia and Mechanisms of Compliance Control (signed on 27 July 1993), Bulletin of the Parliament of the Republic of Georgia (№ 9, 1993) (in Russian) 223–7; A Zverev, 'Ethnic Conflicts in the Caucasus 1988–1994' in B Coppieters (ed), *Contested Borders in the Caucasus* (Vubpress 1996) 54.

[19] Declaration 'On Measures for a Political Settlement of the Georgian-Abkhaz Conflict' (signed in Geneva 4 April 1994); *Free Georgia Newspaper* (№ 52, 5 April 1994) (in Russian).

and Legal Elements of the Comprehensive Settlement of the Georgian–Abkhaz conflict adopted as Annex II of the UN Secretary-General's Report of 3 May 1994.[20] After the 'Five-Day War' in South Ossetia and massive-scale military operations by Russia against Georgia, Abkhazia, together with South Ossetia, declared their independence and were recognized by Russia.

The conflict over the status of Abkhazia has once again become 'frozen'. As yet there have been no further attempts at its settlement, although much is expected after the recent takeover of power in Georgia.

III. Legal Analysis of the Abkhaz Conflict

1. The legality of Abkhazia's external self-determination under international law

The main emphasis should be placed on the legality of the two breakaway regions' right to external self-determination, as well as on Russia's follow-up recognition of the two separatist units.

In the case of South Ossetia and Abkhazia, there were some objections, but there were no strong reactions to Russia's recognition. However, today it can be argued that, along with the Russian recognition, the follow-up recognition of these separatist units by other states, such as Nicaragua,[21] Venezuela,[22] Nauru,[23] Vanuatu,[24] and Tuvalu,[25] makes these cases exceptional in the current international legal system.

It is generally accepted that the right to self-determination in the form of secession from the parent state was originally developed within the colonial context,[26] and the international community does not recognize the right to external self-determination that may lead to the violation of the principle of territorial

[20] Report of the Secretary-General 'On the Situation in Abkhazia, Georgia. Proposals for Political and Legal Elements for a Comprehensive Settlement of the Georgian/Abkhaz Conflict', S/1994/529 (3 May 1994) 11.

[21] El Presidente de la República Nicaragua Decreto No. 47-2008 <http://www.cancilleria.gob.ni/publicaciones/r_abjasia.pdf> accessed 4 May 2010; 'Nicaragua Recognizes South Ossetia and Abkhazia', *Ria Novosti* (4 September 2008) <http://en.rian.ru/world/20080904/116538071.html> accessed 3 May 2010.

[22] 'Chavez Recognizes South Ossetia, Abkhazia as Independent', Radio Free Europe (Radio Liberty), <http://www.rferl.org/content/Chavez_Visits_Russia_To_Discuss_Arms_Energy_Deals/1819273.html> accessed 29 April 2010.

[23] L Harding, 'Tiny Nauru Struts World Stage by Recognising Breakaway Republics', *The Guardian* (14 December 2009) <http://www.theguardian.com/world/2009/dec/14/nauro-recognises-abkhazia-south-ossetia> accessed 3 April 2010.

[24] 'Vanuatu recognizes Abkhazia independence—Abkhaz ministry', *Moscow: RIA Novosti* (31 May 2011) <http://en.rian.ru/world/20110531/164348947.html> accessed 15 September 2011.

[25] 'Tuvalu Recognises Abkhazia's Independence', Lenta Ru Information Agency (23 September 2011) (in Russian) <http://lenta.ru/news/2011/09/23/tuvalu/> accessed 15 September 2011.

[26] UNGA Res 1513 (XV) (14 December 1960), UN Doc A/RES/1513 (XV); M Shaw, *International Law* (5th edn, CUP 2003) 230; R Higgins, *Problems and Process: International Law and How We Use It* (Clarendon Press 1994) 121–3.

integrity, ie impairment of the territorial, political and economic unity of a sovereign state'.[27] However, established practice was departed from in the case of the recognition of Kosovo by the western world and of Abkhazia and South Ossetia by Russia and some other states. In both cases, the parties initiating such recognition claimed that their case had 'a specific no-precedent' character and thus could not serve as grounds for similar action with respect to other situations.[28]

It is generally supported that international law is not friendly to unlawful secession.[29] In fact, there are many precedents of central authorities undertaking military actions against separatist units, and certain clashes leading to civilian deaths have not qualified as acts of genocide. Chechnya is a clear example where it was reported that the Russian regular army killed not only combatants, but also civilians.[30] Nevertheless, Russia's actions were never qualified as acts of genocide by the international community.

In cases where separatist groups illegally exercise the right to external self-determination, the parent state is entitled to prevent this process within its constitutional law framework.[31] Therefore, actions of the parent state against the separatist groups within the framework of that state and in compliance with humanitarian law requirements cannot be considered as grounds for separatist groups to claim external self-determination.

The Declaration on Principles of International Law Concerning Friendly Relations and Cooperation among States in Accordance with the Charter of the United Nations ('the Declaration on Principles of International Law') provides that the right to self-determination shall not be used for impairment of the territorial integrity of a sovereign state if such a state, in reality, creates all conditions for the exercise of the right to internal self-determination.[32] From this it can be argued that external self-determination is admissible only in certain 'special cases' exercised with support of the international community.[33]

For Abkhazia and South Ossetia, no such circumstances ever existed. These minority groups were not subject to acts of genocide or gross violation of human

[27] UNGA Res 2625 (XXV) (24 October 1970), UN Doc A/8018.

[28] President Medvedev's Statement of 26 August 2008 <http://archive.kremlin.ru/eng/speeches/2008/08/26/1543_type82912_205752.shtml> accessed 29 December 2009; UNSC, 'Statements by UK and US Representatives at the Emergency Session of the Security Council', 5839th Meeting (PM) (18 February 2008) UN Doc SC/9252; Bureau of International Information Programs, US Department of State <http://www.america.gov/st/washfile-english/2007/March/20070321142711MVyelwarC0.6473047.html#ixzz0mwCi6HA8> accessed 7 June 2009.

[29] JE de Arechaga, 'International Law in the Past Third of a Century' (1978) 159 RCADI 111; JP Humphrey, *Human Rights and the United Nations: A Great Adventure* (Transnational Publishers 1984) 129; A Buchanan, *Secession: The Legitimacy of Political Divorce From Fort Sumter to Lithuania and Quebec* (Westview Press 1991) 11; Higgins (n 26) 125.

[30] S Richard, 'Introduction: Why Chechnya?' in R Sakwa, *Chechnya: From Past to Future* (Anthem Press 2005) 1–42.

[31] J Crawford, *The Creation of States in International Law* (2nd edn, Clarendon Press 2006) 390.

[32] UNGA Res 2625 (XXV) (24 October 1970), UN Doc A/8018.

[33] M Kohen, *Secession: International Law Perspectives* (CUP 2006) 300–12; J Castellino, 'The Secession of Bangladesh in International Law: Setting New Standards' (2000) 7 AYIL 83; de Arechaga (n 29) 111; D Raic, *Statehood and the Law of Self-Determination* (Martinus Nijhoff 2002) 314; *Reference re Secession of Quebec* [1998] 2 SCR 217 para 123; Buchanan (n 29) 227.

rights. Russia often compares these two Georgian cases with that of Kosovo. However, the Kosovo conflict was a purely ethnic conflict resulting in the genocide of the Albanian ethnic civilians residing in this region,[34] whereas the conflicts in Abkhazia and South Ossetia had a strong political nature without intentional discrimination against any groups or crimes against humanity. There are no proven facts providing grounds to argue that the central authorities in Georgia systematically and extensively violated the human rights of the Abkhazians.[35] Moreover, the Abkhazians were granted the right to internal self-determination during the Soviet times,[36] and from the beginning of the conflicts Georgia has periodically offered extensive autonomy to Abkhazia.[37]

Although Georgia's arguments that South Ossetia was never attacked by Georgia are disputable, it cannot be proven that Georgia was planning to commit an act of genocide and slay all civilians in South Ossetia. While under the Convention on the Prevention and Punishment of the Crime of Genocide (GA Resolution 260 (III) (1948)) ('the CPPCG'), the act of genocide is qualified as intent to destroy certain ethnic, religious, or racial groups, the attack on South Ossetian and Russian combatants cannot be qualified as an act of genocide against South Ossetia.[38] In the case of Abkhazia, although there was no attack by Georgia, the separatist unit claims that external self-determination was exercised in response to a potential Georgian military threat. Even if Georgia used force against South Ossetia, under no circumstances can it be treated as an attack against Russia giving the latter the right to use force against Georgia. It cannot be accepted in light of the prohibition of the use of force as a *jus cogens* norm in international law.[39] Since Abkhazia is recognized as part of Georgia, arguably any military action undertaken by Georgia was a matter of internal affairs.

Abkhazia claims that it exercised its right to external self-determination and held a referendum that expressed the will of the Abkhazians in response to the gross human rights violations by Georgia.[40] In Abkhazia and South Ossetia,

[34] UNSC Res 1244 (1999) (30 June 1999), UN Doc S/RES/1244; K Borgen, 'Kosovo's Declaration of Independence: Self-Determination, Secession and Recognition' 12 ASIL Insights 2 <http://www.asil.org/insights/volume/12/issue/2/kosovos-declaration-independence-self-determination-secession-and> accessed 3 April 2010.

[35] A Nußberger, 'The War between Russia and Georgia—Consequences and Unresolved Questions' (2009) 1(2) GJIL 360.

[36] Lakoba and Bgajba (n 16) 190–210.

[37] *Report of the Secretary-General on the situation in Abkhazia, Georgia* (2 April 2008) UN Doc S/2008/219 para 18.

[38] ICJ, *Application of the International Convention on the Elimination of All Forms of Racial Discrimination (Georgia* v *Russia)* [2008] <http://www.icj-cij.org/docket/index.php?p1=3& p2=1&case =140> accessed 12 September 2009.

[39] ICJ, *Military and Paramilitary Activities in and against Nicaragua (Nicaragua* v *United States)* [1986] ICJ Reports 14, 100–1; J Frowein, 'Recognition' in R Bernhardt, *Encyclopaedia of Public International Law* (North Holland Publishing 2000) 628.

[40] G Hewitt, 'Abkhazia and South Ossetia, A Year On' *Opendemocracy* (11 August 2009) < http://www.opendemocracy.net/article/abhazia-and-south-ossetia-a-year-on > accessed 27 January 2010; E Adzhindzhal, *Abkhazia's Liberation and International Law* (Sukhum 2007) < http://www.abkhaziya.org/foreign/liberation.html > accessed 19 October 2009; G Hewitt, 'Abkhazia and South Ossetia: Heart of Conflict, Key to Solution' *Opendemocracy* (18 August 2008) < http://www.opendemocracy.net/article/abkhazia-and-south-ossetia-heart-of-conflict-key-to-solution > accessed 29 November 2009.

neither the Abkhazians nor the South Ossetians were majority groups. Nowadays, these groups exceed the number of Georgians only as a result of violent ethnic cleansing.[41] The referendums held by the separatist units were not attended by the displaced Georgians who constitute two-thirds of the indigenous population of these breakaway regions. Therefore, the legitimacy of the results of such referendums is in doubt.

In the doctrine of modern international law there is a certain view that the right to external self-determination can be exercised if certain groups are subject to a repressive regime ('Remedial Theory').[42] According to some commentators, the right to self-determination can be transformed into the right of secession if certain minority groups are oppressed and eliminated from participation in state political life,[43] and if all this have led to gross violations of human rights, including acts of genocide.[44] However, the Remedial Theory is not well developed and lacks support in international law. In fact, based on state practice it can be argued that secession can take place in 'special' cases when the parent state agrees with the unit's secession and there is broad support within the international community, such as the cases of Bangladesh or South Sudan.[45] In the case of Abkhazia, Georgia never agreed to Abkhazia's secession; nor was it supported by the international community.[46]

[41] US State Department, 'Country Reports on Human Rights Practices for 1993' (February 1994) 619; Human Rights Watch, 'Georgia/Abkhazia: Violations of the Laws of War and Russia's Role in the Conflict' (Helsinki, March 1995) <http://www.hrw.org/reports/pdfs/g/georgia/georgia953.pdf > accessed 14 February 2009.

[42] D Raiç, *Statehood and the Law of Self-Determination* (Martinus Nijhoff 2002) 366–372; A Randelzhofer, 'Article 51' in B Simma et al. (eds), *The Charter of the United Nations. A Commentary* (Vol I, 2nd edn, OUP 2002) 58.

[43] A Cassese, *Self-determination of Peoples: Legal Reappraisal* (CUP 1995) 118–22; T Franck et al., 'L'intégrité territoriale du Québec dans l'hypothèse de l'accession à la souveraineté' in *Commission d'étude des Questions afférentes à l'accession du Québec à la Souveraineté: Projet de Rapport* (Quebec, Annete 1992) 51–2; G Marchildon and E Maxwell, 'Quebec's Right of Secession under Canadian and International Law' (1992) 32 VJIL 583; *Katangese Peoples' Congress* v *Zaire Case* [1994] 75/92 Communication of the African Commission on Human and Peoples' Rights 66; *Katangese People's Congress* v *Zaire* (2000) 75/92 African Commission of Human and Peoples' Rights in R Murray and M Evans (eds), *Documents of the African Commission of Human Rights and Peoples' Rights* (Hart Publishing 2001) 389.

[44] K Doehring, *Völkerrecht* (2nd edn, CF Müller 2004) 347.

[45] Kohen (n 33) 300–12; J Castellino (n 33) 83; K Borgen (n 34); C Know, 'The Secession of South Sudan: A Case Study in African Sovereignty and International Recognition' (College of Saint Benedict and Saint John's University 2012) <http://digitalcommons.csbsju.edu/cgi> accessed 7 August 2012.

[46] 'OSCE Chair Condemns Russia's Recognition of Abkhazia, S. Ossetia' *Civil Georgia* (Tbilisi 2008) <http://www.civil.ge/eng/article.php?id=19296> accessed 6 April 2010; 'US Condemns Russia over Georgia', BBC News (4 September 2008) <http://news.bbc.co.uk/2/hi/europe/7597336.stm> accessed 4 December 2009; 'Statement of the Meeting of the North Atlantic Council at the Level of Foreign Ministers Held at NATO Headquarters, Brussels' (19 August 2008) <http://www.nato.int/cps/en/natolive/official_texts_29950.htm> accessed 28 August 2008; S Castle, 'EU Agrees to Support Georgia, but Stalls over More Severe Action', *New York Times* 28 August 2008 <http://www.nytimes.com/2008/08/28/world/europe/28iht-union.4.15721770.html?_r=1> accessed 17 April 2010.

Even if Abkhazia can claim to possess some features of statehood as provided by the Montevideo Convention,[47] this breakaway region can hardly be regarded as a real sovereign independent state.

It can be argued that the authorities of Abkhazia are dependent on Russia. Today Russian troops guard the territories of this self-proclaimed state and all of its high officials are approved by the Russian political administration. It is generally accepted that a state can be recognized if it is stable, independent, and effective, as shown by the League of Nations in Finland's case.[48] One example of a lack of effective government in Abkhazia is citizenship. The separatist unit compels the inhabitants of this breakaway region (including ethnic Georgians) to accept either Abkhazian or Russian citizenship. Abkhaz authorities established dual citizenship and are forcing those Georgians wishing to return to their homes in Abkhazia to apply for separatist unit citizenship in order to enjoy the full scope of rights and freedoms. The main requirement for the Georgians is to officially reject Georgian citizenship and produce confirmation of such refusal.[49] In fact, such discriminatory and forceful granting of dual Abkhaz–Russian citizenship can be considered illegal.

A capacity to enter into relations with other states and communicate with them independently without the support of any third states is a key feature of an independent state. Other features include an ability to communicate independently with other states on the issue of recognition.[50] Based on previous precedents and qualifications for effective control available in international law,[51] Abkhazia arguably depends hugely on Russia and is under its effective control. Undoubtedly, neither Abkhazia nor South Ossetia were able to enter into relations with the states which recognized them. It is believed that all of those countries recognizing Abkhazia's independence received certain dividends from Russia, either in the form of hugely favourable credits or Russian arms at privileged/discounted rates.[52]

[47] V Chirikba, 'The International Legal Status of the Republic of Abkhazia In the Light of International Law', AbkhazWorld (2 September 2009) < http://www.abkhazworld.com/articles/analysis/285-int-legal-status-abkhazia-vchirikba.html > accessed 27 January 2010; V Margiyev and S Kesayev, *Statehood of South Ossetia: Past, Present and Future* (in Russian) (Vladikavkaz 2009); *Report of the Committee on CIS of the Council of Federation of the Russian Federation* < http://www.council.gov.ru/files/journalsf/item/20090916154932.pdf > (in Russian) accessed 13 February 2010.

[48] DJ Harris, *Cases and Materials on International Law* (5th edn, Sweet & Maxwell 2010) 147; D Devine, 'The Requirements of Statehood Re-Examined' (1971) 34 MLR 410–15; W Vitzthum, *Völkerrecht* (Walter de Gruyter 1997) 227.

[49] Council of the European Union, 'Independent International Fact-Finding Mission on the Conflict in Georgia' (September 2009) 18 <http://www.ceiig.ch> accessed 19 October 2009.

[50] Crawford (n 31) 62–3; 'State Defined' in *Restatement of the Law, Third of the Foreign Relations Law of the United States* (1986) para 201.

[51] *Lotus Case (France* v *Turkey)* [1927] PCIJ Series A No. 10; Dissenting Opinion of Judge Anzilotti in *Austro-German Customs Union Case (Austria* v *Germany)* [1931] PCIJ Series A/B, No 53, 83.

[52] Radio Free Europe, 'Tiny Nauru in $50 Million Russia Gambit' (14 December 2009) <http://www.rferl.org/content/Tiny_Nauru_In_50_Million_Russia_Gamble/1903967.html> accessed 19 March 2010; Y Maofeng and L Jingli, 'Russia, Venezuela Talk Weapons, Oil, Lubricate Relations' Xinhua World News Agency (11 September 2009) < http://news.xinhuanet.com/english/2009-09/11/content_12033727.htm > accessed 7 January 2010; 'Why Nicaragua Recognised South Ossetia and Abkhazia', interview of Foreign Minister of Nicaragua Samuel Santos Lopez with *Russia Today* < http://rt.com/About_Us/Programmes/Spotlight/2008-11-11/359190.html > accessed 29 March 2010.

Abkhazia's incapacity to enter into relations with other states in the light of the existing dispute with Georgia is arguably evidence of its lack of sovereignty and independence and, in turn, grounds for its non-recognition by the international community.

The existence of a sufficient number of persistent objectors to Abkhazia's secession is another ground justifying the argument that secession has no support under customary international law. However, precedents such as Kosovo, South Ossetia, and Abkhazia have given grounds for further speculation arguing in favour of external self-determination.

2. Territorial integrity and *uti possidetis* in support of the Georgian boundaries and territory

While Georgia considers Abkhazia to be an integral part of its territory, the breakaway region claims that it has exercised, based on the principle of self-determination, the right to secession. Like other separatist units in the post-Soviet territory under the provisions of the Soviet Constitution(s), Abkhazia had no constitutional right to claim independence. As argued under the principle of *uti possidetis juris*, the internal administrative borders of the 15 constitutional units of the USSR transformed into the international boundaries of newly established independent states.[53]

Abkhazia was among 20 autonomous republics in the USSR which constituted an integral part of the Georgian SSR, and this was reflected in Article 85 of the 1977 USSR Constitution. Evidently, all Soviet Constitutions (including the latest one, from 1977) explicitly determined the subjects of the right to secession, limiting their number to the 15 Soviet republics as constitutional parts of the USSR.[54] Neither the Constitution of the Georgian SSR[55] nor the Constitution of the Abkhazian ASSR[56] provided the right for this autonomous unit to secede either from the Georgian SSR or from the USSR. Accordingly, the secession of Abkhazia in the early 1990s should be regarded as a serious violation of the Soviet legislation.

As with all separatist units in the post-Soviet area, Abkhazia claims that the USSR's Law 'On Procedure on Solution of Issues Related to the Secession of Union Republic From the USSR' adopted on 3 April 1990 ('the Secession Law')[57] was one of the main legal grounds for its right to external self-determination. Article 3 thereof established procedures for secession of only the union republics through

[53] FS Mirzayev, *Contemporary Problems of State Frontiers Delimitation in Modern International Law* (Ganun 2004) (in Russian); FS Mirzayev, 'Azerbaijan on the Crossroads: Legal Evaluation of the Contemporary Territorial Issues. Self-Determination v. Territorial Integrity': Summer University's Best Papers' Digest (University of Fribourg Press, September 2005) 53–72.

[54] AL Unger, *Constitutional Development in the USSR* (Methuen 1981) 60.

[55] 'Constitution of the Georgian Soviet Socialist Republic' (adopted on 15 April 1978), 'The Collection of the Constitutional Acts of the Georgian SSR' (1921–1978) (Tbilisi 1983) (in Russian) 249–293. English text: < http://www.rrc.ge/law/Gkon_1978_04_15_e.htm?lawid=1387&lng_3=en> accessed 13 February 2010.

[56] 'Congresses of the Soviets of the USSR, Union and Autonomous Soviet Socialist Republics of the Transcaucas', collection of documents, 1923–1937 (vol VI, Moscow 1964) (in Russian) 686–700.

[57] Full text in *New Laws of the USSR* (Issue 1) (Yuridicheskaya Literatura 1990) 124.

referendums. However, referring to the above legal analysis on the Secession Law's compliance with the 1977 USSR Constitution, if the USSR Constitution provided a right to secession only for the 15 union republics, the Secession Law granted such rights also to the autonomous units of the Soviet Union. In fact, Article 76 of the USSR Constitution provided that the union republics are sovereign states, and under Article 78 their territory could be changed only with their consent, whereas Article 3 of the Secession Law specifically provided that referendums on secession from the union republics by the autonomous republics and *oblasts* could be held by the latter. It can be argued that the Secession Law was not properly complied with by Abkhazia.

Moreover, under the requirements of the Secession Law, referendums on secession by the autonomous units within the Soviet Union republics could be recognized as valid if no less than two-thirds of the USSR citizens residing in this territory voted for such secession. In the case of Abkhazia, subsequent to the ethnic cleansing of the Georgians, the referendums held by the separatist units were not attended by two-thirds of the indigenous ethnic Georgian population of this region. Undoubtedly, the results of such referendums could not be regarded as lawful. As mentioned above, the Secession Law was severely criticized by most scholars.[58] It can be concluded that under the Soviet legislation, Abkhazia did not possess a right to secession, and any references by it to the Soviet laws as legal grounds for secession from Georgia lack substance.

Based on the principle of *uti possidetis juris*, it can be argued that since the declaration of independence by the Republic of Georgia, the former administrative boundaries of the Georgian SSR (which included also Abkhazia and South Ossetia) have been transformed into the internationally recognized boundaries of sovereign Georgia.[59] The provision of the right to secession by the Soviet Constitution, granting such a right to the union republics, is solid grounds for the exercise of external self-determination by the union republics and, on the basis of the principle of *uti possidetis*, for determining the boundaries of the independent Republic of Georgia within the frameworks of the Georgian SSR.

The international community has already expressed its position on the right to external self-determination by the constitutional units of the collapsed state without approving the right of autonomous regions to enjoy the same right. The Badinter Commission on the former Yugoslavia explicitly argued in favour of the application of the *uti possidetis* principle to the administrative boundaries of the former constitutional units of the SFRY.[60] Based on this, it can be argued that the two Georgian separatist units' claims to exercise the right to secession from Georgia are

[58] A Cassese (n 43) 264–5; R Mullerson, *International Law, Rights and Politics: Developments in Eastern Europe and the CIS* (Routledge 1994) 75.

[59] FS Mirzayev, 'The *Uti Possidetis* Principle in Modern International Law and its Application to the Post-Soviet Area: Theory and Practice' (2004) 6 Law and Politics (in Russian) 54, 43–53; FS Mirzayev, 'The *Uti Possidetis* Principle: History and Modern Reality' (2004) 3 UYIL 36–47.

[60] EC Yugoslav Arbitration Commission (Opinion No 2) (1992) 3 EJIL 183–5; C Szacz, 'The Fragmentation of Yugoslavia' (1994) PASIL 34; M Weller, 'The International Response to the Dissolution of the Socialist Federal Republic of Yugoslavia' (1992) 86 AJIL 591.

legally groundless. As observed by some commentators, there could be no 'secession from secession' by the autonomous units of the former Soviet republics, including Abkhazia and South Ossetia, since these units have a right to secession under neither international nor domestic law.[61]

Georgia was a member of the Commonwealth of Independent States (CIS) before the 'Five-Day War' in South Ossetia and had a solid argument in referring to the various CIS legal instruments to justify its legal position regarding the conflicts in Abkhazia and South Ossetia. Considering the historical background of the USSR's collapse, the whole procedure of the former Soviet republics' delimitation clearly indicates that the former constitutive parts of the USSR agreed to apply the principle of *uti possidetis* with respect to their boundaries and territories. Like other international and regional legal instruments, the acts signed within the CIS format also confirmed the recognition of the prevailing force of the principles of territorial integrity and inviolability of frontiers over external self-determination targeting the territorial unity of sovereign states. It can be argued that recognition of the former Soviet administrative boundaries as international boundaries of the newly established independent states in 1992 strongly supports the argument that the principle of *uti possidetis* was applied by the former constitutional units of the USSR, notwithstanding the absence of any direct references to the principle in the Minsk and Almaty Declarations and the CIS Charter.

Debates around the determination of boundaries of the newly established CIS member states strongly encouraged the concerned parties to fix their positions in the agreements that would guarantee the inviolability of boundaries existing within the former USSR.[62]

Article 5 of the 8 December 1991 Agreement on Establishment of the CIS signed in Minsk proclaims that the parties recognize and respect the territorial integrity and the inviolability of existing boundaries within the CIS.[63] This was affirmed again in the 21 December 1991 Alma-Ata Declaration signed by 11 former republics of the former USSR, which affirmed CIS member states' obligations to recognize and respect the territorial integrity and inviolability of the existing boundaries of member states.[64] The CIS Charter adopted on 22 January 1993 in Minsk in Article 3 affirms the respect for the territorial integrity of member states and the recognition of existing boundaries, ie the transformation of the administrative boundaries of the former USSR republics into international boundaries.[65] Moreover, in 1994 the CIS member states signed the new Declaration on Respect of Sovereignty, Territorial Integrity and Inviolability of Boundaries of Member

[61] M Weller, 'Settling Self-Determination Conflicts: Recent Developments' (2009) 20 EJIL 1, 111–65.

[62] Weller (n 61) 119.

[63] 'Agreement on the Establishment of the Commonwealth of Independent States' (signed on 8 December 1991 in Minsk) (1992) 31 ILM 138.

[64] Almaty Declaration (21 December 1991) (1992) 31 ILM 148.

[65] Charter of the Commonwealth of Independent States (22 January 1993) (1995) 34 ILM 1283.

States,[66] which reinforced the application of the principle of *uti possidetis* to the territory and boundaries of the former USSR republics.

The EC Guidelines on Recognition of New States in Eastern Europe and the Soviet Union of 16 December 1991 ('the Guidelines') explicitly provided for the respect for all existing boundaries that could be changed only through mutual consent.[67] As Shaw rightly observes, such agreements within the CIS and the position of the EC expressed in the Guidelines support the application of the principle of *uti possidetis* in the post-Soviet area. [68] Even the absence of a direct reference to the principle of *uti possidetis* in the key legal instruments adopted within the CIS format provides an argument that one of the primary goals of the former USSR republics was the intention to apply the principle of *uti possidetis* for legitimization of the transformation of former administrative boundaries inherited from the Soviet Union into the international boundaries of the newly independent states.[69] Accordingly, it is arguable that under the CIS Charter and other agreements jointly signed and adopted by the former USSR republics, the principle of *uti possidetis* is applicable and was applied by such former republics.[70]

Although the right to self-determination has been formed as a fundamental norm of international law, the international acceptance of this principle in the form of secession from an independent state has not been recognized.[71] The position of the international community in the process of the USSR and SFRY dissolution through support of the territorial integrity of newly independent states has shown that it was seriously concerned with matters of international peace and stability, which may be threatened by boundary and territorial conflicts. In fact, the dissolution of the Soviet Union raised the question of the current status of the right to self-determination in the form of secession.[72] Obviously, by signing without any reservation the UN Charter, the CIS Foundation Agreement, the Almaty Declaration, the CIS Charter, and a number of other relevant legal instruments, Russia has recognized the territorial integrity and inviolability of the boundaries of the Republic of Georgia, which certainly implied that Abkhazia is part of Georgia's territory.

[66] CIS Declaration on Respect of Sovereignty, Territorial Integrity and Inviolability of Boundaries of Member States (15 April 1994) (1994) 7 Bulletin of International Agreements (in Russian) 9–10.

[67] EC Declaration on Recognition of New States in Eastern Europe and the Soviet Union (16 December 1991) (1992) 31 ILM 1487.

[68] Shaw (n 2).

[69] M Shaw, 'Supplément à la duplique: Rapports additionnels des experts de l'amicus curiae' in *The Matter of the Reference re Secession of Quebec* (Montreal 1998) 5 para 11.

[70] Shaw (n 2); R Mullerson, 'New Developments in the Former USSR and Yugoslavia' (1993) 33 VJIL 299; FS Mirzayev (n 59).

[71] G Fox, 'Self-Determination In the Post-Cold War Era: A New Internal Focus?' (1995) 16 MJIL 738; D Cass, 'Re-Thinking Self-Determination: A Critical Analysis of Current International Law Theories' (1992) 18 SJILC 27–29.

[72] L Eastwood, 'Secession: State Practice and International Law After the dissolution of the Soviet Union and Yugoslavia' (1993) 3 JCIL 300.

In fact, within the CIS format under the bilateral and multilateral agreements both Georgia and Russia undertook to recognize and respect the territorial integrity and inviolability of boundaries which emerged as a result of the USSR's collapse. The above-mentioned CIS instruments declared that each member state would respect the sovereignty and inviolability of the state borders of other member states and recognize the existing borders and the territorial integrity of the member states.[73] Legally speaking it meant that, despite the existing territorial disputes, the former Soviet constitutional units, including Georgia and Russia, applied *uti possidetis* as a legal instrument for establishing stability and as a preventive tool against the defragmentation of newly independent states, meaning the principle was a prevailing force over the right of such newly independent states to external self-determination. As discussed above, the practice of the former USSR republics and the legal grounds expressed in the instruments signed and adopted within the CIS format contributed greatly to the strengthening of the principle of *uti possidetis* that could be used by Georgia to strengthen its legal position on the Abkhaz conflict with reference to such state practice.[74]

The Badinter Commission's opinions on the correlation of the right to external self-determination and the principle of *uti possidetis* in the case of Yugoslavia, and the inadmissibility of the use of the former to change the existing boundaries of newly independent states that were constitutional units of the SFRY,[75] can be similarly applied to the USSR. Undoubtedly, there are many similarities between these two socialist federations, their constitutions, and their federal organizational structures. Similar to the dissolution of Yugoslavia,[76] during the USSR's collapse the international community did not recognize the right of autonomous *oblasts* and republics to external self-determination.[77] In the case of Yugoslavia it was expressly stated that former autonomous units, as parts of six former constitutional units of the Socialist Yugoslav Federation, were entitled to the right to self-determination neither under the Yugoslav Constitution (which did not provide a right of secession for such units) nor under modern international law protecting territorial integrity and internationally recognized boundaries of sovereign states.[78] The position of

[73] Agreement 'On the Establishment of the Commonwealth of Independent States' (signed on 8 December 1991 in Minsk) (1992) 31 ILM 138; Almaty Declaration (21 December 1991) (1992) 31 ILM 148; CIS Declaration 'On Respect of Sovereignty, Territorial Integrity and Inviolability of Boundaries of Member States' (15 April 1994) (1994) 7 Bulletin of International Agreements (in Russian) 9–10.

[74] M Shaw, 'The Heritage of States: The Principle of Uti Possidetis Juris Today' (1997) 77 BYIL 110–11; A Eide, 'Territorial Integrity of States, Minority Protection and Guarantee for Autonomy Arrangements: Approaches and Roles of the United Nations' in UniDem Seminar (eds), *Local Self-government, Territorial Integrity and Protection of Minorities* (COE Publishing 1996) 282; L Weerts, 'Heurs et malheurs du principe de l'uti possidetis: le cas du démembrement de l'URSS' in O Corten et al. (eds), *Démembrements d'États et délimitations territoriales: l'uti possidetis en question(s)* (Bruylant 1999) 79–142, 107.

[75] EC Yugoslav Arbitration Commission (1993) 92 ILR 168.

[76] EC Yugoslav Arbitration Commission (n 75).

[77] EC *Declaration on Recognition of New States in Eastern Europe and the Soviet Union* (16 December 1991) (1992) 31 ILM 1487.

[78] EC Yugoslav Arbitration Commission (Opinion No 2) (1992) 3 EJIL 182–5; S Sharma, *Territorial Acquisition, Disputes and International Law* (Martinus Nijhoff 1997) 228–9.

various states and international organizations remains unchanged and there is no support for external self-determination impairing the territorial integrity of existing sovereign states.[79]

IV. External Self-determination or Third-state Factor: Russia's 'Special' Role

The 15 years of peace negotiations led essentially by Russia, and passively by the UN and other international organizations, added nothing to the settlement of the Abkhaz or the South Ossetian conflicts. The only success of such mediation was the ceasefire that stopped the deaths of innocent people and the return of a few thousand internally displaced persons (IDPs) to the Ghali region of Abkhazia, which was recently left again by the Georgians as a result of Russia's military actions against Georgia.

If Russian-dominated CIS peacekeeping forces played some positive role in the early stages of the conflict, but in the later stages they were used by Russia to show support for the separatists. All forms of Russian support to these two breakaway regions were considered by Georgia as aggression against its territorial integrity, boundaries, and sovereignty. Georgia opposed Russia's strong political and economic presence in the breakaway regions and demanded to replace the Russian peacekeeping forces, blaming them for the lack of neutrality.[80]

After the 'Rose Revolution' and Saakashvili's political triumph, Georgia's relations with Russia steadily worsened. Georgia undertook certain measures to bring the conflicts into the international arena and condemned Russia's non-constructive role as a mediator.[81]

The 'Five-Day War' in South Ossetia and the ceasefire between Georgia and Russia dramatically changed the whole picture of these two conflicts. During the Russian–Georgian war, the Russian troops not only pushed back the Georgian troops from the breakaway region, but also took and further passed under the control of the Abkhazians some other Georgian territories.[82] Such actions were strongly condemned.[83] Georgia itself considered Russian military interference as an occupation of its territory. Therefore, immediately after the war, Georgia declared South Ossetia and Abkhazia as occupied territories and passed the

[79] *Reference re Secession of Quebec* [1998] 2 SCR 217; *Katangese Peoples' Congress* v *Zaire* (2000) 75/92 African Commission of Human and People's Rights in R Murray and M Evans (eds), *Documents of the African Commission of Human Rights and Peoples' Rights* (Hart Publishing 2001) 389; *United Communist Party of Turkey and Others* v *Turkey* (ECHR Judgments 30 January 1998) 63 (1998-I) Reports 26–7.

[80] G Sepashvili, 'Resolution on Peacekeepers Leaves Room for More Diplomacy', *Civil Georgia* (16 February 2006) < http://www.civil.ge/eng/article.php?id=11833 > accessed 26 December 2009.

[81] 'M Saakashvili's UN Speech Focuses on Conflict Resolution, Relations with Russia', *Civil Georgia* (21 September 2004) < http://www.civil.ge/eng/article.php?id=7888 > accessed 25 December 2009.

[82] M Schwirtz et al., '1,500 Reported Killed in Georgia Battle', *New York Times* (9 August 2008) <http://www.nytimes.com/2008/08/10/world/europe/10georgia-2.html> accessed 16 February 2010.

[83] n 46.

respective law 'On Occupied Territories',[84] which governed the legal status of these lands and which was welcomed by the Council of Europe.[85]

Along with recognition of South Ossetia, Russia recognized Abkhazia after defeating Georgia in the 2008 military campaign. Immediately afterwards the separatist unit signed and ratified an agreement with Russia regarding a military base to be located in Abkhazia.[86] Abkhazia has also granted Russian troops the right to guard its borders.

Russia's recognition of South Ossetia and Abkhazia was expressed in the Presidential Decree of 26 August 2008.[87] Announcing this Decree, Russian President Medvedev referred to various international legal instruments such as the UN Charter, the 1975 Helsinki Final Act, and the 1970 Declaration on Principles of International Law. This came as a great surprise to the entire international community, since Russia had been the main persistent objector to recognition of Kosovo's independence.

The actions of the Russian Federation clearly constitute a direct violation of the fundamental norms and principles of international law. Furthermore, Russia's military actions against Georgia was nothing but an armed attack and interference with the internal affairs of another sovereign UN member.[88] Moreover, use of force by a UN member state against another member state without UNSC authorization should be qualified as illegal use of force.[89] In order to justify the use of force against Georgia, Russia referred to the Remedial Theory[90] and claimed that the Russian humanitarian intervention in Georgia was a response to the latter's military actions against South Ossetia. President Medvedev justified Russia's actions as an opportunity to save the lives of innocent civilians.[91]

It may be assumed that Russia's actions on recognition of Abkhazia and South Ossetia were some kind of 'revenge action' in response to the west's categorical and uncompromised support of Kosovo's independence,[92] which was declared 'a special case' by the west.[93]

[84] No 431-IIs 23 October 2008. The official website of the Parliament of the Republic of Georgia. Available in English at < http://www.parliament.ge/index.php?lang_id=ENG&sec_id=69&info_id=18768 > accessed 18 December 2009.

[85] Council of Europe. Venice Commission, 'Opinion on the Law on Occupied Territories of Georgia' Opinion No 516/2009. CDL-AD(2009)015, 78th Plenary Session (Strasbourg, 17 March 2009) < http://www.venice.coe.int/docs/2009/CDL-AD(2009)015-e.asp > accessed 19 November 2009.

[86] News, Official Website of the President of Abkhazia < http://www.abkhaziagov.org/en/news/detail.php?ID=28673 > accessed 18 November 2009.

[87] President Medvedev's Statement of 26 August 2008 (n 28).

[88] Dissenting Opinion of Judge Simma in *Uganda* v *DRC Case* [2005] ICJ Reports 334–5.

[89] *Military and Paramilitary Activities in and against Nicaragua (Nicaragua* v *United States)* [1986] ICJ Reports 14, 100–1; A Nußberger (n 35) 341–364.

[90] A Buchanan, 'Theories of Secession' (1997) 26 Philosophy and Public Affairs 1 34–5.

[91] President Medvedev's Statement (n 28).

[92] J Devdariani, 'Russian Diplomacy Uses "Kosovo Precedent" for Tactical Advantage on Abkhazia', Central Asia-Caucaus Analyst (2 August 2006) < http://www.cacianalyst.org/?q=node/3722v > accessed 28 November 2009; A Aksenock, 'Self-Determination between Law and Realpolitick' (2006) 5 Rossiya v Globalnoy Politike <http://www.globalaffairs.ru/articles/6214.html> (in Russian) accessed 18 December 2009.

[93] UNSC, 'Statements by UK and US Representatives at the Emergency Session of the Security Council', 5839th Meeting (PM) (18 February 2008) UN Doc SC/9252; Bureau of International

Despite Russia's and some other states' subsequent recognition, the majority of states have recognized neither Abkhazia nor South Ossetia as independent states. Russian recognition of Abkhazia and South Ossetia was heavily criticized by the international community, stating that Georgia's territorial integrity and boundaries could not be violated under the norms and principles of international law.[94]

It is still disputable on what basis Russia used military force against Georgia, since only Russian peacekeeping forces' presence in the territory of Georgia was consented to by the latter, based on two agreements: the Bilateral Agreement of 24 June 1992 between Russia and Georgia, Agreement 'On Principles of Georgian-South Ossetian Conflict Settlement' ('Sochi Agreement'),[95] and the Agreement on the Ceasefire and Secession of Forces of 14 May 1994 signed between Georgia and Abkhazia ('Moscow Agreement') with Russian mediation.[96] For instance, Article 3(5) of the Sochi Agreement stipulated a peaceful solution of any violations thereof. Therefore, the entrance of regular Russian troops into the territory of Georgia within its internationally recognized boundaries, without the latter's consent, can be considered as an act of aggression. Additionally, Russia's refusal to withdraw its peacekeeping troops from Georgia after termination of their mandate can be considered as continuing occupation.

Moreover, the general view is that the use of force under modern international law is acceptable only if necessary to exercise the right of self-defence (Article 51 of the UN Charter). In the case of Georgia, Russia cannot claim to have used force in self-defence since all operations took place in the territory of Georgia, with a huge difference in military powers between the two. Russia does not therefore justify its actions by self-defence, but claims that it was engaged in nothing but the defence of its citizens and peacekeepers.[97] The use of force can be acceptable in international law in certain exceptional cases, such as self-defence.[98] Modern international law grants to states specific forms of protection of their citizens, essentially in the form of diplomatic or consular protection, including judiciary and many other means. However, it is almost impossible to justify such an argument here, since international law does not allow the use of force against other states for the protection of one's own citizens. Therefore, the use of such force should be considered as a breach of Article 2(4) of the UN Charter.

Information Programs, US Department of State < http://www.america.gov/st/washfile-english/2007/March/20070321142711MVyelwarC0.6473047.html#ixzz0mwCi6HA8 > accessed 7 June 2009.

[94] 'Reaction of the International Community to Russia's Recognition of Abkhazia and South Ossetia', Collection of Statements and Press-Releases, Ministry of Foreign Affairs of the Republic of Georgia < http://mfa.gov.ge/index.php?lang_id=ENG&sec_id=511 > accessed 25 April 2010.

[95] Agreement 'On Principles of Georgian- South Ossetian Conflict Settlement' (signed on 24 June 1992 in Sochi) < http://smr.gov.ge/uploads/file/Dagomis%20Accord.pdf> (in Russian) accessed 12 January 2009.

[96] 'Declaration on Measures for a Political Settlement of the Georgian-Abkhaz Conflict' (signed in Geneva, 4 April 1994) *Free Georgia Newspaper* (№ 52, 5 April 1994) (in Russian).

[97] News, Official Website of the President of Abkhazia < http://www.abkhaziagov.org/en/news/detail.php?ID=28673.>.

[98] *Military and Paramilitary Activities in and against Nicaragua (Nicaragua* v *United States)* [1986] ICJ Reports 14, 100–1.

During Soviet times Abkhazia was part of the Georgian SSR, and the latter was a unit of the Soviet federal state. Arguably, under the Soviet constitutional system, the Georgian SSR was not a federal state, while the USSR itself was formed on a federal basis. Therefore, unlike the 15 former Soviet republics, Abkhazia did not possess a right to secession. As mentioned above, self-determination is primarily the right of ethnic minorities to exercise their political, economic, social, and cultural rights, ie the right to internal self-determination. In the case of Abkhazia such rights were exercised by the Georgian unit within the Georgian SSR.

Remarkably, Russia recognized Georgia's territorial integrity and international boundaries under the principle of *uti possidetis* through recognition of the former administrative boundaries of the Georgian SSR, which also included Abkhazia, as boundaries of the independent Georgia. This was done by Russia within the international framework and within the CIS. Moreover, as a permanent member of the UNSC, Russia directly participated in adopting a substantial number of the UNSC's Resolutions recognizing and reaffirming Georgia's territorial integrity.[99] The UN General Assembly also recognized Georgia's jurisdiction over Abkhazia through the adoption of Resolution No 62/249 on 15 May 2008.[100] Considering that under Article 25 of the UN Charter, UNSC resolutions have binding force on all UN members, any such resolution can only be overruled by another resolution adopted by the same UNSC. Therefore, Russia's unilateral action against Georgia and further recognition of the two separatist units constitute serious violations of the UN Charter and the fundamental principles of international law. Such a position and behaviour on the part of a UNSC permanent member can set a dangerous precedent that can seriously affect the current international law system.

A completely new factor in post-Soviet territorial and boundary conflicts is the granting of citizenship of third states to inhabitants of the separatist units. This

[99] UNSC Res 876 (1993) (19 October 1993), UN Doc S/RES/876; UNSC Res 881 (1993) (November 1993), UN Doc S/RES/881; UNSC Res 892 (1993) (22 December 1993), UN Doc S/RES/892; UNSC Res 896 (1994) (31 January 1994), UN Doc S/RES/896; UNSC Res 906 (1994) (25 March 1994), UN Doc S/RES/906; UNSC Res 937(1994) (21 July 1994), UN Doc S/RES/937; UNSC Res 971 (1995) (12 January 1995), UN Doc S/RES/971; UNSC Res 993 (1995) (12 May 1995), UN Doc S/RES/971; UNSC Res 1036 (1996) (12 January 1996), UN Doc S/RES/1036; UNSC Res 1065 (1996) (12 July 1996), UN Doc S/RES/1065; UNSC Res 1096 (1997) (30 January 1997), UN Doc. S/RES/1096; UNSC Res 1124 (1997) (31 July 1997), UN Doc S/RES/1124; UNSC Res 1150 (1998) (30 January 1998), UN Doc S/RES/1150; UNSC Res 1187 (1998) (30 July), UN Doc S/RES/1187; UNSC Res 1225 (1999) (28 January 1999), UN Doc S/RES/1255; UNSC Res 1255 (1999) (30 July 1999), UN Doc S/RES/1255; UNSC Res 1287 (2000) (31 January 2000), UN Doc S/RES/1287; UNSC Res 1311 (2000) (28 July 2000), UN Doc S/RES/1311; UNSC Res 1339 (2001) (31 January 2001), UN Doc S/RES/1339; UNSC Res 1364 (2001) (30 March 2001), UN Doc S/RES/1364; UNSC Res 1393 (2002) (31 January 2002), UN Doc S/RES/1393; UNSC Res 1427 (2002) (29 July 2002), UN Doc S/RES/1427; UNSC Res 1462 (2003) (30 January 2003), UN Doc S/RES/1462; UNSC Res 1494 (2003) (30 July 2003), UN Doc S/RES/1494; UNSC Res 1524 (2004) (30 January 2004), UN Doc S/RES/1524; UNSC Res 1554 (2004) (29 July 2004), UN Doc S/RES/1554; UNSC Res 1582 (2005) (28 January 2005), UN Doc S/RES/1582; UNSC Res 1615 (2005) (29 July 2005), UN Doc S/RES/1615; UNSC Res 1666 (2006) (31 March 2006), UN Doc S/RES/1666; UNSC Res 1752 (2007) (13 April 2007), UN Doc S/RES/1752; UNSC Res 1781 (2007) (15 October 2007), UN Doc S/RES/1781; UNSC Res 1808 (2008) (15 April 2008), UN Doc S/RES/1808.

[100] UNGA Res 62/249 (15 May 2008) UN Doc A/RES/62/249.

can be observed in the case of Abkhazia, where Russia granted citizenship to the residents of this breakaway region. Even during war, the Russian troops, together with the separatist forces, forced the ethnic Georgians to either accept Russian citizenship or leave their places of residence.[101] This device was also used by Russia in the Abkhaz and South Ossetian conflicts. According to some sources, about 80% of Abkhazians have been issued Russian passports, but do not pay taxes or serve in the Russian Army.[102] It can be argued that unique Soviet citizenship was transferred into citizenship of newly independent states—15 constituent units of the Soviet Union. In this regard the inhabitants of Abkhazia automatically became citizens of the Republic of Georgia, and still possess Georgian citizenship unless they legally reject it. Russia used its granting of citizenship to justify its military actions as protection of Russian citizens. However, even if the inhabitants of these regions had freely chosen Russian citizenship, it can hardly be considered lawful justification for Russia's military actions. This was also confirmed by the Council of European Union's Independent International Fact-Finding Mission on the Conflict in Georgia:

> The mass conferral of Russian citizenship to Georgian nationals and the provision of passports on a massive scale on Georgian territory, including its breakaway provinces, without the consent of the Georgian Government runs against the principles of good neighbourliness and constitutes an open challenge to Georgian sovereignty and an interference in the internal affairs of Georgia.[103]

Effective control exercised over the region by Russia could be observed not only in its military involvement but also in its economic support, including the use of the Russian rouble in Abkhazia. Russia's effective control was confirmed by the OSCE: for instance, in July 2008 the OSCE Parliamentary Assembly passed a resolution calling upon Russian authorities to cease its maintenance provided to the separatist unit expressed in military, economic, and political support, and to respect other OSCE member states' territorial integrity and refrain from the threat or use of force.[104]

The issues stressed by the European Court of Human Rights ('ECHR') in the *Ilaşcu* case[105] can be similarly applied to the Abkhazia and South Ossetia situations. Undoubtedly Russia, its state agencies, and its officials and officers are directly involved in the actions of the separatist units. Similar to the case in Transnistria, Russia exercises effective control over Abkhazia, expressed in full political, economic,

[101] D McElroy, 'South Ossetian Police Tell Georgians to Take a Russian Passport, or Leave Their Home', *Telegraph* (30 August 2008) < http://www.telegraph.co.uk/news/worldnews/europe/georgia/2651836/South-Ossetian-police-tell-Georgians-to-take-a-Russian-passport-or-leave-their-homes.html > accessed 30 April 2010.

[102] UNGA Res 10708 (15 May 2008), UN Doc A/62/L.45; International Crisis Group, 'Europe Report N°176' (15 Sep 2006, accessed 30 May 2007) 10.

[103] Council of the European Union, 'Independent International Fact-Finding Mission on the Conflict in Georgia' (September 2009) 18 <http://www.ceiig.ch> accessed 19 October 2009.

[104] OSCE Parliamentary Assembly, Resolution 'On the Security Environment in Georgia' (adopted at 17th Annual Session in Astana, 29 June–3 July 2008) < http://www.oscepa.org/oscepa_content/documents/Astana/Declaration/2008-AS-Final%20Declaration%20ENG.pdf > accessed 7 March 2010.

[105] *Ilaşcu and others* v *Moldova* (Application no. 48787/99) 8 July 2004.

and military control over the breakaway region.[106] It can be argued that, as in the case of Transnistria,[107] Russia plays a considerable role in the existence of these breakaway regions that have seceded from Georgia. All the legal features related to Russian effective control and emphasized by the ECHR in the *Ilaşcu* case are also evident in the case of Abkhazia, as evidenced by the Russian military campaign against Georgia in the course of the 'Five-Day War'. Moreover, Georgia is trying to get its own 'Georgian *Ilaşcu* case', which will give it the legal arguments to prove Russia's negative role in the conflicts in the territory of Georgia and effective control over the separatist units of Georgia. For instance, the Georgian Young Lawyers' Association (supported by European Human Rights Advocacy Centre) has submitted applications against Russia on behalf of 132 applicants, representing 34 groups who suffered during the heavy Russian military campaign in the course of the 'Five-Day War'.[108] The applications claim that Georgian civilians residing in the territory of the breakaway region of South Ossetia were killed and injured and that their property was damaged or destroyed during the Russian attacks in 2008. Georgians are pursuing the goal of legally proving Russia's exercise of effective control over the separatist unit.[109] The complaints refer to certain provisions of the European Convention of Human Rights that were violated by Russia and the separatist forces controlled by it.[110] The ECHR's decision is eagerly awaited by the legal community, which is wondering whether the 'Georgian *Ilaşcu* case' will permit Georgia to argue over Russia's effective control. Should the Court decide on Russia's effective controller role, it will give Georgia grounds to claim Russian responsibility for violations committed by its army and the separatist forces.

It is undeniable that the independence of Abkhazia was not achieved through democratic means, and that it was the result of a powerful third state's interference. It can be argued that Russia, as a power exercising effective control[111] over Abkhazia, should bear full responsibility for the actions against Georgia in the course of the military campaign in 2008. Based on these facts, Georgia initiated proceedings in the International Court of Justice (ICJ) concerning alleged acts of racial discrimination against the Georgians of Abkhazia and South Ossetia.[112]

[106] *Loizidou* v *Turkey* (Application no. 15318/89) ECHR 23 March 1995.

[107] *Ilaşcu and others* v *Moldova* (n 105).

[108] 'Financial. Georgians Lodge Suit Against Russia at ECHR over August War' (16 February 2010) <http://www.finchannel.com/Main_News/Politics/58427_Georgians_Lodge_Suit_Against_Russia_at_ECHR_over_August_War> accessed 18 April 2010.

[109] EHRAC, 'Georgians take Russia to European Court of Human Rights over August 2008 Armed Conflict', London Metropolitan University <http://www.londonmet.ac.uk/londonmet/fms/MRSite/Research/HRSJ/EHRAC/Press%20releases/EHRAC%20Press%20Release%2062%20Russia-Georgia%20conflict%20apps%20lodged%2010_2_10.pdf> accessed 27 March 2010.

[110] Radio Netherlands Worldwide, 'Georgia Takes Russia to Court over 2008 War' (15 February 2010) < http://www.rnw.nl/international-justice/article/georgia-takes-russia-court-over-2008-war > accessed 28 April 2010.

[111] S Talmon, 'The Responsibility of Outside Powers for Acts of Secessionist Entities' (2009) 58 ICLQ 493–517; S Barbour and Z Salzman, 'The Tangled Web: The Right of Self-Defence against Non-State Actors in the Armed Activities Case' (2008) 40 NYUJILP 70–9; A Abbas, 'Proving State Responsibility for Genocide: The ICJ in Bosnia v Serbia and the International Commission of Inquiry for Darfur' (2008) 31 FILJ 890–6.

[112] ICJ, Press Communication of 12 August 2008 < http://www.icj-cij.org/docket/files/140/14659.pdf > accessed 23 April 2010.

In this case, Georgia was attempting to prove the exercise of effective control by Russia in Abkhazia and South Ossetia and its negative role in these unresolved conflicts. In its application, Georgia claimed that Russia, through its state authorities, agents, and officers, and through the separatist forces of Abkhazia and South Ossetia, engaged in ethnic cleansing of the Georgians residing in breakaway regions. Georgia considers such Russian actions as an intentional plan aimed at the impairment of Georgia's territorial integrity and the violation of its sovereignty and independence.[113] Georgia requested the ICJ to indicate provisional measures. On 15 October 2008, the ICJ in its Order indicated provisional measures urging all parties to refrain from any acts of racial discrimination and from assisting, supporting, and sponsoring racial discrimination, and to facilitate humanitarian assistance.[114] In its judgments the ICJ held that it had no jurisdiction to hear the Application filed by Georgia on 12 August 2008.[115] It also concluded that although there was a legal dispute between the parties with respect to Russia's compliance with the norms of the Convention on the Elimination of All Forms of Racial Discrimination, Georgia did not fulfil a precondition for the Court to be seized of the case, ie Georgia had not endeavoured to amicably negotiate the dispute and not all remedies to address the dispute had been exhausted before referring the case directly to the ICJ.[116] For these reasons, the ICJ stated that it would not perform a legal evaluation of the questions raised in Georgia's application and referred to international humanitarian law and international human rights law.[117] The position of the ICJ, an authoritative international legal forum, was disappointing not only for the Georgians, but also for many international legal experts who were expecting to receive a judgment of the 'World Court' in the light of today's conflicts in Kosovo, Abkhazia, South Ossetia, Nagorno-Karabakh, Transnistria and many other places. Unfortunately, Georgia could not rely upon this case to strengthen its international legal arguments.

Georgia also brought the legal dispute with Russia regarding breakaway regions before other forums. It instituted interstate proceedings against the Russian Federation with the ECHR, alleging discrimination and violation of the rights of Georgians who were residing in the Russian Federation following the arrest in Tbilisi on 27 September 2006 of four Russian service personnel on suspicion of espionage against Georgia.[118] Its application was filed in April 2009 under Article 33 (Inter-State cases) of the European Convention of Human Rights, and essentially alleged the violation by Russia of various articles of the European Convention of Human Rights.[119]

[113] S Ghandhi, 'International Court of Justice: Application of the International Convention on the Elimination of All Forms of Racial Discrimination (*Georgia v Russian Federation*) Provisional Measures Order of 15 October 2008' 58 ICLQ 3 713.

[114] ICJ, Press Communication of 12 August 2008.

[115] ICJ, *Georgia* v *The Russian Federation*, Judgment of 1 April 2011 < http://www.icj-cij.org/docket/files/140/16398.pdf > accessed 17 May 2011.

[116] *Georgia* v *The Russian Federation* (n 115).

[117] *Georgia* v *The Russian Federation*, n 115.

[118] ECHR, State Complaint Georgia v the Russian Federation (*Georgia* v *Russia)* (No 1) (Application no. 13255/07) 2009.

[119] *Georgia* v *Russia* (n 118).

Georgia initiated these proceedings in the ECHR in order to prove the intentional nature of the Russian government's policy against the Georgians residing in the territory of Russia, and their collective expulsion therefrom. Moreover, Georgia claims that Russia's actions deprived Georgian nationals deported from Russia of various transportation means due to the closing of borders with Georgia.[120] In total, Georgia lodged three interstate applications against Russia with the European Court of Human Rights in connection with the August Russian–Georgian war.[121] Georgia alleges that Russia 'allowed, or caused to develop, an administrative practice through indiscriminate and disproportionate attacks against civilians and their property in the two autonomous regions of Georgia—Abkhazia and South Ossetia—by the Russian military forces and the separatist forces under their control'.[122] However, the final judgment is still pending, and continues to attract much attention.

It can be argued that all of Russia's attempts to justify its actions in Abkhazia with arguments regarding the protection of the Russian border and of its citizens and peacekeepers, as well as those regarding the prevention of an act of genocide, lack any solid legal basis under international law, and that Russia's stance on Abkhazia and South Ossetia is nothing but a response to the west with respect to the Kosovo case. Although the Russian authorities stated that Abkhazia and South Ossetia were 'special' based on the exercise of the right to self-determination,[123] the political grounds can be clearly assumed. Even the statements of high Russian officials that 'Abkhazia and South Ossetia are unique cases and should not be a precedent for other secessionist situations'[124] cannot guarantee the current international system against the risk of similar scenarios taking place in the future. All these facts and arguments give strong grounds to claim that in the cases of Abkhazia and South Ossetia, the main factor is a 'special' role of a third state rather than an attempt to exercise the right to external self-determination.

V. Conclusion

The background of the Abkhaz conflict suggests that this is not simply a conflict over the legal issues arising under international law, including the collision between certain principles—territorial integrity and *uti possidetis* on the one hand and external self-determination on the other—but rather a highly politicized

[120] *Georgia* v *Russia* (n 118).

[121] ECHR, Inter-State Applications Table < http://www.echr.coe.int/NR/rdonlyres/5D5BA416-1FE0-4414-95A1-AD6C1D77CB90/0/Requ%C3%AAtes_inter%C3%A9tatiques_EN.pdf> accessed 12 October 2011.

[122] ECHR, Registrar of ECHR, Press Release 150 (2011) (22 September 2011).

[123] Ministry of Foreign Affairs of the Russian Federation, 'Transcript of Remarks by Sergey Lavrov, Minister of Foreign Affairs of the Russian Federation' (presented at an Enlarged Meeting of the Federation Council International Affairs Committee) (Moscow 18 September 2008) MID Doc 1387-18-09-2008 < http://www.un.int/russia/new/MainRoot/docs/off_news/180908/newen1.htm > accessed 23 October 2008.

[124] Russian Federation Foreign Ministry (n 123).

geopolitical issue hidden under the cover of self-determination. Therefore, all other reasons are only aggravating circumstances, not the key grounds on which this conflict is carried out. However, since the political analysis of the Abkhaz conflict is beyond the scope of this article, the main emphasis is on legal issues arising out of the secession of this unit and its recent recognition by Russia and a few other states.

Based on the above analysis, it can be concluded that in the conflict between the right to self-determination and the principle of territorial integrity, the former is limited in favour of the latter. External self-determination in the form of secession is not recognized in international law and primacy has been given to the principle of territorial integrity. Any attempts to change the balance in favour of external self-determination will result in a threat to international peace and stability. Under the Soviet Constitution, only the 15 former republics had a right to exercise their right to external self-determination and exercise of this right was accompanied by application of the principle of *uti possidetis* under which the transformation of former administrative borders of the Soviet republics into international boundaries took place. Therefore the principles of *uti possidetis* and self-determination were mutually supportive upon the obtaining of independence by the 15 republics of the former USSR. Shaw aptly comments that upon the obtaining of independence by the non-self-governing territory, the principle of self-determination coupled with the principle of *uti possidetis* will serve for the protection of territorial unity of the new state.[125] Crawford aptly concludes that the principle of self-determination has arisen in the colonial context, harmonizing with the doctrine of stability,[126] ie the principle of *uti possidetis*.

The dissolution of the Soviet Union was accompanied by numerous secessionist movements in the territories of newly independent states. In this case, the conflict between *uti possidetis* and the principle of self-determination can be clearly seen where the unrecognized separatist units declared independence and claimed exercise of the right to external self-determination. In this context there are strong grounds to argue that the principle of *uti possidetis*, which acts to strengthen the principle of territorial integrity, has primary force over the right to self-determination. Nevertheless, case speaking about the right to self-determination in this, we have to imply external self-determination, ie separatism leading to the impairment of the internationally recognized territorial integrity and political, economic, and cultural unity of the former USSR republics.

Thus, it may be argued that the principle of self-determination upon the process of obtaining independence serves, together with the principle of *uti possidetis*, to protect the territorial integrity of new states—former USSR republics. In addition, on the next level these principles collide due to the intention of some ethnic or other groups to exercise the right to external self-determination and *eo ipso* impair the territorial integrity and unity of these newly independent states. It is obvious

[125] M Shaw, 'Territory in International Law' 13 NYBIL (1982) 71.
[126] Crawford (n 31) 101–2.

that in this case, the principle of *uti possidetis* is called upon to protect the territorial integrity of a state against groundless claims to external self-determination.

In fact, the Russian arguments on Abkhazia's right to secession due to the threat to human rights cannot be accepted under modern international law. The general policy line of the Russian authorities after recognition of Kosovo by the western world was to respond by undertaking similar measures and recognizing certain separatist units in the post-Soviet area. Russia systematically warned the international community that it reserved a right to use the Kosovo precedent.[127]

Clearly, Russia's actions in Georgia should be considered a serious challenge to the system of international law and its fundamental principles such as territorial integrity, non-interference in internal affairs, and inviolability of internationally recognized boundaries.

The resumption of peace negotiations, the restoration of the spirit expressed in economic cooperation, the reinstalment of all communications, the return of all IDPs, the investigation of war crimes, and the cessation of all hostilities are the only ways to achieve peaceful solutions to the Abkhazia conflict within the legal framework. However, above all, a solution to this conflict can take place only within the framework of international law, ie only by complying with the principle of the territorial integrity of Georgia and its internationally recognized boundaries determined on the basis of the principle of *uti possidetis* that transformed the boundaries of the Georgian SSR into the international boundaries of the Republic of Georgia. Undoubtedly, respect for human rights and granting of the effective exercise of the right to internal self-determination ought not to be ignored by the parties under any circumstances.

[127] New Region, 'Statements of President v. Putin and the Deputy Speaker of the Russian Parliament v. Jirinovsky' cited in 'Kosovo's Independence Could be a Precedent for Abkhazia and South Ossetia' (22 February 2006) < http://www.nregion.com/txt.php?i=85 > (in Russian) accessed 17 October 2009; Radio Free Europe, 'Russia Says Kosovo Could Be a Precedent for Georgia' (22 June 2006) < http://www.rferl.org/content/article/1069389.html > accessed 12 December 2009.

11

Nagorno-Karabakh

Heiko Krüger[1]

I. Introduction

The Caucasus is the setting for four territorial disputes which put long-term stability and balanced growth in the region at risk.[2] Currently, the dispute over Nagorno-Karabakh appears to be the conflict with the greatest potential to explode. Although there have been no major outbreaks of violence since 1994, the conflict has not yet been resolved. To this day, young recruits from the hostile parties face each other in the trenches along the armistice line. Despite years of international attempts at mediation, the republics of Armenia and Azerbaijan have not found a way to come to a resolution.

This case study is primarily concerned with the key legal aspects of the Nagorno-Karabakh conflict, which have seemingly become blurred over recent years due to the great difficulty in resolving the conflict and balancing the interests involved. First, the study concentrates on the question of whether the Armenian side may invoke a right to secession which might have arisen either from Soviet or international law. Second, the case study is concerned with the question of what legal status Nagorno-Karabakh currently possesses. Is it a part of the Republic of Azerbaijan or has the region already gained independence?

II. Factual and Historical Background

As part of the Caucasus, for thousands of years Nagorno-Karabakh has been a transit and settlement zone for many ethnic groups and, as such, has seen innumerable campaigns of conquest and ethnic dislocations. Armenians and Azerbaijanis have divergent views on the ethnic history of the region. However, it can be assumed that in the nineteenth century Nagorno-Karabakh was ethnically mixed when several massive population movements took place caused by the struggle for supremacy between Russia, Persia, and the Ottoman empire. This struggle and the ensuing

[1] Dr Heiko Krüger is an attorney at law specializing in international and European legal affairs.

[2] As regards the conflicts in South Ossetia and Abkhazia, see the case studies contributed to this volume by Christopher Waters (175 et seq.) and Farhad Mirzayev (191 et seq.).

Russian rule led to a heavy influx of Armenians into Nagorno-Karabakh and other regions, and eventually to their predominance.[3] Russia envisaged consolidating its control over the whole Caucasus region by means of a policy of Christianization and settlement of Armenians. The influx of Armenians was a key reason for early antipathies and tensions, which were further intensified by preferential Russian treatment of Armenians, Armenian radicalization, and the emergence of a state of social underdevelopment and an exaggerated sense of threat amongst Azerbaijanis.[4] In the wake of the 1905 revolutionary movement in Russia, widespread violence broke out in Transcaucasia for the first time. Violent attacks cost the lives of thousands of Armenians and Azerbaijanis.[5]

Later, when Russian supremacy in the Caucasus region was weakened through the February and October revolutions in 1917, various local groups attempted to fill the power vacuum. Independent republics for the territories of Armenia, Azerbaijan, and Georgia were declared in 1918. Both Armenians and Azerbaijanis laid claim to Nagorno-Karabakh and other disputed areas. The situation was further aggravated by the Bolsheviks' struggle for power in the Caucasus region. There were armed clashes and attacks on both sides' civilians: for instance, during the so-called 'March Events' and 'September Events' in 1918, the 'Shusha Events' in 1920, and the expulsions in the Erevan province.[6] Thousands of people were killed on both sides.[7]

In 1920, the Russian Red Army invaded the Southern Caucasus and expanded Bolshevist rule throughout the whole region. In 1921 the Caucasian Bureau, installed by Moscow to safeguard Russian rule, decided to keep Nagorno-Karabakh within the newly established Azerbaijan Soviet Socialist Republic (Azerbaijan SSR), which later became part of the Soviet Union.[8] This territorial decision was ultimately incorporated into the Soviet Constitution.

The ensuing decades passed relatively peacefully, although the Armenian side repeatedly demanded annexation of Nagorno-Karabakh to the Armenian Soviet Socialist Republic (Armenian SSR). Tensions continued to exist more latently and became apparent in several acts of violence.[9]

In the course of *perestroika*, nationalist movements across the Soviet Union were strengthened, as was also the case in Nagorno-Karabakh. The conflict began in 1988 with mass demonstrations in support of transfer of the region to the Armenian SSR. The situation increasingly escalated, amid much state propaganda,

[3] See for details and further references T Potier, *Conflict in Nagorno-Karabakh, Abkhazia and South Ossetia, A Legal Appraisal* (Kluwer Law International 2001) 2; R Kipke, *Das armenisch-aserbaidschanische Verhältnis und der Konflikt um Berg-Karabach* (VS Verlag 2012); H Krüger, *The Nagorno-Karabakh Conflict, A Legal Analysis* (Springer 2010) 8 et seq.

[4] See Krüger (n 3) 8–11.

[5] Human Rights Watch, *Playing the 'Communal Card': Communal Violence and Human Rights* (1995).

[6] See Human Rights Watch (n 5).

[7] See Human Rights Watch (n 5); UN ECOSOC doc. E/CN.4/1997/139, annex.

[8] According to the minutes of the secession of the Caucasian Bureau of 5 July 1921 no. 12 point 2. See also T de Waal, *Black Garden* (New York University Press 2003) 130.

[9] See Krüger (n 3) 17, 77; Kipke (n 3).

and led to a conflict between paramilitary units and government forces which later became a war between the young republics of Armenia and Azerbaijan. Acts of violence, homicides, and expulsions occurred on both the Armenian and Azerbaijani sides. Overall, an estimated 25,000 Armenian and Azerbaijani casualties and the creation of mono-ethnic areas were the tragic consequences of the conflict. It is estimated that some 350,000 Armenians and 750,000–800,000 Azerbaijanis became refugees and internally displaced persons.[10]

The weapons have been silent since 1994. Since then, Nagorno-Karabakh and seven surrounding administrative districts have been under Armenian control, strictly speaking under the joint control of Karabakh Armenians and the Republic of Armenia. The region has been administered by the unrecognized 'Republic of Nagorno-Karabakh'. However, the Republic of Armenia's military, political, and financial involvement and assistance still form the backbone of the community established in Nagorno-Karabakh.[11] The negotiation process is led by the OSCE Minsk Group, which mediated the Prague Negotiation Process and proposed the Madrid Principles as the basis on which to settle the conflict. Despite some progress in recent years, the Presidents of Armenia and Azerbaijan, both under considerable political pressure at home, have nevertheless been unable to reach a final resolution.

III. Legal Analysis

1. Right to secession under national law

The assessment concentrates first on whether Nagorno-Karabakh had a right to secede from the Azerbaijan SSR and the USSR under national law—namely, the law of the USSR. The Armenian side argues that this was actually the case in accordance with the 1990 Soviet Law on Secession. Armenians refer to the fact that in September 1991, Nagorno-Karabakh declared itself an independent republic, ratified this in a referendum, and thereby satisfied the requirements of the Law on Secession.[12] Azerbaijan rejects this view on the grounds that Nagorno-Karabakh did not fulfil the requirements of the Law on Secession.

In order to shed light on the Soviet Law on Secession we must go back, strictly speaking, to the time of the break-up of the Soviet Union. In the transitional years of 1989–1991, events came thick and fast in Nagorno-Karabakh and across the entire territory of the USSR. National movements flared up in many Union

[10] Cf. Human Rights Watch, *Azerbaijan, Seven Years of Conflict in Nagorno-Karabakh* (1994) 99. In 2011, the CIA cited 120,000 Armenian and 580,000–690,000 Azerbaijani refugees and internally displaced persons; see Central Intelligence Agency, 'The CIA World Factbook: Transnational Issues in Country Profiles of Armenia and Azerbaijan' <https://www.cia.gov/library/publications/the-world-factbook/geos/aj.html#Issues> accessed 29 November 2011.

[11] For details see section IV.2.

[12] Cf. note verbale dated 21 March 2005 from the Permanent Mission of Armenia to the United Nations Office at Geneva and the UN High Commissioner for Human Rights, E/CN.4/2005/G/23, 7 et seq.

Republics and their subdivisions. The Soviet Union seemed about to collapse in the wake of these movements, and this ultimately came to pass. Faced with this situation, Moscow first resorted to the use of the Soviet army, which led to clashes in Baku, Tbilisi, and Vilnius, where scores of people died.

Nevertheless, Gorbachev was not able to control the situation. In fact, his attempts to maintain the old order by force even reinforced these nations' movements for independence. In this dilemma, he did something remarkable. Instead of using military force, Gorbachev tried to rebuild the political system and the federal structure of the Soviet Union through a number of acts.[13] One of these was the adoption of the aforementioned Law on Secession, which concerned the procedure of a Union Republic's secession from the USSR. The Soviet Constitution already included a right to secession for Union Republics, but Gorbachev had now introduced a way to exercise this right.

However, the Law on Secession was remarkable in another respect. Upon closer examination, it appears to be only another strategic move with which Gorbachev attempted to prevent the foreseeable dissolution of the USSR.[14] Even though the Law on Secession offered a way to independence, the procedure set out in this act was so complex, cumbersome, and disadvantageous that it would not only have delayed secession for years but also could have made it impossible (details are provided later in the chapter).

The clumsiness of the secession procedure designed by the Gorbachev administration brought up the question of whether the Law on Secession was in conformity with the Soviet Constitution. As opposed to the Law on Secession, Article 72 of the Constitution expressly determined that Union Republics retain the right to secede *freely* from the Soviet Union. As no further requirements were provided for in Article 72, we must assume that the Soviet Constitution excluded, at least, the establishment of any substantial conditions for the procedure of secession.

Ultimately, Article 72 confirmed the Constitution's general concept that the Soviet Union was legally constituted as a voluntary association of equal Union Republics (see Articles 70 and 76). Exercising the right to secession was, of course, inconceivable for political reasons and would have been blocked prior to 1989. However, the idea of a voluntary association and a free right to secession for Union Republics nevertheless remained an integral part of the Soviet Constitution and therefore had real force of law.[15] This basic idea had to be observed once secession became an issue. Thus, it must be assumed that, at least in parts, the procedure

[13] See also B Meissner, 'Die erste Phase der Verfassungsreform Gorbacevs und ihre Auswirkungen auf das Verhältnis von Partei und Staat' (1989) Recht in Ost und West 385; F Mett, *Das Konzept des Selbstbestimmungsrechts der Völker* (2004) 229; Krüger (n 3) 17–22.

[14] Cf. MG Kohen (ed), *Secession, International Law Perspectives* (Cambridge University Press 2006) 16; H Hannum (ed), *Documents on Autonomy and Minority Rights* (Martinus Nijhoff 1993) 742; A Cassese, *Self-Determination of Peoples: A Legal Reappraisal* (Cambridge University Press 1995) 264 et seq.; Potier (n 3) 41.

[15] See also Henn-Jüri Uibopuu, who has not expressed doubts in this respect, in M Fincke (ed), *Handbuch der Sowjetverfassung* (Vol 2, Duncker & Humblot 1983) art. 72, note 8 with further references.

of secession as elaborated by the Gorbachev administration did not conform with the Constitution.[16]

Nonconformity with the Soviet Constitution also accrues from another section of the Law on Secession. Under its Article 3, autonomous regions, such as Nagorno-Karabakh, were also granted a right to decide on their own legal status once a Union Republic resolved to secede from the Soviet Union. In contrast to this, the Soviet Constitution established in Articles 78 and 86 that autonomous regions were constituent parts of their Union Republic and that territorial alterations required the consent of the Union Republic. Consequently, an interpretation under which the Law on Secession entitled autonomous regions to freely secede without the consent of their Union Republic violated the Soviet Constitution. Pursuant to Article 173 of the Constitution, constitutionality could only be maintained if Article 3 of the Law on Secession was read in accordance with the provisions of the Constitution, meaning that in the case of Nagorno-Karabakh, the Azerbaijan SSR had to agree on the secession of the region.

All these doubts as to the constitutionality of the Law on Secession piled on the pressure within the Union Republics. In the end none of them selected the route presented by Gorbachev.[17] Instead they took the bull by the horns and broke away from Moscow in line with the previously mentioned right to secession provided in the Soviet Constitution.

Karabakh Armenians have nevertheless invoked the Law on Secession as its Article 3, as mentioned above, included the opportunity for autonomous regions to determine their own legal status once their Union Republic decided to follow the road of secession under the Law of Secession. At first sight, reference to this Article makes sense, despite doubts regarding its constitutionality. Ultimately, union laws regarded as unconstitutional did not lose their validity per se. They had to be revoked by the Congress of People's Deputies.[18] The rapid developments of that time, however, also took the Congress by surprise and it did not repeal the Law on Secession. Therefore, we must consider it to have remained valid until the final dissolution of the USSR. Of course, this does not mean that pertinent provisions of the Constitution could have been waived by the Law on Secession. According to Article 173 of the Constitution, its provisions had to be given priority when applying the Law on Secession.

Ultimately, Nagorno-Karabakh could have achieved independence only if it satisfied the complete, cumbersome procedure of the Law on Secession. Furthermore, as just elaborated, when applying the yardstick of the Law on Secession, relevant provisions of the Soviet Constitution had to be observed.

The secession procedure which was considered to apply to an autonomous region was in principle equivalent to the procedure applicable to its Union Republic. The

[16] See Krüger (n 3) 31 et seq. [17] See also Hannum (n 14) 742.

[18] See S Reinhardt, 'Das Gesetz über die Verfassungsaufsicht im Kontext der Umgestaltung in der UdSSR' (1990) Recht in Ost und West 298, 300; E Paetzold, 'Die Diskussion zum Entwurf der neuen sowjetischen Verfassung' (1989) Recht in Ost und West 38, 41; in detail Krüger (n 3) 33–5.

following list contains an overview of the conditions of the Law on Secession which the Karabakh Armenians had accordingly to meet:[19]

- Secession procedure of the Azerbaijan SSR under the Law on Secession (necessarily implied by the Law on Secession concerning the procedure of secession of a Union Republic from the USSR);
- Approval by the Supreme Soviet of the Union Republic to conduct a referendum (Article 2, para. 2 of the Law on Secession);
- Organization of the referendum and review of its results by an electoral commission set up by the Supreme Soviet of the Union Republic (Article 4 of the Law on Secession);
- Monitoring by election observers officially sent by Moscow with the consent of the Union Republic (Article 5 of the Law on Secession);
- Carrying out of the complex multi-institutional procedure provided for in the Law on Secession in order to evaluate possible consequences for each of the union's Soviet and autonomous republics as well as autonomous entities (Articles 8 and 9 of the Law on Secession);
- Adoption of a final act by the Congress of People's Deputies of the USSR in order to set out a transitional phase which would result in secession (Article 9 of the Law on Secession).

In the end, Karabakh Armenians did not meet the list of required conditions. It was simply impossible to remove all the obstacles Gorbachev had put in the way of secession. First, an official secession procedure of the Azerbaijan SSR was not initiated as required.[20] Second, the referendum held in Nagorno-Karabakh was conducted and organized without the involvement of the Azerbaijan SSR as required by the Law on Secession. Its participation was mandatory especially in light of the Soviet Constitution, which even explicitly required the consent of a Union Republic in the case of a territorial alteration. At this point it was obligatory to take account of the mentioned relevant provisions of the Constitution. This is particularly true for Article 78 and its consent requirement. Third, the complex multi-institutional procedure following a referendum could not be carried out, because the Soviet Union ceased to exist. At the end of 1991, the Soviet Union collapsed, and the institutions which would have needed to be involved in the case of a secession attempt disappeared. Karabakh Armenians simply ran out of time, as did all the autonomous regions. None achieved independence during Soviet times on the basis of a right to secession under the Law on Secession. Their fate was therefore linked to that of their Union Republic.

Lastly, Karabakh Armenians could not even appeal to the fact that the Azerbaijan SSR did not meet all of the conditions of the Law on Secession for its part. On the one hand, the Azerbaijan SSR could refer to its constitutional right to secession, which was freely granted—meaning without the imposition of any

[19] See Krüger (n 3) 35–40. [20] See also Potier (n 3) 41.

substantial conditions.[21] On the other hand, a violation of the Law on Secession at best would have meant that Azerbaijan was not able to secede from the USSR until its dissolution in December 1991. Nagorno-Karabakh could not have gained any benefit from this. According to the *uti possidetis* principle of international law, Nagorno-Karabakh would still have become a constituent part of the Republic of Azerbaijan under these terms.[22]

2. Right to secession under international law

For this reason, it is essential to examine whether Nagorno-Karabakh could invoke a right to secession under international law. Whether this is the case is the primary object of the legal dispute between Armenians and Azerbaijanis. In order to counter the Azerbaijani territorial claim, the Armenian side primarily refers to an external right to self-determination, which is a right to secession. Such a right to secession is rejected firmly by the Azerbaijani side. The Republic of Azerbaijan refers to the principle of territorial integrity and asserts that Nagorno-Karabakh is a part of its territory.

Remedial secession?

Whether international law confers rights to secession to ethnic groups is highly disputed.[23] Rights to secession are generally only accepted in the context of colonialism, in situations involving foreign occupation, or where national law or national agreements allow secession. With these exceptions, many legal authors reject rights to secession.[24] It is said that international law is silent on secession in other situations. Neither international treaties nor customary international law pertaining to state practice provide a solid basis for such rights.

On the other hand, a considerable number of other legal scholars and some states hold that there might be a right to secession, ie a right to external self-determination, as a last resort for ethnic groups in the event of the most severe, massive, and systematic human rights violations,[25] meaning that the given state

[21] Cf. WN Kudrjawzew et al., *Verfassung der UdSSR—Erläuterungen zur Verfassung der UdSSR vom 7. Oktober 1977* (1980) 172; Krüger (n 3) 31 et seq., 36.

[22] See Krüger (n 3) 41 et seq. and section IV.1. As regards the *uti possidetis* principle in general, see A Peters, 'The Principle of Uti Possidetis Juris: How Relevant is it for Secession?', (in this volume) 95 et seq.

[23] Cf. ICJ, *Advisory Opinion on the Accordance with International Law of the Unilateral Declaration of Independence in Respect of Kosovo* (22 July 2010) para 82.

[24] Cf. EJ Cárdenas/MF Cañás 'The Limits of Self-Determination' in W Danspeckgruber (ed), *The Self-Determination of Peoples* (Lynne Rienner Publishers 2002) 113; O Corten, 'Are there gaps in the international law of secession?' in MG Kohen (ed), *Secession, International Law Perspectives* (Cambridge University Press 2006) 231 et seq.; Kohen (n 14) 10; Potier (n 3) 36; G Welhengama, *Minorities' Claims: From Autonomy to Secession* (Ashgate Publishing 2000) 313 et seq. With regard to this point of view, even though holding a different opinion, see C Tomuschat, 'Secession and Self-determination' in MG Kohen (ed), *Secession, International Law Perspectives* (Cambridge University Press 2006) 37 et seq., 42; M Herdegen, *Völkerrecht* (5th edn, C.H. Beck 2006) 256 et seq.

[25] Cf. K Doehring in B Simma (ed), *The Charter of the United Nations* (2nd edn, Oxford University Press 2002) art. 1, annex: Self-Determination, note 40; H-J Heintze in K Ipsen, *Völkerrecht* (5th edn,

apparatus has developed into a tyrannical system (the so-called 'remedial secession').[26] If an ethnic group is faced with such persecution and there is no way out other than secession, this group may be entitled to secede. This view mainly refers to the Friendly Relations Declaration.[27]

Whether the Friendly Relations Declaration in particular or other soft law documents provide sufficient grounds to assume the existence of a right to secession for ethnic groups is questionable and should still be rejected. First, the interpretation of these documents in favour of a right to secession is conceivable but nevertheless casts many doubts. Even though the wording of the so-called 'Saving Clause' of the Friendly Relations Declaration provides an argument for secession as an exception,[28] the section neither precisely defines the entitled groups nor determines clear-cut conditions in which secession might be permissible. The concept of remedial secession as referred to above is not even clearly addressed. Hence, the interpretation of the Declaration in favour of a right to secession is open to abuse and, therefore, also seems to be doubtful in the light of the Declaration's primary aim: to maintain international peace and security. Furthermore, conditions assumed by experts on the basis of the Declaration frequently do not correspond with the complex reality of current secession conflicts, which are, for instance, characterized by the reciprocity of violence, the creation of mono-ethnic areas even by the party claiming self-determination, the involvement of third countries supporting secessionist movements, or the dissolution and succession of states.

Second, it would be necessary for any interpretation of the Friendly Relations Declaration in favour of an exceptional right to secession to reflect a fundamental principle of international law, and this would have to be supported by a combination of clearer documents. Otherwise one would unjustifiably convert soft law into hard international law. There are many documents cited by proponents of remedial secession in order to support their viewpoint, eg the CSCE Final Act (Helsinki Final Act) of 1975 and the OSCE Charter of Paris of 1990. However, upon closer consideration none of these documents sheds much more light upon the issue of remedial secession than the Friendly Relations Declaration does, and therefore it is hard to assume that remedial secession has emerged as a fundamental principle of international law.

Besides, the theory of remedial secession was not verified by the International Court of Justice's advisory opinion on Kosovo, either.[29] Although the ICJ found that international law contains no 'prohibition on declarations of independence',

C.H. Beck 2004) 414; Herdegen (n 24) 257; C Tomuschat, 'Self-Determination in a Post-Colonial World' in C Tomuschat (ed), *Modern Law of Self-Determination* (Martinus Nijhoff 1993) 9; Tomuschat (n 24) 38 et seq., 42.

[26] Cf. Tomuschat (n 25), 9; Tomuschat (n 24) 42.

[27] Reference is made to *Friendly Relations Declaration* 1970, 'The Principle of Equal Rights and Self-determination of Peoples' para 7 (the 'saving clause').

[28] *Friendly Relations Declaration* 1970, 'The Principle of Equal Rights and Self-determination of Peoples' para 7 (the 'saving clause').

[29] ICJ, *Advisory Opinion on the Accordance with International Law of the Unilateral Declaration of Independence in Respect of Kosovo* (22 July 2010).

the judges even explicitly avoided saying anything about the legal conditions and consequences of declarations of independence. The ICJ did not state that such declarations require a right to secession or any other particular prerequisite; nor did it find that such declarations necessarily or even immediately lead to the creation of independent states.[30] The judges did not shed any light on the various controversial issues of secession.[31]

Ultimately, it is clear that if the question of separation should be legally resolved in favour of ethnic peoples, groups, or minorities, it is incumbent upon the community of states to create clear rules corresponding to the complexity of secession conflicts. As we know, so far it has deliberately failed to do so. State practice can instead be described as unfavourable towards secession, even in cases of massive human rights violations.[32] Even in the Kosovo case, many recognizing states excluded the confirmation of a general right to secession.

According to the view held here, the Karabakh Armenians have no right to secession since such a right is not provided for ethnic groups under international law. However, we should not forget that the other view mentioned above (theory of remedial secession) has renowned advocates in international jurisprudence.[33] We shall examine whether the documented facts would justify the secession of Nagorno-Karabakh on the basis of this opinion. As mentioned above, this view considers a right to secession if an ethnic group is faced with severe, massive, and systematic human rights violations and if there is no way out other than secession. Karabakh Armenians claim to have been discriminated against by Azerbaijan SSR or Azerbaijanis—a view Azerbaijan categorically rejects. In order to throw light on this allegation, let us go back in time again, to the late 1980s.

The cycle of violence and counter-violence

In the course of *perestroika*, nationalist movements across the Soviet Union were strengthened and in many cases became violent. Detailed studies by de Waal show that as early as 1986, the Armenian side within and outside Karabakh began strategic planning to effect a transfer of the region to the Armenian SSR.[34]

[30] See also T Burri, 'Secession in the Caucasus: Causes, Consequences, and Emerging Principles' (in this volume) 138 et seq. with further references as to the interpretation of the ICJ's Kosovo opinion. As regards the absence of a statement on the right to secession, in particular, see also C Walter, 'The Kosovo Advisory Opinion: What It Says and What it Does Not Say' (in this volume) 13 et seq.

[31] See H Krueger, 'Was Kosovo's Split-off Legitimate? Background, Meaning and Implications of the ICJ's Advisory Opinion' (2010) CRIA 294; ICJ, *Advisory Opinion on the Accordance with International Law of the Unilateral Declaration of Independence in Respect of Kosovo* (22 July 2010), paras 82 and 83.

[32] See Tomuschat (n 24) 31; A Tancredi, 'A Normative "Due Process" in the Creation of States through Secession' in MG Kohen (ed), *Secession, International Law Perspectives* (Cambridge University Press 2006) 187 et seq.; Krüger (n 3) 62–8; H Krueger, 'Implications of Kosovo, Abkhazia and South Ossetia for International Law: The Conduct of the Community of States in Current Secession Conflicts' (2009) CRIA 125–8, 134–7.

[33] Cf. Doehring (n 25) art. 1, annex: Self-Determination, note 40; Heintze (n 25) 414; Herdegen (n 24) 257; Tomuschat (n 25) 9; Tomuschat (n 24) 38 et seq., 42.

[34] For details see de Waal (n 8) 15 et seq., 20 et seq.

The heart of the matter seemed to be political and historical issues. Armenians perceived the affiliation of Nagorno-Karabakh with the Azerbaijan SSR to be incorrect in historical, ethnic and, to a certain extent, economic terms. Even though most ordinary Armenians and Azerbaijanis had lived in peaceful coexistence in Soviet times, these considerations led to tensions. Such tensions between ethnic groups, however, were not unusual in the Soviet Union, a multi-ethnic state, and were even reinforced by the central government in Moscow. Furthermore, the political establishment in the Soviet Union dealt harshly with its critics. As the political establishment in the Azerbaijan SSR was largely occupied by Azerbaijanis, typical problems of the political system of the USSR may have been seen as Azerbaijani restrictions or harassment from the Armenian point of view.

Besides, there is debate as to whether the living conditions in Karabakh were worse or even better than in other regions of the Azerbaijan SSR.[35] A detailed study by Kipke at least shows that the development of Nagorno-Karabakh was not neglected in Soviet times.[36] However, whether these perceptions were correct or incorrect is actually not important for the question of secession. It is clear that the high threshold of discrimination of the remedial secession theory was not reached before the period of *perestroika*. The tensions in question did not reach the extent of most severe, massive, and systematic human rights violations, such as the murder of entire sections of the population, ethnic cleansing, or widespread torture.[37] If the discrimination threshold were to be set much lower, then numerous other regions of the former Soviet Union would run the risk of being overrun with secession claims. This means that the Karabakh Armenians were not entitled to secession, irrespective of the legal view one may follow.

Armenians nevertheless tried to exploit the moment of *perestroika*, as was the case with other national movements across the Soviet Union. At the beginning of 1988, the Armenians of Nagorno-Karabakh and the Armenian SSR were mobilized and mass demonstrations were initiated to demand the transfer of Nagorno-Karabakh to the Armenian SSR.[38] Beginning with these initial mass demonstrations, and in view of the growing anti-Azerbaijani mood, Azerbaijanis fled or were driven into exile from the Armenian SSR, many settling in the Azerbaijani capital Baku and the neighbouring city of Sumgayit.[39] These events were behind the acts of violence against Armenians committed by Azerbaijanis in Sumgayit in 1988.[40] Between 26 and 32 Armenians died and many were injured in these events.[41]

Without a doubt, these events represent a black day in Armenian–Azerbaijani history. They were also one further reason why both ethnic groups subsequently became entangled in a cycle of violence and counter-violence. Acts of violence, killings, and expulsions ultimately occurred on both the Armenian and the

[35] Cf. Krüger (n 3) 76.

[36] R Kipke, *Das armenisch-aserbaidschanische Verhältnis und der Konflikt um Berg-Karabach* (VS Verlag 2012).

[37] See Krüger (n 3) 75–7.

[38] See de Waal (n 8) 20 et seq., 22 et seq.

[39] See Krüger (n 3) 19; SE Cornell, 'The Nagorno-Karabakh Conflict' (1999), report no. 46, Department of East European Studies 14.

[40] For details see de Waal (n 8) 32 et seq.

[41] See de Waal (n 8) 34, 40; Cornell (n 39) 17.

Azerbaijani sides in the course of the conflict. Both sides cite pogroms in several cities and regions.[42] According to estimates, several tens of thousands of people were killed, and some 350,000 Armenians and 750,000–800,000 Azerbaijanis became refugees and internally displaced persons.[43] Hardly any Azerbaijanis now live in Nagorno-Karabakh and the seven adjacent districts since the expulsions. One of the most tragic events was the massacre of a considerable number of Azerbaijani civilians by Armenian units in 1992 in Khojaly, Nagorno-Karabakh. Azerbaijan claims the death toll numbered 613[44] and Human Rights Watch reported that as many as 500–1,000 may have died.[45] Reports by international journalists and the Azerbaijani investigation spoke of dead women and children and in some cases corpses disfigured beyond recognition.[46]

Ultimately, this can hardly be a scenario imagined by scholars of international law representing the view under consideration here (theory of remedial secession), ie where an ethnic group is hopelessly exposed to measures of suppression. This is rather a conflict over the territorial affiliation of a certain area which was perceived as unjust. Humanitarian reasons were in fact not the primary source of the conflict. This is also underlined by the fact that the Armenian side did not refrain from violence against, or the expulsion of, the other side's civilians. The conflict rather has its origin in the secessionist plans and initial propagandistic measures of proponents of a group which was not entitled to secession. This group was also to a large extent responsible for the fact that the violence continued to escalate. This is why, for instance, the Council of Europe has deliberately refused to say that the Karabakh Armenians have lawfully achieved independence, despite the clear fact that thousands of Armenians were also killed by Azerbaijanis in the course of the conflict.[47] As a consequence, a right to secession should also be rejected here irrespective of the legal dispute over the general existence of rights to secession. However, apart from that, it also remains clear that the injustices committed on both sides should be punished under criminal law, human rights law, and international laws of war.

[42] Human Rights Watch, *Playing the 'Communal Card': Communal Violence and Human Rights* (1995); M Quiring, 'Schwelende Konflikte in der Kaukasus-Region' (1999) APuZ 19; Summary of the Armenian Parliamentary Hearings, 'The Karabakh Conflict: Settlement Scenarios' March 2005, <http://www.regnum.ru/english/584766.html> accessed 20 October 2012; letter dated 23 December 2009 from the Permanent Representative of Azerbaijan to the United Nations addressed to the Secretary-General, A/64/608–S/2009/670; letter dated 9 April 1997 from the Permanent Representative of the Republic of Azerbaijan to the United Nations Office in Geneva addressed to the Secretariat of the Commission on Human Rights, UN ECOSOC doc. E/CN.4/1997/139, annex.

[43] Cf. Human Rights Watch (n 10) 99. As noted, in 2011 the CIA cited 120,000 Armenian and 580,000–690,000 Azerbaijani refugees and internally displaced persons; see CIA (n 10).

[44] See Krüger (n 3) 100 et seq.

[45] Cf. Human Rights Watch (n 10) 6, n 28.

[46] Cf. eg reports in *The Sunday Times*, 1 and 8 March 1992; *The Boston Globe*, 3 March 1992; *New York Times*, 3 and 6 March 1992; *The Times*, 2 and 3 March 1992; *taz*, 7 March 1992; *Frankfurter Rundschau*, 2 March 1992. See also de Waal (n 8) 169 et seq.

[47] See Council of Europe Parliamentary Assembly Resolution 1416 (2005).

IV. Legal Status of Nagorno-Karabakh

The legal dispute between the Armenian and Azerbaijani side concerns not only the issue of a right to secession but also the question of the present legal status of Nagorno-Karabakh. Whereas the question of a right to secession pertains only to the legality of a claim, the status question goes further and asks whether the exercise of a given right or even the occurrence of certain other events have already changed the legal character and affiliation of the region.

Ultimately, the present legal status of a region aspiring to independence, like Nagorno-Karabakh, is subject to two basic questions: first, was the region an original component of the parent country in question? Second, has the original affiliation to the parent country changed in the meantime due to the exercise of a right to secession or the occurrence of other relevant events?

1. Nagorno-Karabakh as an initial component of the Republic of Azerbaijan?

Of course, the second question, asking whether the process of secession was effective, makes sense only if Nagorno-Karabakh became an initial component of Azerbaijan. If this is not the case, then there is no legal reason to insist on the necessity of secession at all. Accordingly, the initial affiliation of Nagorno-Karabakh to Azerbaijan is also an object of contention between the two sides.[48]

In order to establish clarity on this point we must take the principle of *uti possidetis* into account. It says, in particular, that in the event of dissolution of a state, the units of that state come to independence within their former administrative boundaries.[49] These boundaries attain the status of international borders. The principle of *uti possidetis* was originally established within the context of decolonization, but today it must be considered part of customary international law beyond the colonial context,[50] especially with regard to the former USSR and the former Yugoslavia.[51]

The application of the *uti possidetis* principle to the Karabakh case shows quite clearly that the region became an initial component of the Republic of Azerbaijan. Before the break-up of the Soviet Union, Nagorno-Karabakh lay within the administrative borders of the Azerbaijan SSR. The Azerbaijan SSR was constituted as a

[48] Cf. 'The Karabakh Conflict: Settlement Scenarios' (n 42).

[49] See MN Shaw, *International Law* (5th edn, Cambridge University Press 2003) 446 et seq.; Tomuschat (n 24) 37 et seq.; Herdegen (n 24) 38; V Epping and C Gloria in K Ipsen (ed), *Völkerrecht* (5th edn, C.H. Beck 2004) 283; S Hobe and O Kimminich, *Einführung in das Völkerrecht* (8th edn, A. Francke Verlag 2004) 78.

[50] See ICJ, *Case Concerning the Frontier Dispute (Burkina Faso/Republic of Mali)*, ICJ Reports 1986, 554, 566; A Peters, 'The Principle of *Uti Possidetis Juris*: How Relevant is it for Secession?' (in this volume) 95 et seq.; Shaw (n 49) 448 et seq.; T Hillier, *Sourcebook on Public International Law* (Cavendish Publishing Limited 1998) 218; T Schweisfurth, *Völkerrecht* (Mohr Siebeck 2006) 283; C Simmler, *Das uti-possidetis-Prinzip, Zur Grenzziehung zwischen neu entstandenen Staaten* (Duncker & Humblot 1999) 293; Hobe and Kimminich (n 49) 78 et seq.

[51] See Shaw (n 49) 448; Heintze (n 25) 421.

Union Republic and was therefore one of the top-level units of the USSR, ranking right below the union level. The administrative borders of the Azerbaijan SSR inside the Soviet Union, which were defined in the Soviet Constitution, applied for decades. After the secession of the Azerbaijan SSR from the Soviet Union, these borders were converted, pursuant to the *uti possidetis* principle, into the international borders of the Republic of Azerbaijan, including Nagorno-Karabakh. This process of border transformation applied to all former Union Republics of the Soviet Union and should not leave any room for doubt in the Karabakh case.

The Armenian side nevertheless questions the application of the *uti possidetis* principle. It is said that the affiliation of Nagorno-Karabakh to Azerbaijan was conditioned exclusively by the formation and existence of the Soviet Union.[52] However, there was no provision of the Soviet Constitution or of Soviet law on which such an argument could be based. Ultimately, an exception to the *uti possidetis* principle would at best be conceivable if, first, the Armenians acquired a legitimate claim over Nagorno-Karabakh in pre-Soviet times which, second, has to be respected even today. The presence of both requirements is more than questionable.

Regarding the first requirement: one can hardly assume that the Armenians possessed a legitimate claim over Nagorno-Karabakh before the foundation of the Soviet Union. Under the rule of the Russian Tsar, Nagorno-Karabakh was assigned to the administrative districts from which the Republic of Azerbaijan later emerged. When Russian supremacy was weakened as a result of the revolutions in 1917, both Armenians and Azerbaijanis laid claim to Nagorno-Karabakh. The region's affiliation was disputed and not determined at that time. Moreover, the proclaimed Armenian and Azerbaijani republics could not be considered as independent states and their recognition was, therefore, refused by the League of Nations in 1920 due to the lack of recognized borders, of a constitution, and of a stable government.[53] In the absence of sovereign states, Armenians even lacked the ability to acquire a legitimate claim over Nagorno-Karabakh under the principles of traditional international law of the nineteenth century, which was still applicable at that time.

Regarding the second requirement: even if such a claim had been given, it would have lost its validity and therefore have no bearing today. When the Russians returned in 1920, they founded the Caucasian Bureau, which ultimately decided that Nagorno-Karabakh was to remain in the Azerbaijan Soviet Republic. This decision was then incorporated into the Soviet Constitution. The Soviet Union had to be considered as the new sovereign in the region, and as such it was allowed to define and redefine internal subdivisions and their borders. The fact that the Russians resumed power over the Caucasus through the threat of military force was not relevant to the legal situation. The prohibition on the threat and use of force as we know it today was not applicable at that time[54] and, in addition, no

[52] Cf. 'The Karabakh Conflict: Settlement Scenarios' (n 42).

[53] See League of Nations Assembly Doc 20/48/206, 20/48/209 and 20/48/251; United Nations Commission on Human Rights Doc E/CN.4/2005/G/23.

[54] See Shaw (n 49) 422 et seq.; Hobe and Kimminich (n 49) 37; Krüger (n 3) 2 et seq.

sovereign Caucasian states were established which might have been protected under such a prohibition. Hence, the territorial decisions taken by the Soviets in those days had to be respected, and they still form the basis of current state structure in the region. Therefore, there are no doubts about the international borders of the Republic of Azerbaijan, which included Nagorno-Karabakh at the time it was founded according to the principle of *uti possidetis*.

2. Alteration of the affiliation of Nagorno-Karabakh?

However, the affiliation of a certain region to a given parent country is not irrevocable. There are two instances under discussion in which the original affiliation ceases and the breakaway region may be recognized as an independent state. The first instance under discussion is the exercise of a right to secession. The second is the factual status that a breakaway region may achieve over the course of time. It is internationally accepted that an entity may gain independence if it meets all requirements of statehood.[55] Accordingly, secession can also be the product of factual events (de facto secession).[56]

As regards the first instance, it was already established above that Nagorno-Karabakh may not fall back on any right to secession that could be exercised either under national or under international law. Therefore, let us proceed with the question of whether the region has already emerged as a state of its own over the years on the basis of factual events.

Nagorno-Karabakh Republic—statehood over time?

The Republic of Armenia has tried to make the international community of states accept the assertion that a stabilized entity has developed in Nagorno-Karabakh, the Nagorno-Karabakh Republic, making a right to secession redundant. As noted above, secession may indeed be achieved as a matter of fact over the course of time. According to the classic concept of statehood, a new state is born and may be recognized as such if an entity meets all requirements of statehood.[57] These include at least the following three criteria: the entity must have a defined territory, a permanent population, and an effective government. Initially, this seems to be the case in Nagorno-Karabakh, since we have a defined territory, a permanent population, and an administration.

But there are two indications that Nagorno-Karabakh has not yet achieved statehood. The first point is that the administration established in Nagorno-Karabakh cannot be considered an effective government under the classic concept of statehood, because it is not able to maintain and administer the created entity on its

[55] See J Crawford, *The Creation of States in International Law* (2nd edn, Clarendon Press 2006) 45 et seq.; Epping and Gloria (n 49) 266, 271 et seq.; Hobe and Kimminich (n 49) 67, 71.

[56] See also Tomuschat (n 24) 44.

[57] See Crawford (n 55) 45 et seq.; Epping and Gloria (n 49) 266, 271 et seq.; Hobe and Kimminich (n 49) 67, 71.

own. To date, the Republic of Armenia's military, political, and financial assistance form the main pillar of the 'Nagorno-Karabakh Republic'.[58] Nagorno-Karabakh is significantly dependent upon the military involvement of Armenia. Armenia took an active part in the military occupation of Karabakh and the seven surrounding districts between 1993 and 1994. To this day, these regions are controlled by one joint military body consisting of troops from Armenia and Karabakh.[59] According to the International Crisis Group, Armenian nationals shall make up half of the defence and occupying forces.[60] The presence of soldiers of the Armenian army is also assumed by reports of the Council of Europe,[61] the OSCE,[62] and the US Department of State[63]. On closer examination, Armenia has formed the backbone of the occupation of the region and its surrounding districts over the entire course of the conflict. The Parliamentary Assembly of the Council of Europe even characterized the situation as a de facto annexation of this territory to another state.[64]

Furthermore, Armenia has supported a large part of the Karabakh budget over the whole course of the conflict through the granting of loans.[65] It is said that this amounts to 50% of the Karabakh budget.[66] Moreover, it can be assumed that the political systems of Armenia and Nagorno-Karabakh are closely intertwined with one another, considering the exchange of political leaders and the massive capital flow originating from Armenia. In the final analysis, the given situation hardly resembles that of an independent effective government.

The second point is that the classic concept of statehood applies only with certain restrictions. International law in particular does not accept a status which rests upon an illegal armed intervention by a third state.[67] Otherwise the prohibition on the use of force and the prohibition of military occupation following such use of force would fail to have the desired effect. Therefore, it is necessary to

[58] See Krüger (n 3) 93–114.

[59] See also H Langner, 'Der politische Status von Berg-Karabach—Aus Sicht des Völkerrechts' (2011) WeltTrends, Zeitschrift für internationale Politik 28.

[60] Cf. International Crisis Group, *Europe Report no. 166* (2005), <http://www.crisisgroup.org/en/regions/europe/south-caucasus/azerbaijan/166-nagorno-karabakh-viewing-the-conflict-from-the-ground.aspx> accessed 10 February 2014.

[61] See *Report of the Political Affairs Committee of the Parliamentary Assembly of the Council of Europe*, 29 November 2004, Doc 10364, III para 6.

[62] OSCE election observers expressed their strong suspicion that during the Armenian elections in 1998, one of the mobile election boxes was brought to Armenian soldiers in Kelbajar. See OSCE—Office for Democratic Institutions and Human Rights, *Republic of Armenia Presidential Elections March 16 and 30 1998, Final Report*, 8.

[63] See Country Reports on Human Rights Practices—2006 released by the Bureau of Democracy, Human Rights, and Labor, 6 March 2007 <http://www.state.gov/g/drl/rls/hrrpt/2006/78799.htm> accessed 20 October 2012.

[64] Council of Europe Parliamentary Assembly Resolution 1416 (2005). See also A Tancredi, 'Secession and the Use of Force' (this volume) IV.2.

[65] Cf. *Report of the Political Affairs Committee of the Parliamentary Assembly of the Council of Europe*, 29 November 2004, Doc 10364, III. para 6; Human Rights Watch (n 10) 110; de Waal (n 8) 246; interview with Armenian President Kotscherian from 10 July 2007 <http://www.spiegel.de/politik/ausland/0,1518,493351,00.html> accessed 20 October 2012.

[66] See International Crisis Group (n 60).

[67] See V Epping in K Ipsen (ed), *Völkerrecht* (5th edn, C.H. Beck 2004) 63; Epping and Gloria (n 49) 302; Council of Europe Parliamentary Assembly Resolution 1416 (2005). Differently see Kohen (n 14) 11.

scrutinize whether the intervention of Armenia must be considered illegal under international law. In this case Nagorno-Karabakh could not attain its own statehood over time.

As the international sources already cited above show, there is no doubt that Armenia occupies Azerbaijani territories. Such a military occupation of territories belonging to another state clearly represents violations of both the prohibition on the use of force and the prohibition on intervention.[68] Consequently, the Armenian intervention is illegal if Armenia is not able to invoke reasons to justify its action. But whether it can do so is very questionable. Armenia can neither appeal to a mandate from the UN Security Council nor invoke Article 51 of the UN Charter regarding measures of individual and collective self-defence. Armenia has never been attacked by Azerbaijan and Nagorno-Karabakh is not a member of the United Nations as required by Article 51; rather, it is recognized as part of Azerbaijan.

Apart from these written justifications, one may consider whether Armenia can invoke unwritten justifications as these are discussed in international jurisprudence. We may ask whether Armenia can refer to reasons of external self-determination or humanitarian reasons. In terms of external self-determination, however, reference falls short because international law, in general, does not allow for an armed external intervention that aims at fostering the separation of an existing state against the will of the central government.[69] Furthermore, we have seen above that the right to external self-determination or secession is not met in the case of Nagorno-Karabakh.

As concerns humanitarian reasons, we know that there is debate about whether a humanitarian intervention by a third state can be considered lawful. The majority of states and legal scholars require in any case authorization by the UN Security Council,[70] which was not available in the Karabakh case. To the contrary, the UN Security Council demanded the immediate withdrawal of all occupying forces from Azerbaijani territory.[71]

But even with the opposing view, which does not require authorization by the UN Security Council, the Armenian intervention cannot be considered as justified. The situation we are confronted with in Nagorno-Karabakh does not resemble that of a humanitarian intervention. Even though the humanitarian situation of the Armenian civilians confronted with the war and Azerbaijani measures has surely played a role for Armenia, humanitarian factors have never been the main reason for the Armenian intervention. The first clearly documented direct intervention by Armenia in 1993, the Kelbajar offensive, was mainly concerned with preventing loss of territory and recapturing recently lost territory.[72] It was meant

[68] Cf. Krüger (n 3) 93 et seq., 110.

[69] Cf. Shaw (n 49) 1038 et seq.; G Nolte, 'Secession and external intervention' in MG Kohen (ed), *Secession, International Law Perspectives* (Cambridge University Press 2006) 88–93; Tomuschat (n 24) 43 et seq.; Kohen (n 14) 11.

[70] See eg Hobe and Kimminich (n 49) 332, 339 et seq.; H Fischer, in K Ipsen (ed), *Völkerrecht* (5th edn, C.H. Beck 2004) 1084.

[71] UN Security Council Resolution 822 (1993).

[72] See Human Rights Watch (n 10) 68; Krüger (n 3) 101 et seq., 109.

to sustain the process of secession and to bring it to a successful end. This is also why no consideration was paid to the humanitarian situation on the other side. Expelled Azerbaijanis were not given the chance to return to their homes in Karabakh. Even today, humanitarian concerns do not seem to be the main reason for the Armenian intervention. Azerbaijani offers of autonomy and humanitarian guarantees are categorically dismissed by Armenia. Therefore the Armenian occupation cannot be considered as justified under international law.

Correspondingly, the lack of its own effective government and the presence of illegal occupying forces reveal that Nagorno-Karabakh has not been able to secede legally from Azerbaijan. In summary it can be said, therefore, that Nagorno-Karabakh still belongs to the Republic of Azerbaijan. Moreover, Azerbaijan may refer to the principle of territorial integrity in view of the fact that Nagorno-Karabakh and the seven surrounding districts are to a large extent illegally occupied by the Republic of Armenia.

However, this finding does not mean that a possible Azerbaijani assault on Nagorno-Karabakh and Armenia would be lawful, in particular with respect to the prevailing line of ceasefire, which is also protected by the prohibition on the use of force.[73]

As a consequence, Azerbaijan is obliged to refrain from violence while facing a continuing violation of international law by Armenia. Azerbaijan is not ready to accept the Armenian occupation of Nagorno-Karabakh in the long run, and this is what makes the Karabakh conflict so dangerous. Therefore, help from the community of states is crucial to maintain peace in the Southern Caucasus and to resolve the Karabakh conflict.

V. Conclusion

The legal assessment above has shown that neither Soviet law nor international law has provided a right to secession for Karabakh Armenians. Furthermore, because of the deep and illegal involvement of the Republic of Armenia in the occupation of territories, the so-called Nagorno-Karabakh Republic cannot be considered as an entity that has already gained its own statehood. For this reason, Nagorno-Karabakh continues to belong to the Republic of Azerbaijan, and this should be respected within the framework of conflict resolution. Apart from that, it is also imperative to find an effective and reliable way to safeguard the rights of Karabakh Armenians and, especially, their autonomy within Azerbaijan.

Despite the clear legal situation, attempts at conflict resolution are ambiguous as far as legal issues are concerned. This legal ambiguity concerns both conflicting parties' positions. On the one hand, the Azerbaijani legal position that Nagorno-Karabakh still belongs to the Republic of Azerbaijan does not form the basis for negotiations.

[73] See *Friendly Relations Declaration 1970*, 'The Principle that States shall Refrain in their International Relations from the Threat or Use of Force', para 5; Fischer (n 70) 1081 et seq.

Despite the fact that the region's belonging to Azerbaijan is internationally confirmed and that Armenia is clearly violating international law, the legal status is considered a subject of negotiation instead of the basis with which to start.

On the other hand, the legal prospects are also not clear for Armenians. Even though the Minsk Group proposes a referendum, it is obvious that such a referendum is not based on the Minsk Group's conviction that Karabakh Armenians already have a right to secession. In the absence of such a conviction, the Minsk Group is not prepared to recognize any elections or the referendum on the status issue already carried out in Nagorno-Karabakh. The Minsk Group, rather, urges the parties to conclude an agreement, which will only form the basis for a referendum.[74] Such an agreement has to be negotiated, and therefore also the exact subject of a referendum and the participants in it (only current Armenian residents or Armenian residents and Azerbaijani internally displaced persons). The crucial point is that in the course of these negotiations, each conflicting party is now attempting to establish preconditions for a referendum under which the own side's victory can be ensured. This is one reason why negotiations are in deadlock.

Ultimately, impartial guidance concerning the conflicting legal positions is needed. Theoretically, relevant legal issues and therefore the guiding principles of conflict resolution could be clarified by an authoritative legal institution like the International Court of Justice.[75] However, even though the conflicting parties and the Minsk Group members frequently confirm their commitment to international law, none of these players seems to be prepared to rigorously seek authoritative legal guidance. The involvement of the ICJ is considered inappropriate to solve complex conflicts like that of Nagorno-Karabakh.

This argumentation reveals, of course, quite a typical pattern of today's international management of secession conflicts, pursuant to which resolution is primarily to be brought about by diplomatic measures while the involvement of legal institutions is excluded. This was also exemplified by the Kosovo case, where, for instance, the United States and Germany were anything but supportive when Serbia finally decided to bring the case to the ICJ.[76] Unfortunately, the ICJ backed this approach when it consciously followed a narrow interpretation of the Serbian request for an advisory opinion. In that way it avoided a decision on the real status questions evidently at issue ('the elephant in the room')[77] and thus left conflict resolution to a later political stage.[78] One may seriously question, therefore, whether the ICJ is

[74] See White House press release from 26 June 2010, 'G8 Summit: Joint Statement On The Nagorno-Karabakh Conflict by Dmitry Medvedev, President Of The Russian Federation, Barack Obama, President Of The United States Of America, and Nicolas Sarkozy, President Of The French Republic' <http://www.whitehouse.gov/the-press-office/g8-summit-joint-statement-nagorno-karabakh-conflict-dmitry-medvedev-president-russi>, accessed 20 October 2012.

[75] See also Council of Europe Parliamentary Assembly Resolution 1416 (2005), para 7.

[76] See Krueger (n 31) 296.

[77] T Burri, 'The Kosovo Opinion and Secession: The Sounds of Silence and Missing Links' (2010) GLJ 889, see also pp. 885 et seq. in this respect, http://www.germanlawjournal.com/index.php?pageID=11&artID=1273 accessed 20 October 2012.

[78] See Krueger (n 31) 295; M Bothe, 'Kosovo—So What? The Holding of the International Court of Justice is not the Last Word on Kosovo's Independence' (2010) GLJ 839, <http://www.germanlawjournal.com/index.php?pageID=11&artID=1269> accessed 20 October 2012.

really ready to take greater responsibility. As a result, legal instruments have little say in current cases of secession, which is particularly true in the Karabakh case. This finding is surely striking considering the western nations' calls to uphold the rule of law within the countries affected by secession.

Ultimately, the present purely diplomatic approach is quite questionable. The case of Nagorno-Karabakh, in particular, reveals that the involvement of foreign states is even one crucial reason why secession conflicts are so complex and difficult to resolve. Contradictory and inconsistent foreign interests strengthen the positions of both conflicting sides and make it harder for the parties to give in and to compromise, irrespective of the current legal status. As regards the Karabakh case, the Minsk Group Co-Chair countries, Russia, France, and the United States, are torn, as mediators, between the strategic importances of both conflicting sides. Russia, for its part, in particular seems to pursue a policy of maintaining a situation of 'controlled instability' through the assistance of both sides.[79] Moreover, a historical bond between Russia and Armenia and strong Armenian diasporas in France and the United States make it difficult to clearly oppose Armenian positions.

To find the key to conflict resolution, it therefore seems to be inevitable that the status issue or any other particular intractable legal question must be referred to an impartial institution such as the International Court of Justice. This is true for the Karabakh case, but also for other cases of secession. However, the inclusion of the ICJ does not mean that conflict management provided by foreign states necessarily becomes redundant—quite the contrary. International conflict management and procedures before the court must ultimately be combined. Whereas the ICJ shall decide on the crucial legal issues, international mediators shall primarily assume the responsibility to ensure that cases are brought to the ICJ and that its findings are enforced through the given conflict resolution procedures later on. However, to achieve this realistically, it is of paramount importance that the international community assumes far more responsibility to resolve secession conflicts and helps implement international law. This especially applies to the Karabakh case, where the danger of a new, major outbreak of violence is still present.

[79] H Langner, *Krisenzone Südkaukasus* (Verlag Dr. Köster 2009) 57.

PART III
COMPARATIVE STUDIES

12

Kosovo

James Summers

I. Introduction

This case study will focus on Kosovo and its legal position in the domestic law of Serbia, the legal regime established by the United Nations, and international law. Kosovo divides the world almost equally. For 98 states in the UN, it is an independent state, but for others it is part of Serbia.[1] At the root of the controversy is Kosovo's position in 2008 as the most significant entity since Bangladesh to unilaterally declare independence. Bangladesh was eventually recognized by its parent state, Pakistan, in 1974, paving the way for its admission into the UN. However, Serbia does not recognize Kosovo and has actively campaigned against recognition. An important part of this was a request for an Advisory Opinion from the International Court of Justice on the legality of the declaration of independence by Kosovo's provisional institutions. This Opinion, delivered in 2010, significantly did not find that the declaration violated international law. The Kosovo Opinion is also important for submissions from a number of interested states to the Court during the proceedings, which provide a rich picture of international law concerning Kosovo's status.

The position of Kosovo has important implications for post-Soviet states. Russia backs Serbia and has argued that Kosovo's declaration of independence set a dangerous precedent. Moreover, as Farhad Mirzayev and Christopher Waters note in their case studies,[2] it has itself applied this precedent in its relations with former Soviet states. In 2008 it recognized the Georgian breakaway regions of Abkhazia and South Ossetia as independent, explicitly citing Kosovo in that decision.[3] Kosovo has obvious relevance among the post-Soviet states as an autonomous area which fell short of the status of a federal unit entitled to independence when the federal state dissolved. The question of where to draw the line in the break-up of a state

[1] <http://www.kosovothanksyou.com> accessed 31 May 2013.

[2] F Mirzayev, 'Abkhazia' (in this volume) 191; C Waters, 'South Ossetia' (in this volume) 175.

[3] Statement by the Ministry of Foreign Affairs of the Russian Federation, 26 August 2008; Statement by the President of Russia Dimitry Medvedev, 26 August 2008; UN Doc S/PV.5969 8.

gives Kosovo resonance for regions such as Abkhazia, South Ossetia, Tatarstan, Chechnya, and Nagorno-Karabakh. At the same time, Kosovo has its own distinct features, most notably its experience under international administration.

II. Factual and Historical Background

Kosovo is a small and landlocked territory of 10,887 square kilometres. Until 1999 it was clearly under the political control of Serbia, which lies to the north. However, most of its population have ethnic ties to Albania, in the south-west. Kosovo's population has changed dramatically over its violent history, but is currently 2.1 million (2006) and predominantly ethnic Albanian (92%) and Muslim, with Serbs the largest minority (5.3%). Prior to NATO intervention in 1999, Kosovo's Serbian population was over twice that size.[4] Economically Kosovo is the poorest region of former Yugoslavia, with a per capita income of $6,500 and marked by high unemployment.

Kosovo was annexed by the Kingdom of Serbia with the break-up of the Ottoman empire in 1912. With the establishment of the Federal Socialist Republic of Yugoslavia in 1945 it was first an autonomous region and then a province of Serbia, one of six republics in the communist federation. These republics (with the exception of Bosnia-Herzegovina) corresponded with a Yugoslav nation: Serbs, Croats, Slovenes, Macedonians, and Montenegrins. Albanians, by contrast, were classified as a 'nationality', along with Hungarians, who formed a large minority in another Serbian autonomous province, Voijvodina.[5] Nationalities in the Yugoslav system did not have a right to self-determination or their own republics.[6] The theory was that Albanians and Hungarians had already established their own states outside Yugoslavia, but this underlay the political reality that Serbs, who had already seen Macedonia carved out of their territory, would not tolerate any further reductions, especially in relation to Kosovo. Serbs regard Kosovo as the cradle of their nation and the Battle of Kosovo in 1389, in which they lost their independence to the Ottomans, as a defining moment in their history. They retain an intense attachment to this territory despite demographic changes that produced an Albanian majority, most likely from the mid-nineteenth century.[7] The Albanians themselves considered their position as a nationality discriminatory, especially as they outnumbered Montenegrins and Macedonians.[8] Moreover, unlike Voijvodina, where Hungarians remained a minority, Kosovo was a viable basis for an Albanian state

[4] Statistical Office of Kosovo, *Demographic Changes of the Kosovo Population 1948-2006* (Statistical Office of Kosovo 2008) 7.

[5] M Vickers, *Between Serb and Albanian: A History of Kosovo* (Hurst and Co. 1998) 160.

[6] V Vujacic and V Zaslavsky, 'Causes of the Disintegration of the USSR and Yugoslavia' (1991) 88 Telos 124; SP Ramet, *Nationalism and Federalism in Yugoslavia, 1962-1991* (Indiana University Press 1992) 20; T Judah, *Kosovo: What Everyone Needs to Know* (OUP 2008) 53–54.

[7] N Malcolm, *Kosovo: A Short History* (MacMillan 1994) 196. See also Vickers (n 5) 164–76, 182.

[8] Judah (n 6) 53; Vickers (n 5) 175.

within Yugoslavia. The demand for its elevation to a republic provided the focus for Albanian nationalism within Yugoslavia.[9]

The republic/autonomy, nation/nationality distinction was a product of the internal politics of Yugoslavia, but it had dramatic international legal consequences when the federation broke up in 1991. Only republics were entitled to statehood. However, in constitutional practice the distinction between republics and autonomies became increasingly blurred, and this has led to arguments that Kosovo was a de facto republic.[10] In the 1974 Constitution nations and nationalities were held to have equal rights. Kosovo acquired its own constitution, government, legislature, judiciary, police, and bank. It held a veto over Serbian legislation and was represented alongside the republics in federal legislative and judicial organs.[11] With the death of Yugoslav leader Josep Tito in 1980, Kosovo became part of an eight-member collective presidency, made up equally of representatives of the six republics and two autonomies[12] (a Kosovar was President from May 1986 to May 1987).[13] This multinational system was supposed to hold the country together, but proved weak and complex. Moreover, it institutionalized the power of the republics and autonomies, which vied with each other for control of the state. Kosovo would play a central role in this struggle.

Serbia under Slobodan Milošević sought to create a Serb-led centralized Yugoslavia. The first steps included a coup in Montenegro in January 1989 and the reestablishment of direct control over the two autonomies in March.[14] This gave Milošević control of two republics and two autonomies, and thus four of the eight seats in the collective presidency.[15] On 28 June 1989—the 600th anniversary of the Battle of Kosovo—addressing a huge crowd on the battlefield, he warned of battles ahead, possibly armed ones.[16] This was a clear threat to the other republics, especially Slovenia and Croatia, which were pressing for a looser federation. As a result of the conflicting goals of these republics and the failure of negotiations, within two years the Yugoslav federation would no longer exist.

On 25 June 1991 Slovenia and Croatia declared independence. Bosnia and Macedonia followed. Serbia and Montenegro claimed to continue the federation as the Federal Republic of Yugoslavia (FRY). On 21 September the Kosovo Albanians also made a declaration of independence, supported by a referendum which endorsed independence by 99.87% on a turnout of 87.01%.[17] However, the

[9] Vickers (n 5) 164, 167. [10] See Section 2.1.

[11] Vickers (n 5) 145–6, 160, 169–70; Judah (n 6) 57.

[12] V Meier, *Yugoslavia: A History of Its Demise* (Routledge 1999) 3–4; I Goldstein, *Croatia: A History* (Hurst and Co. 1999) 187–9; Vickers (n 5) 194.

[13] AS Trbovich, *A Legal Geography of Yugoslavia's Disintegration* (OUP 2008) 234.

[14] Judah (n 6) 67; P Radan, *The Break-Up of Yugoslavia and International Law* (Routledge 2002) 197; Trbovich (n 13) 232–3; Vickers (n 5) 234–5.

[15] Ramet (n 6) 69; C Bennett, *Yugoslavia's Bloody Collapse: Causes, Course and Consequences* (Hurst and Co. 1995) 100; Judah (n 6) 67.

[16] M Glenny, *The Fall of Yugoslavia: The Third Balkan War* (Penguin Books 1992) 35; Malcolm (n 7) 213; Judah (n 6) 67–8; Vickers (n 5) 238–40.

[17] 'Central Board of Kosova for the Conduct of the Referendum, Result, 7 October 1991' in M Weller (ed), *The Crisis in Kosovo 1989-1999* (Documents and Analysis Publishing 1999) 72.

international policy on recognition, expressed most notably by the then European Community (EC)'s Badinter Arbitration Commission, was that Yugoslavia was in the process of dissolution.[18] This reflected the Community's position in its Declaration on Yugoslavia on 16 December 1991, which laid out conditions for the recognition of Yugoslav Republics but not for other political units.[19] The Badinter Commission also applied the principle of *uti possidetis* to republic boundaries and considered that self-determination had to be interpreted within that framework, precluding the possibility for autonomous regions in republics to secede.[20] An application by the de facto authorities in Kosovo on 22 December 1991 for recognition by the EC was rejected.[21] The Republic of Kosovo only gained recognition from Albania.[22]

The proclaimed state of Kosovo, though, notably lacked control of its territory. Serbian authorities began a campaign of 'Serbianization' in the province.[23] The ethnic Albanian leadership, in turn, established parallel governing institutions.[24] However, this non-violent resistance contained Kosovo and allowed it to be overlooked by an international community more concerned with the war in Bosnia. This conflict concluded with the Dayton Accords 1995, which recognized Yugoslavia (FRY) including Kosovo. The result was the rise of more militant groups, notably the KLA, which began a guerrilla insurgency against Serbia.[25] In spring 1997 the collapse of Albania's government in the wake of a financial crisis and the looting of government armouries provided the weapons for a mass insurrection.[26]

In March 1998 armed rebellion broke out in Kosovo, initially led by the KLA, but taking on its own momentum as Albanian villages armed themselves and took control of their territory. In SC Res. 1160 of 31 March the UN Security Council condemned the KLA as terrorists, but also called on the Yugoslav government to enter into a dialogue with the Albanian leadership. The Council proposed that a political solution involved substantially greater autonomy and meaningful self-administration for Kosovo within the territorial integrity of Yugoslavia.[27] However, in July Serbian forces were able to counterattack and swiftly drove back the KLA, and with them the Albanian population, leaving an estimated 200,000 ethnic Albanians displaced by August.[28]

[18] Arbitration Commission of the Peace Conference on Yugoslavia, Opinion No. 1, (1992) 31 ILM 1495–7.

[19] Declaration on Yugoslavia (1992) 31 ILM 1485–6.

[20] Arbitration Commission of the Peace Conference on Yugoslavia, Opinion No. 2, (1992) 31 ILM 1498, para 1.

[21] 'Letter from Dr. Rugova to Lord Carrington, Peace Conference on Yugoslavia, 22 December 1991', in Weller (n 17) 81; Vickers (n 5) 252.

[22] Radan (n 14) 200; Vickers (n 5) 254.

[23] R Caplan, 'International Diplomacy and the Crisis in Kosovo' (1998) 74 IA 751; Malcolm (n 7) 350–353; Vickers (n 5) 252; Juliane Kokott, 'Human Rights Situation in Kosovo 1989-1999' in C Tomuschat (ed), *Kosovo and the International Community: A Legal Assessment* (Kluwer 2002) 15–26.

[24] Judah (n 6) 73.

[25] Judah (n 6) 79.

[26] C Hedges, 'Kosovo's Next Masters?' (1999) 78 FA 3, 37; Judah (n 5) 80.

[27] UNSC Res 1160 (31 March 1998) UN Doc S/RES/1160 para 5.

[28] T Judah, *Kosovo: War and Revenge* (Yale University Press 2000) 140–71.

Indirect negotiations began under the Contact Group,[29] a diplomatic body composed of US, Russia, France, Germany, Italy, and Britain.[30] This process, though, had stalled by December and the situation was further inflamed by a new Yugoslav offensive and the Racak massacre in January 1999.[31] On 29 January the Contact Group summoned the two sides for negotiations in Rambouillet in France. These negotiations were to be based on non-negotiable principles: an interim agreement, with a final settlement after three years; no unilateral changes to the interim status; international involvement; respect for the territorial integrity of the FRY and neighbouring countries; a high degree of Kosovo self-government under democratically accountable institutions. The next day NATO called on the parties to comply with the Rambouillet process, observe a ceasefire, and end disproportionate force or face air strikes.[32]

Talks took place from 6 to 23 February, with the assistance of three negotiators from the Contact Group. The resulting Accords provided for the deployment of an international force in Kosovo operating under a NATO chain of command.[33] They also provided for democratic self-government in Kosovo, though clearly within the sovereignty of Yugoslavia (FRY), which retained powers over defence and foreign affairs.[34] This self-government was an interim system and after three years a meeting would be convened to determine a final settlement based on the will of the people of Kosovo, the opinions of the relevant authorities, the parties' efforts to implement the agreement, and the Helsinki Final Act 1975.[35] This combination of elements did not rule out any particular outcome, but was orientated towards autonomy within Yugoslavia. The reference to the will of the people might be seen as a reference to self-determination, but in the Final Act this is explicitly contained by territorial integrity. However, only the Kosovo delegation signed the Rambouillet Accords on 18 March,[36] and ethnic cleansing continued.[37]

On 24 March 1999 NATO began an air campaign against Yugoslavia.[38] This was not authorized by the Security Council due to Russian and Chinese opposition, but NATO justified it as 'necessary to avert a humanitarian catastrophe' following Yugoslavia's refusal to accept the Rambouillet Accords and its disproportionate use of force.[39] Serbian forces, in turn, intensified attacks on Albanians,[40] and by the end of the campaign 1.3 million Albanians were refugees or internally displaced.

[29] See SL Burg and PS Shoup, *The War in Bosnia-Herzegovina: Ethnic Conflict and International Intervention* (M. E. Sharpe 1999) 298–300.

[30] See UNSC Res 1199 (23 September 1998) UN Doc S/RES/1199; UNSC Res 1203 (24 October 1998) UN Doc S/RES/1203.

[31] M Weller, 'The Rambouillet Conference on Kosovo' (1999) 75 IA 219–20.

[32] Weller (n 31) 222–6.

[33] Chapter 7, Article 1, UN Doc S/1999/648 58.

[34] Chapter 1, Preamble, Article 1 and Article 3.

[35] Chapter 8, Article 1.

[36] AJ Bellamy, *Kosovo and International Society* (Palgrave MacMillan 2002) 120–55.

[37] Bellamy (n 36) 155.

[38] Judah (n 6) 87, 90.

[39] Javier Solana, Secretary General of NATO, Press Statement, 23 March 1999 <http://www.nato.int/cps/en/natolive/opinions_27615.htm> accessed 14 October 2010.

[40] See E Herring, 'From Rambouillet to the Kosovo Accords: NATO's War against Serbia and Its Aftermath' (2000) 4 IJHR 228–32.

The Kosovo conflict concluded with a peace agreement on 3 June.[41] On 10 June, the Security Council, by 14 votes to 0 and China's abstention,[42] adopted SC Res. 1244, which laid out the framework for the international administration of Kosovo. The resolution authorized the deployment of an international security presence,[43] the Kosovo Force (KFOR), with substantial NATO participation,[44] which replaced Yugoslav forces in the territory.[45] KFOR policed Kosovo's borders and aimed to provide a secure environment for the civilian mission, the United Nations Mission in Kosovo (UNMIK), as well as the return of refugees.[46] UNMIK was responsible for establishing an interim political framework that allowed substantial autonomy and self-government for Kosovo.[47] It would perform basic civilian administrative functions in Kosovo, while organizing and overseeing the development of, and then elections to, provisional, democratic self-governing institutions. It would then transfer responsibilities to those provisional institutions, retaining oversight.[48] Kosovo's self-government was to be exercised within the sovereignty and territorial integrity of Yugoslavia (FRY), though that country was prevented from exercising that sovereignty. Nonetheless, this regime was explicitly interim.[49] SC Res 1244 provided for a political process, facilitated by UNMIK, for determining Kosovo's final status, but it provided little indication of when or how that would occur, aside from taking into account the Rambouillet Accords.[50] This can be compared with the international administration established around the same time in East Timor (UNTAET), in which the method of termination, East Timorese independence, and a timeframe were provided. By contrast, UNMIK was mandated to continue until the Security Council agreed to end it.[51]

UNMIK presented the construction of self-governing institutions as a 'contract' with the Kosovo people,[52] whose fulfilment required meeting prescribed standards. The transfer of authority to self-governing institutions took place in two stages: first, elected municipal authorities in 2000; second, an elected assembly in 2001. However, its initial challenge was to support the return of 800,000 refugees and 500,000 internally displaced persons (from a population of 1.8 million) who had been driven from their homes.[53] In addition, KFOR and the administration had to re-establish law and order in a territory from which the previous authorities had fled and which was now controlled by armed gangs. Kosovo had become a centre for trafficking in drugs and women,[54] and there was widespread violence

[41] L Sell, *Slobodan Milosevic and the Destruction of Yugoslavia* (Duke University Press 2002) 308–16.

[42] UN Doc S/PV.4011 9.

[43] UNSC Res 1244 (10 June 1999) UN Doc S/RES/1373 paras 7–9.

[44] Annex 2 para 4.

[45] Paras 3 and 15.

[46] Para 9 (c), (g), and (h).

[47] Paras 11(a), 10, and Preamble.

[48] Para 11 (b)–(d).

[49] Para 10.

[50] Para 11(e).

[51] '[T]he international civil and security presences are established for an initial period of 12 months, to continue thereafter unless the Security Council decides otherwise'. Para 19.

[52] UN Doc S/2000/538 para 132; UN Doc S/2000/878, para 9; UN Doc S/2000/1196, para 108.

[53] UN Doc S/1999/779 paras 8–9. H Strohmeyer, 'Collapse and Reconstruction of a Judicial System: The United Nations Mission in Kosovo and East Timor' (2001) 95 AJIL 48.

[54] UN Doc S/1999/779 paras 4–5; UN Doc S/1999/1250 para 19; UN Doc S/2000/177 para 61; UN Doc S/2000/878 para 40.

aimed particularly at the minority Serbs and Roma. In reverse ethnic cleansing, 220,000 internally displaced persons retreated to Serbia and Montenegro[55] and Serb-majority enclaves in Kosovo.[56] This process was most prominent in the town of Mitrovica, which divided along the Ibar River, with Serbs on the north bank and Albanians on the south.[57] In addition, Albanian irredentist violence briefly spilled over Kosovo's borders into the Presevo Valley of southern Serbia and the Tetevo region in Macedonia.[58]

Municipal elections were held in October 2000, with a high level of participation among Albanians, a much lower one from minorities, and non-participation by Serbs.[59] On 15 May 2001 the Special Representative of the Secretary-General (SRSG) promulgated the Constitutional Framework on Interim Self-Government in Kosovo, which established the institutions of self-government, including the Kosovo Assembly, government, and presidency.[60] Elections for the Kosovo Assembly followed in November and authority was transferred to the new provisional institutions.[61] By the end of 2003, all non-reserved responsibilities had been transferred,[62] though the SRSG still retained reserved powers, such as external relations.[63] The SRSG held a veto over the Provisional Institutions and exercised it a number of times.[64] The new institutions, according to the UN, showed 'an increasing desire to encroach on the powers reserved for the Special Representative…rather than concentrating on the urgent matters over which these bodies have responsibility'.[65] The construction of an impartial multi-ethnic civil service also proved problematic. Serbia at that time was also in transition to full democracy, with Milošević being forced to stand down from the Yugoslav Presidency in October 2000. Serbia could argue that concerns over repression under its authority longer applied.[66]

The development of self-government in Kosovo and transfer of authority to provisional institutions was guided by a series of benchmarks expressed under the 2002 formula 'standards before status'.[67] Albanians saw this as an obstacle to independence,[68] but in January 2003 the UN's assessment was that 'Kosovo is still

[55] See UNHCR, 'Federal Republic of Yugoslavia' [2000] Global Appeal 218.

[56] UN Doc S/1999/779 paras 5, 9.

[57] UN Doc S/2000/177 paras 20–1.

[58] UN Doc S/2000/538 para 24; UN Doc S/2000/878 para 19; UN Doc S/2000/1196 paras 21, 113; UN Doc S/2001/218 para 11; UN Doc S/2001/565 paras 9–12; UN Doc S/2001/926 paras 11–14.

[59] UN Doc S/2000/1196 paras 2 and 4.

[60] Article 1.5, Constitutional Framework for Provisional Self-Government, UNMIK Regulation 2001/9.

[61] UN Doc S/2002/62 para 3.

[62] UN Doc S/2002/62 para 3; UN Doc S/2004/71 para 5.

[63] UN Doc S/2002/1126 para 9.

[64] UN Doc S/2002/779 para 8; UN Doc S/2003/421 para 5; UN Doc S/2004/71 para 9; UN Doc S/2004/348 para 28.

[65] UN Doc S/2003/113 para 8.

[66] Serbia: 'the Republic of Serbia…since 2000 has been an entirely democratic State in which human rights are widely respected and in which all the inhabitants, regardless of their national origin, language or religion, can participate in public life.' Written Statement of Serbia, 15 April 2009, para 646.

[67] UN Doc S/2002/1126 para 2; B Knoll, 'From Benchmarking to Final Status? Kosovo and the Problem of an International Administration's Open-Ended Mandate' (2005) 16 EJIL 641–2; UN Doc S/PV.4518 4.

[68] Judah (n 6) 109. UN Doc S/2003/113 para 9; UN Doc S/2002/1376 para 19; UN Doc S/2003/113 para 9.

a considerable way from reaching the individual benchmarks and targets set out in the benchmarks matrix'.[69] One more notable failure could, however, be attributed to UNMIK: economic reform. Limited privatization of Kosovo's socially owned enterprises had only started in February 2003, and was then delayed due to legal uncertainty.[70] Unemployment stood at 60% and GDP at just €700 per capita.[71] The territory also remained ethnically polarized and in March 2004 those tensions erupted in riots, which were initially spontaneous but quickly became directed against minorities, forcing 4,100 people from their homes.[72] The riots threw into question the UN strategy and in April the Secretary-General requested that the Norwegian Ambassador to NATO, Kai Eide, review the situation. Eide's August report turned UNMIK's underlying assumption of progress on its head. Its motif was a complaint from an Albanian student: 'you gave us freedom but not a future'.[73] Instead of stable self-government built through benchmarks, it envisaged economic decline and growing political instability.[74] Moreover, the international presence was losing its security capacity as KFOR reduced its strength and the UNMIK police struggled to maintain theirs.[75] Rather than focusing on standards, it was time to consider 'a workable exit strategy',[76] which meant final status negotiations. Achieving European standards in Kosovo was a long-term project which would have to continue after those negotiations.

In 2005 the Secretary-General and Security Council moved towards the final status negotiations with the appointment of a Special Envoy, former Finnish President Martti Ahtisaari. The process was led by the Contact Group, which on 7 October 2005 issued a declaration of ten Guiding Principles.[77] The goals in these were similar to those of UNMIK: a democratic Kosovo complying with European standards on human rights and the rule of law; sustainable multi-ethnicity; the return of refugees and the displaced; and integration into Euro-Atlantic institutions. They also set specific dimensions for the settlement: no return to Kosovo's pre-March 1999 status; no partition or union with another state (ie no greater Albania); no unilateral or forcible measures; and respect for the territorial integrity of neighbours. The Group later added that the settlement also had to be acceptable to the population of Kosovo. Moreover, regardless of the form of the settlement, an international civil and military presence would remain to supervise compliance with its terms and to monitor and support the implementation of standards. However, the Contact Group was itself divided on the final status, between the US, France, Italy, Germany, and the UK on one side, and Russia, with its special relationship with Serbia, on the other.[78]

[69] UN Doc S/2003/113 para 61.

[70] HH Perritt, 'Economic Sustainability and Final Status for Kosovo' (2004) 25 UPJIEL 288; Knoll (n 67) 651–2.

[71] UN Doc S/2004/71 paras 36–7.

[72] UN Doc S/2004/348 para 22.

[73] UN Doc S/2004/932 3 and 9, para 5.

[74] UN Doc S/2004/932 3 and 9, 43–4.

[75] UN Doc S/2004/932 3 and 9, para 12.

[76] UN Doc S/2004/932 3 and 9, para 14.

[77] Guiding Principles of the Contact Group for a Settlement of the Status of Kosovo <http://www.unosek.org/docref/Contact%20Group%20-%20Ten%20Guiding%20principles%20for%20Ahtisaari.pdf> accessed 17 October 2010.

[78] M Weller, *Contested Statehood: Kosovo's Struggle for Independence* (OUP 2009) 195, 207, 210.

In 2006 15 rounds of negotiations took place;[79] during this time, in June, Serbia's union with Montenegro ended. Nonetheless, a settlement remained elusive. In September Contact Group ministers, without Russian support, called on the Special Envoy to draw up proposals for a comprehensive settlement.[80] Martti Ahtisaari presented his Comprehensive Proposal to the two parties on 2 February 2007.[81] This was formally neutral on Kosovo's status, though it gave Kosovo attributes normally associated with statehood, such as the ability to conclude international agreements and join international organizations.[82] It was rejected by Serbia.[83] Ahtisaari forwarded his proposal to the Security Council, together with the blunt assessment that the potential for negotiation had been exhausted[84] and that the only viable option was independence, supervised for an initial period by the international community.[85] Reintegration with Serbia was unacceptable to the overwhelming majority of Kosovo's people and could not be achieved without 'violent opposition'. However, these proposals were not accepted due to Russian opposition.[86] Further negotiations between Belgrade and Pristina failed[87] and there was a sense, reflected in the report by the Secretary-General in January 2008, that 'events on the ground could take on a momentum of their own, putting at serious risk the achievements and legacy of the United Nations in Kosovo'.[88]

On 17 February 2008, a special session of the Kosovo Assembly attended by the President adopted a Declaration of Independence.[89] Its opening sentence sparked a legal debate about who exactly had declared independence: 'We, the democratically elected leaders of our people, hereby declare Kosovo to be an independent and sovereign state'.[90] However, this independence was subject to international supervision. It accepted Ahtisaari's Comprehensive Proposal and recommendations[91] and invited an international presence to supervise their implementation, as well as an EU-led rule of law mission, EULEX, and a NATO-led military force.[92] This international involvement was established shortly after the Declaration, on 28 February, with the International Civilian Office for Kosovo, headed by an International Civilian Representative (ICR).[93] The ICR's role was to supervise the implementation of the Ahtisaari Plan. He was also invested with extensive powers, including the annulment of laws and government decisions and the authority to

79 Weller (n 79) 203.

80 Contact Group Ministerial Statement, 20 September 2006 <http://www.unosek.org/unosek/en/docref.html > accessed 6 February 2014.

81 Comprehensive Proposal for the Kosovo Status Settlement, UN Doc S/2007/168/Add.1.

82 Article 1(5).

83 Weller (n 78) 210–11.

84 *Report of the Special Envoy of the Secretary-General on Kosovo's Future Status*, UN Doc S/2007/168 paras 1 and 3.

85 Special Envoy's Report (n 84) para 5, 10–14.

86 Weller (n 78) 216–17.

87 Weller (n 78) 220–9.

88 UN Doc S/2007/768 para 33.

89 UN Doc S/2008/211 para 3.

90 Article 1, Kosovo Declaration of Independence, 17 February 2008, 47 (2008) ILM 467.

91 Articles 3, 4, 5, 8, and 12, Declaration.

92 Article 5, Declaration.

93 Press Statement, First Meeting of the International Steering Group (ISG) for Kosovo, 28 February 2008. See International Steering Group <http://www.ico-kos.org/ico/?id=10> accessed 28 September 2010.

sanction and remove public officials.[94] This raised the question of whether Kosovo was really a sovereign state.[95] There was also a shift in the international administration from the UN to the EU, with the EU's rule of law mission, EULEX, taking on responsibility for policing, the administration of justice, and customs.[96] UNMIK was reconfigured in 2009 to perform a more limited range of functions including monitoring, reporting, and assisting in dialogue between Pristina and Belgrade.[97]

Kosovo was recognized the same day by Costa Rica and the following day by the US, France, Albania, Turkey, the UK, and Afghanistan. Over the next few weeks it was recognized by most European countries. However, after an initial burst of support, the pace slowed, with a clear majority of countries not extending recognition. Serbia launched a diplomatic offensive to prevent further recognition, including a request from the UN General Assembly on 8 October 2008 for the International Court to deliver an Advisory Opinion on the legality of the independence declaration.[98] On 22 July 2010 the International Court delivered its Opinion. By a clear 10–4 majority, the Court considered that the declaration did not violate international law. This was a blow to Serbia, but did not produce a boost in recognition for Kosovo either. States have remained wary of recognizing an entity created by unilateral secession. In the four years after its declaration Kosovo experienced a slow trickle of recognition, bringing it to the level of 98 UN states at the time of writing. On 19 April 2013 Serbia and Kosovo reached an EU-brokered deal on normalization of their relations by which Serbia accepted the legal authority of the Kosovo authorities, though this did not amount to recognition of Kosovan statehood.[99] It remains to be seen how this will be viewed by other states considering recognition. Nonetheless, while Kosovo has undoubtedly been controversial, it does contrast with Abkhazia, South Ossetia, Nagorno-Karabakh, and Transdniestria in obtaining a broad measure of international recognition.

III. Legal Analysis

1. Right of secession under national law

The population of Kosovo has never had any specific right of self-determination or secession under the national law of either Yugoslavia or Serbia. The preamble of

[94] Article 2(1), Annex IX, Comprehensive Proposal for the Kosovo Status Settlement, S/2007/168/Add.1.

[95] See C Warbrick, 'Kosovo: The Declaration of Independence' (2008) 57 ICLQ 689; J Vidmar, 'International Legal Responses to Kosovo's Declaration of Independence' (2009) 42 VJTL 820–1, 849.

[96] Council Joint Action 2008/124/CFSP, 4 February 2008, OJEU L42/92 (2008). See E de Wet, 'The Governance of Kosovo: Security Council Resolution 1244 and the Establishment and Functioning of EULEX' (2009) 103 AJIL 83–96.

[97] UN Doc S/2008/354 paras 16, 19. UN Doc S/2009/497 para 2.

[98] UNGA Res 63/3 (8 October 2008) UN Doc A/RES/63/3.

[99] 'A Breakthrough at Last', *The Economist* (20 April 2013) <http://www.economist.com/blogs/easternapproaches/2013/04/serbia-and-kosovo-0>, accessed 31 May 2013.

the Constitution of the Socialist Federal Republic of Yugoslavia 1974 recognized the right of self-determination and secession for nations. However, Albanians were classed as a nationality and, in principle, not entitled to exercise this right, though the Constitution is ambiguous, referring to nations and nationalities as having equal rights.[100] Kosovo is defined in Article 2 of the 1974 Constitution as an autonomous province in the Republic of Serbia. Arguments have been made that the authority of Kosovo was politically similar to that of a republic. In submissions to the ICJ, a number of states, such as Finland and Ireland, considered that Kosovo's status was comparable to that of a republic within Yugoslavia.[101] Albania noted that Albanians were the 'third nation' in Yugoslavia in terms of population.[102] Nonetheless, for the most part these were subsequent critiques of the international response to the dissolution of Yugoslavia in 1991, in which Kosovo was treated as an autonomous region of Serbia and not considered to have a right to independence.

With the dissolution of Yugoslavia, Serbia formed the Federal Republic of Yugoslavia along with Montenegro. Its 1992 Constitution makes no reference to self-determination, but refers only to the rights of national minorities.[103] In the Constitution of the State Union of Serbia and Montenegro which succeeded the FRY in 2002, Kosovo is described as an Autonomous Province of Serbia under international administration.[104] While Serbia or Montenegro had the right to terminate this union in Article 60—and Montenegro did, in 2006—there was no such right for Kosovo. On 30 September 2006, an independent Serbia adopted a new Constitution which, in Article 182 offered Kosovo substantial autonomy within Serbia—though this has been questioned as it is still subject to laws made by the Serbian National Assembly.[105] Thus, at the time that Kosovo authorities declared their independence on 17 February 2008, Kosovo did not have the right to secede under national law.

2. Right to secession under the regime of SC Res. 1244

Kosovo from 1999 remained formally under the sovereignty of Yugoslavia (FRY), but the legal framework for its governance was that of the United Nations administration (UNMIK). Regulations by UNMIK and the Constitutional Framework proclaimed in 2001 took precedence over existing national laws.[106] The foundational instrument in the legal regime for Kosovo was SC Res. 1244 (1999). In contrast

[100] Articles 1 and 3, Constitution of the Socialist Federal Republic of Yugoslavia 1974.

[101] Statement of Finland, 16 April 2009, para 10; Statement of Ireland, 17 April 2009, para 33; Written Statement of Denmark, 17 April 2009, para 2.5; Written Statement of Poland, 14 April 2009, para 3.5. But see Written Statement by Russia, 16 April 2009, para 90; Written Statement of Serbia, 15 April 2009, para 573.

[102] Written Statement of Albania, April 2009, para 75. But see Written Statement of Russia, 16 April 2009, para 91.

[103] Article 11, Constitution of the Federal Republic of Yugoslavia 1992.

[104] Preamble, Constitutional Charter of the State Union of Serbia and Montenegro 2002.

[105] European Commission for Democracy through Law (Venice Commission), Opinion on the Constitution of Serbia, Opinion No. 405/2006, 17–18 March 2007, CDL-AD(2007)004, para 8.

[106] S. 3, UNMIK Regulation 1999/1, 25 July 1999.

to SC Res. 1272 on East Timor, this resolution did not specify a final status for Kosovo. The matter was left unresolved, and correspondingly both sides in the debate over Kosovo's independence have seized on different parts of the resolution to support their own interpretations of that status.

Those who believed that the resolution prohibited independence cited, in particular, paragraph 10 of the preamble, which referred to 'the commitment of all Member States to the sovereignty and territorial integrity of the Federal Republic of Yugoslavia and the other States of the region, as set out in the Helsinki Final Act'.[107] This provision did reflect the desire of several Security Council members that Kosovo should be resolved within the territorial integrity of Yugoslavia.[108] However, other states questioned whether this was limited to the interim period of self-government rather than the final status. Territorial integrity could be read together with phrases in the resolution, such as 'pending a final settlement',[109] to demonstrate its temporary nature.

States in favour of the possibility of independence highlighted two features of SC Res. 1244. First, there was the reference to the Rambouillet Accords (para. 11(a)), which based a settlement for Kosovo on the will of the people.[110] However, the Accords equally contained other provisions which could limit this will, such as territorial integrity.[111] Moreover, the resolution established only a commitment to take the Accords 'into account'. Second, there was what the resolution did not contain: any express prohibition on independence.[112] If the Security Council wanted to foreclose the possibility of independence it could have done so within the text of the resolution. Nonetheless, even with these arguments, it is clear that Kosovo did not have a right to independence, as East Timor did under SC Res. 1272.

In the Kosovo Opinion the Court controversially considered that the provisions on territorial integrity in SC Res. 1244 did not prevent Kosovo authorities from declaring their independence and by extension pursuing their secession. This related to two aspects: the scope of SC Res. 1244 and the authority of institutions created under its provisions.

[107] Written Statement of China, 2; Written Statement by Cyprus, 17 April 2009, paras 90, 92; Note by Libya; Written Statement by Russia, 16 April 2009, para 58; Written Statement of Serbia, 15 April 2009, para 928; Written Statement of Spain, April 2009, para 37; Written Statement of Slovakia, para 20; Statement of Venezuela. See also Dissenting Opinion of Judge Koroma para 13.

[108] Namibia, UN Doc S/PV.4011 7; China, UN Doc S/PV.4011 9; Argentina, UN Doc S/PV.4011 19; Russia, UN Doc S/PV.4011 7.

[109] Written Statement of Czech Republic, April 2009, 10; Written Statement by Denmark, para 2.6; Written Statement of Estonia, April 2009, para 3; Statement of Ireland, 17 April 2009, para 25; Written Statement of Poland, April 2009, para 7.2.

[110] Written Statement of Albania, April 2009, para 50; Written Statement by Denmark, para 2.6; Statement of Germany, April 2009, 39; Statement of Ireland, 17 April 2009, para 25; Written Statement of Luxembourg, 30 March 2009, para 21; Written Statement of United States of America, April 2009, 64–8; Written Contribution of Kosovo, 17 April 2009, para 4.17, 9.12. But see Written Statement of Argentina, 17 April 2009, para 99.

[111] Written Statement by Cyprus, 17 April 2009, para 93; Written Statement of Romania, para 48; Written Statement by Russia, 16 April 2009, para 55; Written Statement of Spain, April 2009, para 37.

[112] Written Statement by Switzerland, para 48; Written Statement of United Kingdom, 17 April 2009, para 6.12; Written Contribution of Kosovo, 17 April 2009, para 9.04.

First, the Court considered that SC Res. 1244, despite its references to sovereignty and territorial integrity, did not prohibit a declaration of independence. The resolution established a temporary regime that did not prejudice agreement on its future status.[113] The Court highlighted the fact that the Security Council had 'remained silent' on a final status,[114] whereas when it wanted to restrict options on a territorial settlement it had specified those conditions (eg in Cyprus).[115] Thus, there were two levels to the resolution: the interim administration and the final status, and the independence declaration related to the latter.[116]

Second, there was the question of whether the Provisional Institutions of Self-government—the Assembly, President, and Prime Minister, who issued the declaration—were acting *ultra vires*.[117] As an objection this was not necessarily insurmountable. If the Provisional Institutions were prohibited from declaring independence, the Kosovars could have formed a new constituent assembly and reissued the declaration.[118] A simple alternative was to argue that they had already done this. For a brief period they had stepped outside their official role to sit as a constituent assembly, or, as it was phrased, 'the democratically elected representatives of the people of Kosovo'. The argument that the declaration's authors were representatives of the people rather than Provisional Institutions evolved with proceedings.[119] In the General Assembly debate on the Advisory Opinion, no state actually questioned whether the declaration was issued by the Provisional Institutions.[120] The General Assembly's question itself asserted that the declaration was by the Provisional Institutions, which the Court significantly did not consider itself bound to respect.[121] However, in written statements, states supporting Kosovo's independence commonly asserted that the declaration was not by the Provisional Institutions,[122] but by a constituent body.[123]

[113] [2010] ICJ Rep paras 97–100.

[114] [2010] ICJ Rep para 114.

[115] UNSC Res 1251 (29 June 1999) UN Doc S/RES/1251.

[116] [2010] ICJ Rep para 114.

[117] See eg Written Statement of Argentina, 17 April 2009 paras 61–4, 116.

[118] See Written Comments of the United States, 17 July 2009 para 38.

[119] See Written Comments of Cyprus, 8 July 2009 para 5. See also Oral Submission of Serbia (Djeric), (1 December 2009) CR 2009/24 41, para 18.

[120] See objections by US, UN Doc A/63/PV.22 5; Albania, UN Doc A/63/PV.22 4.

[121] [2010] ICJ Rep para 54. See MD Öberg, 'The Legal Effects of United Nations Resolutions in the Kosovo Advisory Opinion' (2011) 105 AJIL 84.

[122] Written Contribution of Kosovo, 17 April 2009 paras 4.22, 6.13–6.20, 7.07; Written Statement of Albania, 14 April 2009 para 71; Written Statement by Austria, 16 April 2009 para 16; Written Statement of Estonia, 13 April 2009 para 1; Written Statement of Germany, 15 April 2009 6–7; Written Statement of Luxembourg, 30 March 2009 para 13; Written Statement of Norway, 16 April 2009 para 13; Written Statement of United Kingdom, 17 April 2009 paras 0.24, 1.12; Oral Submission of Croatia (Metelko-Zgombić), (7 December 2009) CR 2009/29, para 75.

[123] Written Comments of Albania, 17 July 2009 paras 67 and 79; Written Comments of Germany, 14 July 2009 7; Oral Submission of Finland (Kaukoranta), (8 December 2009) CR 2009/30, para 9. See also Written Statement of Germany, 15 April 2009 6; Further Written Contribution of Kosovo, 17 July 2009 para 5.63; Oral Submission of Germany (Wasum-Rainer), (2 December 2009) CR 2009/26, para 7; Oral Submission of Albania (Frowein), (2 December 2009) CR 2009/26, para 11; Oral Submission of Norway (Fife), (9 December 2009) CR 2009/31 para 14; Oral Submission of United Kingdom (Bethlehem), (10 December 2009) CR 2009/32, para 16.

This argument was adopted in the majority opinion, to the obvious bemusement of several judges.[124] It found that the authors of the declaration did not act as one of the Provisional Institutions, but as 'persons who acted in their capacity as representatives of the people of Kosovo outside the framework of the interim administration'.[125] This was not without problems. The Court itself recognized that when the declaration was issued, both the President of the Kosovo Assembly and the Prime Minister referred to the Assembly of Kosovo and the Constitutional Framework.[126] The SRSG, in his report to the Secretary-General, referred to the declaration as the work of 'the Assembly of Kosovo'.[127] Nonetheless, the Court also drew attention to the language of the Declaration, which proceeded with 'We…' rather than 'The Assembly of Kosovo…', as would normally be used. The procedure was also different, with the involvement of the President. The Court's reasoning here is open to the charge of selectiveness.[128] It emphasized the distinctive wording of the declaration, but merely noted references to the Assembly of Kosovo and the Constitutional Framework.[129] Nonetheless, this reference to the representation of the people is significant. It is tempting to see a new variation on the self-determination rhetoric emerging here, whereby individuals invoke a people to escape from legal restrictions—in this case, imposed by the UN Security Council. Kosovo's Declaration of Independence can be seen to be aimed at UNMIK as much as Serbia. Nonetheless, even if this can be considered a self-determination argument, it does not amount to a positive right to independence.

3. Right to secession under international law

A general right to secede

There is broad support for the idea that, even if the principle of self-determination applies to peoples within states, it does not establish a general right of secession.[130]

124 See Decl. of Judge Tomka paras 12, 20; Diss. Op. of Judge Bennouna para 60; Sep. Op. of Judge Sepulvéda-Amor para 24; Sep. Op. of Judge Yusuf para 20; Diss. Op. of Judge Skotnikov para 12; Diss. Op. of Judge Koroma paras 4–5, 19.

125 [2010] ICJ Rep para 109.

126 [2010] ICJ Rep para 104.

127 [2010] ICJ Rep para 108.

128 See MG Kohen and K Del Mar, 'The Kosovo Advisory Opinion and UNSCR 1244 (1999): A Declaration of "Independence from International Law"?' (2011) 24 LJIL 114–18; R Tricot and B Sander, 'The Broader Consequences of the International Court of Justice's Advisory Opinion on the Unilateral Declaration of Independence in Respect of Kosovo' (2011) 49 CJTL 356–61; R Muharremi, 'A Note on the ICJ Advisory Opinion on Kosovo' (2010) 11 GLJ 871–3; D Jacobs, 'International Court of Justice, Accordance with International Law of the Unilateral Declaration of Independence in Respect of Kosovo, Advisory Opinion of 22 July 2010' (2011) 60 ICLQ 807–8; S Trifunovska, 'The Impact of the "Kosovo Precedent" on Self-Determination Struggles' in J Summers (ed), *Kosovo: A Precedent?* (Martinus Nijhoff 2011) 389–90.

129 [2010] ICJ Rep para 104.

130 See J Crawford, 'State Practice and International Law in Relation to Unilateral Secession' in AF Bayefsky (ed), *Self-Determination in International Law: Quebec and Lessons Learned* (Kluwer 2000) 42–3, 57; R Higgins, *The Development of International Law Through the Political Organs of the United Nations* (OUP 1963) 105; A Cassese, *Self-determination of Peoples: A Legal Reappraisal* (CUP 1995) 123.

This is also reflected in the ICJ's comments in *Kosovo* that a general right to independence based on self-determination was 'a subject on which radically different views were expressed by those taking part in the proceedings',[131] suggesting a lack of *opinio juris*. In fact, there was not so much disagreement in states' statements to the Court on a right to secede as an obvious lack of support for independence as anything other than an exceptional measure.[132] Comments by the ICJ in *Kosovo* point to the formation of states (outside the colonial context) as part of the rough-and-tumble of international politics:

> During the eighteenth, nineteenth and early twentieth centuries, there were numerous instances of declarations of independence, often strenuously opposed by the State from which independence was being declared. Sometimes a declaration resulted in the creation of a new State, at others it did not.[133]

The suggestion is that the formation of a new state is not a right, but is a political possibility.

If there is no general right to secession, is it prohibited? There is significant support for the idea that international law is essentially neutral on secession, not laying down any specific prohibitions.[134] However, there is also opinion from a number of states that territorial integrity does restrict secession.[135] The problem with such a position, though, is that the firm application of the principle would prevent any unilateral state-formation from existing states. But states do sometimes break up due to their own internal pressures, and other states may be unable to prevent this.

If territorial integrity does not absolutely prohibit secession, it does appear to weigh against it. For example, in response to the Declaration of Independence by the Republika Srpska from Bosnia, in SC Res. 787 the Security Council called on 'all parties and others concerned to respect strictly the territorial integrity of the Republic of Bosnia and Herzegovina, and affirms that any entities unilaterally declared or arrangements imposed in contravention thereof will not be accepted'.[136] There is considerable practice to support the idea that territorial integrity could

[131] [2010] ICJ Rep para 82.

[132] eg Estonia: 'Certainly the right to self-determination does not contain an automatic right to secession.' Written Statement of Estonia, 13 April 2009 5.

[133] [2010] ICJ Rep para 79.

[134] *Re Secession of Quebec* (1998) 161 DLR 4th para 112; J Crawford, *The Creation Of States In International Law* (OUP 2006) 417; MG Kohen, 'Introduction' in MG Kohen (ed), *Secession: International Law Perspectives* (CUP 2006); O Corten, 'Territorial Integrity Narrowly Interpreted: Reasserting The Classical Inter-State Paradigm of International Law' (2011) 24 LJIL 88; H Hannum, 'The Advisory Opinion on Kosovo: An Opportunity Lost, or A Poison Chalice Refused?' (2011) 24 LJIL 155.

[135] Written Statement of Argentina, 17 April 2009 paras 75–82; Written Statement of Iran, 17 April 2009 paras 3.1–3.6; Written Statement of Serbia, 15 April 2009 paras 431–91; Written Comments of Argentina, 17 July 2009 paras 39–40; Written Comments of Serbia, 14 July 2009 paras 225, 231–2; Written Comments of Spain, 17 July 2009 paras 4–5; Oral Submission of Serbia (Shaw) (1 December 2009) CR 2009/24, paras 7–12; Oral Submission of Romania (Aurescu) (10 December 2009) CR 2009/32, paras 10–11.

[136] UNSC Res 787 (16 November 1992) UN Doc S/RES/787, para 3.

limit the scope of the right to self-determination. This can be found in international instruments such as the Declaration on Granting Colonial Independence 1960, the Declaration on Friendly Relations 1970, the Helsinki Final Act 1975, and the Declaration on the Rights of Indigenous Peoples 2007. This is also supported by the practice of national courts and international bodies.[137] In *Western Sahara* the ICJ suggested that territorial sovereignty, of which territorial integrity is considered an element,[138] could affect the range of options for the right of self-determination.[139]

The position taken by the ICJ in *Kosovo* was curious: 'the scope of the principle of territorial integrity is confined to the sphere of relations between States'.[140] This was delivered in the context of Kosovo's authorities as non-state actors making a declaration of independence, but should, in principle, also apply to acts of secession.[141] It made no distinction between the principle as a source for negative prohibitions and its role in tempering positive rights: it simply did not apply within states. This arguably runs counter to previous and subsequent practice. It also makes it hard for the Court to legally justify a distinction it makes itself between peoples subject to alien subjugation, who have a right to independence, and other populations, who apparently do not. If self-determination is a right of 'all peoples', as instruments assert, why is it not applied without distinction, unless there is a countervailing principle that tempers its application? The Court's reasoning was also curious, referring to instruments on territorial integrity in relation to the use of force between states rather than self-determination: Principle 1 of the Declaration on Friendly Relations instead of Principle 5, and Principle IV of the Helsinki Final Act, not Principle VIII(1).[142] It appeared to reach the conclusion that territorial integrity was a principle of interstate relations by only looking at its role in interstate relations. It was also hard to square with the Court's previous stance in *Western Sahara*, which may account for that opinion's strange absence when the ICJ recalled its previous jurisprudence on self-determination.[143]

It appears that Kosovo does not have a general right to independence, but equally, the role of territorial integrity as a prohibitive principle is also divisive. In such circumstances it is hard to argue that Kosovo is prohibited from secession through any customary rule, though any right it might claim to do so could be negated by territorial integrity. Given an absence of illegality, it can be argued that a duty of non-recognition is not applicable. Articles 40 and 41 of ILC Articles on

[137] *Re Secession of Quebec*, (1998) 161 DLR 4th para 122. *Katangese People's Congress* v *Zaire*, Communication No. 75/92; *Tatarstan* (1994) 30:3 Statutes and Decisions of the USSR and Its Successor States 40–1; *Chechnya* (1995) 31:5 Statutes and Decisions: The Laws of the USSR and Its Successor States 52; *Kevin Mgwanga Gunme et al* v *Cameroon*, Communication No. 266/2003 paras 190–1.

[138] See eg Written Statement of the Czech Republic, 15 April 2009 7.

[139] *Western Sahara* (Advisory Opinion) [1974] ICJ Rep 68, para 162.

[140] [2010] ICJ Rep para 80.

[141] See R Wilde, 'Self-Determination, Secession, and Dispute Settlement after the Kosovo Advisory Opinion' (2011) 24 LJIL 152; M Weller, 'Modesty Can be a Virtue: Judicial Economy in the ICJ Kosovo Opinion?' (2011) 24 LJIL 135.

[142] See Sep. Op. of Judge Cançado Trindade, para 179.

[143] By contrast, in the *Wall in Occupied Palestinian Territory* (Advisory Opinion) the Court referred to its previous decisions in *Namibia, Western Sahara*, and *East Timor* [2004] ICJ Rep 172, para 88.

State Responsibility 2001 refer to such a duty in relation to serious violations of peremptory norms. In reviewing Security Council practice on non-recognition of declarations of independence, the ICJ appeared to support this position.[144] However, this was not considered to apply to Kosovo.

Remedial secession

There appears to be general agreement among states that Kosovo does not have a general right to independence, but a more divisive matter is whether Kosovo obtained one as a result of Serbian oppression culminating in the ethnic cleansing of 1999. The case studies on Abkhazia,[145] South Ossetia,[146] Nagorno-Karabakh,[147] and Transdniestria[148] suggest that Kosovo would have a stronger claim on this basis than those territories would, but remedial secession is a shadowy concept in international law. The Canadian Supreme Court mentioned it as a possibility in *Re Secession of Quebec*, while cautioning that 'it remains unclear whether this... actually reflects an established international law standard'.[149] The Kosovo Advisory Opinion, though, does represent a significant development in relation to this right, as it allowed a significant airing of the doctrine in the submissions of interest states.

The general point of reference in discussions of remedial secession is Principle 5(7) of the Declaration on Friendly Relations 1970. This provides that:

> Nothing in the foregoing paragraphs [on self-determination] shall be construed as authorizing or encouraging any action which would dismember or impair, totally or in part, the territorial integrity or political unity of sovereign and independent States conducting themselves in compliance with the principle of equal rights and self-determination of peoples as described above and thus possessed of a government representing the whole people belonging to the territory without distinction as to race, creed or colour.

A similar provision can be found in the Vienna Declaration 1993 and the UN Fiftieth Anniversary Declaration 1995.

The understanding of this paragraph amongst states varied considerably and depended on the words emphasized. A number of states saw the conditionality of the phrasing on territorial integrity as allowing some scope for secession. Much of this was expressed in equivocal terms. Albania argued it provided neither 'a passport to secession' nor an 'unconditional prohibition of secession',[150] but something in between. The Kosovo authorities believed it did not expressly encourage secession, 'but it certainly does not exclude it'.[151]

144 [2010] ICJ Rep para 81. 145 Mirzayev (n 2). 146 Waters (n 2).

147 H Krüger, 'Nagorno-Karabakh' (in this volume) 214.

148 B Bowring, 'Transnistria' (in this volume) 157.

149 *Re Secession of Quebec* (1998) 161 DLR 4th para 135.

150 Written Comments of Albania (17 July 2009) paras 56–60; Written Statement of Albania, 14 April 2009 para 81; Oral Submission of Albania (Gill) (2 December 2009) CR 2009/26, para 9.

151 Further Written Contribution of Kosovo, 17 July 2009 para 4.39. See also Written Statement of Switzerland, 15 April 2009 paras 60-68; Written Statement of Romania, 14 April 2009 paras 133, 138; Written Statement of Poland, 14 April 2009 paras 6.8-6.9; Written Statement of Estonia, 13 April 2009 5; Written Statement by Russia, 16 April 2009 paras 83–8; Written Statement of Netherlands, 17 April 2009 para 3.7.

States such as Argentina and Serbia, conversely, argued that the possibility of secession only derived from an *a contrario* reading of the paragraph. The provision was framed to protect territorial integrity of states, not the opposite of a right to independence, and the drafting did not support an alternative reading.[152] Cyprus and China noted that it referred back to the previous paragraphs on self-determination which were focused largely on colonial situations.[153] Cyprus focused on the word 'authorizing' as indicating the lack of a positive rule which would allow secession.[154] Slovakia saw nothing 'encouraging' dismemberment to support the view that the provision was focused on participation in a political system on the basis of equality.[155] Even if oppression took place, some states did not consider secession the answer.[156] Slovakia argued that the law did not provide for the 'punishment' of states by the loss of territory for human rights violations.[157]

A number of states, such as Finland and Germany, did lay out the conditions for the possible exercise of remedial secession.[158] This typically comprised two elements. First, a denial of human rights and participation in government, often expressed as internal self-determination, of a serious nature and which had been going on for a considerable period of time. Second, that secession was the only option, the *ultima ratio* for resolving this crisis. This meant the exhaustion of other forms of resolution, such as negotiations between the parties, as well as the frustration of international involvement. What was striking, however, about these conditions was how much discretion they left. What was a serious violation of internal self-determination? How long was a considerable period of time? When have dispute resolution measures been exhausted? In relation to Kosovo, these were points of fundamental disagreement between states in the proceedings.

As with secession generally, the Court recorded 'differences' over the possibility of remedial secession and the circumstances in which it might apply. The court also noted that this possibility was raised 'in almost every instance only as a secondary argument',[159] suggesting states' lack of confidence in this position. The Court did

[152] Written Statement of Argentina, 17 April 2009 para 97; Written Statement of Cyprus, 17 April 2009 para 142; Written Statement of Serbia, 15 April 2009 paras 589–625; Written Comments of Serbia, 14 July 2009 paras 342–5; Oral Submission of China (Xue) (7 December 2009) CR 2009/29, paras 22–6; Written Statement of Spain, 14 April 2009 para 24; Written Statement of Brazil, 17 April 2009 para 2.

[153] Written Statement of Cyprus, 17 April 2009 para 142; Oral Submission of China (Xue) (7 December 2009) CR 2009/29, para 24.

[154] Written Comments of Cyprus, 8 July 2009 para 15.

[155] Written Statement of Slovakia, 16 April 2009 paras 8-10.

[156] Written Comments of Serbia, 14 July 2009 para 348; Written Statement of Cyprus, 17 April 2009 para 139.

[157] Written Statement of Slovakia, 16 April 2009 para 28; Written Statement of Egypt, 16 April 2009 paras 63–74; Written Statement of Iran, 17 April 2009 para 4.1; Written Comments of Bolivia, 17 July 2009 para 12.

[158] See Written Statement of Albania, 14 April 2009 paras 71–112; Written Statement of Estonia, 13 April 2009 para 2.1; Statement of Finland, 16 April 2009 paras 8–12; Written Statement of Germany, 15 April 2009 33–4; Statement of Ireland, 17 April 2009 paras 28–32; Written Statement of Netherlands, 17 April 2009 paras 3.1–3.20; Written Statement of Poland, 14 April 2009 paras 6.1–6.10; Written Statement of Switzerland, 15 April 2009 paras 60-68; Oral Submission of Jordan (Al Hussein), (9 December 2009) CR 2009/31, paras 33–8.

[159] [2010] ICJ Rep para 82.

not draw express conclusions, but this is still a more insightful reflection on the state of the law than the tentative reference by the Canadian Court to the assertion of the right by a 'number of commentators'.[160]

In addition to questions over the status of remedial secession in international law, the ICJ also noted a sharp difference of views as to whether the circumstances for remedial secession were actually present in Kosovo.[161] Proponents of remedial secession for Kosovo point to the periods of considerable oppression of its population as well as the failure of the international community to resolve its status. However, there are three particular problems posed by a remedial claim in relation to Kosovo. First, the initial response to Serbia's oppression was not support for independence, but an autonomous international regime that lasted for over eight years.[162] At the time that independence was declared, it could not be argued that it was necessary to stop acts of oppression. It may be true that the memory of oppression precluded the possibility of a peaceful restoration of Serbian authority, but this was more of a political question of how to terminate the international presence. Second, Serbia changed its government and its political standards.[163] Third, abuses suffered by minorities in Kosovo undermine the legitimacy of Kosovo's claim and could even, following the same standard, legitimize separatist claims by those minorities.[164]

4. Legal status of Kosovo

There are two alternative perspectives on the legal status of Kosovo: either that it is part of Serbia or that it is an independent state. States are almost evenly divided between these two positions. The first position is that Kosovo, despite the Declaration of Independence, remains an autonomous province of Serbia. Serbia has not exercised control in the territory (except Serb-majority areas in the north) since 1999. However, this is not necessarily fatal to Serbia's claim. SC Res. 1244, while preventing Yugoslavia from exercising sovereign rights in Kosovo, recognized its continuing sovereignty. Serbia could be seen as the successor to Yugoslavia in respect of Kosovo. The continuing loss of control following the Declaration of Independence 2008 likewise does not prevent Serbia from claiming sovereignty. A number of states have lost control of parts of their territory for extended periods without losing their title to it.

[160] *Re Secession of Quebec* (1998) 161 DLR 4th 440, para 134.

[161] [2010] ICJ Rep para 82.

[162] Written Statement of Romania, 14 April 2009 para 147; Written Statement by Russia, 16 April 2009 para 92.

[163] See Z Oklopcic, '*Populus Interruptus*: Self-Determination, the Independence of Kosovo, and the Vocabulary of Peoplehood' (2009) 22 LJIL 688; R Müllerson, 'Precedents in the Mountains: On Parallels and Uniqueness of the Cases of Kosovo, South Ossetia and Abkhazia' (2009) 8 Chinese JIL 7.

[164] See Serbia, UN Doc S/PV.5839 4. See also M Goodwin, 'From Province to Protectorate to State? Speculation on the Impact of Kosovo's Genesis upon Doctrines of International Law' (2007) 8 GLJ 6.

The second position is that Kosovo is an independent state. The usual formula for determining the existence of a state is Article 1 of the Montevideo Convention 1933, which has four elements: permanent population, defined territory, government, and capacity to enter relations with other states. The most serious challenge to Kosovo's claim to fulfil these criteria relates to the authority of its government. There are two aspects to this. First, Kosovo's government does not exercise effective control over all of its territory. The area around Mitrovica in the north remains outside government control, though the April 2013 Agreement provides for the establishment of Kosovar authority, while respecting autonomous Serbian structures. However, this does not fundamentally challenge the operation of the Kosovo state. Indeed, other entities from former Yugoslavia, Croatia and Bosnia-Herzegovina, gained international recognition with a loss of territory posing a more serious threat to their viability. The second aspect is the involvement of international institutions in the governance of Kosovo. The most significant of these was the International Civilian Office, led by the International Civilian Representative, who held extensive powers over Kosovo's governance and law-making. However, a meeting of the International Steering Group in Vienna on 24 January 2012 concluded that Kosovo was in the final stages of implementing the Comprehensive Status Proposal and agreed to end its international supervision. The International Civilian Office was terminated on 10 September 2012,[165] removing perhaps the most significant objection to Kosovo as an independent entity. An international presence remains in the form of EULEX, which is mandated to continue to 2014, as well as KFOR and UNMIK, but Kosovo is moving away from a position where it could be seen as just an international protectorate.

[165] International Civilian Office Website <http://www.ico-kos.org/?id=61> accessed 21 October 2012.

13

Western Sahara

Sven Simon

I. Introduction

Having been largely forgotten, the Western Sahara conflict appeared to be heating up again in early 2012 when the German multinational, Siemens, landed an order for the construction and maintenance of 22 windmills to be built on a wind farm in Moroccan-occupied Western Sahara.[1] The Western Sahara conflict has lasted more than 40 years now but has yet to see a definitive solution. However, the situation in this part of the world sporadically attracts the attention of the international community. For example, on 14 December 2011 this dispute once again became relevant to the question of where the fish consumed by Europeans comes from. In December 2011, the European Parliament had to take a decision on the extension of the Fisheries Partnership Agreement between Morocco and the European Union (EU).[2] Somewhat surprisingly, a narrow majority of members of the Parliament voted against the Commission's proposal, which led to the result that the European Parliament rejected the proposed extension of this controversial agreement.[3] It called on the Commission to negotiate a new, more environmentally and economically beneficial deal, which should take account of the interests of the Sahrawi population. The protocol, which has applied provisionally since 28 February 2011, ceased to apply immediately. A new protocol was signed on 18 November 2013 and adopted by Council[4] and Parliament.[5]

[1] Siemens, 'First Wind Orders for Siemens from Africa' (Press statement) (30 January 2012) <http://www.siemens.com/press/en/pressrelease/?press=/en/pressrelease/2012/energy/wind-power/ewp201201025-wp.htm> accessed 10 November 2012.

[2] <http://www.europarl.europa.eu/oeil/popups/sda.do?id=20895&l=en> accessed 10 November 2012.

[3] Results of vote in Parliament (final vote 14 December 2011) (For: 296, Against: 326, Abstentions: 58) <http://www.europarl.europa.eu/oeil/popups/sda.do?id=20895&l=en> accessed 10 November 2012.

[4] Council decision 2013/720/EU of 15 November 2013 (OJ L 328 of 7 December 2013) on the signing of the new protocol and Council decision 2013/785/EU of 16 December 2013 (OJ L 349 of 21 December 2013) on its conclusion.

[5] Results of vote in Parliament (final vote 10 December 2013) (For: 310, Against: 204, Abstentions: 49). <http://www.europarl.europa.eu/pdfs/news/expert/infopress/20131206IPR30021/20131206IPR30021_en.pdf> accessed 5 February 2014.

As far as the interrelation with the developments in the CIS states of Transnistria, South Ossetia, Abkhazia, and Nagorno-Karabakh is concerned, one has to make it very clear from the beginning: the nature of the dispute surrounding Western Sahara is unique and it is hard to compare it to the developments in the CIS states discussed in the other case studies in this volume. However, before mentioning its fundamental differences from the situation in Transnistria, South Ossetia, Abkhazia, and Nagorno-Karabakh, it seems necessary to analyse the legal status of Western Sahara and to work out the differences regarding the right to self-determination, secession, and autonomy, as well as to provide an overview of the historical background of this conflict. Finally, the question of using natural resources will be discussed, since it is an ongoing problem.

II. Factual and Historical Background

The territory of Western Sahara encompasses an area of about 280,000 square kilometres with an estimated population of just over 500,000,[6] many of whom live in Laâyoune, the largest city in Western Sahara. It is situated in the north-west of the African continent, bordered by Morocco to the north, Algeria to the north-east, Mauritania to the east and south, and the Atlantic Ocean to the west, with a coastline of more than 1,000 km. The climate is predominantly a desert environment: hot and dry in summer, cold in winter, with little or no rainfall. While the Sahrawis were originally nomads, most of the population today lives in small towns and villages. The economy is based on agriculture and fishing, primarily destined for local consumption. Rich phosphate deposits are the main export commodity and most probably part of the problem. There also seem to be oil deposits off the Atlantic coast.[7]

Of the territory of Western Sahara, 85% is today occupied and *de facto* administered by Morocco. The remaining parts of the territory are under the control of the *Polisario Front* and administered by the so-called 'Sahrawi Arab Democratic Republic'. The United Nations, however, still considers Spain the administering power of the entire territory,[8] awaiting the outcome of the ongoing negotiations and the resulting election to be overseen by the United Nations Mission for the Referendum in Western Sahara (MINURSO).

'Spanish Sahara', the former moniker of Western Sahara, was colonized by Spain in 1884.[9] At this time Spain declared Western Sahara a 'protectorate' and later, in 1958, it was declared a Spanish province.[10] Beginning in 1962, Spain

[6] Population Division of the Department of Economic and Social Affairs of the United Nations Secretariat, World Population Prospects: The 2010 Revision, <http://esa.un.org/unpd/wpp/unpp/panel_population.htm>.

[7] H-P Gasser, 'The Conflict in Western Sahara—An Unresolved Issue from the Decolonization Period' (2002) 5 *Yearbook of International Humanitarian Law* 375.

[8] Since United Nations General Assembly Resolution 34/37 (21 November 1979) UN Doc A/RES/34/37 and UNGA Res 35/19 (11 November 1980) UN Doc A/RES/35/19.

[9] See *Western Sahara Case* (Advisory Opinion) ICJ Reports 1975, para 77.

[10] T Hodges, *Western Sahara: The Roots of a Desert War* (Lawrence Hill Books 1983) 42 and 153.

as administering power transmitted technical and statistical information on the territory under Article 73 lit. e) of the Charter of the United Nations. This information was examined by the Special Committee with Regard to the Implementation of the Declaration on the Granting of Independence to Colonial Countries and Peoples.[11]

In 1963, Western Sahara was included as a Non-Self-Governing Territory under Chapter XI of the UN Charter, after which Spain came under pressure from the UN General Assembly and the Organization of African Unity (AOU) to decolonize Western Sahara and to allow the free exercise of the right to self-determination.[12] Morocco, claiming historical ties with the territory, urged the UN General Assembly to seek an Advisory Opinion from the International Court of Justice (ICJ). At the request of the UN General Assembly, the ICJ issued an Advisory Opinion on 16 October 1975. The Court ruled that the Western Sahara could not be considered *terra nullius* and concluded that there were no legal ties preventing the decolonization of Western Sahara and the self-determination of the Saharawi people in accordance with the Declaration on the Granting of Independence to Colonial Countries and Peoples (UNGA Res 1514 [XV]). On the same day that the Opinion of the Court was given, the situation escalated, with Morocco threatening the so-called 'Green March'—which eventually took place in early November 1975, when 350,000 Moroccans crossed the border of Western Sahara.[13]

The dispute intensified when Spanish control over Western Sahara came to an end on 27 February 1976. The following day, the Sahrawi Arab Democratic Republic (SADR) was proclaimed by the Polisario Front, notwithstanding the occupation by Moroccan and Mauritanian troops. But the Sahrawi people did not gain their independence, and no sovereign state of Western Sahara was born. The SADR was first recognized by Algeria on 6 March 1976 and subsequently by more than 70 states—more than 20 of which, however, have withdrawn their recognition.[14] In 1979, the UN General Assembly recognized the Frente Polisario as the representative of the Saharawi people (UNGA Res 34/37), but the SADR does not have representation at the UN.

After Morocco had annexed the northern two-thirds of Western Sahara in 1976, it claimed the rest of the territory in 1979 when Mauritania gave up its claim and withdrew from the southern part of Western Sahara. A war with the Polisario Front contesting Morocco's sovereignty ended in 1991 in a UN-brokered ceasefire. In the same year the UN peacekeeping mission MINURSO was established. MINURSO's mission was to monitor the ceasefire and to organize and

[11] H Corell, 'Letter dated 29 January 2002 from the Under-Secretary-General for Legal Affairs, the Legal Counsel, addressed to the President of the Security Council' (12 February 2002) UN Doc S/2002/161.

[12] On inclusion as Non-Self-Governing territory, see 'Letter dated 29 January 2002 from the Under-Secretary General for Legal Affairs, the Legal Counsel, addressed to the President of the Security Council' (12 February 2002) UN Doc S/002/161, 5. On the OAU's role, see Hodges (n 10) 307–20.

[13] T Marauhn, 'Sahara' in R Wolfrum (ed), *The Max Planck Encyclopedia of Public International Law* (OUP online 2010), para 9 <www.mpepil.com> accessed 10 November 2012.

[14] Marauhn (n 13).

conduct a referendum, in accordance with the so-called Settlement Plan,[15] which would enable the Sahrawis of Western Sahara to choose between integration with Morocco and independence. The independence referendum was originally scheduled for 1992, but conflicts over voter eligibility prevented it from being held. Both sides blamed each other for stalling the process. In 1997, the Houston Agreement[16] was supposed to restart the process; however, it failed again. In 2003 the Baker Plan[17] was launched to replace the Settlement Plan, but while accepted by the Polisario and unanimously endorsed by Security Council Resolution 1495 (2003), it was rejected by Morocco.

The UN has since 2007 sponsored intermittent talks between representatives of the Government of Morocco and the Polisario Front to negotiate the status of Western Sahara. Morocco has put forward an autonomy proposal for the territory which would allow for some local administration while maintaining Moroccan sovereignty. The Polisario, with Algeria's support, demands a popular referendum that includes the option of independence. Today, MINURSO is still deployed, the UN Special Representative is still trying to find a solution to the contentious issues, and the Security Council continues to appeal to the concerned parties to accept a peaceful solution to the conflict. The MINURSO mandate has been extended 41 times since 1991,[18] most recently by Security Council Resolution 2099 (2013) of 25 April 2013.[19] The Security Council decided to extend the mandate of MINURSO through 30 April 2014 and called 'upon all the parties to cooperate fully with MINURSO, including its free interaction with all interlocutors, and to take the necessary steps to ensure the security of, as well as unhindered movement and immediate access for, United Nations personnel in carrying out their mandate, in conformity with existing agreements'. However, presently there is no plan to hold a referendum, and the viability of the ceasefire is coming into question.

[15] The Settlement Plan was an agreement between the Polisario Front and Morocco on the organization of a referendum which would constitute an expression of self-determination for the people of Western Sahara, leading either to full independence or integration with the kingdom of Morocco. It resulted in a cease-fire which remains effective to this day, and the establishment of the MINURSO peace force to oversee it and to organize the referendum. It was based on an earlier peace proposal by the Organization of African Unity, but this time was organized by the United Nations. Originally introduced in the late 1980s and in 1990 in Security Council Resolution 658, the plan was signed in 1991.

[16] The Houston Agreement was the result of negotiations between the Polisario Front and Morocco on the organization of a referendum which would constitute an expression of self-determination for the people of Western Sahara, possibly leading to full independence or integration within Morocco. The talks were conducted in Houston, USA, under the auspices of UN representative James Baker, in the framework of the 1991 Settlement Plan. The agreement was supposed to lead to a referendum in 1998 after it had been prevented from taking place in 1992 as originally envisioned. This never happened, and the Houston Agreement produced few tangible results.

[17] The Baker Plan (formally, 'Peace Plan for Self-Determination of the People of Western Sahara') is a UN initiative to grant self-determination to Western Sahara. It was intended to replace the Settlement Plan of 1991, which was further detailed in the Houston Agreement of 1997.

[18] UNSC Res 179 (27 April 2011), UN Doc S/Res/179; see also UNSC 'Report of the Secretary-General on the situation concerning Western Sahara' (2012) UN Doc S/2012/197.

[19] The latest document is UN SC Res 2099 (25 April 2013) UN Doc S/Res/2099.

Morocco informed the Secretary-General on 10 May 2012 that it had a number of reservations regarding the current negotiating process and indicated a week later that it had lost confidence in the Secretary-General's Personal Envoy for Western Sahara, Christopher Ross, describing his work as 'unbalanced and biased.' Following this announcement, the Secretary-General asserted that he had complete confidence in Ross. On 25 August 2012, during a phone conversation with King Mohammed VI, Secretary-General Ban Ki-moon stated that the UN did not intend to modify the terms of its mediation and reaffirmed his confidence in Ross. On 15 June 2012, the Secretary-General appointed Wolfgang Weisbrod-Weber (Germany) as his Special Representative and head of MINURSO to succeed Hany Abdel-Aziz (Egypt), who completed his assignment on 30 April 2012.[20]

III. Legal Analysis

From a legal perspective, three main questions have to be answered: the status of the territory of Western Sahara, the status of Morocco in relation to this territory, and— likewise relevant due to the current situation—the principles of international law governing the use of natural resources in Non-Self-Governing Territories.

1. Legal status of the territory of Western Sahara

According to international law, Western Sahara has the legal status of a Non-Self-Governing Territory. In 1963 Western Sahara was listed as a Non-Self-Governing Territory by the United Nations. Non-Self-Governing Territories are territories that have not yet attained full self-government.[21] Chapter XI of the UN Charter, entitled 'Declaration Regarding Non-Self-Governing Territories', deals in two articles with the main obligations of the states that control such territories (administering powers). Article 73 states that member states that have assumed responsibilities for the administration of Non-Self-Governing Territories will recognize the interests of the inhabitants of these territories as paramount and accept the obligation to promote, to the utmost, their well-being. The initial 'List of Non-Self-Governing Territories' was created by compiling lists of dependent territories submitted by the administering states themselves. Further, in Article 73 lit. e) of the Charter, member states agree to report annually to the United Nations on the development of Non-Self-Governing Territories under their control.

After Western Sahara's listing as a Non-Self-Governing Territory, Spain was considered the administering power of the territory, and this has not changed to

[20] See UNSC, 'Letter dated 12 April 2012 from the Secretary-General addressed to the President of the Security Council' (14 June 2012) UN Doc S/2012/441.

[21] J Brink, 'Non-Self-Governing Territories' in R Bernhardt (ed), *Encyclopedia of Public International Law III*, (Elsevier 1997) 629.

date. Thus, Spain is *de jure* still the administering power of the Non-Self-Governing Territory, Western Sahara.

2. Moroccan occupation and annexation

Simultaneously, it is also well known that Morocco rejected the ICJ's findings in which the Court rejected the claims of sovereignty made by Morocco and Mauritania over Western Sahara.[22] Just days after the decision by the International Court, Morocco occupied (and later annexed) Western Sahara through the famous 'Green March', in which more than 350,000 Moroccans invaded the territory.[23] The UN Security Council responded by adopting three resolutions. The first two reaffirmed UN General Assembly Resolution 1514 and called on the concerned parties to exercise restraint. The third deplored the Green March and called for Moroccan withdrawal.[24]

UN Security Council Resolution 380 'deplored the holding of the march' and 'call[ed] upon Morocco immediately to withdraw from the Territory of Western Sahara all the participants in the march'. However, this did not dissuade Morocco, which has strengthened its occupation of the territory through military, economic, and other repressive means.

In legal terms, the Moroccan occupation and annexation of the territory constitutes a serious violation of a fundamental, peremptory norm of international law, namely the prohibition of the use of force and aggression.[25] International law provides that '[n]o territorial acquisition or special advantage resulting from aggression is or shall be recognized as lawful'.[26]

Shortly thereafter, in November 1975, a weakened Spanish government secretly agreed to relinquish Western Sahara to Morocco and Mauritania. Morocco, Mauritania, and the colonial power, Spain, entered into an agreement (the Madrid Agreement) which—in convoluted terms—transferred the administration of the territory to Morocco and Mauritania. Mauritania withdrew in 1979.

This Declaration was subsequently registered with the UN Secretariat as a treaty. The agreement did not, however, transfer sovereignty explicitly; nor could it have done so, since Spain had no right to dispose of a territory that belonged to the people of that territory. Nor did it confer upon any of the signatories the status of an administering power—a status which Spain alone could not have unilaterally

[22] *Western Sahara Case* (Advisory Opinion) ICJ Reports 1975, 12, para 162.

[23] S Koury, 'The European Community and Member States' Duty of Non-Recognition under the EC-Morocco Association Agreement: State Responsibility and Customary International Law' in K Arts and P Pinto Leite (eds), *International Law and the Question of Western Sahara* (IPJET 2007) 165, 166.

[24] UNSC Res 377 (22 October 1975) UN Doc S/Res/377; UNSC Res 379 (2 November 1975) UN Doc S/Res/379; UNSC Res 380 (6 November 1975) UN Doc S/Res/380.

[25] Presentation by Associate Professor Pål Wrange, Stockholm University, Seminar 'The EU and Western Sahara: Trading Fish, Ignoring Rights?', European Parliament (7 December 2011); see also RS Clark, 'Western Sahara and the United Nations Norms on Self-Determination and Aggression' in Arts and Leite (n 23) 45, 54.

[26] The UN General Assembly's Definition of Aggression, UNGA Res 3314 (XXIX) (14 December 1974) A/Res/3314(XXIX).

transferred.[27] As Western Sahara was included in the List of Non-Self-Governing Territories and the people of Western Sahara had the right to self-determination, Spain could no longer unilaterally decide to change the legal status of the territory.[28] Spain, as a member of the United Nations, had accepted its responsibilities as the administering power of the territory and as such had to respect the interests and wishes of the people of Western Sahara and acknowledge the role of the United Nations in realizing their right to self-determination. Therefore, Spain could transfer neither sovereignty nor its responsibilities for the territory to another state or states.[29] Thus, the legal basis for the Western Sahara self-determination entitlement lies in its relationship with the former colonial power (Spain) and not with the occupying power (Morocco),[30] even if one argues that the 1975 agreement as such is in accordance with international law. Given the developments since then, this question is only of limited relevance. It should be sufficient to conclude that under the agreement, Spain would remain responsible.

However, on 26 February 1976, Spain informed the Secretary-General that as of that point it had terminated its presence in Western Sahara and relinquished its responsibilities over the territory, thus leaving it in fact under the administration of both Morocco and Mauritania in their respective controlled areas. Following the withdrawal of Mauritania from the territory in 1979, upon the conclusion of the Mauritano-Sahraoui agreement of 19 August 1979 (S/13504, Annex I), Morocco has administrated the territory of Western Sahara alone. 'Morocco however, is not listed as the administering Power of the territory in the United Nations 'List of Non-Self-Governing Territories', and has, therefore, not transmitted information on the territory in accordance with Article 73 lit. e) of the United Nations Charter.'[31]

Since then, Morocco has exercised its de facto authority in the territory. It has used its military power to control the territory, to suppress the quest of the people of Western Sahara for self-determination, and to claim the territory as part of Morocco. It has neither claimed the role of administering power nor has it been granted such a role by the United Nations under Article 73 of the Charter. Despite the fact that its presence in the territory started with consent under the legal authority of Spain as the administering power, from the outset—and as a result of its claims that the territory is part of Morocco—it must be regarded as an occupying power rather than as an administering power under the UN Charter.

Consequently, the annexation of Western Sahara was not lawful and has therefore not been recognized by any state.[32] Western Sahara is occupied, as confirmed twice by the General Assembly.[33] In Resolution 34/37 (1979), the General

[27] Corell (n 11); L Hannikainen, 'The Case of Western Sahara from the Perspective of Jus Cogens' in Arts and Leite (n 23) 59, 66.

[28] M Brus, 'The Legality of Exploring and Exploiting Mineral Resources in Western Sahara' in Arts and Leite (n 23) 201, 205.

[29] Brus (n 23).

[30] C Drew, 'The Meaning of Self-Determination: "The Stealing of the Sahara" Redux?' in Arts and Leite (n 23) 87, 92.

[31] Corell (n 11).

[32] Hannikainen (n 27) 59, 68.

[33] UNGA Res 34/37 (21 November 1979) UN Doc A/RES/34/37; UNGA Res 35/19 (11 November 1980) UN Doc A/RES/35/19.

Assembly 'deeply deplore[d] the aggravation of the situation resulting from the continued occupation of Western Sahara by Morocco and the extension of that occupation to the territory recently evacuated by Mauritania'.[34] In Resolution 35/19 (1980), the General Assembly again declared that it is 'deeply concerned at the aggravation of the situation deriving from the continued occupation of Western Sahara by Morocco and from the extension of that occupation to the part of Western Sahara which was the subject to the peace agreement concluded on 10 August 1979 between Mauritania and the Frente Popular para la Libercón de Saguia el-Hamra y de Río de Oro...'.[35]

The laws of occupation limit Morocco's actions towards the occupied population and its territory, while enabling it to ensure the security of its military presence. Article 43 of the 1907 Hague Regulations Respecting the Laws and Customs of War on Land stipulates:

> The authority of the legitimate power having in fact passed into the hands of the occupant, the latter shall take all the measures in his power to restore, and ensure, as far as possible, public order and safety, while respecting, unless absolutely prevented, the laws in force in the country.[36]

To sum up the legal status: Western Sahara is not a part of Morocco and Morocco has no legal title or claim to the territory. Since the annexation is illegal, it is null and void, and Morocco is therefore, legally speaking, an occupying power. Morocco has an obligation to respect the right of the people of Western Sahara according to the law of occupation and to end its illegal annexation and occupation of Western Sahara.

3. Right to self-determination

Furthermore, the people of Western Sahara have a right to self-determination which can be realized through the creation of a fully sovereign state or in any other modality that the people of Western Sahara choose.[37] Therefore, in 1966 the UN General Assembly adopted its first resolution[38] on the territory, urging Spain to organize, as soon as possible, a referendum under UN supervision on the territory's right to exercise its right to self-determination.

[34] UNGA Resolution 34/37 (21 November 1979) UN Doc A/RES/34/37, 5.

[35] UNGA Resolution 35/19 (11 November 1980) UN Doc A/RES/35/19, 3.

[36] This is translated from the French text, the only authentic version of the 1907 Hague Regulations Respecting the Laws and Customs of War on Land, annexed to the 1907 Hague Convention Respecting the Laws and Customs of War on Land, the Hague, 18 October 1907. The English 'public order and safety' is not an adequate translation of the French 'l'ordre et la vie public'. Several provisions make this duty more concrete, such as Arts 55–56 of the IV Geneva Convention, on food and health care. See also Arts 72–79, Protocol Additional to the Geneva Conventions of 12 August 1949, and relating to the Protection of Victims of International Armed Conflicts (Protocol I).

[37] P Wrange, 'The Swedish Position on Western Sahara and International Law' in Arts and Leite (n 23), 299, 300; see also UNGA Res 1514 (XV) (14 December 1960) UN Doc A/RES/1514(XV); Res 1541 (XV) (15 December 1960) UN Doc A/Res/1541(XV); *Western Sahara Case* (Advisory Opinion) ICJ Reports 1975, paras 57–58.

[38] UNGA Res 2229 (XXI) (20 December 1966) UN Doc A/RES/2229(XXI).

The right to self-determination, a fundamental principle of human rights law,[39] is an individual and collective right to 'freely determine... political status and [to] freely pursue... economic, social and cultural development'.[40] The International Court of Justice refers to the right to self-determination as a right held by people rather than a right held by governments alone[41] and has further elaborated the status and scope of the right in international law:

> The principle of self-determination as a right of peoples, and its application for the purpose of bringing all colonial situations to a speedy end, were enunciated in the Declaration on the Granting of Independence to Colonial Countries and Peoples... The validity of the principle of self-determination defined as the need to pay regard to the freely expressed will of the peoples is not affected by the fact that in certain cases the General Assembly has dispensed with the requirement of consulting the inhabitants of a given territory...[42]

In the case of Western Sahara, the ICJ concluded by 14 votes to two that while there had been precolonial ties between Morocco and some tribes in the territory of Western Sahara, these ties did not imply sovereignty:

> ... the Court's conclusion is that the materials and information presented to it do not establish any tie of territorial sovereignty between the territory of Western Sahara and the Kingdom of Morocco or the Mauritanian entity. Thus the Court has not found legal ties of such a nature as might affect the application of General Assembly resolution 1514 (XV) in the decolonization of Western Sahara and, in particular, of the principle of self-determination through the free and genuine expression of the will of the peoples of the Territory.[43]

Therefore, the ICJ rejected the claims of sovereignty made by Morocco and Mauritania over Western Sahara.[44] It became clear that the Court made two significant findings: first, it found that the territory was not a territory unoccupied by any people and thus not *terra nullius*; second, the Court asserted that no links of sovereignty existed between the territory of Western Sahara and its neighbours Morocco and Mauritania. Thus there were no ties that would affect the application of General Assembly Resolution 1514 (XV) granting the right to self-determination.

[39] The Universal Declaration of Human Rights provides that the will of 'the people shall be the basis of the authority of government'. Universal Declaration of Human Rights, UNGA Res 217A (III) (10 December 1948) UN Doc A/RES/3/217A, Art. 21; The International Covenant of Civil and Political Rights (adopted 16 December 1966, entered into force 23 March 1976) 999 UNTS 171 (ICCPR), Art. 1; The International Covenant on Economic, Social and Cultural Rights (adopted 19 December 1966, entered into force 3 January 1976) 999 UNTS 3 (ICESCR), Art. 1.

[40] ICCPR, Art. 1; ICESCR, Art. 1; see also K Parker and L Neylon, 'Jus Cogens: Compelling the Law of Human Rights' (1989) 12 HICLR 411, 440, drawing on discussion of the right to self-determination in A Critescu, 'The Right to Self-determination' UN Doc E/CN.4/Sub.2/404/Rev. 1 (1980) UN Sales No E.80.XIV.3; H. Gros Espiell, 'The Right to Self-Determination' UN Doc E/CN.4/Sub.2/405/Rev.1 (1980) UN Sales No E.79.XIV.5.

[41] *Western Sahara Case* (Advisory Opinion) ICJ Reports 1975, 31.

[42] *Western Sahara Case* (Advisory Opinion) ICJ Reports 1975, para 59.

[43] *Western Sahara Case* (Advisory Opinion) ICJ Reports 1975, 68 [162].

[44] *Western Sahara Case* (Advisory Opinion) ICJ Reports 1975, 12 et seq.; see also Hannikainen (n 27) 59, 65.

Resolution 1514[45] is the famous resolution on decolonization adopted by the General Assembly on 14 December 1960 and subtitled 'Declaration on the Granting of Independence to Colonial Countries and Peoples'. It provides for the granting of independence to colonial countries and peoples in providing an inevitable legal linkage between self-determination and its goal of decolonization, and postulated a new international law-based right of freedom also in economic self-determination. Article 5 states:

Immediate steps shall be taken in Trust and Non-Self-Governing Territories, or all other territories which have not yet attained independence, to transfer all powers to the peoples of those territories, without any conditions or reservations, in accordance with their freely expressed will and desire, without any distinction as to race, creed or colour, in order to enable them to enjoy complete independence and freedom.

Moreover, on 15 December 1960 the General Assembly adopted UN General Assembly Resolution 1541 (XV), subtitled 'Principles Which Should Guide Members in Determining Whether or Not an Obligation Exists to Transmit the Information Called For Under Article 73 Lit. E) of the UN Charter'.[46] Article 3 provided that '[i]nadequacy of political, economic, social or educational preparedness should never serve as a pretext for delaying independence'.[47] In 1961 the General Assembly created the Special Committee popularly referred to as the Special Committee on Decolonization to ensure decolonization in complete compliance with the principle of self-determination in the UN General Assembly Resolution 1541 (XV), with 12 principles of the Annex defining free association with an independent state, integration into an independent state, or independence as the three legitimate options of full self-government compliance with the principle of self-determination.

Following the decision of the ICJ, the right to self-determination of the people of Western Sahara has been reaffirmed many times by the General Assembly[48] and by the Security Council,[49] most recently in Resolution 2099 of 25 April 2013. In para. 7, the Security Council calls again

[u]pon the parties to continue negotiations under the auspices of the Secretary-General without preconditions and in good faith, taking into account the efforts made since 2006 and subsequent developments, with a view to achieving a just, lasting, and mutually acceptable political solution, which will provide for the self-determination of the people of Western Sahara in the context of arrangements consistent with the principles and purposes

[45] UNGA Res 1514 (XV) (14 December 1960) UN Doc A/RES/1514(XV) (Declaration of the Granting of Independence of Colonial Countries and Peoples).

[46] UNGA Res 1541 (XV) (15 December 1960) UN Doc A/RES/1541(XV) (Principles which should guide members in determining whether or nor an obligation exists to transmit the information called for under Article 73e of the Charter).

[47] UNGA Res 1541 (XV) (15 December 1960) UN Doc A/RES/1541(XV) Article 3.

[48] UNGA Res 3458 (XXX) (10 December 1975) UN Doc A/RES/3458(XXX) declared unequivocally that the GA '1. Reaffirms the inalienable right of the people of Spanish Sahara to self-determination, in accordance with GA Res 1514 (XV)'.

[49] UNSC Res 377 (22 October 1975) UN Doc S/Res/377, UNSC Res 379 (2 November 1975) UN Doc S/Res/379 and UNSC Res 380 (6 November 1975) UN Doc S/Res/380, on the situation concerning Western Sahara.

of the Charter of the United Nations, and noting the role and responsibilities of the parties in this respect...[50]

Consequently, there is no doubt whatsoever that the people of Western Sahara have a right to self-determination; however, this is yet to be realized.

4. The role of the United Nations, MINURSO and the Referendum

Initially the Organization for African Unity sought to help the people of Western Sahara to exercise their right, but when the OAU admitted the SADR as a member in 1981, Morocco left the organization and African efforts were stymied. In 1988, the OAU handed the issue to the United Nations, which agreed to handle it in conformity with its GA Resolution 1514 (XV) on self-determination under Chapter VI of the Charter, requiring the consent of the parties concerned.

Its settlement plan, accepted by the parties in 1988, focused on a ceasefire and a final-status referendum. The Security Council later set up a UN Mission for the Referendum in Western Sahara (MINURSO) in 1991 and appointed a succession of Special Representatives of the Secretary-General (SRSGs) and Special Envoys to oversee the process. Those currently in place are Wolfgang Weisbrod-Weber (Germany),[51] Special Representative of the Secretary-General for Western Sahara and Head of MINURSO, and Christopher Ross[52] (United States), Personal Envoy of the Secretary-General for Western Sahara.

From 1976 until the ceasefire in September 1991, following the 1988 Settlement Plan brokered by the United Nations and the Organization of African Unity, Sahrawi combatants, backed by Algeria, fought Moroccan and until 1979, Mauritanian troops. On 19 April 1991 the UNSC finally passed Resolution 690, which outlined a detailed plan for the holding of a free and fair referendum and the setting up of a UN Mission (MINURSO) to conduct the referendum. However, the situation remained at stalemate.

In April 2006, in a more or less radical departure from erstwhile UN policy, the United Nations Secretary-General recommended that the United Nations should 'step back'[53] from its attempts to formulate a 'Plan' for self-determination for Western Sahara in favour of direct negotiations between the parties.[54] In his report S/249/2006,[55] the Secretary-General, among other things, endorses his Personal Envoy's recommendation for direct negotiations among the parties, to be

[50] UNSC Res 2099 (25 April 2013) UN Doc S/Res/2099.

[51] See 'Letter dated 12 April 2012 from the Secretary-General addressed to the President of the Security Council' (14 June 2012) UN Doc S/2012/441.

[52] See 'Letter dated 6 January 2009 from the Secretary-General addressed to the President of the Security Council' (8 January 2009) UN Doc S/2009/19.

[53] *Report of the Secretary-General on the situation concerning Western Sahara* (19 April 2006) UN Doc S/2006/249 [35].

[54] *Report of the SG on the Situation Concerning Western Sahara* (19 April 2006) UN Doc S/2006/249.

[55] *Report of the SG on the Situation Concerning Western Sahara* (19 April 2006) UN Doc S/2006/249.

held 'without preconditions'. The negotiations should work out a compromise that would produce a just, lasting, and mutually acceptable political solution, providing for the self-determination of the people of Western Sahara. Against the background of occupation and annexation described above, the wording is surprising:

> 32. … Once the Security Council recognized the political reality that no one was going to force Morocco to give up its claim of sovereignty over Western Sahara, it would realize that there were only two options left: indefinite prolongation of the current deadlock in anticipation of a different political reality; or direct negotiations between the parties. . .
>
> 34. What remained therefore was a recourse to direct negotiations, which should be held without preconditions. Their objective should be to accomplish what no 'plan' could, namely to work out a compromise between international legality and political reality that would produce a just, lasting and mutually acceptable political solution, which would provide for the self-determination of the people of Western Sahara.
>
> 35. After years of reliance on United Nations-sponsored plans, it should be made clear to the parties that the United Nations was taking a step back and that the responsibility now rested with them.[56]

Thereby the Secretary-General's recommendation followed the briefing of his former Personal Envoy Peter van Walsum,[57] who concluded that, due to Moroccan opposition, holding a referendum that included the option of independence was no longer possible, and that a new approach of direct negotiations was necessary as 'the only alternative to the indefinite prolongation of the impasse'.[58] One year later, the recommendation of Secretary-General Kofi Annan was reiterated by his successor,[59] and on 30 April 2007 the Security Council unanimously adopted Resolution 1754, calling upon the parties:

> [t]o enter into negotiations without preconditions in good faith, taking into account the developments of the last months, with a view to achieving a just, lasting and mutually acceptable political solution, which will provide for the self-determination of the people of Western Sahara.[60]

The UN Security Council, in realistic desperation, dropped the idea of a referendum and called on the parties to negotiate a solution. However, the Secretary-General was well advised when he made it very clear that:

> 37. … The Security Council would not be able to invite parties to negotiate about Western Saharan autonomy under Moroccan sovereignty, [since] such wording would imply

[56] *Report of the SG on the Situation Concerning Western Sahara* (19 April 2006) UN Doc S/2006/249, 32f.

[57] For a summary of the Personal Envoy's reasoning, see *Report of the Secretary-General on the Situation concerning Western Sahara* (19 April 2006) UN Doc S/2006/249, 31–46.

[58] See 'Briefing to the Security Council' (18 January 2006) summarized in *Report of the Secretary-General on the Situation concerning Western Sahara* (16 October 2006) UN Docs S/2006/817 [14].

[59] *Report of the Secretary-General on the Situation concerning the Western Sahara*, UN Doc S/2007/2002, 13 April 2007, para 47.

[60] UNSC Res 1754 (2007), 30 April 2007, no 2.

recognition of Moroccan sovereignty over Western Sahara, which was out of the question as long as no Member States of the United Nations had recognized that sovereignty...[61]

Consequently, he recalled the Advisory Opinion of the ICJ, which concluded that there were no valid reasons why the rules for decolonization and self-determination, as contained in General Assembly Resolution 1514 (XV), should not apply to Western Sahara. In this context, the Secretary-General observed that the Advisory Opinion had been handed down more than 30 years previously and the resolution had still not been implemented. In reference to that inordinate lapse of time, he observed that a solution to the question of Western Sahara could only be achieved if the parties worked to seek a mutually acceptable compromise based upon relevant principles of international law and current political realities.

However, the observation by the Secretary-General that the Security Council would not be able to invite parties to negotiate about Western Saharan autonomy under Moroccan sovereignty was urgently needed, because 'on the traditional understanding of self-determination, for the Security Council to abandon its commitment to a referendum in favour of negotiations between the parties runs contrary to the international law of self-determination'.[62]

The International Court of Justice famously interpreted the 1960 Colonial Declaration[63] as 'confirming' and 'emphasizing' 'that the application of the right of self-determination requires a free and genuine expression of the will of the peoples concerned'.[64] Its 'essential feature'[65] was free choice.[66] In other words, 'it is to the Western Sahara Advisory Opinion that self-determination scholars turn for authority that, despite the pro-independence proclivities of some provisions of early resolutions, the proper interpretation of the right of self-determination is that it confers a right, not to a particular *outcome*, but to a particular *process*—one that entails "the freely expressed will of peoples".'[67] However, since a referendum does not in fact seem to be a promising approach in order to solve the problem, one has to follow the way of direct political negotiation.

5. Comparison with the Situation in the CIS

As previously mentioned, the conflict in the Western Sahara is hard to compare with any other situation presented in the case studies discussed in this volume. Western Sahara is a case of decolonization in an otherwise predominantly autonomist and secessionist era. Neither Transnistria nor South Ossetia, Abkhazia, or

[61] *Report of the SG on the Situation Concerning Western Sahara* (19 April 2006) UN Doc S/2006/249 [37].

[62] Drew (n 30) 88.

[63] *Declaration on the Granting of Independence to Colonial Countries and Peoples* (14 December 1960) UNGA Res 1514 (XV).

[64] *Western Sahara Case* (Advisory Opinion) ICJ Reports 1975, para 55; A Cassese, *Self-Determination of Peoples: A Legal Reappraisal* (Cambridge University Press 1995) 88.

[65] *Western Sahara Case* (Advisory Opinion) ICJ Reports 1975, para 57.

[66] Drew (n 30) 91.

[67] See Drew (n 30) 91; eg Cassese (n 64) 89.

Nagorno-Karabakh have a decolonization background. The question of whether the Soviet Constitution established a right to secession for autonomous regions has to be answered by former national law.

As far as international law is concerned, one cannot, however, transfer the above described rules concerning the right to self-determination to a situation of decolonization. The ICJ in the *Western Sahara Case*[68] referred first to the right to self-determination as a right held by people rather than a right held by governments alone. It further elaborated the status and scope of the right in international law. The Court made it very clear that its interpretation of the right to self-determination was done in the context of 'its application for the purpose of bringing all colonial situations to a speedy end, [which was] enunciated in the Declaration on the Granting of Independence to Colonial Countries and Peoples. . . '.[69]

When discussing the right to 'external self-determination' in connection with Transnistria, South Ossetia, Abkhazia, or Nagorno-Karabakh, the fundamental difference lies in the historical and factual background of decolonization.

Beyond the context of colonialism or alien occupation, the existence, scope and meaning of the right to self-determination remains contentious.[70] Antonio Cassese, for example, argues that what normatively distinguishes the international rules on self-determination relating to colonial peoples is that they 'specify the techniques for ascertaining the wishes of the population concerned (plebiscites or referendums)'[71] and, together with the rules relating to peoples subject to alien or foreign occupation, confer the right to choose independence:

> . . . the right to external self-determination which entails the possibility of choosing (or restoring) independence, has only been bestowed upon two classes of people (those under colonial rule or foreign occupation) . . .[72]

This was, for example, different when the recommendation of the Special Envoy of the Secretary-General in favour of 'supervised' secession of Kosovo was accompanied by repeated statements in favour of its uniqueness and non-precedential value:[73]

> More crucially, it is only in the decolonisation context that there is disciplinary consensus on the content of self-determination–that it confers on a people a right to a free choice that includes the option of independent statehood.[74]

[68] *Western Sahara Case* (Advisory Opinion) ICJ Reports 1975, para 31.

[69] *Western Sahara Case* (Advisory Opinion) ICJ Reports 1975, para 59.

[70] *Western Sahara Case* (Advisory Opinion) ICJ Reports 1975, 93 et seq.; see eg J Crawford, 'The Right of Self-Determination in International Law: Its Future and Development' in P Alston (ed), *Peoples' Rights* (OUP 2001) 38.

[71] Cassese (n 64) 88.

[72] Cassese (n 64) 334. This was recognized by the UN Secretary-General in relation to the Western Sahara in 2003: 'It is difficult to envision a political solution that, as required by Security Council resolution 1429 (2002) provides for self-determination but that nevertheless precludes the possibility of independence as one of several ballot questions'. *Report of the Secretary General on the Situation Concerning Western Sahara* (23 May 2003) UN Doc S/003/565, 52.

[73] 'Kosovo is a unique case that demands a unique solution. It does not create precedent for other unresolved conflicts.' *Report of the Special Envoy of the Secretary-General on Kosovo's Future Status* (26 March 2007) UN Doc S/2007/168, 15.

[74] Drew (n 30) 87, 94.

The UN Charter states (Article 1) that the principle of equal rights and self-determination of peoples is one of the purposes of the Organization, and Chapter VI of the Charter makes clear that the primary concern is to support self-government and development of those people who have 'not yet attained a full measure of self-government'. The Declaration on the Granting of Independence to Colonial Territories of 1960[75] points out that this notion was to be interpreted as 'decolonization'.[76] The General Assembly also specified in a later resolution that the right of peoples to self-determination cannot be interpreted as 'authorising or encouraging an action, no matter what it is, which would disrupt or threaten, partially or totally, the territorial integrity or political unity of an independent and sovereign State'.[77] From this development the conclusion is to be drawn that the United Nations law recognizes self-determination in the context of decolonization, but expressly rejects self-determination as a justification for secession.

In short, on the Western Sahara understanding of the meaning of the right to self-determination, identifying colonialism as the legal basis for self-determination is significant because it places that entitlement of Western Sahara at the very top of a normative hierarchy both in terms of the status and the content of the right.[78] Therefore, because of its exclusive colonial background, no conclusion can be drawn from the case study of the Western Sahara concerning the right to self-determination for the CIS states, or any other situation without a colonial background.

6. Use of natural resources

In the light of recent developments, there is one other aspect of self-determination that should not remain unconsidered: the sovereignty over and use of natural resources.[79] In November 2001, the Members of the Security Council requested the opinion of the United Nations Legal Counsel on 'the legality in the context of international law, including relevant resolutions of the Security Council and the General Assembly of the United Nations, and agreements concerning Western Sahara of actions allegedly taken by the Moroccan authorities consisting in the offering and signing of contracts with foreign companies for the exploration of mineral resources in Western Sahara'.[80]

As mentioned, Morocco is, legally speaking, an occupying power. The basic principles of belligerent occupation apply: the occupying power may not change

[75] UNGA Res 1514 (XV) (14 December 1960) UN Doc A/RES/1514(XV).

[76] M Craven, 'Statehood, Self-determination, and Recognition' in M Evans (ed), *International Law* (3rd edn, OUP 2010) 231.

[77] *Friendly Relations Declaration*, UNGA Res 2625 (XXV) (24 October 1970) UN Doc A/Res/2625(XXV).

[78] Drew (n 30) 87, 94.

[79] A basic source on the status of the natural resources of peoples who have not had the chance to exercise their right of self-determination is common Art. 1(2) of the 1966 Covenants on Civil and Political Rights and on Economic, Social and Cultural Rights.

[80] See 'Letter dated 29 January 2002 from the Under Secretary-General for Legal Affairs, the Legal Counsel, addressed to the President of the Security Council' (12 February 2002) UN Doc S/2002/161.

the legal and political framework and should proceed from the premise that the occupation is a temporary status and that the occupying power may not introduce permanent changes into the occupied territory.[81] Furthermore, Western Sahara is still a Non-Self-Governing Territory in UN terms, and its people have a right to permanent sovereignty over its natural resources and the right to 'freely dispose of their natural wealth and resources', as provided in Article 1(2) of the two UN Covenants on Human Rights.

Since Morocco has no legal right to govern the territory, it has no legal title to the natural resources of Western Sahara. Consequently, Morocco has no right as a sovereign to dispose of such natural resources for her own purposes. Furthermore, any agreement that Morocco enters into with other countries cannot cover Western Sahara as a part of Morocco.

Nevertheless, under some circumstances Morocco may use the natural resources of the territory. Morocco has a responsibility to uphold order as well as the *vie public* (public life and welfare), as is provided in the Hague Convention of 1907 and in the 1949 Fourth Geneva Convention.[82] This means that Morocco must offer basic public goods to the population of Western Sahara, which entails that there must be income to pay for these goods. Consequently, Morocco may make arrangements with regard to the resources of Western Sahara, provided that they benefit the Sahrawi people. This would be particularly appropriate with regard to renewable resources, such as sustainable and reasonable fishing. The principle of self-determination further requires that the people of Western Sahara should be able to influence how this is done.

In a situation where it is clear that the administering power is not interested in the aspiration of the people of the territory, but has other interests which dominate its agenda, it is not easy to distinguish between economic activities undertaken in the territory that are in the interests of the people of the territory and those that are not. However, it should be clear that these economic activities and investments are in the interest and to the benefit of the people of the territory and are undertaken, as far as possible, in collaboration with the representatives of the people of the territory.

Even if Western Sahara, contrary to my argument above, was not occupied but merely 'administered', the fact remains that the rules governing the administration of Non-Self-Governing Territories point in the same direction as the law of occupation. This is provided for in Article 73 of the UN Charter and was developed in a legal opinion by the then UN Legal Counsel, Hans Corell, in 2002.[83] The opinion concluded, with regard to oil exploration, that if:

[81] See Article 43 of the 1907 Hague Regulations and in particular concerning the 'Change of Legislation and Changes to Institutions'; M Sassòli, 'Legislation and Maintenance of Public Order and Civil Life' (2005) 16 EJIL 4, 661, 671.

[82] Wrange (n 37) 299, 301.

[83] 'Letter dated 29 January 2002 from the Under Secretary-General for Legal Affairs, the Legal Counsel, addressed to the President of the Security Council' (12 February 2002) UN Doc S/2002/161.

further exploration and exploitation activities were to proceed in disregard of the interests and wishes of the people of Western Sahara, they would be in violation of the international law principles applicable to mineral resource activities in Non-Self-Governing Territories.

Consequently, 'Morocco may not dispose of the resources of Western Sahara for her own benefit; any agreement entered into by Morocco in her own name does not cover Western Sahara, since Western Sahara is not a part of Morocco; Morocco may enter into agreements regarding the use of natural resources as an occupying or *de facto* administering power with regard to the territory of Western Sahara *but only provided that* any such agreement must be for the *benefit* of the *people* of Western Sahara *and* according to the *wishes* of that people'.[84]

A significant source of controversy in this regard concerns the inclusion of fishing in the waters off Western Sahara and the Fisheries Partnership Agreement (FPA) between the European Union and Morocco.[85] One of the issues to consider is whether or not the local population of Western Sahara has been benefitting from the agreement. Because according to the 2002 opinion by the then UN Legal Counsel *Hans Corell*, mentioned above, any exploration or exploitation activities in Western Sahara can only proceed if they are to the benefit of, and in accordance with, the wishes of the people of Western Sahara.

In late 2009, the legal service of the European Parliament provided an opinion about the FPA and Western Sahara. The legal service found that 'compliance with international law requires that economic activities related to the natural resources of a Non-Self-Governing Territory are carried out for the benefits of the people of such Territory, and in accordance with their wishes'. Further,

> [i]n the event that it could not be demonstrated that the FPA was implemented in conformity with the principles of international law concerning the rights of the Saharawi people over their natural resources, principles which the Community is bound to respect, the Community should refrain from allowing vessels to fish in the waters off Western Sahara by requesting fisheries licences only for fishing zones that are situated in the waters off Morocco.[86]

Consequently, it is illegal to enter into an agreement with Morocco which explicitly or implicitly recognizes the annexation of Western Sahara; any agreement that covers Western Sahara must clarify that the territory is legally not under Moroccan sovereignty. Further, it means that any such agreement should not strengthen the Moroccan occupation and hence should not support measures that strengthen Moroccan control or that facilitate Morocco's transfer of settlers into the territory. In addition, as was explained above, if an agreement is concluded that covers fishing or other natural resources, it must be to the *benefit* of the Sahrawi *people* and in accordance with their wishes.

[84] Wrange (n 25) (italics in original).

[85] Council Regulation (EC) No 764/2006 'Fisheries Partnership Agreement between the European Communities and the Kingdom of Morocco' [2006] OJ L 141/4–8; for the current status see <http://ec.europa.eu/fisheries/cfp/international/agreements/morocco/index_en.htm>.

[86] 'Legal Opinion regarding the Fisheries Partnership Agreement between the European Community and the Kingdom of Morocco by the European Parliament's Legal Service' [2009] SJ-0269/09, D(2009)37828 of 14 July 2009.

Otherwise the EU should consider either the suspension of the agreement or its application in such a way that EU-flagged vessels are excluded from the exploitation of the waters of Western Sahara. A legally sound example is the 2004 Free Trade Agreement (FTA) between the United States and Morocco, which explicitly excludes Western Sahara from its operation.[87] This FTA does not include services or goods originated in the Western Sahara due to the latter's status as a Non-Self-Governing Territory[88] and as the US does not recognize Moroccan sovereignty over the disputed territory.[89]

Since any exploitation of its natural resources must be in accordance with the wishes and interests of the people of Western Sahara, the European Parliament made the right choice in 2011 when it decided to draw attention to that point. If the agreements stay in line with the wishes and interests of the people of Western Sahara, there is no reason not to conclude them. However, if exploration and exploitation activities were to proceed in disregard of the interests and wishes of the people of Western Sahara, they would be in violation of the principles of international law applicable to the use of natural resources in Non-Self-Governing Territories.

[87] See <http://www.moroccousafta.com/index_ang.htm> accessed 10 November 2012.

[88] 'Rep. Pitts Lauds Protection of Sahrawis in Morocco Trade Pact' (22 July 2004) <http://web.archive.org/web/20110629044535/http://www.house.gov/pitts/press/releases/040722r-FTAwsahara.htm> accessed 10 November 2012.

[89] Hannikainen (n 27) 59, 69.

14

Eritrea

Gregory Fox

I. Introduction

Eritrea is one of the newest countries in Africa, achieving independence in 1993 after a 30-year war of secession against Ethiopia. Eritrea sits on the west coast of the Red Sea, bordering the Sudan, Ethiopia, and Djibouti. Its population of just over 6 million is roughly divided between those living on the lowlands coastline, who are predominantly Muslim, and those in the highlands, who are predominantly Coptic Christian.[1] Post-independence Eritrea is well known to international lawyers for the arbitrations that resulted from its disputes with Yemen and Ethiopia, as well as for litigation in United States courts arising from Ethiopia's 1998 mass expulsion of Eritreans.[2] But the success of its independence struggle has left the origins of that struggle somewhat lost to history.

The Eritrean claim to self-determination had two critical legal features. The first is the central role played by the United Nations. An Italian colony since the late nineteenth century, Eritrea was occupied by Britain in 1941, excised from Italian sovereignty by the Four Powers in 1947 and federated with Ethiopia in 1952 by the UN General Assembly. Dissatisfied with the arrangement, Ethiopia dissolved the federation and absorbed Eritrea as a province in 1962. The war for independence ensued. The legal arguments supporting the Eritrean case rested primarily on unfulfilled UN obligations: to ensure that Eritrea received the same autonomy options as other non-self-governing territories, to remedy Ethiopia's dissolution of the federation created by the General Assembly, and to respond to the atrocities committed by Ethiopian forces against Eritrean civilians.

[1] See CIA World Factbook, Eritrea (Skyhorse Publishing 2013), available at <https://www.cia.gov/library/publications/the-world-factbook/geos/er.html>.

[2] See Permanent Court of International Arbitration, Eritrea/Yemen, available at <http://www.pca-cpa.org/showpage.asp?pag_id=1160>; Permanent Court of International Arbitration, Eritrea-Ethiopia Claims Commission, available at <http://www.pca-cpa.org/showpage.asp?pag_id=1151>; Eritrea-Ethiopia Boundary Commission, available at <http://www.pca-cpa.org/showpage.asp?pag_id=1150>; *Nemariam* v *Commercial Bank of Ethiopia*, 315 F.3d 390 (DC Cir. 2003); *Nemariam* v *Commercial Bank of Ethiopia*, 491 F.3d 470 (DC Cir. 2007).

The second is the question of whether self-determination rights, once created, can ever be extinguished. Ethiopia's dismantling of the federal arrangement provoked no response whatever from the UN or any other international actor, and the Eritrean rebels received virtually no external support during the civil war. Did this resounding silence and full Ethiopian control over Eritrea for 30 years cause Eritrean autonomy rights to lapse? Or were they simply dormant during adverse political circumstances?

This chapter will first review Eritrea's various political configurations from colonial times until full independence. It will then examine the Eritrean case for self-determination, first under national law and then under international law. It will conclude by asking whether the various Eritrean claims, their reception by the international community, and their resonance in international law provide any lessons for self-determination conflicts in the Commonwealth of Independent States (CIS).

II. The Eritrean Path to Independence

Prior to the late nineteenth century Eritrea existed under the loose control of a variety of outside powers: the Ethiopian empire, the Ottoman empire, and Egypt.[3] With a history of shifting imperial control by regional powers and its use as a strategic buffer zone, Eritrea during this period lacked the opportunity to consolidate a clear national identity. As Trevaskis observes, prior to the Italian colonial presence, 'Eritrea had never enjoyed any form of unity, had never had a government of its own, had never even had a name'.[4]

1. From colony to occupied territory—1869 to 1941

Starting in 1869 the Italian Rubattino Navigation Company bought tracts of land near Assab in the south of the country, which became the property of the Italian government in 1882.[5] In 1889 Italy and Emperor Yohannes of Ethiopia signed the Treaty of Uccialli, which ceded Eritrea to Italy. A year later the colony of Eritrea came into existence by royal decree.[6]

Despite the treaty's focus on Eritrea, Italy sought to add the Ethiopian province of Tigre to its colonial holdings. Tensions escalated and war erupted in December 1894; two years later, however, the forces of Emperor Menelik defeated Italy at the battle of Adawa. But Menelik was in no position to expel Italians from Eritrea and in fact needed the security of peace with Italy in order to consolidate control elsewhere in Ethiopia. On 26 October 1896 Menelik signed the Treaty of Addis

[3] See generally R Sherman, *Eritrea: the Unfinished Revolution* (Greenwood Publishing Group 1980) 4–10.

[4] G Kennedy and N Trevaskis, *Eritrea: a Colony in Transition* (Oxford University Press 1960) 4.

[5] Sherman (n 3) 11. [6] Sherman (n 3) 11.

Ababa, which abrogated the Treaty of Ucciali and confirmed Italian control over Eritrea.[7]

The defeat at Adawa stung the Italians and in 1932 Mussolini began preparations for an invasion of Ethiopia. The Italian population of Eritrea increased dramatically, as did the construction of infrastructure. In October 1935 Mussolini's troops entered Ethiopia and in 1936 they conquered Addis Ababa, forcing Emperor Haile Selassie into exile.[8] Despite Haile Selassie's plea for international assistance before the League of Nations, Italy remained in Ethiopia until April 1941, when British forces occupied all the Italian territory in Africa.[9]

2. Postwar disposition—1941–1952

At the Potsdam Conference on 1 August 1945 the four victorious powers decided to conclude a treaty of peace with Italy that would address the status of Italy's colonial possessions.[10] The decision taken at Potsdam came only a few months before the UN Charter entered into force, on 24 October 1945. The peace treaty with the Allied and Associated Powers of 10 February 1947 compelled Italy to renounce all title to its possessions in Africa: Libya, Italian Somaliland, and Eritrea. For Eritrea, the treaty provided that final disposition would be determined by the Four Powers within one year 'in the light of the wishes and welfare of the inhabitants and the interests of peace and security, taking into consideration the views of other interested Governments'.[11] If the Four Powers could not agree, however, the matter would be referred to the General Assembly for a recommendation, and the Four Powers agreed 'to accept the recommendation and to take appropriate measures for giving effect to it'.[12] The Four Powers convened a Committee of Investigation and consulted widely but after three years they were unable to agree on a solution, meaning debate shifted to the General Assembly.[13]

On 21 November 1949 the General Assembly created a five-member Commission to make recommendations on Eritrea's final status.[14] The Commission was instructed to meet with all interested parties in Eritrea and to take into account the 'wishes and welfare of the inhabitants of Eritrea', the 'interests of peace and security in East Africa', and 'the rights and interests of Ethiopia based on geographical,

[7] Sherman (n 3) 11.

[8] B Davidson, 'Historical Note' in B Davidson, L Cliffe, and B Habte Selassie (eds), *Behind the War in Eritrea* (Spokesman 1980) 12–13.

[9] Trevaskis (n 4) 18.

[10] The Berlin (Potsdam) Conference (July 17–August 2, 1945), in H Bhebre-Ab (ed), *Ethiopia and Eritrea: A Documentary Study* (Red Sea Press 1993) 29, 31.

[11] Treaty of Peace, Allies et al.–Italy, Feb. 10, 1947, Art. 23 (renunciation of colonies), Annex XI (disposition of colonies).

[12] Treaty of Peace (n 12) Annex XI, para 3.

[13] AA Schiller, 'Comment, Eritrea: Constitution and Federation with Ethiopia' (1953) 2 AJCL 375, 376.

[14] UNGA Res 289 (IV) (Nov 21, 1949). The members were Burma, Guatemala, Norway, Pakistan, and South Africa. In the same resolution the General Assembly declared that Libya and Italian Somaliland would become independent sovereign states.

historical, ethnic or economic reasons, including in particular Ethiopia's legitimate need for access to the sea'.[15] The Committee was to report back by 15 June 1950. The General Assembly would then make a final decision that the Four Powers would accept.[16]

The Commission performed its work diligently. It held 70 meetings in total, 40 of which were public. It consulted the British administrators, other governments, and 'representatives of the population, including minorities, organizations and individuals'.[17] The Commission found significant divisions among the population, with highland Copts largely in favour of a union with Ethiopia, while much of the lowland Muslim population favoured Eritrean independence.[18] Despite agreeing on these basic facts, the Commission was divided on its final recommendations. Burma and South Africa recommended a close association with Ethiopia in the form of a federation under Ethiopian sovereignty;[19] Norway proposed that Eritrea be fully absorbed into Ethiopia;[20] and Guatemala and Pakistan proposed full independence to be preceded by a ten-year trusteeship under United Nations supervision.[21]

On 2 December 1950 the General Assembly agreed with the Burmese and South African view and determined that Eritrea 'shall constitute an autonomous unit federated with Ethiopia under the sovereignty of the Ethiopian crown'.[22] The General Assembly based its decision on the same three considerations underlying its mandate to the Commission: the wishes of Eritrean citizens, the interests of peace and security in the region, and the rights and claims of Ethiopia.[23] Under the federal arrangement, Ethiopia was to have authority over matters of defence, foreign affairs, currency, finance, and foreign and internal commerce. The autonomous Eritrean government was given jurisdiction over 'all matters not vested in the Federal Government', ie everything else.[24] The resolution also prescribed a structure for the federal system, rules on nationality (a single nationality would prevail throughout the federation), and a comprehensive set of human rights protections.[25] All these internal constitutional norms of the federation were to constitute a Federal Act to be ratified by the Ethiopian Emperor. The federation would thus come into existence as a matter of both international law and Ethiopian national law.

The resolution also created a United Nations Commissioner for Eritrea, tasked with establishing an administrative structure for Eritrea and drafting an Eritrean constitution. The constitution was to be ratified by the Ethiopian crown along with the Federal Act, after which they would both enter into force.[26] The Commissioner and his staff held extensive consultations with citizens and political groups, as well as with representatives of the Ethiopian government. Ethiopia objected to many

[15] UNGA Res 289 (IV) (n 14) para C(2).
[16] UNGA Res 289 (IV) (n 14) para C(4).
[17] *Report of the United Nations Commission for Eritrea*, UN GAOR 5th Session No. 8 (UN Doc A/1285) (1950).
[18] UN Doc A/1285 (n 17) 57–60.
[19] UN Doc A/1285 (n 17) 79.
[20] UN Doc A/1285 (n 17) 81.
[21] UN Doc A/1285 (n 17) 84.
[22] UNGA Res 390A (1950).
[23] UNGA Res 390A (n 22) preamble.
[24] UNGA Res 390A (n 22).
[25] UNGA Res 390A (n 22) paras 1–7.
[26] UNGA Res 390A (n 22) para 13.

aspects of the draft constitution, reflecting an 'apprehension that an Eritrea too autonomous and democratic might militate against the stability of the Federation and indeed of Ethiopia'.[27] For the most part the Commissioner rejected the proposed changes. The final draft reflected the General Assembly's wish in Resolution 390A that the constitution 'be based on the principles of democratic government' and include the human rights guarantees outlined in the Federal Act.[28]

The transition to local rule proceeded rapidly. Elections for the Eritrean Representative Assembly took place in late March 1952, resulting in a division of power among three parties. The Assembly convened in late April and on 10 July adopted the Commissioner's draft constitution. Emperor Haile Selassie ratified the constitution on 11 August and the federation was formally established on 11 September. On 15 September the British occupation authority relinquished all control over Eritrea.[29]

3. Federation with Ethiopia—1952–1962

Throughout the General Assembly's deliberations leading up to Resolution 390A, Ethiopia had lobbied hard for maximum control over Eritrea.[30] The compromise of a federation represented a setback. But in the years following the departure of foreign actors and international scrutiny, Addis Ababa undertook an escalating series of measures to undermine Eritrean autonomy within the federation. Only two weeks after the British ceded control, the Emperor issued a proclamation providing that the Ethiopian Supreme Court would be the court of final appeal for Eritrea. This appeared contrary to Article 90 of the new Eritrean constitution that described its Supreme Court as a 'court of last resort'.[31] In the succeeding years, Addis Ababa relocated several critical Eritrean manufacturing facilities to Ethiopia and exerted pressure on foreign investors to locate in Ethiopia rather than Eritrea.[32] More critically, a new Ethiopian constitution in 1955 made no mention of the federation.[33] In 1956 Ethiopia decreed that Amharic (the Ethiopian language) would be the only official language of the entire country, displacing Tigrinya and Arabic, the two most widely spoken languages in Eritrea,[34] and in the same year virtually all political parties were banned.[35] In 1959 Ethiopian laws were extended to Eritrea and in 1960 the Ethiopian flag replaced the Eritrean flag at all official buildings.[36]

Finally, on 14 November 1962, with a large Ethiopian military contingent surrounding the administration building in Asmara, the Eritrean Assembly voted to

[27] Schiller (n 13) 381. Schiller served as Legal Advisor to the UN Commissioner.

[28] UNGA Res 390A (n 22) para 12.

[29] *Final Report of the United Nations Commissioner in Eritrea*, UN Doc A/2188 (1952), paras 760–8.

[30] See O Yohannes, *Eritrea, A Pawn in World Politics* (University Press of Florida 1991) 189–93; R Iyob, *The Eritrean Struggle for Independence* (Cambridge University Press 1995) 88–94.

[31] M Ayoob, *The Third World Security Predicament* (Lynne Rienner Publishers 1995) 88.

[32] D Pool, *Eritrea—Africa's Longest War* (Anti-Slavery Society 1982) 37.

[33] H Erlich, *The Struggle over Eritrea 1962–1979* (Hoover Inst Press 1983) 8.

[34] Pool (n 32) 37. [35] Erlich (n 33) 9. [36] Erlich (n 33) 9.

accept Haile Selassie's decree annulling the federation, dissolving the Assembly and constituting Eritrea as Ethiopia's 14th province.[37]

4. The civil war—1962–1991

Small Eritrean independence movements had emerged even prior to Haile Selassie's dissolution of the federation,[38] but organization of an armed resistance began in earnest after 1962. The first significant group, the Eritrean Liberation Front (ELF), had limited success and was riven by internal rivalries. In 1970 these divisions led a group of younger guerilla fighters to split from the ELF and form the Eritrean People's Liberation Front (EPLF). After a bitter armed struggle in the early 1970s the EPLF emerged ascendant and began to enjoy success against the Ethiopian military.[39] As a result, much of Eritrea was placed under martial law.

In 1974 a group of Ethiopian military officers, known eventually as the Dergue, deposed and murdered Emperor Haile Selassie. The Dergue mounted a series of brutal counter-insurgency campaigns against both EPLF and ELF fighters that included massacres of civilians and the destruction of entire villages.[40] Nevertheless Eritrean fighters enjoyed success in defeating a series of garrisoned towns and by the late 1970s they controlled most of the small towns and villages in the territory.[41] But a counter-offensive saw this situation reversed by 1980.[42]

There were two factors complicating the civil war during this period. The first was the reversal of superpower alignments in the region. With the human rights situation in Ethiopia deteriorating under Dergue rule, the United States began to terminate aid in 1977. The Dergue's Marxist political agenda soon resulted in a significant flow of aid from the USSR, including sophisticated weapons systems.[43] Within two years the Ethiopian army went from fighting Eritrean insurgents with American aid and weapons to fighting with Soviet aid and weapons. Second, in 1975 an entirely separate guerilla group, the Tigrean People's Liberation Front (TPLF), began an insurgency campaign aimed not at secession but at overthrow of the Dergue. In the late 1980s it enjoyed such success that 'the government began to be more preoccupied with it than the EPLF'.[44]

Despite extensive superpower involvement on the Ethiopian side, Eritrean efforts to enlist outside support were almost uniformly unsuccessful.[45] No United Nations body took up the question of Eritrea during the civil war. The official

[37] Yohannes (n 30) 194. [38] Ayoob (n 31) 98–110.

[39] Sherman (n 3) 40–72; Yohannes (n 30) 95–6. [40] Yohannes (n 30) 196–7.

[41] Sherman (n 3) 72–89.

[42] T Negash, *Eritrea and Ethiopia* (Transaction Publishers 1997) 160.

[43] Sherman (n 3) 89–90. [44] Negash (n 42) 166–7.

[45] As the new Eritrean government stated in 1993, 'The long war in Eritrea unfolded in international isolation... The primary obstacle to recognition of the Eritrean conflict was the Cold War. The US and USSR forged alliances based on national interests, with little regard for local realities. Despite the legal basis for Eritrean self-determination and the illegal violation of the UN federal agreement, no government formally recognized Eritrea's right to self-determination until the war's end in 1991'. Government of Eritrea, *Eritrea: Birth of a Nation* (1993), available at <http://www.dehai.org/conflict/history/birth_of_a_nation.htm>.

UN publication on its involvement in Eritrea, which reprints all critical documents, includes no materials between 1952 and 1990.[46] The Organization of African Unity, headquartered in Addis Ababa, was similarly silent. Human rights organizations decried Ethiopian scorched-earth policies but had little influence over government policy. The dominant external actors in Eritrea were the two superpowers, who provided massive amounts of aid to allied Ethiopian regimes.[47]

5. Independence 1991–1993

The conflict took a decisive turn in 1984 when the EPLF captured a large cache of Soviet-made weapons, which transformed its ability to conduct offensive operations.[48] In May 1988 the Eritreans captured the town of Afabet, where the largest and most skilled Ethiopian regiment was headquartered. The TPLF made similar gains in Ethiopia proper. On 21 May Dergue President Mengistu went into exile and one week later TPLF forces entered Addis Ababa.[49] On 24 May EPLF forces entered Asmara following the departure of Ethiopian troops and on 27 May the EPLF announced the formation of a provisional government of Eritrea, headed by its leader Issaias Afwerki.

In early July the new Eritrean and Ethiopian regimes held a Conference on Peace and Democracy in Addis Ababa and affirmed Eritrea's right to determine its own political future. The Conference agreed that 'the future status of Eritrea should be decided by the Eritrean people in a referendum to be conducted in the presence of international observers'. The new TPLF-led government of Ethiopia agreed to respect the outcome of the referendum and invited the United Nations to supervise the vote.[50]

In October 1992 the Secretary-General recommended that the General Assembly approve the creation of a UN observer mission to Eritrea.[51] On 16 December the Assembly gave its approval, creating the United Nations Observer Mission to Verify the Referendum in Eritrea (UNOVER).[52] UNOVER oversaw voter registration, a campaign period, and the voting itself, which took place in late April 1993. Of

[46] United Nations, *The United Nations and the Independence of Eritrea* (1996) 45.

[47] Dan Connell reports that 'Washington provided Addis Ababa over half its total aid to Africa from 1952 to 1976, including the first supersonic jet fighters on the continent and Special Forces units to train the Ethiopians in counterinsurgency techniques'. After the Dergue took power, the Soviet Union 'promptly escalated the conflict by pumping in over $11 bn in new arms. This massive arsenal was accompanied by high level military advisors'. D Connell, 'Eritrea: Starting from Scratch' (1994) 21 Rev African PE 587, 588.

[48] HM Adam, 'Formation and Recognition of New States: Somaliland in Contrast to Eritrea' (1994) 21 Rev African PE 21, 30.

[49] B Habte Selassie, 'Self-Determination in Principle and Practice: The Ethiopian-Eritrean Experience' (1997) 29 CHRLR 91, 120–1.

[50] Letter dated 13 December 1991 from the President of the Transitional Government of Ethiopia to the Secretary-General of the United Nations Concerning the Results of the Conference on Peace and Democracy held in Ethiopia in July 1991, UN Doc A/C.3/47/5, Annex II (1992).

[51] *Report of the Secretary-General on the Request to the United Nations to Observe the Referendum Process*, UN Doc A/47/544 (1992).

[52] UNGA Res 47/114 (1992).

those voting, 99.8% favoured independence, and UNOVER reported that the referendum had been free and fair at every stage.[53] On 29 April the Ethiopian government accepted the results and recognized Eritrean independence.[54] Formal independence came on 24 May and on 28 May Eritrea was admitted as a member state of the United Nations.[55]

III. Eritrean Legal Claims to Self-Determination under National Law

A variety of legal systems operated in Eritrea during the long run-up to its independence: Italian law applicable to its colonies; the Italian system modified by decrees of the British occupation authority; Eritrean law under the federation; and Ethiopian law after the federation was dissolved. None of the many claims for self-determination made by Eritreans appealed to national law. This was true for four reasons. First, none of the legal systems provided a right to self-determination for Eritrea, let alone a right to secession. Indeed, acquiring political authority over Eritrea was a central political goal of each system and providing an opportunity for exit would have undermined this goal.[56] Second, during the post-World War II era, the deliberative processes created by the Four Powers and then the UN General Assembly seemed to offer the real possibility of independence. An appeal to national law would have missed these critical international opportunities. Third, the federal period from 1952 to 1962, enshrined in the Ethiopian Federal Act, offered autonomy, if not full sovereignty, under Ethiopian law. As long as the federation appeared politically viable, Eritreans had an incentive to hold Ethiopia to the terms of the Federal Act rather than seek to abrogate the arrangement. Finally, when Ethiopia itself terminated the federation pursuant to a national decree annexing Eritrea, any appeal to national law would have been pointless.

IV. Eritrean Legal Claims to Self-Determination under International Law

Eritreans created a rich political and legal literature during their 30-year war for independence. In these writings, three distinct claims to statehood appear,

[53] *Report of the Secretary-General on UNOVER*, UN Doc A/48/283 (1993).

[54] Statement of 4 May 1993 by the Ministry of Foreign Affairs of the Transitional Government of Ethiopia on the Recognition by Ethiopia of the Sovereignty and Independence of Eritrea, in The United Nations and the Independence of Eritrea (n 46) 214.

[55] UNGA Res 47/230 (1993).

[56] This is well captured by Article 1 of the 1955 Ethiopian constitution: 'The Empire of Ethiopia comprises all the territories, including the islands and the territorial waters, under the sovereignty of the Ethiopian Crown. Its sovereignty and territory are indivisible. Its territories and the sovereign rights therein are inalienable.' Revised Constitution of the Empire of Ethiopia (1955), Art. 1, available at <http://www.angelfire.com/ny/ethiocrown/Constitution.html>.

roughly coinciding with different periods in Eritrean history after World War II. The first is that Eritrea was entitled to independence at the beginning of the UN era on the same terms as the other Italian possessions and colonial territories more generally. The second is that Ethiopia's abrogation of the federation in 1962 constituted a breach of its legal obligations to the international community and the Four Powers in particular. Eritrea's remedy for that breach should have been independence. The third is a claim of remedial secession: Eritrea suffered grievous oppression during the entire postwar period, with no hope of remediation from the states that controlled its political destiny. In these circumstances it should not have been compelled to remain subordinate to Ethiopia, particularly after 1962. The following sections will examine and critique each of these claims.

Before proceeding, two points of clarification are necessary. First, the Eritrean claims to a legal entitlement to independence all predate the UN-supervised process of 1991–3. No one in the Eritrean camp claims that actual independence was achieved pursuant to a legal right against continued Ethiopian territorial integrity. The TPLF-led Ethiopian government that took power in 1991 consented to Eritrean independence following the UN-sponsored referendum. The international community deferred to this consensual arrangement, with no state objecting either to the UN monitoring mission in 1993 or to Eritrea's subsequent admission to the United Nations.[57] The claims examined here address only Eritrea's situation from 1945 to 1991.

Second, I will not examine in detail the specific Ethiopian responses to these claims. While the Ethiopian position was multifaceted and varied somewhat over time, the central recurring theme of its replies was a claim of historic title. This is well captured in an article by a former official of the Haile Selassie government: 'Had Italy not wrenched it from Ethiopia, Eritrea would have remained an administrative province of Ethiopia. It is important to remember that Eritrea never existed as its own nation. It did not exist at all prior to its colonization by Italy... Prior to colonization by Italy, Eritrea had formed an integral part of Ethiopia since the Aksumite period in the first century A.D.'.[58] International law generally does not credit historic title as a counter to a people's right to self-determination.[59] While other responses to the Eritrean claims are legally quite persuasive, and will be examined below, this one is not.

[57] J Crawford, *The Creation of States in International Law* (2nd edn, Oxford University Press 2006) 402–3.

[58] M Haile, 'Legality of Secessions' (1994) 8 EILJ 479, 528–9.

[59] See *Sovereignty over Pulau Ligitan and Pulau Sipadan (Indonesia* v *Malaysia)*, 2001 ICJ 575, 652 (separate opinion of judge ad hoc Thomas M Franck) ('historic title, no matter how persuasively claimed on the basis of old legal instruments and exercises of authority, cannot—except in the most extraordinary circumstances—prevail in law over the rights of non-self-governing people to claim independence and establish their sovereignty through the exercise of bona fide self-determination').

1. First Eritrean argument: entitlement to independence after World War II

The first argument is that in the aftermath of World War II the United Nations Charter made clear that colonial territories had a right to self-determination, which could take the form of independent statehood if desired by the population. Evidence suggests that an overwhelming percentage of Eritreans favoured independence.[60]

According to this view, two Charter provisions were relevant to Eritrea. The first is Chapter XII of the Charter dealing with trusteeships. Article 77(1)(b) provides that the trusteeship system shall apply to 'territories which may be detached from enemy states as a result of the Second World War'. Eritrea was detached from Italy pursuant to the 1947 peace treaty. Like all trust territories, those under Article 77(1)(b) were to make 'progressive development towards self-government or independence'.[61] Even if former enemy territories were not converted into trust territories, it was argued, Chapter VII could not sanction any lesser degree of autonomy than self-government or independence, since that would permit the entire system to be circumvented.

Second, apart from Eritrea's connection to a defeated enemy power, colonial territories of all kinds were entitled to self-determination.[62] Designating colonies of enemy states as mandate territories was not obligatory, but that did not mean they were not entitled to self-determination.[63] It simply meant that the obligation to promote their self-determination derived from Chapter XI of the Charter rather than Chapter XII. Proponents concede, as they must, that the legal obligation to emancipate non-mandate colonies did not become clear until General Assembly Resolution 1514 of 1960.[64] But thereafter the General Assembly made clear that self-determination for colonial territories would mean full independence if desired by the population.[65]

That the Charter provided all other colonies with an entitlement to independence is well illustrated by the fate of Libya and Somaliland, both former Italian colonies. The peace treaty with Italy placed disposal of all three Italian colonies in

[60] Several sources cite British estimates that in the late 1940s 75% of Eritreans favoured independence. See eg GH Tesfagioris, 'Note, Self-Determination: Its Evolution and Practice by the United Nations and its Application to the Case of Eritrea' (1987) 6 WILJ 75, 106 n 164; *Eritrea, Birth of a Nation* (n 45).

[61] UN Charter, Art. 76(b).

[62] *Legal Consequences for States of the Continued Presence of South Africa in Namibia (South West Africa) Notwithstanding Security Council Resolution 276 (1970)*, 1971 ICJ 16, 31 (Advisory Opinion of June 21) ('the subsequent development of international law in regard to non-self-governing territories, as enshrined in the Charter of the United Nations, made the principle of self-determination applicable to all of them').

[63] *International Status of South-West Africa*, 1950 ICJ 128, 139 (Advisory Opinion of July 11) (given the permissive language of Chapter XII of the Charter, states are under no obligation to designate territories as mandates).

[64] D Raič, *Statehood and the Law of Self-Determination* (Kluwer Law International 2002) 202–3.

[65] UNGA Res 1541 (XV) (1960).

the hands of the Four Powers. As with Eritrea, the four failed to agree on dispositions for Libya and Somaliland, and so along with Eritrea their fate was referred to the General Assembly. There the paths diverged. The Assembly recommended that Libya become independent no later than 1 January 1952.[66] It further recommended that Italian Somaliland be subject to a ten-year trusteeship, after which it would become independent.[67] Eritrea, as we have seen, was first referred to an investigative commission that divided in its recommendations and then ultimately federated with Ethiopia. Viewed in this context, it is argued, the failure to provide Eritrea a path to full statehood appears a deviation from the norm of independence for all colonies rather than a laudably nuanced approach that weighed all factors counselling for and against full statehood.

Proponents of this argument do not contest the Allies' ability to dispose of the former Italian colonies in a peace treaty. They argue instead that the process by which the Allies reached their decision should be no different than that for any other colony: a free and fair vote by the inhabitants. In the Western Sahara case the Court defined the principle of self-determination as 'the need to pay regard to the freely expressed will of peoples'.[68] Eritreans had many specific complaints about the two investigations that preceded the 1952 federal arrangement, but their central claim was that Eritreans were not consulted in the only reliable manner recognized elsewhere in decolonization practice—an internationally monitored referendum—before a status short of full independence was chosen for them.

Under contemporary international law this argument has some appeal, though as explained below, even its contemporary salience may be limited. But the inter-temporal law doctrine requires that Eritrean claims be evaluated under the law in force at the time, which was the period from the Italian peace treaty of 1947 to the decision to federate with Ethiopia in 1952.[69] It is certainly true that after 1945 all former mandate territories (save south-west Africa) were placed into the trusteeship system. It is also true that some non-self-governing territories (non-trust colonies) achieved independence between 1945 and 1960 and that after 1960 virtually all the remaining colonies followed.[70] But in the peace treaty with Italy, the Four Powers chose a different route: giving themselves the power of disposition and, failing agreement, seeking a recommendation from the UN General Assembly that they committed to accept. The treaty contains no substantive constraints on the power of disposition. The question, then, is whether international law in the immediate postwar period permitted the Four Powers to exercise this authority without recourse to a referendum or, as in the case of Somaliland and Libya, a clear intention to provide independent statehood? Importantly, final dispositive authority was not ceded to the United Nations upon the Four Powers' failure to agree. The treaty was clear that the powers themselves were the ultimate decision-makers.[71]

[66] UNGA Res 289A (IV) (1949). [67] UNGA Res 289A (IV) (1949) (n 67).

[68] *Western Sahara* (Advisory Opinion), 1975 ICJ 12, para 59.

[69] See TO Elias, 'The Doctrine of Intertemporal Law' 75 AJIL 285 (1980).

[70] See generally S Hasan Ahmad, *The United Nations and the Colonies* (Asia Pub. House 1974).

[71] Italian Peace Treaty (n 11), Annex XI, para 3 ('If with respect to any of these territories the Four powers are unable to agree upon their disposal within one year from the coming into force of the

Collective dispositions through peace treaties have been a common practice in international law. They are the basis for numerous international borders and are often said to have acquired an objective basis, immune from alteration except through consent of the nations involved or a revision by the original treaty parties.[72] In the *Southwest Africa* Advisory Opinion, for example, the ICJ held that the mandate for south-west Africa outlived the demise of the League of Nations, its creator. As Sir Arnold McNair observed in his separate opinion, such a collective territorial disposition has frequently acquired 'a degree of acceptance and durability extending beyond the limits of the actual contracting parties, and giving it an objective existence'.[73] There is little basis, therefore, for challenging the Four Powers' authority to dispose of Eritrea and thereby subject it to a 'default' rule of full independence.

Even if one were to reject this broad fiat power, there are two additional problems with the Eritrean claim. First, it was not clear in the immediate postwar era that colonies were entitled to full independence. Britain and France were particularly fierce in disputing such an obligation through the 1950s, only clearly losing the argument with the adoption of Resolution 1514 in 1960.[74] Second, given the indeterminacy of the law at the time, it is difficult to view the UN's consideration of Eritrean interests as inadequate, either procedurally or substantively. The General Assembly's Commission of Inquiry conducted an extensive investigation and found the Eritrean population split on the desirability of independence versus affiliation with Ethiopia. The Commission was itself divided in its recommendations, proposing four alternative solutions. The General Assembly adopted the federation plan on a vote of 46 to 10, with four abstentions. The plan gave Eritrea its own constitution and full autonomy over all matters other than defence, foreign affairs, currency, finance, and foreign and internal commerce. Eritrean and Ethiopian partisans predictably took opposing positions on the plan.[75] But the process did take Eritrean interests into account, garnered a substantial majority among UN member states, and produced a compromise outcome that rejected the maximalist demands of either side. The federal outcome, moreover, was recognized even after Resolution 1514 as one of the valid ways for colonies to exercise their right to self-determination.[76]

Treaty of Peace with Italy, the matter shall be referred to the General Assembly of the United Nations for a recommendation, and the Four powers agree to accept the recommendation and to take appropriate measures for giving effect to it.').

[72] See J Crawford, *The Creation of States in International Law* (2nd edn, Oxford University Press 2007) 536.

[73] *International Status of South-West Africa* (n 63) 153 (separate opinion of Judge McNair).

[74] See MS Rajan, *The United Nations and Domestic Jurisdiction* (Orient Longmans 1958).

[75] See Haile (n 58) 488 (Report of Commission for Eritrea 'records a wealth of factual findings which fully justify the General Assembly's decision to federate Eritrea with Ethiopia, instead of recommending the independence of Eritrea'); Ayoob (n 31) 2 (federation resolution 'ran roughshod over a series of unaddressed Eritrean grievances and eliminated what little remained of the façade of Eritrean autonomy').

[76] See UNGA Res 1541 (XV) (1960).

One might respond that while the inquiry and resolution did take Eritrean interests into account, the Four Powers and the General Assembly also considered other factors as equally important.[77] As a result, the value of Eritrean independence was marginalized in a way that would not have been permitted under the law of self-determination, where it would have been the *only* relevant factor. This view is effectively another challenge to the Four Powers' authority to dispose of territory, perhaps conceding that while the power itself is valid, its exercise must privilege the inhabitants' interests over all others. International law of the late 1940s provided little support for this view.

2. Second Eritrean argument: Ethiopian abrogation of federation creates entitlement to independence

The second Eritrean argument is that Ethiopia's abrogation of the federation arrangement in 1962 violated the 1950 General Assembly Resolution and created an entitlement to independence as a remedy for that violation. One certainly cannot deny that Ethiopia's annexation of Eritrea violated both the resolution and the Ethiopian Federal Act that delimited the terms of the federal relationship. One also cannot deny that the United Nations did nothing in response.

The argument faces two difficult questions. First, did Ethiopia have an international legal obligation to respect the federal arrangement? Second, assuming Ethiopia did have such an obligation, to whom was it owed? Specifically, if Eritrea argues it was entitled to independence as a remedy for Ethiopia's breach, and even if the obligation was owed to others, was it also owed to Eritrea?

Regarding the first question, the General Assembly is not usually understood as capable of creating binding obligations, though its resolutions may begin or contribute to the development of customary norms. This includes the power to dispose of territory.[78] One possibility is that Ethiopia owed obligations *erga omnes* by virtue of the federal arrangement acquiring the objective character often ascribed to general territorial settlements.[79] Another is that the Four Powers and not the General Assembly were ultimately responsible for creating the federation. In the Italian peace treaty the Four Powers referred the Eritrean question to the General Assembly for a 'recommendation' that they agreed to accept.[80] This is not

[77] The peace treaty provided that Eritrea's disposition would take into account not only the views of its inhabitants but 'the interests of peace and security, taking into consideration the views of other interested Governments'. Similarly, the General Assembly directed its Commission of Inquiry to consider the 'interests of peace and security in East Africa' and 'the rights and interests of Ethiopia based on geographical, historical, ethnic or economic reasons, including in particular Ethiopia's legitimate need for access to the sea'. The last Chief Administrator of the British occupation authority in Eritrea commented, 'No one can say that, during the prolonged consultations and negotiations out of which the final solution evolved, the wishes and welfare of the inhabitants, the interests of peace and security, and the views of other interested Governments were not given full consideration'. DC Cumming, 'The Disposal of Eritrea' (1953) 7 MEJ 18, 19.

[78] Crawford (n 57) 551 ('the Assembly does not possess any broad dispositive powers under the Charter').

[79] Crawford (n 57) 536–7.

[80] Italian Peace Treaty (n 11) Annex XI, Art. 3.

an uncontroversial reading,[81] but it would bring the Eritrean settlement within the ambit of territorial dispositions by groups of powerful states that are generally taken to transcend the normal process of consent in the interest of long-term stability. Under either theory, Ethiopia would be obliged to respect the federal scheme.

A final theory is that the Eritrean right to self-determination antedated both the peace treaty and the General Assembly's action, deriving instead from a general entitlement in international law.[82] On this view, the Four Powers gave particular form to the Eritrean right by mandating the federation but did not thereby extinguish the right. Rather, the right remained extant, awaiting a time when it might be needed if Eritrean autonomy were limited or extinguished.[83] This view is consistent with the common characterization of self-determination as an 'inalienable' right.[84] It is also consistent with international law's hesitancy to automatically accept a state's extinction after its annexation.[85] Ethiopia's central justification for terminating the federation—a claim of historic title to Eritrea—was rejected by the ICJ in the Western Sahara case as a valid counterweight to a non-self-governing territory's right of self-determination.[86]

Obviously this third theory provides a ready answer to the second question of whether Eritrea was a beneficiary of an Ethiopian obligation. If Eritrea held a right to self-determination then that right was opposable to the entire international community. The question must be answered somewhat differently if either of the first two theories are accepted, since their focus is on an Ethiopian obligation to respect the federation rather than an Eritrean entitlement to its continuation. But the answer is straightforward. By the time the federation was abrogated in 1962, international law had clearly endowed self-determination units like Eritrea with rights vis-à-vis states that would deny or limit their autonomy.[87] Whether the obligation is derived from the peace treaty or the objective character of the territorial settlement, the demise of the federation would not relieve Ethiopia of the obligation.

[81] See Cumming (n 77) 18 (provision of Italian peace treaty sending Eritrean question to General 'was a clear renunciation of the privileges of the four powers in favor of a fully international settlement'.)

[82] As noted above, the law of self-determination in the 1940s was rather opaque. For this argument to be credible, Eritrea would need to have acquired the right after the UN Charter's entry into force on 24 October 1945 (when colonial self-determination arguably entered international law) but before the Italian peace treaty was signed on 10 February 1947 (when the Four Powers co-opted the power of disposition). In the *Wall* Opinion the ICJ held that self-determination rights are owed *erga omnes* but did not pinpoint the historical origin of that status. *Legal Consequences of the Construction of a Wall in the Occupied Palestinian Territory* (Advisory Opinion of July 9), 2004 ICJ Rep. 136, para 155.

[83] Both the *Western Sahara* and *East Timor* cases involved related circumstances in which former colonial territories whose rights to self-determination remained unextinguished awaited the political moment in which they could be fully exercised. *Western Sahara Case* (Advisory Opinion), 1975 ICJ 12; *Case Concerning East Timor (Port.* v. *Aust.)* (June 30, 1995), 1995 ICJ 90.

[84] For examples, see Raič (n 64) 232.

[85] Crawford (n 57) 704 ('the lapse of time in and of itself does not extinguish title').

[86] *Western Sahara Case* (n 83) 34–6.

[87] Less than one year after the landmark Resolution 1514, the General Assembly decried the refusal of some states to grant independence to their dependent territories and established a Special Committee to oversee the resolution's implementation. UNGA Res 1654 (1961).

Opponents might well reply that even if Eritrea's right to self-determination rested upon the dissolution of the federation, the international community's long refusal to address the situation from 1962 to 1991 signalled its acquiescence to Ethiopian control. They would argue that the *ex injuria jus non oritur* principle is not absolute and that a state's illegal control over territory may in some situations become validated by acquiescence.[88] Here, not only did no state or international organization object to dissolution of the federation, but also, for almost 30 years the world's two superpowers supported successive Ethiopian governments in their war with Eritrean rebels. And during the periods in which the US and Soviet Union was not allied with Ethiopia, neither provided support for the Eritreans.

But cases derogating from the *ex injuria* principle have been rare, especially in the post-Cold War era, and authoritative statements of the principle in this period have been categorical and without exception.[89] The principle has been said to apply with special force where the purported rights acquired arise out of violations of *jus cogens*, such as territorial integrity or self-determination.[90] In its 1995 East Timor opinion, the ICJ affirmed the territory's right to self-determination despite the last protesting Security Council resolution having come 19 years earlier and the last such General Assembly Resolution 13 years earlier.[91] One has a difficult time imagining the ICJ, should it have acquired jurisdiction, sanctioning the Ethiopian annexation and declaring the Eritreans' right to self-determination extinguished.

3. Third argument: right arises as result of oppression during period of Ethiopian domination. Remedial secession.

The third Eritrean argument is for remedial secession. It focuses on the period from 1962 to 1991, during which the struggle for independence took place. The

[88] While Crawford holds that the lapse of time in itself does not extinguish claims to independence in the context of annexed states, he nonetheless acknowledges that claims may be extinguished by 'a general acceptance by the international community as a whole that the situation has been resolved'. Crawford (n 57) 704. See also A Gioia, 'Historic Titles' in *Max Planck Encyclopedia of Public International Law* (OUP 2009) para 24 ('it is now almost generally recognized that territory can no longer be acquired . . . in derogation of other rules of ius cogens, such as the principle of self-determination of peoples. But a territorial annexation which may now appear to be invalid on those grounds might in the future be recognized, or acquiesced in, by a number of interested States').

[89] See *Gabčikovo-Nagymaros Project Case*, 1997 ICJ 7, 76 (facts flowing from unlawful conduct do not 'determine the law. The principle *ex injuria jus non oritur* is sustained by the Court's finding that the legal relationship created by the 1977 Treaty is preserved and cannot in this case be treated as voided by unlawful conduct').

[90] Article 41(2) of the Draft Articles on State Responsibility provides that 'No State shall recognize as lawful a situation created by a serious breach within the meaning of article 40, nor render aid or assistance in maintaining that situation.' Draft Articles on Responsibility of States for Internationally Wrongful Acts, Rep. of the Int'l Law Comm'n, 53rd Sess., April 23–June 1, July 2–August 10, Art. 41(2), reprinted in 2 YBILC pt. 2, 114. Article 40(1) defines a 'serious breach of international law' as one violating 'an obligation arising under a peremptory norm of general international law'. 2 YBILC pt. 2, 112. The commentary to Article 41 makes clear that violations of self-determination fall within the obligation of non-recognition. 2 YBILC pt. 2, 115: '[a]s regards the denial by a State of the right of self-determination of peoples, the advisory opinion of ICJ in the Namibia case is similarly clear in calling for a non-recognition of the situation'.

[91] *Case concerning East Timor* (n 83) 96, 103 (listing resolutions and finding that 'East Timor remains a non-self-governing territory and its people has the right to self-determination').

argument is one of necessity: after the demise of the federation and a scorched-earth anti-insurgency campaign by Ethiopian forces that produced egregious human rights abuses, the only option remaining for Eritreans was independence. This claim faces enormous legal hurdles. In the postcolonial era, self-determination has taken an inward turn, decidedly subordinating claims of independence to the territorial integrity of existing states.[92] This refusal to accept virtually all secessionist claims extended through the period of the Eritrea–Ethiopia civil war, evident in critical documents such as Resolution 1514 and the Friendly Relations Declaration[93], as well as in state practice.[94]

The doctrine of remedial secession is controversial, residing more in theory than practice.[95] But, assuming its presence in international law during the Eritrean civil war, the question is whether the level of Ethiopian oppression was sufficiently egregious to trigger the right.[96] This is an impossible question to answer, involving comparisons of human suffering across different times, cultures, and political contexts. There is little agreement among scholars on this point and their views are generally not based in state practice showing successful secessions to have emerged from some set of brutal state policies but not others.[97] At most, one can make two observations here. First, in the specific setting of Africa, brutal civil wars,

[92] See M Fabry, *Recognizing States* (Oxford University Press 2010) 204–7.

[93] Declaration on Principles of International Law Concerning Friendly Relations and Co-operation Among States in Accordance with the Charter of the United Nations, UNGA Res 2625 (XXV) (Oct. 24, 1970) (describing peoples' right to self-determination with the caveat that '[n]othing in the foregoing paragraphs shall be construed as authorizing or encouraging any action which would dismember or impair, totally or in part, the territorial integrity or political unity of sovereign and independent States conducting themselves in compliance with the principle of equal rights and self-determination of peoples as described above and thus possessed of a government representing the whole people belonging to the territory without distinction as to race, creed or colour'); *Declaration on the Granting of Independence to Colonial Countries and Peoples*, para. 6, UNGA Res 1514 (XV) (Dec. 14, 1960) ('[a]ny attempt aimed at the partial or total disruption of the national unity and the territorial integrity of a country is incompatible with the purposes and principles of the Charter of the United Nations').

[94] J Crawford, 'State Practice and International Law in Relation to Succession' (1999) 69 BYBIL 85, 108 ('[w]here the government of the State in question has maintained its opposition to the secession, such attempts have gained virtually no international support or recognition, and this has been true even when other humanitarian aspects of the situations have triggered widespread concern and action').

[95] See A Cassese, *Self-Determination of Peoples: A Legal Reappraisal* (Cambridge University Press 1995) 121; SE Meller, 'The Kosovo Case: An Argument for a Remedial Declaration of Independence' (2011–2012) 40 GJICL 833, 845–6; M Shaw, 'Peoples, Territories and Boundaries' (1997) 8 EJIL 478, 483 (even if level of human rights violations triggering remedial secession is set quite high, 'practice demonstrating the successful application of even this modest proposition is lacking').

[96] Antonio Cassesse proposes the following threshold: 'Extreme and unremitting persecution and the lack of any reasonable prospect for peaceful challenge'. Cassese (n 95) 120.

[97] One report summarizes the scholarly views as follows: 'Scenarios invoked in this context are violations of basic human rights, especially (attempted) genocide, the exclusion of a minority from the political process, or the outbreak of armed conflicts or despotic governments suppressing the rights of minorities. It is also highlighted that any extraordinary permission to secede would have to be realised following the appropriate procedures, notably having recourse to a free and fair referendum on independence, ideally under international supervision.' (2009) II *Report of the Independent International Fact-Finding Mission on the Conflict in Georgia* 139, available at <http://www.ceiig.ch/pdf/IIFFMCG_Volume_II.pdf>.

occasionally involving secessionist claims, were a common phenomenon during the period of Eritrean–Ethiopian conflict. This suggests the dispiriting conclusion that if remedial secession is to remain truly exceptional, it will be rarer still in a region in which governmental brutality is widespread. Second, the difficult task of sorting exceptional from unexceptional cases is most usefully undertaken by states and international organizations issuing condemnations of governmental practices, providing assistance to the rebels, terminating assistance to particularly brutal governments, promoting mediation, and engaging in other efforts that demonstrate support for the secessionist group. No such efforts occurred in Eritrea.

V. Lessons for Self-Determination in the Commonwealth of Independent States

What lessons does the Eritrean case hold for the 'frozen' conflicts of the CIS? Before identifying similarities between the Eritrean case and those conflicts, two important points of difference must be noted. These are differences of applicable law and differences of factual predicates.

1. Different applicable law

The law applicable to the Eritrean claims differs from that applicable to the CIS cases in two respects. The first involves the inter-temporal law problem. Each of the CIS territories is properly evaluated under contemporary international law, but several Eritrean claims focus on events occurring at a time when the contemporary law on self-determination was in its infancy. Decisions of international tribunals, episodes of precedent-setting significance, and entire doctrines (such as remedial secession) that inform contemporary debates cannot be applied to the Eritrean case, or can only be applied to some of the claims. This limits the range of lessons to be drawn.

The second is a difference of legal categories. Eritrea was a colonial ('non-self-governing') territory subject to a right of self-determination that, after 1960, virtually guaranteed independent statehood. None of the CIS territories has been a colony. While some may argue that their subjugation at certain periods in history was equivalent to colonization, in the post-World War II era the term acquired a particularized meaning and the Special Committee on Decolonization created an authoritative list of non-self-governing territories.[98] None of the CIS territories has ever been on the list.[99] Of course, if one views the Italian peace treaty and General Assembly federalism resolution as wholly displacing the law of self-determination for Eritrea, this distinction may have little relevance. But as

[98] UNGA Res 1654 (XVI) (1961).

[99] See United Nations, Trust and Non-Self-Governing Territories (1945–1999), available at <http://www.un.org/en/decolonization/nonselfgov.shtml>.

we have seen, even the Four Powers' power of disposition can be interpreted by reference to the default entitlement to independence.[100]

2. Different factual predicates

Much of the factual foundation for self-determination claims by CIS territories is simply absent in the Eritrean case:

- Eritrea never claimed a right of secession under Ethiopian law. The Federal Act of 1953, embodying critical portions of the General Assembly Resolution defining the nature of the federation, was obviously Ethiopian law. But after 1962 Eritreans sought not enforcement of the Federal Act and a return to federation but full independence.
- Some of the CIS territories draw on brief periods of past independence or quasi-independence to bolster their current self-determination claims. Eritrea was never independent prior to 1993.
- In several of the CIS cases a third party, Russia, has played a critical role in the political alignment of the territory claiming independence. Indeed, the European Court of Human Rights has held that the PMR was under the effective control of Russia;[101] a similar claim could be made for Abkhazia and South Ossetia.[102] No other state played any significant role in Eritrea's relationship to Ethiopia.[103]
- The question of appropriate boundaries looms large in the CIS cases, resulting in debate over the application of *uti possidetis juris*. During the Eritrean independence struggle there was no debate over its boundaries.

3. Positive lessons

The result of these distinctions is that there are few relevant lessons from the Eritrean case—but several are significant. The first concerns the status of self-determination rights during long periods of disuse. From 1962 to 1991 various Eritrean groups sought recognition of their independence claims from the international community and received no support. Yet one may argue that the rights endured and were ultimately vindicated upon independence in 1993. Some may respond that Eritrea did not achieve its independence by exercising an international legal right but through a combination of military victories against the Derg government of Ethiopia and

[100] The intertemporal law problem intersects with this question. As noted in Section IV.1, the law on colonial territories underwent a substantial evolution from 1945 to 1960. The strength of Eritrea's entitlement to independence depends on which year that law is deemed relevant to.

[101] See *Ivanţoc and Others* v *Moldova and Russia*, Application no. 23687/05, judgment of 15 November 2011, para 10.

[102] See the chapters in this volume by Christopher Waters (175–190) and Farhad Mirzayev (191–213).

[103] One might argue that Italy played a critical role as the colonial power. But for purposes of Eritrea's self-determination claim it was Italy's absence, and the concomitant path to decolonization, that was critical.

consent by the new Ethiopian government, its wartime ally. But assuming the rights were not extinguished and ultimately contributed to the international community's willingness to recognize an independent Eritrea, how is their endurance relevant to the CIS cases?

One might argue that any rights to self-determination possessed by the 'frozen' territories cannot be superseded by factual developments mitigating against their autonomy. These would include lack of widespread recognition, continuing assertions of authority by the parent state, failure to win military victories, and lack of local control over certain governmental functions. While these facts are present in some of the conflicts, the majority seem to involve the opposite situation: territories operating with varying degrees of independence from their parent states but failing to achieve recognition. Because such de facto independence (in varying degrees) appears not to have enhanced the CIS territories' self-determination claims, their very different situation might not alter the relevance of the Eritrea case, for one could argue that just as the *failure* to exercise self-determination rights in Eritrea did not alter their ongoing validity, so the exercise of autonomy in the CIS cases does not *create* rights to independence where none previously existed. That is, facts on the ground do not move a 'people' from right-holder or non-right-holder. As a former colonial territory, Eritrea would always be entitled to self-determination. As territories within sovereign states with internationally recognized borders, the CIS entities may well never be entitled to the right. As is obvious, independence may be achieved or frustrated entirely apart from any legal entitlement. But that is not the phenomenon under discussion here.

A second possible lesson could buttress this conclusion: that a claim of remedial secession cannot be achieved where a group claims no more than (a) subordination within the parent state's political system and (b) violence and killing resulting from fighting a secessionist civil war. Eritrean autonomy rights were wholly extinguished in 1962 and Ethiopia imposed its national political institutions and cultural norms on the territory. The Ethiopian army committed widespread atrocities, but those occurred in the course of fighting in response to the Eritrean independence struggle.[104] But international law clearly permits governments to put down rebel movements, as evidenced by its ongoing preference for territorial integrity over secessionist claims. The mere fact that Eritreans were killed in a war that Ethiopia was entitled to wage, therefore, cannot trigger remedial secession. The justification must come from other acts. Ethiopian forces clearly committed war crimes and crimes against humanity in the course of the conflict, though evidence of genocide is lacking. The question, then, is whether these *jus in bello* violations trigger the right. In the CIS cases, therefore, unlawful *jus in bello* violations must be separated from the fact of the government opposing secession with force.

[104] I do not suggest that Ethiopia's actions were in any way appropriate or legally justified. I am simply distinguishing atrocities that take place in the course of an armed conflict initiated by forces seeking independence from atrocities employed as a means to political ends, such as repressing political dissent or engaging in genocide. It is possible, of course, that a state might experience both.

A third lesson concerns the critical role of international organizations in secessionist struggles. Surely one of the reasons why Eritrean self-determination rights endured was the deep involvement of the United Nations, both in its investigation of the various options for disposition and in the General Assembly's final approval of the federation. The UN considered and rejected full integration into Ethiopia. When Ethiopia took that very step in 1962, its legitimacy was thus easy to determine. The steepest hurdle to independence or any form of *de jure* autonomy for the CIS territories is the lack of international recognition. Just as the endurance of Eritrea's rights can be traced to the General Assembly's collective decision in 1952, so too the CIS territories' lack of rights can be attributed in part to the failure of any international organization to assist in a collective disposition. Of course the barriers to doing so are substantial: the UN acquired authority in Eritrea not on its own initiative but by reference by the Four Powers. But it represents a collective preference for autonomy missing in the CIS cases.

A final lesson concerns the limits of legal argumentation in conflicts that involve the major powers. With the United States and Soviet Union supporting successive Ethiopian regimes opposed to Eritrean independence, the rebels had little chance of success. In most of the CIS cases, Russian influence and interests loom large. In both situations the involvement of a permanent member of the Security Council precludes the most obvious form of collective involvement. This is a particular tragedy for the CIS cases given the Council's now regular involvement in mediating and remediating internal conflicts.

VI. Conclusions

It is possible that the parties to the CIS conflicts have missed the opportunity for international involvement that is the distinguishing feature of the Eritrean case. The General Assembly's validation of Eritrean autonomy rights came at the tail-end of a postwar settlement process which, from the beginning, ensured that Eritrea's fate would be a matter of international concern. That seems impossible to replicate in the CIS cases, largely because of Russian influence. But if the dissolution of the Soviet Union, the terms of independence for its constituent units, and the creation of the CIS had involved an international organization that, in some fashion, could have addressed the claims of minority groups within the new state, then ongoing international involvement in subsequent conflicts could have been legitimized. Another relevant parallel would be the minority protection regimes resulting from the settlements following World War I. Absent such a presence at their creation, carving out a role for international organizations in the CIS cases, let alone one with the sort of authority exercised by the General Assembly in Eritrea, will be a very difficult task.

Postscript: Self-Determination, Secession, and the Crimean Crisis 2014

Christian Walter[1]

When the authors of this book met in February 2012 for the preparatory workshop in Munich, none of the conflicts treated in the case studies was on the front page of the newspapers. All of them had been refrozen after a more or less warm period of thaw.[2] At the time, analysing self-determination and secession basically seemed an academic exercise with the aim of inquiring into the possible consequences of the ICJ's Kosovo Advisory Opinion on the territory of the CIS.

Two years later, in the final stage of checking the proofs of this book, things could not be more different: the developments in the Crimea have put self-determination and secession back at the top of the international agenda. In contrast to many other international crises, international law plays a predominant role in the arguments presented by all players concerned. While many states believe that the 'reunification'[3] between Russia and the Crimea violates international law,[4] Russia and the relevant actors on the peninsula argue in terms of self-determination[5] and the protection of civilians.[6] The United States,[7] the

[1] I am enormously indebted to Stephan Lorentz, Paulus Suh, Antje von Ungern-Sternberg, and Markus Vordermayer for their comments on earlier drafts of this Postscript and their suggestions and ideas when we were discussing the legal issues raised by the developments in the Crimea. The manuscript was finalized on 15 April 2014.

[2] B Bowring, 'Transnistria' (ch 8 in this volume), 161–6; C Waters, 'South Ossetia' (ch 9 in this volume), 176–81; F Mirzayev, 'Abkhazia' (ch 10 in this volume), 191–4; H Krüger, 'Nagorno-Karabakh' (ch 11 in this volume), 214–16.

[3] Term used by President Putin in his speech of 18 March 2014, <http://eng.kremlin.ru/transcripts/6889>, accessed 9 April 2014.

[4] See in particular UNGA Res 68/262 (27 March 2014) (adopted by 100 votes to 11, 58 abstentions): 'calling upon all states [...] not to recognize any alteration of the status of the Autonomous Republic of Crimea and the city of Sevastopol on the basis of the [...] referendum'; see also Joint statement on Crimea by President of the European Council Herman Van Rompuy and President of the European Commission José Manuel Barroso, EUCO 63/14; Joint declaration on Ukraine by the Foreign Ministers of the Triangle of Weimar Frank-Walter Steinmeier (Germany), Laurent Fabius (France), and Radoslaw Sikorski (Poland) on 31 March 2014, <http://www.auswaertiges-amt.de/DE/Infoservice/Presse/Meldungen/2014/140331_Gemeinsame_Erklärung_zur_Ukraine.html>, accessed 9 April 2014.

[5] See eg Speech by President Putin on 18 March 2014 (n 3): ('[...] we had to help create conditions so that the residents of Crimea for the first time in history were able to peacefully express their free will regarding their own future.')

[6] See eg Speech by President Putin on 18 March 2014 (n 3): ('[...] the residents of Crimea and Sevastopol turned to Russia for help in defending their rights and lives, in preventing the events that were unfolding and are still underway in Kiev, Donetsk, Kharkov and other Ukrainian cities.')

[7] Executive Order 13660 of 6 March 2014 blocking Property of certain persons contributing to the situation in Ukraine [2014] Federal Register Vol. 79 No. 46, Executive Order 13662 of 20 March 2014 Federal Register Vol. 79 No. 56.

European Union,[8] and others[9] have decided on sanctions as counter-measures and political analysts speak of a return of the Cold War.[10] In other words: the legal aspects of secession and self-determination have been propelled to new heights in international politics, most probably even beyond their importance during the Kosovo crisis.

Sober legal analysis requires distance and an assessment of the facts which is as comprehensive as possible. Both are difficult at a time where contradictory factual and legal claims are being made by the parties involved. Nevertheless, this book would be incomplete without a perspective on the developments on the Crimea. Thus, a preliminary attempt at analysing the development in the light of the Kosovo Opinion of the ICJ and against the background of the other CIS conflicts treated in this book shall be made in this postscript to the book.

The analysis starts with asking for similarities and differences between the Crimea and the four case studies treated in this book (I). An important difference is seen in the fact that the Crimea does not strive for independent statehood but for integration into Russia. This difference is taken up in the next section, which enquires into the legality of the declaration of independence by the Crimean Parliament and the referendum on joining Russia under the parameters established in the Kosovo Advisory Opinion (II). Here, the interstate obligation to respect the territorial integrity of other states becomes the decisive argument. In a third step, the question of whether the Crimea could rely on self-determination is addressed (III), before arguments relating to the protection of Russians abroad (IV) and the principle of *uti possidetis iuris* (V) are dealt with. The postscript closes by considering legal consequences for the future development of the law on self-determination and secession (VI).

I. The Crimea and the Other CIS Conflicts Treated in this Book: Similarities and Differences

The crumbling of the Soviet Union, as Thomas Burri puts it, serves as the trigger in all four conflicts treated in this book.[11] From a political science perspective all

[8] Council Decision 2014/145/CFSP of 17 March 2014 concerning restrictive measures in respect of actions undermining or threatening the territorial integrity, sovereignty and independence of Ukraine [2014] OJ L78/6.

[9] See eg the Council of Europe's Parliamentary Assembly in its Resolution 1990 (2014) of 10 April 2014 (suspending, among others, the Russian delegation's voting rights until the end of the 2014 session).

[10] See eg S Markov (Moscow Institute of Political Studies), 'Russia Must Stop U.S. Expansion in Ukraine', *The Moscow Times Online* (19 March 2014), <http://www.themoscowtimes.com/opinion/article/russia-must-stop-us-expansion-in-ukraine/496137.html>, accessed 11 April 2014; D Trenin (Carnegie Moscow Centre), 'The Crisis in Crimea Could Lead the World into a Second Cold War', *The Observer Online* (2 March 2014), http://www.theguardian.com/commentisfree/2014/mar/02/crimea-crisis-russia-ukraine-cold-war, accessed 11 April 2014.

[11] T Burri, 'Secession in the CIS: Causes, Consequences, and Emerging Principles' (ch 7 in this volume), 142.

of the conflicts are labelled as 'frozen conflicts', denoting that military hostilities have generally stopped without an overall solution to the roots of the conflict having been found.[12] The term 'frozen' is used to describe the stalemate, which may be due to military, political, economic, or other factors.[13] Usually the moment of freezing is dated to the immediate post-Soviet period when, in the course of the disintegration of the Soviet Union, sub-units of the former Soviet republics fought their own battles of independence, but without succeeding in this endeavour. Being sub-units of third (Abkhazia) or fourth level (South Ossetia, Nagorno-Karabakh) they had to witness the republics, the sub-units of the second order of which they formed part (in the case of Abkhazia: Georgia; in the case of Nagorno-Karabakh: Azerbaijan; in the case of South Ossetia: Georgia and, finally, in the case of Transnistria: Moldova), achieving independence which they, as lower sub-units, were denied.[14]

Will the Crimea become, as some analysts suggest,[15] yet another frozen conflict on the territory of the former Soviet Union? The comparison with the conflicts treated in this volume suggests caution. There are at least two factors which distinguish the situation in the Crimea from the frozen conflicts treated in this book: the claim for independence from Ukraine was not triggered by the disintegration of the Soviet Union (1) and the Crimean movement does not strive for independent statehood but for integration into the Russian Federation (2). The question arises as to whether these distinctions are of relevance for the legal analysis (3).

1. Not triggered by the disintegration of the Soviet Union

Just as all four conflicts analysed in the case studies, the Crimean conflict has its roots in the multi-ethnic composition of the population living on the peninsula. According to the 2001 census 58.5 per cent are Russians, 24.4 per cent Ukrainians, and 12.1 per cent Crimean Tartars, all of which have been ascribed the quality of 'people' for the purposes of the right to self-determination.[16] Ukraine had no history of autonomous statehood prior to its declaration of independence from the Soviet Union in 1990. In all the other four conflicts, claims for independent statehood were made in the immediate period of dissolution of the Soviet Union

[12] S MacFarlane, 'Frozen Conflicts in the Former Soviet Union–The Case of Georgia/South Ossetia', 18 OSCE Ybk 23, (23, footnote 1).

[13] S MacFarlane (n 12), 24 – 25.

[14] In contrast to the Republics none of the entities mentioned, had a right to secession under the former Soviet Constitution, see A Peters, 'The Principle of Uti Possidetis Juris: How Relevant Is It for Issues of Secession?' (ch 6 in this volume), 120.

[15] See eg D Barlow, 'Russians and Ukrainians Battle over Crimea, But What about Tartars? The Tragic Perils of Nationalism', Cato Institute (24 March 2014), <http://www.cato.org/publications/commentary/russians-ukrainians-battle-over-crimea-what-about-tartars-tragic-perils>, accessed 11 April 2014.

[16] B Bowring, 'The Crimean Autonomy – Innovation or Anomaly', in M Weller and S Wolff (eds), *Autonomy, Self-governance, and Conflict Resolution: Innovative Approaches to Institutional Design in Divided Societies* (Routledge 2005), 75.

in the early 1990s.[17] One might thus assume that, just as with the four other conflicts treated in this book, the conflict around the Crimea is a consequence of the dissolution of the Soviet Union. While the parallels with the other conflicts cannot be denied, some important differences also merit attention.

As has been highlighted by President Putin and other Russian officials, the Crimea has historically been associated with Russia.[18] Its allocation to Ukraine in 1954 seems to have been the consequence of a whim of then General Secretary of the Communist Party Nikita Khrushchev, who had strong ties to Ukraine. Immediately after the break-up of the Soviet Union a conflict over the allocation of the Black Sea Fleet and other military installations arose between Ukraine and Russia and nationalist tendencies gained support on both sides.[19] In 1992 the Russian Duma claimed that the transfer of the Crimea to Ukraine had been illegal and in 1993 it declared that the Crimea was part of Russia.[20] The difficulties were finally overcome with the 1996 Ukrainian Constitution, in which the Crimea was granted the unique status of 'Autonomous Republic of Crimea' within Ukraine.[21] This led to the 1997 Treaty on Friendship, Cooperation, and Partnership between Ukraine and the Russian Federation, in which Russia acknowledged the Ukrainian borders.[22] Thus, in contrast to the other four case studies, in 1997 one could assume that the latent conflict about the Crimea was not only frozen but even formally settled by an international treaty between Russia and Ukraine and by a constitutionally guaranteed status of autonomy for the Crimea.[23]

However, since the mid-2000s, stability in the Crimea gradually came under pressure, for a number of reasons. First, and probably most importantly, a policy of 'Ukrainianization' under Presidents Kuchma and Jushtchenko led to growing reservations on the part of the non-Ukrainian population.[24] In June 2009 the OSCE High Commissioner on National Minorities voiced his concerns about reports 'about the tendency towards increasing radicalization and xenophobia on the

[17] B Bowring, 'Transnistria' (ch 8 in this volume), 161; C Waters, 'South Ossetia' (ch 9 in this volume), 176; F Mirzayev, 'Abkhazia' (ch 10 in this volume), 192 et seq.; H Krüger, 'Nagorno-Karabakh' (ch 11 in this volume), 215 et seq.

[18] Speech by President Putin on 18 March 2014 (n 3) ('In people's hearts and minds, Crimea has always been an inseparable part of Russia.').

[19] For details of the development see M Galeotti, 'The Crimea: Russia's Ukrainian peninsula', IBRU Boundary and Security Bulletin, January 1994, 50 et seq.

[20] B Bowring, 'The Crimean Autonomy' (n 15), 82; according to D Wydra, 'The Crimea Conundrum: The Tug of War Between Russia and Ukraine on the Questions of Autonomy and Self-Determination' (2004) 10 International Journal on Minority and Group Rights 111, 115, the following remark was made by then Foreign Minister Kozyrev: 'The donation in 1954 was illegal, as it was only a decision by the communist elite'. See also R Solchanyk, 'Crimea: Between Ukraine and Russia' in M Drohobycky (ed), *Crimea: Dynamics, Challenges and Prospects* (Rowman & Little 1995), 5.

[21] No other region had comparable autonomy. See Chapters IX and X of the 1996 Constitution of Ukraine; English translation available at <http://faolex.fao.org/docs/pdf/ukr127467E.pdf>, accessed 15 April 2014.

[22] For an English translation see DB Stewart, 'The Russian Ukrainian Friendship treaty and the search for stability in Eastern Europe' (1997) accessible at <http://www.dtic.mil/dtic/tr/fulltext/u2/a341002.pdf>, Appendix.

[23] B Bowring, 'The Crimean Autonomy' (n 16), 93 et seq.

[24] F Evers, 'Damaged Prospects/Damaged Dialogue in Ukraine and Crimea: The Current Situation in Ukraine and Future Co-operation with the OSCE' (2010) 16 OSCE Ybk 221, 222–4.

peninsula'.[25] Second, the Ukraine got trapped in an ambiguous strategic position as far as its security interests were concerned. Perspectives for closer association with EU and/or NATO did not materialize and the relations with Russia were largely dependent on respective Ukrainian presidents. In contrast to some of his predecessors, President Janukovich had managed to establish closer ties with Russia.[26] His removal from office in February 2014 thus served as a trigger for the secessionist movement in the Crimea.

In sum, the disintegration of the Soviet Union certainly is a decisive factor in a long-term analysis of the events in the Crimea. However, in contrast to the four other case studies, it cannot be considered the trigger for the Crimean crisis. In the years following the dissolution of the Soviet Union a seemingly stable legal solution had been found which was safeguarded by the 1996 Ukrainian Constitution, and, internationally, by the 1997 Treaty on Friendship, Cooperation, and Partnership between Russia and Ukraine. In the end it was the deterioration of Ukraino–Russian relations following the Majdan demonstrations which triggered the conflict in the Crimea.

2. Claim for statehood is an instrument for accession to Russia

A further difference relates to the purpose of secession. In the four cases treated in this book secession, if achieved successfully, would have resulted in independent statehood. By contrast, Crimean independence was, right from the beginning, instrumental for finally joining Russia. This is made abundantly clear by the wording of the 'Declaration of Independence' which the Crimean Parliament adopted on 11 March 2014 and by the further course of events. The Declaration of Independence was made explicitly subject to a positive referendum on joining Russia.[27] This referendum was held only five days later, on 16 March 2014.

[25] Statement by the OSCE High Commissioner on National Minorities to the Permanent Council of 18 June 2009, available at <http://www.osce.org/hcnm/37812>.

[26] F Evers (n 24), 227–8.

[27] 'Declaration of Independence of the Autonomous Republic of Crimea and Sevastopol:

> We, the members of the parliament of the Autonomous Republic of Crimea and the Sevastopol City Council, with regard to the charter of the United Nations and a whole range of other international documents and taking into consideration the confirmation of the status of Kosovo by the United Nations International Court of Justice on July, 22, 2010, which says that unilateral declaration of independence by a part of the country doesn't violate any international norms, make this decision jointly:
>
> 1. If a decision to become part of Russia is made at the referendum of the March 16, 2014, Crimea including the Autonomous Republic of Crimea and the city of Sevastopol will be announced an independent and sovereign state with a republican order.
> 2. Republic of Crimea will be a democratic, laic and multinational state, with an obligation to maintain peace, international and intersectarian consent in its territory.
> 3. If the referendum brings the respective results, Republic of Crimea as an independent and sovereign state will turn to the Russian Federation with the proposition to accept the Republic of Crimea on the basis of a respective interstate treaty into the Russian Federation as a new constituent entity of the Russian Federation.'; Declaration approved by the Resolution of the Supreme Council of the Autonomous Republic of Crimea at the extraordinary plenary session on March 11, 2014 (signed by the Chairman of the Supreme Council of the Autonomous Republic of Crimea Vladimir Konstantinov) and by the Decision of the Sevastopol City Council at the extraordinary plenary session on March 11, 2014 (signed by the Chairman of the Sevastopol city council Yury Doynikov).

According to the official result, 85 per cent of the Crimean population participated, 97 per cent of which voted in favour of accession to Russia.[28] On 17 March 2014, based on its previous declaration and the outcome of the referendum, the Supreme Council of the Crimea declared the independence of the Crimea,[29] which was immediately recognized by President Putin in an Executive Order.[30] Finally, on 18 March 2014 a treaty between the Crimea and Russia on accession was signed.[31]

Both the clear wording of the Declaration of Independence of 11 March 2014 and the speed with which the next steps were taken underline the main difference from the other conflicts treated here: in the case of the Crimea secession was not an instrument for achieving independent statehood, but a transitory step in the process of integrating into Russia.

3. Consequences for the further legal analysis

In order to avoid misunderstandings it should be stressed that the mere fact that an entity wishes to join another state does not exclude its claim from the scope of self-determination.[32] Nevertheless, the situation is different, because the international legal obligations of the third state must be taken into account. The integration into a neighbouring state invariably results in a change of borders between the two states. What is taken from Ukraine is given to Russia. Concerning claims for secession aiming at independence, international law only has to look at the relation between the seceding entity and its parent state (and thus at an issue which, before secession has become effective, seems purely internal). By contrast, claims for secession in order to be then integrated into another state also affect the international legal relations between the two states concerned. It is to this relationship that the analysis concerning the Crimea must therefore turn.

See <http://www.rada.crimea.ua/app/2988>; an English translation is available at <http://www.voltairenet.org/article182723.html>, accessed 15 April 2014.

28 BBC News, 'Russia's Vladimir Putin Recognises Crimea as Nation' (17 March 2014), <http://www.bbc.com/news/world-europe-26621726>, accessed 10 April 2014. On the question of participation in the referendum see eg *The Economist*, 'Ukraine's Amputation' (17 March 2014), <http://www.economist.com/blogs/easternapproaches/2014/03/crimea-votes-secede>, accessed 10 April 2014.

29 BBC News, 'Crimean Parliament Formally Applies to Join Russia' (17 March 2014), <http://www.bbc.com/news/world-europe-26609667>, accessed 10 April 2014.

30 Executive order of 18 March 2014 <http://eng.news.kremlin.ru/acts/6888>, accessed 9 April 2014.

31 Press Release 'Executive Order on Executing Agreement on Admission of Republic of Crimea into the Russian Federation' (18 March 2014), <http://eng.news.kremlin.ru/acts/6888>, accessed 15 April 2014.

32 S Oeter, 'Self-Determination' in B Simma et al. (eds), *The Charter of the United Nations—A Commentary* (3rd edn, OUP 2012) MN 33.

II. The Principle of Territorial Integrity in the Kosovo Advisory Opinion

The Crimean 'Declaration of Independence' explicitly refers to the Kosovo Advisory Opinion and quotes it as authority in order to demonstrate that it does not violate international law ('taking into consideration the confirmation of the status of Kosovo by the United Nations International Court of Justice on July 22, 2010, which says that unilateral declaration of independence by a part of the country doesn't violate any international norms'). The following section demonstrates that this reference to the Kosovo Advisory Opinion is deficient because it overlooks the norms of international law which govern the interstate relationship between Russia and Ukraine. While it is true that the ICJ in its Kosovo Advisory Opinion holds that international law does not prohibit unilateral declarations of independence (1), the Advisory Opinion refers to limits and conditions, notably the absence of use of force by third states, which are not met in the case of Ukraine (2). In consequence, the Declaration of Independence of Crimea, in contrast to the Kosovo Declaration, is not in conformity with international law (3).

1. No international legal protection against disaggregation from within

The main line of argument of the ICJ in its Kosovo Advisory Opinion is analysed in Chapter 2 of this book. The decisive factor in the Court's reasoning is its limitation of the principle of territorial integrity to the interstate context.[33] As has been pointed out in the analysis in Chapter 2, the approach of the Court must be read as a contribution to the solution of the Kosovo dispute rather than as an attempt at developing the law of self-determination and secession.[34] In doing this, the Court excluded non-state actors from the application of the principle of territorial integrity.

If the inapplicability of the principle of territorial integrity to non-state actors is the decisive factor, then the approach chosen by the Court cannot be limited to declarations of independence only. Rather, any preparatory act of non-state actors on their way to independence must, in principle, be seen as covered by the exclusion from the reach of international law assumed by the ICJ,[35] the

[33] *Accordance with International Law of the Unilateral Declaration of Independence in Respect of Kosovo* (Advisory Opinion) 2010, <http://www.icj-cij.org/docket/files/141/15987.pdf> accessed 9 August 2013, para. 80: '[...] the scope of the principle of territorial integrity is confined to the sphere of relations between States.'

[34] C Walter, 'The Kosovo Advisory Opinion: What It Says and What It Does Not Say' (ch 2 in this volume), 25.

[35] Cf. eg E Cirkovic, 'An Analysis of the ICJ Advisory Opinion on Kosovo's Unilateral Declaration of Independence' (2010) 11 German LJ 895 (905, 912); R Muharremi, 'A Note on the ICJ Advisory Opinion on Kosovo' (2010) 11 German LJ 867 (879); G Anderson, 'Unilateral Non-Colonial Secession and the Use of Force' (2013) 28 Conn J Int'l L 197 (215); R Tricot/B Sander, 'The Broader Consequences of the International Court of Justice's Advisory Opinion on the Unilateral Declaration of Independence in Respect of Kosovo' (2011) 49 Colum J Transnat'l L 321 (337).

application of the use of force or other violations of international law applicable to non-state actors being possible exceptions.[36] As a result, a referendum organized by non-state actors in order to determine the will of the population in the possibly seceding territory is (again, in principle) beyond the scope of the international law principle of territorial integrity. It would result in an unacceptable contradiction if international law, which has been gradually developing an obligation to hold referenda when relying on self-determination[37] and which favours democratic decision-making processes in general,[38] were to prohibit what it tends to promote. In consequence, there are no reasons why the Court's line of argument concerning declarations of independence should not be applied also to referenda. To repeat the conclusion in Chapter 2 on this point: According to the ICJ, international law does not protect states against disaggregation from within.[39]

In consequence, the Court's reasoning in the Kosovo Advisory Opinion is, in principle, applicable also to the Declaration of Independence of the Crimea and the referendum to which it was linked. However, the limits and conditions for the international legal silence on declarations of independence (and referenda) which are to be derived from the Kosovo Opinion must also be respected. In other words, the question is raised: is Crimea really a case of disaggregation from within?

2. Limits and conditions in the Kosovo Advisory Opinion

In dealing with the question of international legal limitations on secession, the Court takes up an argument presented by some states which had referred to several Security Council resolutions in which declarations of independence were condemned. The relevance of these resolutions is, however, denied by the Court in pointing out that in the instances covered by the resolutions, the illegality of the resolutions did not derive from the unilateral character of the declarations of independence in question 'but from the fact that they were, or would have been, connected with the unlawful use of force or other egregious violations of norms of general international law, in particular those of a peremptory character (*jus cogens*)'.[40] The situations concerned are the presence of Turkish troops in Northern Cyprus,[41] the role of Serbia in relation to the Republika Srpska,[42] and the Apartheid regime concerning the declaration of independence of South Rhodesia.[43]

36 See again the discussion in C Walter (n 34), 19–23.

37 A Peters, *Das Gebietsreferendum im Völkerrecht* (Nomos 1995), 75 et seq. and 321 et seq.

38 TM Franck, 'The Emerging Right to Democratic Governance' (1992) 86 AJIL 46; F Ehm, *Das völkerrechtliche Demokratiegebot – Eine Untersuchung zur schwindenden Wertneutralität des Völkerrechts gegenüber den staatlichen Binnenstrukturen* (Mohr Siebeck 2013).

39 C Walter (n 34), 22.

40 *Kosovo* (n 31), para. 81.

41 UNSC Res 541 (18 Nov 1983) UN Doc S/Res/541.

42 UNSC Res 787 (16 Nov 1992) UN Doc S/Res/787.

43 UNSC Res 216 (12 Nov 1965) UN Doc S/Res/216; UNSC Res 217 (20 Nov 1965) UN Doc S/Res/217.

One may ask whether it is really necessary to tie the violations of international law just mentioned (violation of the prohibition of the use of force, massive human rights violations) necessarily to the declaration of independence. Wouldn't it be possible to assess the legality of the respective actions separately, i.e. without these violations of other norms of international law infecting the declarations of independence? The wording of the Kosovo Opinion is quite clear as to the result:

> The Court notes, however, that in all of those instances the Security Council was making a determination as regards the concrete situation existing at the time that those declarations of independence were made; the ***illegality attached to the declarations of independence*** thus stemmed not from the unilateral character of these declarations as such, but from the fact that they were, or would have been, connected with the unlawful use of force or other egregious violations of norms of general international law, in particular those of a peremptory character (*jus cogens*).[44]

It must be concluded from this passage that declarations of independence in which illegal external use of force or threat of use of force is involved are not covered by the Court's opinion. In his contribution to this book, Antonello Tancredi underlines this point regarding the international treatment of the use of force in the four case studies.[45] The Russian intervention in Georgia (with regard to Abkhazia and South Ossetia) and the Armenian intervention in Azerbaijan (with regard to Nagorno-Karabakh) have been qualified as violations of international law.[46] It thus can hardly come as a surprise that the respective claims for secession have been rejected by the majority of states: Abkhazia and South Ossetia were recognized by only a tiny minority of states (Russia, Venezuela, Nicaragua, Nauru, Tuvalu, and—for Abkhazia—also Vanuatu).[47] As a reaction to the developments in the Crimea, Tuvalu has withdrawn its recognition of both South Ossetia and Abkhazia and has instead established diplomatic relations with Georgia.[48] Irrespective of the possible motives for such a withdrawal and also avoiding any legal assessment of the implications of a withdrawal of recognition under the declaratory theory of recognition, the overall number of recognitions of South Ossetia and Abkhazia is so low that the respective claims for independence cannot be accepted as valid practice. Transnistria and Nagorno-Karabakh are not recognized at all.[49]

It should be noted that the Court explicitly attaches the illegality to the declarations of independence as such (and not any other activity related to them).[50] This seems astonishing at first sight. The Court's position can only be explained if neither declarations of independence nor their authors are generally outside the reach

[44] *Kosovo* (n 33), para. 81 (emphasis added).

[45] A Tancredi, 'Secession and Use of Force' (ch 5 in this volume), 92 et seq.

[46] F Mirzayev (n 2), 204 et seq.; C Waters (n 2), 180 et seq.; T Burri (n 11), 143.

[47] For references see F Mirzayev (n 2), 194.

[48] Statement of the Georgian Foreign Ministry regarding the establishment of diplomatic and consular relations on 31 March 2014, <http://www.mfa.gov.ge/index.php?lang_id=ENG&sec_id=59&info_id=17401> accessed 10 April 2014.

[49] H Krüger (n 2), 227; B Bowring (n 2), 165.

[50] See the quotation at n 44.

of international law. This point has already been made in Chapter 2.[51] But even then, an international legal norm needs to be found which specifically addresses either the declarations or their authors. Why should a possible violation of the prohibition of the use of force by a third state affect the legality of a declaration of independence made by a secessionist group? One possible explanation could be that Security Council resolutions may 'internationalize' declarations of independence. Under such a reading, the respective passage in resolution 787 (1992)[52] would not reflect the general position of international law on territorial integrity, but merely follow from the decision of the Security Council to ban such a declaration in the Bosnian context.

However, such a reading of resolution 787 (1992)—and of the other condemnations of unilateral declarations in resolutions 216 (1965), 217 (1965), and 541 (1983)—would miss the larger framework in which the principle of territorial integrity must be situated. The principle of territorial integrity serves the wider purpose of stability and foreseeability in international relations.[53] While international law may not protect against disaggregation from within, it certainly protects against external intervention inciting or fuelling secessionist movements.

3. Consequences for the legal analysis concerning the Crimea

It is against this background that the situation around the Crimean Declaration of Independence must be analysed. The analysis is complicated since, at the time of writing of this postscript, many of the factual circumstances are still unclear and subject to speculation. But even with the precaution just mentioned, the following assessment can be made:

a) Violation of the Prohibition on the Use of Force by Russia prior to the Declaration of Independence?

Rumours of Russian military intervention were heard throughout the hot phase of the crisis prior to the Crimean referendum.[54] These rumours have to some extent been confirmed by OSCE observers in Ukraine, who, however, were denied access to Crimea by Russian-speaking 'self-defence groups'.[55] Apart from that, the broad

[51] C Walter (n 34), 25.

[52] The passage reads: 'The Security Council [...] 3. Strongly reaffirms its call on *all parties and others concerned* to respect strictly the territorial integrity of the Republic of Bosnia and Herzegovina, and affirms that any entities unilaterally declared or arrangements imposed in contravention thereof will not be accepted; [...]' (emphasis added).

[53] Cf. *Case Concerning the Temple of Preah Vihear (Cambodia v Thailand)* (Merits) [1962] ICJ Rep 6 (34); for an historical account of the development of territorial integrity and the underlying concepts, see M Zacher, 'The Territorial Integrity Norm: International Boundaries and the Use of Force' (2001) 55 Int'l Org 215 (esp. 237 et seq.).

[54] See eg S Erlanger, 'Ukrainian Government Rushes to Dampen Secessionist Sentiment', *NY Times Online* (2 March 2014), <http://www.nytimes.com/2014/03/03/world/europe/ukraine.html?_r=0>, accessed 11 April 2014.

[55] See eg P Felstead, 'OSCE Evidence Lifts Lid on "Little Green Men" in Crimea', Jane's Online (12 March 2014), <http://www.janes.com/article/35275/osce-evidence-lifts-lid-on-little-green-men-in-crimea>, accessed 11 April 2014.

authorization by the Russian Federation Council to use military force (potentially within the whole of Ukraine) indicates at least a threat of force.[56] An assessment of the legality of Russian military presence on the Crimea must furthermore take into account the Agreement between Ukraine and the Russian Federation on the Status and Conditions of the Russian Federation Black Sea Fleet's Stay on Ukrainian Territory, which allows for a Russian military presence in Crimea.[57] To the extent that the conditions laid down in the treaty were respected, no violation of Art. 2 (4) UN Charter could be established. However, Ukraine claims that Russia violated the provisions of the Agreement.[58] Given the unclear factual situation, only a hypothetical conclusion operating on the reverse assumption may be formulated: if Russian military presence in the Crimea beyond what Ukraine agreed to can be established, this constitutes a violation of the prohibition of the use of force. Under such circumstances the Crimean Declaration falls directly within the scope of exceptions formulated by the ICJ in its Kosovo Advisory Opinion, and thus has to be qualified as illegal.

b) Valid acquisition of the Crimea by Russia?

If no violation of the prohibition of the use of force prior to the Declaration of Independence can be established, the declaration is not clearly prohibited under the terms of the Kosovo Advisory Opinion. However, this by no means implies that the underlying claim for secession is accepted and produces legal effects. These issues will be addressed in section III. A further important difference between the Kosovar Declaration of Independence and the Crimean Declaration must be seen in the clear legal condition of accession to Russia. Under the terms of the Declaration, secession from Ukraine is a mere transitory step for the final accession to Russia. Hence, the Crimean secession claim by necessity affects the borders between Russia and Ukraine. While non-state actors are, according to the Kosovo Advisory Opinion, not bound by the principle of inviolability of borders, states are.[59] As far as the relations between Russia and Ukraine are concerned, this is not only a consequence of general international law, to which the ICJ referred in its Advisory Opinion, but is also clearly set out in Art. 3 of the 1997 Treaty

[56] See 'Vladimir Putin Submitted Appeal to the Federation Council' (1 March 2014), <http://eng.kremlin.ru/news/6751>, accessed 15 April 2014; with regard to the Federation Council's approval see Washington Post Online, 'Russian Parliament Approves Use of troops in Ukraine' (1 March 2014), <http://www.washingtonpost.com/world/europe/russian-parliament-approves-use-of-troops-in-crimea/2014/03/01/d1775f70-a151-11e3-a050-dc3322a94fa7_print.html>, accessed 15 April 2014.

[57] For an English translation see JL Black (ed.), *Russia & Eurasia Documents Annual* 1997 (1), 129.

[58] See the Statement 'On Violations of Ukraine's Laws in Force and of Ukrainian-Russian Agreements by Military Units of the Black Sea Fleet of the Russian Federation in the Territory of Ukraine' of 3 March 2014, available at <http://mfa.gov.ua/en/news-feeds/foreign-offices-news/18622-shhodo-porusheny-chinnogo-zakonodavstva-ukrajini-ta-ukrajinsyko-rosijsykih-ugod-vijsykovimi-formuvannyami-chf-rf-na-teritoriji-ukrajini>, accessed 10 April 2014.

[59] For a general account of the principle of territorial integrity (encompassing the principle of inviolability of borders), see S Blay, 'Territorial Integrity' in *Max Planck Encyclopedia of Public International Law* (2010), online at <http://opil.ouplaw.com/home/EPIL>, accessed 11 April 2014.

of Friendship, Cooperation, and Partnership between Ukraine and the Russian Federation.[60]

Russia and the actors in the Crimea seem to qualify the developments as having occurred in two distinct legal steps: 1) secession and creation of the 'Republic of Crimea' as a new state,[61] 2) accession and incorporation of that new state into the Russian Federation.[62] However, the two-step theory cannot operate solely on the basis of the declaration of independence. It requires that a new state has indeed been created, which means that all criteria for statehood would have had to be established prior to the act of incorporation. However, in spite of the recognition of the 'Republic of Crimea' by Russia,[63] this was not the case. The 'Republic of Crimea' never had the possibility to acquire independent public power.[64] Given the condition contained in the Declaration of Independence, it could be argued that there was not even the intention to exercise independent and sovereign power. Apart from this, the extremely short period of time between the referendum on accession to Russia (16 March 2014) and the Execution of the Agreement on Admission of Republic of Crimea into the Russian Federation (18 March 2014) practically excludes that the 'Republic of Crimea' managed to effectively establish independent public authority. As far as independent authority is concerned, the criteria set up by the Independent Commission of Jurists in the Åland-Islands dispute are still relevant. The Commission considered that 'a stable political organisation' is necessary and that the public authorities must be 'strong enough to assert themselves throughout the territories of the State without the assistance of foreign troops'.[65] Under these criteria, the 'Republic of Crimea' lacked independent public authority and could not be qualified an independent state.

In consequence, as a matter of law, the territory of the Crimea continues to belong to Ukraine. A change of borders cannot, therefore, legally become effective without Ukrainian consent. The acquisition of territory against the

[60] The provision reads: 'The High Contracting Parties shall base their relationship on the principles of mutual respect; sovereign equality; territorial integrity; immutability of borders; peaceful settlement of disputes; nonuse of force or the threat of force including economic and other means of pressure; the right of their peoples to freely decide their fate; noninterference in internal affairs…'; reprinted in JL Black (ed.), *Russia & Eurasia Documents Annual* 1997 (1), 217; see also Art. 5 of the 'Minsk Agreement' (establishing the Commonwealth of Independent States) of 8 December 1991, (1992) 31 ILM 143, and the subsequent 'Alma Ata Declaration' of 21 December 1991, (1992) 31 ILM 148.

[61] Executive Order on recognizing Republic of Crimea (17 March 2014), <http://eng.news.kremlin.ru/acts/6884>, accessed 15 April 2014.

[62] See the Speech by the Russian Foreign Minister S Lavrov before the State Duma (20 March 2014), <http://www.mid.ru/brp_4.nsf/0/94D6676508BC6C4844257CA2005B0613>, accessed 15 April 2014 and the Press Release 'Executive Order on executing Agreement on Admission of Republic of Crimea into the Russian Federation' (18 March 2014), <http://eng.news.kremlin.ru/acts/6888>, accessed 15 April 2014.

[63] See again n 61.

[64] On the relationship between public authority and independence, see J Crawford, *Brownlie's Principles of International Law* (8th edn, OUP 2012), 129 et seq.

[65] League of Nations, *Official Journal* (1920) Sp Supp No 3, 9.

will of Ukraine as the legitimate territorial state must hence be qualified as illegal.[66]

c) Consequences for the international legal assessment of the referendum

What are the consequences of this analysis for the referendum? The referendum is used by Russia as a political and legal argument for legitimizing the territorial acquisition of the Crimea. However, the preceding analysis has shown that the referendum cannot have such a legitimizing effect as far as international legal relations between Ukraine and Russia are concerned. In the context of decolonization, and of self-determination in general, referenda are being treated favourably because they are a means of determining the will of the people concerned.[67] However, in relations between sovereign states they cannot provide for a title for the acquisition of territory against the will of the territorial state.

It is furthermore clear that the referendum was illegal under Ukrainian constitutional law, which does not provide for the possibility of holding a referendum on secession. In its Opinion no. 762/2014 of 21 March 2014, the Venice Commission additionally considered that the circumstances under which the referendum was held were incompatible with European democratic standards.[68] Accordingly, the Parliamentary Assembly of the Council of Europe declared that the outcome of the referendum had 'no legal effect'.[69]

III. Self-Determination and Secession

Leaving aside the Kosovo Advisory Opinion, which did not address substantive issues of self-determination and deliberately side-stepped the hotly disputed question of remedial secession, the Crimean claim for self-determination is nevertheless weak if considered under the law on self-determination as it currently stands. It is still the predominant position in state practice and in literature that self-determination does not grant a general right to secession (1). Even if one follows the growing number of voices claiming a right to remedial secession, the conditions for such a right are not met in the case of the Crimea (2).

1. Self-Determination does not grant a general right to secession

Leaving aside possible questions of who among the different groups in the population of the Crimea might rely on self-determination and assuming that the whole

[66] See generally MG Kohen/M Hébié, 'Territory, Acquisition', paras. 41 et seq., in *Max Planck Encyclopedia of Public International Law* (2011), available online at <http://opil.ouplaw.com/home/EPIL>, accessed 11 April 2014; Badinter Commission, Opinion No. 3 (11 January 1992), 2nd principle, ILM 31 (1992), 1499; EC Declaration on the Guidelines on the Recognition of New States in Eastern Europe and in the Soviet Union (16 December 1991), ILM 31 (1992), 1485.

[67] Peters (n 37), passim.

[68] CDL-AD(2014)002.

[69] Resolution 1988 (2014) of 9 April 2014, para. 16.

of the population of the peninsula might claim a right to self-determination,[70] the main obstacle in the Crimean position remains that there exists an overall consensus both in state practice and among lawyers in literature that self-determination does not grant a general right to secession.

In the Kosovo Advisory Proceedings, none of the states participating argued for a general right to secession. Even those backing the secessionist claim by Kosovo relied on 'remedial secession', which they construed as an exception to the general rule of territorial integrity.[71] Ironically, notably Russia made a specifically strong claim arguing that the principle of territorial integrity was of peremptory character and applied not only to states, but to all subjects of international law.[72] A similarly clear record results from the scholarly work on self-determination. A general right to secession as part of the right to self-determination is overwhelmingly rejected.[73] It also finds no support in international practice.[74] It must therefore be concluded that the Crimea cannot claim a right to secession on the basis of self-determination in general.

2. The conditions for 'remedial secession' are not met

The self-determination claim thus hinges on an alleged right to remedial secession. Even if one follows the proponents of such a right, the Crimean claim cannot be upheld, because the conditions for remedial secession are not met. The most widely accepted position on remedial secession can be found in the Canadian Supreme Court's decision on a possible secession of Quebec. According to the Canadian Supreme Court two constellations may be distinguished in which the right to self-determination may result in secession: colonial and oppressed peoples.[75] A third constellation was discussed which concerns situations where a people is excluded from internally exercising self-determination in a meaningful way.[76] The Court left the international legal acceptance of such a third constellation open, given that nothing indicated that Quebec could arguably claim the denial of internal self-determination.

In the Kosovo Advisory Proceedings it was again Russia which took a much more rigid stand on the question of 'remedial secession'. According to Russia the conditions for remedial secession should be 'limited to truly extreme circumstances,

[70] Bowring, 'The Crimean Autonomy' (n 16), 75 suggests all three (Ukrainians, Crimean Tartars, and Russians) may be qualified as 'people' for the purpose of self-determination.

[71] See, among others, the written submissions of the Kingdom of the Netherlands (17 April 2009, 7 et seq.), Switzerland (15 April 2009, 14 et seq.), Germany (17 April 2009, 32 et seq.) and Ireland (17 April 2009, 8 et seq.).

[72] Oral Statement of the Russian Federation, CR 2009/30 (8 December 2009), 46 (Gevorgian).

[73] J Crawford, *The Creation of States in International Law* (OUP 2006), 388–91; S Oeter, 'The Role of Recognition' (ch 4 in this volume), 45 (53 et seq.), C Tomuschat, 'Secession and Self-determination', in MG Kohen (ed), *Secession: International Law Perspectives* (CUP 2006) 23, 34; L Brillmayer, 'Secession and Self-Determination: A Territorial Interpretation' (1991) 16 Yale J Int'l L 177, 183.

[74] See documentation in J Crawford, *The Creation of States*, 388–418.

[75] *Reference re Secession of Quebec* (1998) 2 S.C.R. 217, paras. 131 et seq.

[76] *Reference re Secession* (n 72), para. 134.

such as an outright armed attack by the parent state, threatening the very existence of the people in question. Otherwise all efforts should be taken in order to settle the tension between the parent state and the ethnic community concerned within the framework of the existing state'.[77] Given the autonomous status of the Crimea within the Ukrainian constitutional order and in the absence of any indications of 'an outright armed attack' by Ukraine against the Crimea, certainly the standard formulated by Russia itself in the Kosovo proceedings was not met.

But even beyond that: the autonomy granted to the Crimea arguably also meets the standard applied by the Canadian Supreme Court in its hypothetical assessment of the situation in Quebec. The Canadian Supreme Court speaks of a situation in which the exercise of the 'right to self-determination internally is somehow being totally frustrated'.[78] Could this be seriously argued in a situation where the province in question enjoyed constitutional autonomy, with no claims of substantive violations having been heard of?[79] There does not seem to be any indication which supports that the autonomy granted under the Ukrainian Constitution was insufficient. This corresponds to the earlier analysis: secession of the Crimea was not about more autonomy, but about autonomy within a different state, Russia instead of Ukraine. To be sure: such a claim does not automatically fall outside the scope of self-determination. It could be argued that self-determination includes the possibility to decide on where to belong. But since the situation in the Crimea did not fulfil even the most generous criteria for remedial secession, a decision on integration into Russia (which necessarily means secession from Ukraine) cannot be taken against the will of Ukraine.

IV. Protection of Russians Abroad?

At the beginning of the Crimean crisis, official Russian statements indicated that military intervention was necessary in order to protect Russians in the Crimea, who were said to be in danger given growing Ukrainian nationalism.[80] This takes up a position which was also voiced immediately after the dissolution of the Soviet Union[81] and was taken up in 2008 in the conflict concerning South Ossetia.[82]

The protection of nationals abroad is a particularly thorny and disputed area of the use of force. A number of authors have generally rejected the concept of protection of nationals abroad as a justification for the use of force.[83] However, it

77 Written Statement of the Russian Federation (17 April 2009), 31 et seq. (para. 88).

78 *Reference re Secession* (n 72), para. 135.

79 For an account of the relationship of the three major groups populating the Crimean region see B Bowring, 'The Crimean Autonomy' (n 16).

80 See n 6.

81 C Gray, *International Law and the Use of Force* (3rd edn, OUP 2008), 157, footnote 187.

82 For a detailed analysis see A Thomson, 'Doctrine of the Protection of Nationals Abroad: Rise of the Non-Combatant Evacuation Operation' (2012) 11 Wash U Gl Stud L Rev 627 (659 et seq.).

83 See eg I Brownlie, *International Law and the Use of Force by States* (Clarendon Press 1963), 298 et seq.; N Ronzitti, *Rescuing Nationals Abroad Through Military Coercion and Intervention on Grounds of Humanity* (Martinus Nijhoff 1985), 65; J Mrazek, 'Prohibition of the Use and Threat of Force: Self-Defence and Self-Help in International Law' (1989) XXVII Canadian Ybk Int'l L 81, 97.

cannot be overlooked that since the 1960s states have used force in order to protect (and usually evacuate) their nationals from situations of imminent danger. The most recent examples of this type are French and Belgian operations in the Central African Republic in 1996 and 2003; in Rwanda in 1990, 1993, and 1994; in Chad in 1992 and 2006; and in the Ivory Coast in 2002/2003.[84] Based on this practice, a more favourable approach to the protection of nationals abroad seems to gain ground as far as so-called 'non-combatant evacuation operations' are concerned.[85] But even among those scholars who accept a right to protect nationals abroad, narrow criteria are established in order to exclude using the protection of nationals as a pretext for broad interventions.[86]

Even on the assumption that a limited exception from the prohibition of the use of force concerning rescue operations for own nationals can be established, the conditions for its exercise are not met in the Crimea for several reasons. First, and most importantly, it is at best unclear whether the operations concerned Russian *nationals*. There are no reliable figures available, but the development since 1991 suggests that most of the 'Russians' among the population of the Crimea are of Russian origin but, nevertheless, Ukrainian nationals. When the Soviet Union fell apart, the successor republics usually granted the new nationality to all their residents irrespective of their ethnic origin and without leaving them any choice.[87] Furthermore, it is unlikely that Russian attempts to establish dual citizenship for its 'compatriots abroad' were successful in the Crimea,[88] since Ukrainian law expressively prohibits its citizens from acquiring a second nationality.[89] The doctrine of protection of nationals abroad refers, however, to nationality only. Extending it to ethnic or other affiliations would create highly dangerous grounds for intervention in all countries with ethnic minorities belonging to majority groups in neighbouring states.[90]

[84] For these and further examples see A Randelzhofer/O Dörr, Art. 2 (4), MN 59, in B Simma (n 32).

[85] For a discussion of this, see, T Ruys, 'The "Protection of Nationals" Doctrine Revisited' (2008) 13 Oxford J Conflict & Security L 233 (esp. 263 et seq.); A Thomson (n 82), 627 (662 et seq.).

[86] See eg O Dörr, 'Use of force, prohibition of' in *Max Planck Encyclopedia of Public International Law*, para. 45, available online at <www.mpepil.com>, accessed 14 April 2014; see also A Thomson (n 82), 627; T Ruys (n 85), 264.

[87] O Shevel, 'The Politics of Citizenship Policy in Post-Soviet Russia' (2013) 28 Post Soviet Affairs 111, 124.

[88] 'On State Policy of the Russian Federation towards Compatriots Abroad' Russian Federal Law No. 99-FZ 24 May 1999, amended by Russian Federal Law No. 179-FZ 23 July 2010. According to O Shevel (n 87) 139–40, the law mostly lay dormant and only in recent years has increasingly become the main legal instrument by which Russia defines the target of its polices in the post-Soviet region. E Lohr, 'Russian Citizenship - Modernization and Population Policy in Historical Perspective' (2013) 60 Problems of Post-Communism 3, 11, however, assumes that there is a 'large population of Russian Federation citizens living outside the borders of the state'. See also I Ziemele, *State Continuity and Nationality – The Baltic States and Russia* (Martinus Nijhoff 2005), 177–86.

[89] OSCE High Commissioner on National Minorities, *The Integration of Formerly Deported People in Crimea, Ukraine* (2013) 7–8 (also available at <www.osce.org/hcnm/78053>).

[90] For a detailed analysis of the comparable problem regarding the conflict in South Ossetia see the Tagliavini Report (Independent International Fact-Finding Mission on the Conflict in Georgia – Report of September 2009; Vol. II, ch 3, 147–83) <http://www.ceiig.ch/Report.html, accessed 19 April 2014.

Secondly, the operations referred to in Rwanda, the Congo, the Central African Republic, and Ivory Coast were designed to rescue and evacuate nationals, i.e. ensure their safe return to their home country. In none of the examples did the intervening state operate with the purpose of establishing a military presence for the protection of their nationals in their country of residence. This may be seen as one of the reasons why the Russian justification for the intervention in South Ossetia in 2008, which also relied on the protection of nationals abroad, was internationally criticized.[91] Thus, even if one assumes that the recent practice resulted in a customary law exception to the prohibition of the use of force for rescuing and evacuating nationals abroad, such an exception would not apply to the Crimea, where a safe return of Russians to Russia was not the aim of the military operations.[92] Since, finally, there are no indications that Russians in the Crimea were in imminent peril,[93] the protection of nationals cannot serve as justification for the (alleged) Russian use of force.

V. Inviolability of Borders and the Relevance of the *Uti Possidetis* Principle

The principle of *uti possidetis* is regularly referred to in the context of secession disputes. Anne Peters' contribution to this book proposes to extend its application to second- and third-order sub-units of the former Soviet Union.[94] However, before prematurely jumping to its application to the Crimea, it should be underlined that *uti possidetis* is confined to determining where exactly to draw the lines of a border. It does not give any answers to the question of whether or not new borders may be created. *Uti possidetis* determines *where* international borders run, not *whether* there should be international borders at all.[95] And even if one were to look at the moment of the dissolution of the Soviet Union as a situation where *uti possidetis* applied in order to determine the borders between the now independent subjects Russia and Ukraine,[96] *uti possidetis* would favour the Ukrainian position as, whatever the reasons for Khrushchev's decision in 1954 may have been, it led to

[91] See again the references by A Thomson (n 82), 660 and 662; and, notably the Tagliavini Report (n 90), 285–9.

[92] For a similar argument regarding the Russian intervention in South Ossetia see T Ruys (n 85), 267.

[93] See the strong rejection of such claims by Parliamentary Assembly of the Council of Europe Resolution 1988 (2014) para. 15.

[94] A Peters, 'The Principle of *Uti Possidetis Juris*: How Relevant Is It for Issues of Secession?' (ch 6 in this volume), 95 (123).

[95] A Peters, 'The Principle of *Uti Possidetis Juris*: How Relevant Is It for Issues of Secession?' (ch 6 in this volume), 95 (137).

[96] See the 'Minsk Agreement' (establishing the Commonwealth of Independent States) of 8 December 1991 (1992) 31 ILM 143, and the subsequent 'Alma Ata Declaration' of 21 December 1991 (1992) 31 ILM 148. For an overall account of the legal questions concerning the USSR's dissolution and the nature of the mentioned agreements, see A Nußberger, 'Russia', in *Max Planck Encyclopedia of Public International Law* (2009), online at <http://opil.ouplaw.com/home/EPIL>, accessed 11 April 2014.

an internally respected border between the two entities during the Soviet period. Finally, here again, the 1997 Treaty on Friendship becomes relevant, in which Russia formally acknowledged the borders as inviolable.[97] In consequence, Russia cannot rely on the principle of *uti possidetis iuris* for its claim for the Crimea.

VI. Consequences and Perspectives

From a legal point of view it results from the foregoing that the integration of the Crimea into the Russian Federation was illegal and may therefore correctly be labelled an 'annexation'.[98] It follows that all states are under a legal obligation to refuse any recognition of the new factual situation.[99] Instead of speculating on future developments concerning the Crimea, it seems preferable to wind up this postscript by asking about the possible consequences for the law of self-determination. Does the development in the Crimea add anything to the law as it currently stands? What are the possible consequences for the position of the ICJ in its Kosovo Advisory Opinion?

Given the fact that the Crimean Declaration of Independence explicitly refers to the Kosovo Advisory Opinion, one might be tempted to assume that the negative reactions both in the Security Council and by the General Assembly might also bring into question the Court's decision. However, the negative reactions in the Security Council and in the General Assembly were carefully drafted so as to avoid any criticism of the main message of the Kosovo Advisory Opinion, namely that international law is silent on internal activities aiming at secession. Both UN organs deny the validity of the referendum, but they do so without explaining why they believe that the referendum does not have international effects. The explanation could either be its purely internal character or a violation of applicable international law, as envisaged in the Court's opinion.[100] The overall approach by the ICJ in its Kosovo Advisory Opinion was thus not put into question by either the General Assembly or those members of the Security Council who voted in favour of the draft resolution.

[97] See n 60.

[98] Parliamentary Assembly of the Council of Europe, Resolution 1988 (2014) of 9 April 2014, para. 12. The traditional doctrine of 'annexation' is mostly concerned with the forcible acquisition of territory, i.e. acquisition of territory by means of force (see eg R Hofmann, 'Annexation', in *Max Planck Encyclopedia of Public International Law* (2013), available online at <http://opil.ouplaw.com/home/EPIL>, accessed 15 April 2014, with further references; see also G Dahm/J Delbrück/R Wolfrum, Völkerrecht, Vol. I/1 (De Gruyter 1989), 359 et seq.; EC Declaration on the Guidelines on the Recognition of New States in Eastern Europe and in the Soviet Union (16 December 1991), ILM 31 (1992), 1485). The situation on the Crimea corresponds to this traditional concept. If Russian military presence prior to the declaration of independence could be established this would constitute a violation of the prohibition of the use of force (see section II 3 a). Alternatively, the Russian military presence and territorial control after the 'reunification' is in contravention to the prohibition of the use of force, because the territorial integration of the Crimea into Russia could not produce legal effects under international law (see section II 3 b).

[99] *Restatement (3rd), Foreign Relations Law of the United States*, § 202 (2); J Crawford (n 64), 155.

[100] See section II 2.

However, the developments in the Crimea illustrate that the approach by the Court, attractive as it may have seemed in contributing to the solution of the Kosovo crisis, had a price attached to it. This price is the result of the latent tension between the Court's dispute settlement function and its law-making function, which has already been analysed in Chapter 2 of this book. When rendering its Kosovo Advisory Opinion in 2010, the Court apparently focused on its dispute settlement function. In pursuing its 'judicial minimalism', the Court not only avoided any general statements on the law of self-determination and on secession as such; it also refrained from any detailed considerations as to possible circumstances under which declarations of independence nevertheless raise issues of international law, in spite of their general exclusion from its scope of application. In the Advisory Opinion, the reference to use of force or other grave violations of international law as possible international legal limits to declarations of independence occurs more or less incidentally, as a reaction to arguments which had been presented by some states during the proceedings.[101] As a result, the exact scope of exclusion of declarations of independence from international law remains unclear. Apart from outright military intervention, the Advisory Opinion does not provide for criteria as to when the involvement of an outside power in an internal struggle renders international law applicable also to internal non-state actors striving for independence.

It cannot be overlooked that Russia's instrumental use of the declaration of independence and the referendum on the Crimea was somehow facilitated by the silence of the Court on possible limits to external involvement. True, secession can hardly be imagined in complete isolation from external developments. However, given the enormous potential for perturbation and destabilization inherent in secessionist movements, the limitations posed by international law on foreign intervention need to be strengthened and clarified. It must be excluded that self-determination can be exploited for unilaterally remapping internationally recognized borders between neighbouring states. In this regard, silence is not an option.

[101] *Kosovo* (n 33), para. 81.

Index